THE SOCIAL MEDIA AGE

Sara Miller McCune founded SAGE Publishing in 1965 to support the dissemination of usable knowledge and educate a global community. SAGE publishes more than 1000 journals and over 800 new books each year, spanning a wide range of subject areas. Our growing selection of library products includes archives, data, case studies and video. SAGE remains majority owned by our founder and after her lifetime will become owned by a charitable trust that secures the company's continued independence.

Los Angeles | London | New Delhi | Singapore | Washington DC | Melbourne

THE SOCIAL MEDIA AGE

ZOETANYA SUJON

Los Angeles | London | New Delhi
Singapore | Washington DC | Melbourne

Los Angeles | London | New Delhi
Singapore | Washington DC | Melbourne

SAGE Publications Ltd
1 Oliver's Yard
55 City Road
London EC1Y 1SP

SAGE Publications Inc.
2455 Teller Road
Thousand Oaks, California 91320

SAGE Publications India Pvt Ltd
B 1/I 1 Mohan Cooperative Industrial Area
Mathura Road
New Delhi 110 044

SAGE Publications Asia-Pacific Pte Ltd
3 Church Street
#10-04 Samsung Hub
Singapore 049483

Editor: Michael Ainsley
Assistant editor: Ozlem Merakli
Production editor: Martin Fox
Copyeditor: Audrey Scriven
Proofreader: Neil Dowden
Indexer: Elizabeth Ball
Marketing manager: Abigail Sparks
Cover design: Lisa Harper-Wells
Typeset by: C&M Digitals (P) Ltd, Chennai, India

Library of Congress Control Number: 2020946447

British Library Cataloguing in Publication data

A catalogue record for this book is available from the British Library

ISBN 978-1-5264-3689-4
ISBN 978-1-5264-3690-0 (pbk)

Praise for *The Social Media Age*

'Social media platforms have changed social life so completely in the past 15 years that it seems impossible to capture all that in a comprehensive book, but Zoetanya Sujon has managed it in this impressive text. Theoretically and geopolitically smart, and crammed full with great examples of social media's role in both our politics and everyday intimacies, this is more than a textbook: it's a primer for living in the age of social media.'

Nick Couldry, Professor of Media, Communications and Social Theory at London School of Economics and Political Science

'Amidst hope, hype, panic and euphoria around social media, this book clears the way – with evidence, and a compelling writing style. A must-read for students and scholars who wish to make sense of a complex and ever-changing landscape.'

Ranjana Das, Reader in Media and Communication, University of Surrey

'Zoetanya Sujon gives us something unique with *The Social Media Age*: a history of the present. It is both a playful and problematic history, one that makes immediate sense from a users' point of view as much as it enables us to step back and reflect.'

Mark Deuze, Professor of Media Studies, University of Amsterdam

'This textbook provides an accessible and incisive overview of how our world has changed in the social media age. Reflecting on milestone events, social movements, and internet trends of the past decade, Sujon deep-dives into case studies to provide illuminating insight on how various social media cultures can be deciphered in the context of useful frameworks, and in light of evolving platform and user cultures.'

Crystal Abidin, Curtin University and Jönköping University

'Social media are full of contrasts. They're at once public and private, commercial and interpersonal, hyperglobal and hyperlocal. Zoetanya's Sujon's *The Social Media Age* navigates these paradoxes with deft precision, balancing the past and the present, the theoretical and the empirical, and the good and the bad of digital connection. The result is a comprehensive overview that prepares readers for every twist and turn of our inescapably networked lives.'

Ryan M. Milner, Associate Professor at College of Charleston

'More than a textbook, *The Social Media Age* gives us invaluable tools for thinking through the complex, elusive, but omnipresent technologies of social media. It weaves together a wide range of stories about what we do with social media and what social media does with us and positions these narratives within neatly described material and theoretical contexts in ways that both illuminate and complicate.'

Kylie Jarrett, Associate Professor of Media Studies at National University of Ireland Maynooth

'*The Social Media Age* is a compelling introduction to the critical study of social media. Students will find a wealth of engagingly written case studies from #BlackLivesMatter to YouTube influencer culture to digital dating in socially conservative countries. With its global and interdisciplinary perspective, this textbook easily fits in undergraduate curricula in sociology, anthropology, and media and communications across national contexts.'

Jonathan Corpus Ong, Associate Professor of Global Digital Media, University of Massachusetts Amherst

'Zo Sujon has written the most detailed yet theoretical framework for the study of social media. This book will be indispensable to students and researchers alike. The scope is impressive, with a huge range of highly original case studies very usefully discussed. Excitingly, Sujon pushes forward theories of the selfie, showing how this new mainstay of online communication is closely linked to platforms, which facilitate public connection in highly specific ways, and mapping out emerging areas demanding ongoing research.'

Mehita Iqani, Professor in Media Studies, University of the Witwatersrand

'*The Social Media Age* perfectly captures the disruptive capacities of social media platforms and user practices. Incorporating historical, political, and technical perspectives Sujon reminds the reader of the need to critically assess the embedded impact of social media in our daily lives. This book should be required reading for all media and communication students.'

Greg Elmer, Professor of Professional Communication at Ryerson University

'*The Social Media Age* is a deeply researched, wonderfully wide-ranging and accessible examination of key contemporary and historical approaches towards understanding social media. Spanning from ideology to infrastructure, from privacy to participation and from memes to selfies, Zoetanya Sujon offers a thorough and critical introduction to how social media permeates and impacts many facets of modern social, cultural, political and economic life. The book's clear structure and objectives, together with its discussion questions and diverse selection of in-depth case studies, lend itself perfectly for use in media and communications classrooms or as an indispensable resource book for any student seeking to better understand our complicated relationship with social media.'

Patrick McCurdy, Associate Professor of Communication, University of Ottawa, Canada

CONTENTS

List of Boxes	xiii
List of Figures	xv
List of Tables	xvii
About the Author	xix
Acknowledgements	xxi
Introduction	xxiii

PART I   WHAT ARE SOCIAL MEDIA AND WHERE DO THEY COME FROM? **1**

1	The Social Media Landscape	3
2	The Historical Origins of Social Media	23
3	Power and Ideology	57

PART II   SOCIALITY AND SOCIAL TECHNOLOGIES **83**

4	Understanding the 'Social' in Social Media	85
5	Material Infrastructures and Platformization	107
6	Participation, Culture and Protest	127

PART III   EVERYDAY LIFE AND SOCIAL MEDIA **153**

7	Selfie and Society: Snapchat and Instagram	155
8	Privacy and Dataveillance	179
9	Social Screens: From YouTube to TikTok	205
10	Love, Intimacy and Personal Connections	229

References	249
Index	297

EXPANDED CONTENTS

List of Boxes	xiii
List of Figures	xv
List of Tables	xvii
About the Author	xix
Acknowledgements	xxi
Introduction	**xxiii**
Welcome to the Age of Social Media	xxiii
Overview of the Book	xxv
A Note on Pedagogical Features	xxx
Key Social Media Journals	xxx
Key Social Media Research Centres	xxxi
PART I WHAT ARE SOCIAL MEDIA AND WHERE DO THEY COME FROM?	**1**
1 The Social Media Landscape	**3**
Introduction	4
Data and Surveillance	5
Cambridge Analytica (CA)	6
China's social credit systems (SCS)	8
Community and Connection	11
Pokémon Go!	12
Memes	16
Conclusion	19
Further Reading and Key Resources	20
2 The Historical Origins of Social Media	**23**
Introduction	24
Life Cycles of Social Media as Products, Technologies and Knowledge	27
Four Stages of Social Media	28
Stage 1: Pre-history (1980s–1990s)	29
Stage 2: Early development (1990s–2006)	34
Stage 3: Consolidation and growth (2007–2012)	44
Stage 4: Maturation (2013–present)	49
Conclusion: What Next?	54
Questions and Activities	56
Further Reading	56

3 Power and Ideology   **57**

Introduction   58

Power: The Basics   59

   Marx, capitalism and ideology   60

   Forms of power   62

   Power/knowledge   64

   Media and symbolic power   67

The Ideology of Connection: From the Culture Industries to Platform Empires   69

   The culture industries   70

   The audience commodity   71

   Platform empires: Every click is capital   73

   The ideology of connection   75

Critiques: The Active Audience Tradition and 'Small Acts of Engagement' (SAOE)   76

Conclusion: Ambivalent Cultures and the Power of Connection   79

Questions and Activities   80

Further Reading   80

PART II SOCIALITY AND SOCIAL TECHNOLOGIES   **83**

4 Understanding the 'Social' in Social Media   **85**

Introduction   86

Defining 'the Social'   87

   The social according to social media: Twitter, Instagram, Facebook,
      Snapchat and YouTube   89

   Unpacking the social: Structure and agency   92

   Infrastructures of everyday life: From structuration to deep mediatization   94

Affordances and Tactics of Belonging   98

   The 'like' button: Metrics in the like economy   100

   New vernaculars and literacies   101

Conclusion: Social Solidarities and the Public Good   103

Questions and Activities   104

Further Reading   105

5 Material Infrastructures and Platformization   **107**

Introduction   108

Embedded Technologies and Overlapping Networks   109

Early Internet History and Internet Infrastructures   110

   The 'stack' and global megastructures   113

   Telephony and mobile social media   118

   Platformization: Extending social media across the web   120

Platform Empires and the Social Landscape: GAFA and BATX   122

Conclusion: Social Media and Shifting Infrastructures   124

Questions and Activities   125
Further Reading   125

6 Participation, Culture and Protest   **127**
Introduction: Media and the Long Promise of Public Participation   128
Thinking Through the Meaning of Participation   130
    Participatory culture and creative agency   133
Participation and Play   135
The Participatory Turn in Culture and Politics   136
    PostSecret   139
    We're Not Really Strangers (WNRS)   140
    2011 Egyptian revolution   142
    Black Lives Matter   147
Conclusion: Making Sense of Participatory Culture   150
Questions and Activities   151
Further Reading   152

PART III EVERYDAY LIFE AND SOCIAL MEDIA   **153**

7 Selfie and Society: Snapchat and Instagram   **155**
Introduction: The Rise of the Selfie   156
What Is a Selfie, Really?   158
Selfie Platforms   163
    Instagram   163
    Snapchat   166
Data Selfies   169
    Filters, lenses and apps   170
    Facial recognition, tagging and artificial intelligence 173
Conclusion: The Visual Logics of Selfie Culture   175
Questions and Activities   176
Further Reading   177

8 Privacy and Dataveillance   **179**
Introduction   180
Privacy from the Twentieth to the Twenty-First Century   181
    Defining privacy: From the right to be let alone to networked
      privacy   184
    Privacy according to social media platforms   186
    Why do we need privacy rights if we have nothing to hide? 192
From Surveillance to Dataveillance   194
    The panopticon, dataveillance and surveillance realism   194
    Shadow profiles and 'People You May Know' (PYMK)   199

Conclusion: 'The Future Is Private'   202
Questions and Activities   203
Further Reading   204

9 Social Screens: From YouTube to TikTok   **205**
Introduction: Social Screens, Social Media Entertainment and YouTube   206
YouTube: Platform, Creation and Affective Labour   207
    Platform origins and features   207
    Content and creators   211
Affective Labour and Social Relations   221
Emerging Trends in Social Video: Rise of Live and TikTok   224
Conclusion   226
Questions and Activities   227
Further Reading   227

10 Love, Intimacy and Personal Connections   **229**
Introduction   230
Personal Connections: Interpersonal Relations Across Social Media   230
Love and Intimacy   231
    Dating industries: From sites to apps   234
    Tinder   238
    Gamification and swipe logic   240
    Abuse and harassment   242
Personal Disconnections: Breaking Up and Defriending on Social Media   244
Conclusion: Shifting Intimacies   246
Questions and Activities   247
Further Reading   247

References   249
Index   297

LIST OF BOXES

3.1 Intersectionality and Kimberlé Crenshaw 61

3.2 Programmed sociality: From Foucault to Bucher 66

4.1 Gendered technologies: Social or individual? 96

5.1 Why infrastructure matters? The case of net neutrality 116

5.2 Facebook Connect and platformization 121

6.1 Debating user-generated content: Free labour or creative agency? 131

6.2 Cute cat theory 137

6.3 Introducing Twitter 142

6.4 Brief timeline of the Egyptian revolution 144

7.1 Erving Goffman and the presentation of self in everyday life 162

7.2 What Essena O'Neill has to teach us about Instagram and authenticity 165

7.3 Facetune: Photoshop for your selfies 171

7.4 Joy Buolamwini and Timnit Gebru's work on algorithms and bias, 'Gender Shades' 174

8.1 From revenge porn to non-consensual image sharing 182

8.2 'Your Rights' in Twitter's Terms of Service 187

8.3 Police dataveillance: Social media monitoring, data harvesting and racial profiling 196

8.4 Subverting dataveillance on Instagram 198

9.1 YouTube's Partner Programme (YPP), minimum entry requirements 211

9.2 Issa Rae and PewDiePie 215

10.1 Dating in socially conservative countries 236

10.2 Tinder: Key info 238

LIST OF FIGURES

1.1 Pokémon Go! Game play in Helsinki, Finland   13

1.2 The first emoticon   17

1.3 'Lolspeak: I furst language born of I intertubes'   18

2.1 Number of peer-reviewed academic publications and newspaper articles using the exact term 'social media', 2007–2017   44

2.2 The rise in millions of worldwide monthly active users on Facebook, WhatsApp, WeChat, Instagram, Snapchat and TikTok   50

4.1 Word cloud showing the most frequently occurring words on Twitter, Instagram, Facebook, Snapchat and YouTube in their 'about us' and 'what is' pages (September 2019)   91

4.2 Representing social action through structure and agency   93

4.3 Tier 3 meme, illustrating the everyday vernacular of memes   102

5.1 Paul Baran's 'Centralized, Decentralized and Distributed Networks' (1964)   112

5.2 'The stack': Models of the layered architecture of the internet, comparing Lessig (2001) and Cath et al. (2017) 'layers of the internet' with the technical models of OSI/TCP/IP   114

5.3 Submarine cable map   116

6.1 Industrial production value chain   131

6.2 Produser as hybrid producer/consumer in individual UGC value chain   131

6.3 'PostSecret' home page   139

6.4 We're Not Really Strangers – a sample of the cards   141

6.5 Jack Dorsey's first tweet   142

6.6 Internet, Facebook and Twitter penetration rates in Egypt, 2010   146

6.7 #BlackLivesMatter surges in use on Twitter over time   149

7.1 Number of global news articles in English with 'Selfie' in the headline, 2013–2019   157

7.2 A small selection of headlines about selfies   160

7.3 Some of the author's Snapchat selfies   168

8.1 Three kinds of privacy: Social and interpersonal; Public institutional; Commercial institutional 186

8.2 Bentham's plan of the panopticon 195

9.1 YouTube front page, featuring the motto 'YouTube: Your Digital Video Repository' 208

10.1 Selection of headlines identifying Tinder and other dating apps as cause for a decline in the quality of dating relationships 239

LIST OF TABLES

2.1 Overview of shared stages across different models for the life cycles of products, technology and knowledge 27

2.2 Four stages of social media: Social technologies, key scholars, related concepts and parallel fields 30

2.3 Overview of early social network sites (SNSs) and social media (1990s–2006) 39

3.1 'Forms of power' 63

4.1 How social media platforms present themselves in their 'About' pages and what this means for understanding the social 90

8.1 Privacy policies across social media 190

8.2 'Data given' across social media platforms according to their privacy policies (February 2020) 191

9.1 Comparing YouTube's 'most viewed channels worldwide' with the 'most viewed videos globally' and the 'top earners' in 2019 213

9.2 From parasocial relations to perceived interconnectedness 222

10.1 Top ten dating apps on the App Store and Google Play Store 236

10.2 Intimate internet use in the Muslim world 237

ABOUT THE AUTHOR

Dr Zoetanya Sujon is a Senior Lecturer and the Programme Director for Communications and Media at London College of Communication (LCC), University of the Arts London. Before joining LCC in 2018, Zoetanya was a Senior Lecturer in Media and Communications at Regent's University London (2010–2018) and Lecturer/Fellow in Media and Communications at the London School of Economics and Political Science where she completed her PhD.

Originally trained as a sociologist, Zoetanya draws from an interdisciplinary lens to address the relationships between new technologies and social life, particularly as related to everyday political and social life. Currently, these interests are based around four themes: social media, technologies and platform politics; the intersections between dataveillance, privacy and sharing culture; innovation and emerging technologies; and the impact of digital media on changing skill sets and digital literacies.

Zoetanya has published in leading media journals such as *New Media and Society*, *Social Media + Society* and the *International Journal of Communication*. Zoetanya also currently serves on the programme committee for the International Conference on *Social Media and Society*, and is on the editorial board for *Digital Culture and Education*.

Links:

- Twitter: @jetsumgerl
- Email: z.sujon@lcc.arts.ac.uk
- Institutional home page: https://www.arts.ac.uk/colleges/london-college-of-communication/people/zoetanya-sujon
- LCC Communications and Media programme home page: https://www.arts.ac.uk/colleges/london-college-of-communication/about-lcc/media-school
- International Conference on Social Media and Society: https://socialmediaandsociety.org/
- *Digital Culture and Education*: https://www.digitalcultureandeducation.com/

ACKNOWLEDGEMENTS

Writing a book requires monumental effort, and writing one on social media is no different, save that it also requires paying close attention to the world, and thus balancing conflicting motivations: writing which is intensely introspective and engagement with the world which demands a much more extroverted and open mindset. The process of writing this book has reflected the nature of social media, which is also intensely personal and inward focused, as well as outward and public facing. That nature is not easily contained within a single topic. Instead, it is interdisciplinary, overlapping with multiple perspectives.

This book has taken three years to write. When I first wrote the proposal for what you are now holding in your hands, I imagined it would take a year. It would be closely related to my teaching, and indeed would be the book that wasn't yet on the market and that I could work through with my students to challenge and open up all that social media encompassed. Of course life has intervened, children, new jobs, endings and beginnings, as well as a pandemic that continues as I finalize edits, but the real reason this book has taken three years to write is because the subject demands careful thought, which can only take place over time. Many thanks go to Michael Ainsley, my editor, whose patient encouragement helped me through this project.

I am grateful to be part of a much wider community of thinkers and practitioners focused on digital culture, new technologies, social life and political culture. I am indebted to this community and the many people with whom I've shared conversations about social media and their impact, which have directly and indirectly led to the contents of this book. *The Social Media Age* is the result of a deep engagement with other researchers, thinking through and making sense of a complex field while it takes shape around us. It is not just about what I think, but also about the debates and issues that surfaced. While there are too many within this community to name individually, I am especially thankful for those who commented on and supported my work, and the work that informed these chapters. I would like to thank Justine Gangneux and Stevie Docherty for inviting me to the seminar on surveillance capitalism at the University of Glasgow (June 2019), where feedback on some of my earlier work was remarkably helpful. As well, many thanks go to Harry Dyer, my co-organizer for the 'Understanding the Social in a Digital Age' conference (January 2019) and special issue of *New Media & Society* on the same theme. We learned so much from our colleagues and contributors, and this has helped me work through really difficult questions on the nature of sociality in the contemporary moment. I have also been incredibly fortunate for those who have taken the time to read and comment on chapters, including Patrick McCurdy, Chiara Minestrelli, Rebecca Bramall, Steve Cross, Sophie Bishop, Tara Molloy and the anonymous reviewers at Sage who all provided detailed comments and constructive criticisms which helped me strengthen the focus and flow for this book. There are also many others with whom I debated and discussed a number of points which inevitably shaped the thinking that is reflected throughout the pages of this book: Nick Couldry, Crystal Abidin, Sonia Livingstone, the Social Media and Society conference organizers Anotoliy Gruzd and Philip Mai, my co-researchers on the 'Domesticating Facebook' project, Leslie Viney and Elif Toker-Turnalar, as well as Lisette Johnston who I worked with on the 'privacy and sharing culture' project. My thoughts on social media have been greatly enhanced by all of these collaborations and exchanges.

My colleagues at London College of Communication and especially those in the Communications and Media programme have been critical friends, in co-teaching and in sharing larger conversations about the field of media and communication. In addition to those I've already mentioned, I would like to especially thank Adrian Crookes, Sara Marino, Maitrayee Basu, Simone Hinde, Lee MacKinnon, Corrine De Silva, Berfin Emre Cetin, Tereza Pavlíčková and, most recently, Jonathan Hardy. Much thanks also go to my dear friends who offered editorial feedback and vital encouragement at many points throughout the writing process: Bob Ooboberto, Elizabeth Kim and, again, Tara Molloy. I also owe a huge debt to John Verdon, for nurturing my curiosity and instilling a life-long love of knowledge. Of course, the structure of this book comes from designing courses on social media, work which I began in 2012, and I am grateful for all my students at Regent's University London, as well as those at London College of Communication. This book would not be what it is without you.

I would like to thank Izaak and Felix from the bottom of my heart. You have both been so patient with me as I spent many weekends, early mornings and evenings writing and editing chapters rather than adventuring with you, which I know you would have preferred. This book is for you. May the lessons I have learned and uncovered help you navigate the complications of the social media age.

Finally, this book would not be here without my mother, Susan Fripp, who not only supported my projects at every turn, but also made writing time and space appear out of nothing.

I stand on the shoulders of giants, and this book is dedicated to you.

INTRODUCTION

Social media are all around us. We find them on almost every page of the web, on our small and big screens, and tucked into our pockets. Through them, we can find our favourite and most reviled public figures, we can find and make news, and we can see and even interact with them on almost every form of digital communication. Social media are also in the corners of our relationships, linking our personal connections, facilitating romance and break-ups, helping or hindering our family communications, consolidating our public and professional identities, and they can often help us feel connected or disconnected. Social media have become integrated into our everyday lives, and are embedded in those lives as intimate technologies. For many, they are the first things to look at upon waking and the last thing to do before sleeping. And there is more. Social media are also at the forefront of cultural, social and economic change, marking a shift from twentieth-century industrialism to twenty-first-century networked societies. Social media are no longer merely used for occasional entertainment and escapist pleasures; instead they have become crucial platforms for human connection as well as for cultural and economic exchange. Indeed, in an era where we use media more than we sleep, social media have become the dominant communications systems as well as a key platform for connecting with others and with the world.

Many feel an intense familiarity with social media brought on by everyday use, and while this familiarity is important, there is much more to social media than what we experience on an interpersonal level or from a user's perspective. Users often face a screened experience of social media, limiting perception of the data infrastructures and platform exchanges. Social media are made up of familiar interfaces, but they also include specific platforms, technologies, infrastructures, algorithms, business models, partnerships, data collection and extraction systems, behavioural analytics, social networks and many other aspects operating behind those familiar screens. Social media reflect broader cultural shifts and industry trends, often defining both the media landscape and the social landscapes within which contemporary life takes place.

Welcome to the Age of Social Media

Social media are the dominant information technologies of our time. There are still many questions about what social media include and exclude, and many ongoing debates about their meaning and their impact. In terms of defining social media, drawing boundaries can be problematic. Some take a broad view, arguing all media are social (e.g. Humphreys 2016;

Van Dijck 2013), dating from the first cave paintings to the almost 6 million apps available for download as of August 2020 (a figure which has doubled from March 2017; see Statista 2017a; also Clement 2020d). Others take a much narrower view, arguing that social media include only specific technologies used for specific purposes. Yet, despite many contrasting definitions, the term 'social media' is often unquestioned and understood as referring to specific digital platforms enabling some kind of public-facing social interaction. In addition to exploring these debates, a review of the scholarship on social media reveals that it is much harder to locate a comprehensive definition of social media than it has been for other dominant communication technologies like the telephone or television. Ultimately, social media do not have easily fixed boundaries and they are constant in their movement, blurring complete visibility. This may explain why there has been so much debate around the meaning of social media, but it also shows rapid-fire integration across every dimension of social life, industry and public communications.

Regardless of these debates, social media are embedded and seamless objects. By this I mean that they are embedded technologies – embedded within internet and mobile network infrastructures, embedded within computers and mobile devices, and embedded within the social and interpersonal dimensions of our lives. Social media are also seamless objects, simultaneously networked and hyperlinked. By their very nature, the edges between social media and not-social media are blended and overlapping. Their frictionless edges blend across many aspects of our lives, creating what seems like barely-there transitions across the web, across social and cultural contexts, and across personal connections. Social media are often invisible, increasingly present across the web and in many aspects of our digital experiences. It is important to remember this is no accident. Expensive user design teams, engineers, computer and data scientists, and product designers, to name but a few, coordinate sophisticated efforts to make this happen, to make social media look and feel seamless.

The intense familiarity with social media brought on by everyday use may seem equivalent to digital literacy, but use is not the same. This book aims to provide both a generalist view of social media, and an in-depth analysis of platform specific cases. This work has been partially driven by the importance of history and context, and these are offered within every chapter. Cases and ideas are historically contextualized. It is impossible to understand what something really is if it is too clouded by the shine of novelty, so this book aims to direct the reader to historical precedents, mapping continuities and discontinuities across the social and technological landscape. New technologies carry with them the great promises and terrible fears of older generations, carving out social norms for younger generations who may not know any other kinds of communication paradigms. Many of my own students objected to detailed examination of the shift from analogue to Snapchat photography, or the shift from sheet music to the easy shareability of music on Soundcloud. At first, students claim 'but it's always been that way', implying that they don't really want or need to know. And then, as the connections are made between then and now, the magic happens. With greater understanding of where things come from, students seem to more easily cast a critical eye on the media technologies of the moment. This book aims to account for change in relation to the social technologies around us, providing a foundation for that greater understanding and more critical eye.

This book is also incomplete, as perhaps are all books, even those on social media. There are chapters on networks, social media methods and platform interest in payment systems all unwritten. There is a whole other book in my notes files, which accompanied me throughout the writing process. There are also constant social and technological changes, some of which may mean that the cases or platforms I have chosen are suddenly obsolete, or replaced by the next tech iteration. Social media are moving targets, and this is a condition of the territory. Even if (or, perhaps more precisely, when) this happens, there are still important lessons to be learned about the particulars of a site or app, details which can help map, trace, challenge and understand the next iteration, the next stage of mediated social interaction.

It is also worth saying that this book has been written based on years of teaching social media, both a privilege and a challenge. I learn from my students as much as they learn from me. Many of the exercises and questions have evolved from work and exercises I asked them to do, and this means that students have helped me work out the most compelling questions and the best thought-provoking exercises. It has been hard to find that one book that covers all I needed for my classes on social media, and it is fair to say that, for me, this is that book. It would not be what it was without my students, their engagement, their feedback and their amazing questions. I do love a good question.

While this book is intended to support students in the social sciences and humanities, it offers a comprehensive and interdisciplinary overview of social media as everyday technologies, as platforms, as industries and as a dedicated field of scholarship. This means it is also intended to be useful for anyone interested in knowing more about social media and their social, cultural and economic impacts. While it is intended to introduce readers to the key debates surrounding social media and their uses from a broad perspective, it also includes original research drawn from my own practice. This approach is intended to integrate evidence with context, but in such a way that readers are encouraged to make up their own minds about the meaning and consequences of social media.

Overview of the Book

The book is divided into three parts: Part I, 'What are social media and where do they come from?'; Part II, 'Sociality and social technologies'; and Part III, 'Everyday life and social media'. These parts can be read consecutively from cover to cover, or select parts or chapters can be dipped into as desired by the reader. This book has been written as a whole, but each chapter is self-contained enough to read on its own.

Part I begins with simple but challenging questions: What are social media and where do they come from? In **Chapter 1**, I draw from four game-changing cases that changed the ways we think about and understand social media. There are two themes, data and surveillance, and community and connection. These are complementary, often linked through social media in intersecting and interesting ways. Yet, they are intended to focus the reader on the most impactful aspects of each case. The first case unpacks the Cambridge Analytica events and provides an overview of what happened along with some context on surveillance culture more broadly. The second case is China's social credit systems, providing background information on the Chinese context and outlining key features of these apps, where they come from, how they relate to national plans for a social credit system and what they mean for surveillance.

Moving towards the community and connection theme, the third case is Pokémon Go. This is one of those cases that may seem more closely aligned with gaming, but provokes interesting forms of sociality and raises important questions about culture, connection and play, all of which are 'social media' features. As such, this is an important example. The last case is memes. Memes are not necessarily a social technology, but they are the lingua franca of digital culture and make up an impressive proportion of social media content.

There are so many other cases which could be considered game changers, and choosing only four had to be done very carefully. Other cases in the running were digital advertising, YouTube's adpocalypse(s), fake news and disinformation, and current events in the changing regulatory practices of social media and big tech. While these are all important, they touch on themes covered elsewhere in the book. The cases presented in this chapter are meant to intrigue readers, while providing a detailed analysis of four different cases that can be further explored as suits those readers. You will notice these cases are intentionally presented without a theoretical framework, and this is because each of them applies to multiple theories, multiple social platforms and multiple moments of use. Indeed, each of these game-changing cases connect with recurring themes throughout this book.

The historical chronology of social media in **Chapter 2** aims to achieve two goals. First, it provides a forty-year history mapping the development of social media, as technologies and as a field(s) of scholarship. In addition, this chapter provides a framework for making sense of change and the life cycle of technologies. This is an important framing which better compensates for where a technology is in relation to its first iteration, rather than beginning with a platform from its launch date. This is a lengthy chapter, appropriate to the rich history of social technologies, and details what I've called 'the four stages of social media': prehistory (1980s–90s), early development (1990s–2006), growth and consolidation (2007–12), and maturation and the critical turn (2013–present). Each stage includes three levels: the social technologies themselves, the key concepts and thinkers working on those technologies, and the most relevant cognate concepts and parallel fields. Taken together, this chapter maps the development of social media as a field, illustrating a much longer and vastly interdisciplinary history than commonly reported. Although it is ambitious and covers a vast literature, there will still be some absences. And while extensive, this chapter is also narrowly focused on social media, within the context of internet and networked technologies. Indeed, many of the historical cases, like Napster or social software, mirror current issues and debates.

Chapter 3 turns to issues of power and the ideology of connection. Introducing foundational concepts essential to the study of power, it begins with an overview of capitalism, ideology, forms of power (economic, political, coercive and symbolic), the Foucaldian theory of power as productive, and media and symbolic power. Next, the chapter unpacks the ideology of connection, a kind of hidden logic driving social media platforms and articulated in different ways by users. To better understand and contextualize this ideology, I trace the historical continuities from critical political economy traditions, such as: Max Horkheimer and Theodor Adorno's work on the culture industries; Dallas Smythe's theory of the audience commodity; and integrate work on platform capitalism (Srnicek 2017), surveillance capitalism (Zuboff 2019) and data colonialism (Couldry and Mejias 2019a, 2019b). Finally, drawing from the active audience tradition, the chapter closes with critiques of these critical theories, considering how social media enable 'small acts of engagement' (Picone et al. 2019).

Part II focuses on sociality and social technologies. **Chapter 4** grounds this section in questions about what it means to be social in an age of social media. For example, it focuses on the increasingly elusive meaning of the 'social' – a concept that has a long history in sociology, anthropology and the social sciences. The purpose of this chapter is to think through core theories of the social as they apply to social media. Beginning with key definitions of the social, it introduces the structure/agency model as a useful starting point for making sense of social complexity. Both structuration theory and deep mediatization offer insights on how social media are rewriting social relations and the tactics of belonging. From here, we look at affordances, i.e. those behaviours or actions made possible by the design of a thing. In particular, 'like' buttons, metrics and new vernaculars provide fascinating case studies for explaining the link between affordances, belonging and 'the social'.

Chapter 5 introduces the material infrastructure of networked and social technologies, providing an overview of just how embedded social media are in the wires and cables of the internet. Although social media are one of many 'new' technologies, the chapter begins with the history of the early internet, including the impact of distributed communication networks on internet infrastructures. This history sheds light on the layered architecture of the internet, an influential model about how the internet works and upon which standards for interoperability were set. This model, known as 'the stack', provides a useful way to visualize the internet's layered architecture, and how social media fit into this architecture, from its content layers to its physical layers, like the undersea network cables. This chapter also introduces the network developments of social media, including the rise of mobile social media, apps and platformization – all of which situate social media within digital culture and the digital environment more broadly. It highlights the seamless nature of social technologies, particularly as we have come to use and engage social media. Finally, like the networks of networks they come from, social media are intensely embedded in social, technological, mediated and increasingly networked ways.

Chapter 6, the last in Part II, looks at participation in popular culture and political protests. Although there is a focus on Twitter, this chapter also includes other social platforms like Instagram, Facebook and cross-platform communities. It is informed by the participatory turn, which may not feel as urgent as it once did, but its call for seeking out the potential is as urgent as ever. Hope is a radical act, and this scholarship provides an essential contribution to understanding what there is to be hopeful about and on social media. The chapter covers four cases, two of which come from popular culture, providing support for the mental health of their community members. The first is a community art project called PostSecret, launched in the early 2000s through the sharing of anonymous postcards, before making the switch to social media more recently. The second is an Instagram community called We're Not Really Strangers (WNRS), which is entirely geared towards fostering meaningful connections, as well as selling WNRS products. The next two cases address political protest, the first of which is the 2011 Egyptian revolution. Although this took place years ago now, it was one of the first political revolutions on social media and establishes some important precedents. The last case is #BlackLivesMatter, currently one of the longest movements on social media, and most recently recharged by the police murder of an unarmed Black man, George Floyd. In addition to detailing key elements of this case, this chapter presents evidence for readers to critically evaluate the relationship between social media, collective protest, participation and social action.

In **Part III**, on everyday life and social media, the chapters focus on unpacking the role of social media in shaping and informing our everyday lives. **Chapter 7** looks at selfies which, like memes, are not platform specific, but do account for content that is easily circulated across the web and social platforms. Snapchat and Instagram, however, are two of the most well-known selfie-oriented sites, and as such this chapter introduces these platforms, working through their platform-specific affordances. For example, Snapchat often features more private 'ugly selfies', whereas Instagram features public-facing, highly polished aesthetics aligning with 'perfect' Instagram. One of the key theoretical findings from this chapter is that selfies are not a sign of narcissism or selfishness. Instead, more thoughtful accounts suggest that the selfie breaks down creative barriers, allowing selfie-takers to easily express themselves in deep and meaningful ways, as well as documenting their presence in everyday life. This chapter also looks at data selfies, facial recognition, filters and lenses as part of the selfie assemblage. It concludes with a reflection on how these practices inform the visual logics of selfie culture.

Chapter 8 examines privacy and dataveillance across social media. This is a big topic. Beginning with a brief historical example on the rise of 'surreptitious photography' around the turn of the twentieth century, this example provides a point of comparison for twenty-first-century privacy. In the twenty-first century, privacy is more networked, more contextual and more personal than it was in the twentieth century. Based on a review of how social media platforms define privacy (spoiler alert, not very accurately), it is clear that these platforms are misdirecting users to believe they are in control of their privacy when this is not the case. While there are some features which allow users to hide some content or decide who can see what, this is only for other users. Researchers have defined this user-facing idea of privacy as social or interpersonal privacy. There are no or very few user controls for privacy from platforms and third parties, what researchers have called institutional privacy. This is an important distinction and has important consequences for how we understand and are able to negotiate privacy. The other key shift related to privacy is the one from surveillance to dataveillance as a form of social control. For example, as part of widespread dataveillance practices, social media companies collect contact data to create shadow profiles, sometimes about non-users, so that they can enrich the 'discover' option, offer better friend recommendations and build up their lucrative databases of users' personal information.

Although focused on YouTube, **Chapter 9** introduces social screens and the convergence between social media, streaming, internet distributed video, second (and third) screens and creative video practice. This is a complex and rapidly changing landscape. In order to make sense of this dense space, I briefly introduce this market, before explaining the highly contested origins of YouTube. Given the vibrant range of creator content on YouTube, I provide an overview of top content and YouTubers to get a feel of the YouTube environment. However, influencers on YouTube are not always looking just to promote themselves. Indeed, based on two cases of red-pilling and radicalization, and child sexual exploitation through comments, it is possible to see how harmful content is as spreadable and profitable for YouTube as non-harmful content. Notably, YouTube creators embrace an entrepreneurial logic widely associated with social media, and have high rates of burn-out. Part of this challenging and precarious work environment is the rise of affective labour, which has a big impact on the kinds of social relations afforded to YouTube. As part of their affective labour, creators must personally connect with their audiences, providing the feeling of intimacy with their audiences. In closing, affective labour is as important for harmless content creators as it is for harmful content creators like white supremacists and extremists seeking out audiences on and through YouTube.

Chapter 10 features Tinder and other dating apps to make sense of the ways that personal connections and interpersonal relations unfold on social media. Drawing from theories of liquid love and hyperconnective modernity, this chapter considers dating and relational patterns on social media. A few things become clear. Tinder and other social media, like Facebook, widen the dating pool but do not necessarily promote hook-up culture. Instead, it is easier to find romantic interests and friendships, and also to be subject to antagonistic and harmful interactions. The last section of this chapter looks at breaking up and disconnecting on social media, both actions which require working in opposition to social platforms' ideology of connection. That said, even with the proliferation of many different social media platforms, dating apps and social media can help people negotiate and make sense of their personal relationships. Social media have impacted on the way that people are intimate with each other and how they maintain relationships or disconnect from their personal connections. Based on an overview of the emergence and state of the online dating industry, the rise of Tinder and dating apps, readers are asked to reflect on what they think love means in a digital age.

A Note on Pedagogical Features

Based on a learner-centred approach, this textbook uses a series of pedagogical features to engage readers and provide applied insights into the role, purpose and use of social media beyond the user experience. Each chapter includes a summary of chapter objectives, as well as call-out boxes where important cases, examples and histories are used to provide context and insight for the topic at hand. Following the end of each chapter is a section with 'Questions and Activities', supplying steps for further thinking or to inform class exercises or written assignments for coursework. Additional exercises, such as debates, further questions, web-links and guided tours through the back end of ad preferences, follow each chapter's conclusion. These have been designed to provoke and engage readers and students beyond the chapters. Although some would benefit from group discussion, they can also be explored individually. Each chapter also includes a 'Further Reading' section. Many of these carefully selected recommendations come from core readings informing parts of the chapter, but at times they also include important readings which haven't been covered but will guide the reader to a more advanced exploration of the topics at hand.

This book aims to introduce and examine the social media age in all its glory and wonder, from a critical, research-informed perspective, one that seeks out promise as well as its negative consequences. The content of this book has been written to be both educational and stimulating. It has been inspired by a longstanding interest not only in social technologies, but also in the ways that social technologies come bundled up in our own social and psychological processes for making sense of the world around us. It is my hope that the pages ahead help deepen your understanding of social media, and provide conceptual tools to also help you make sense of the world around us, as well as to raise the next questions and critiques of that world as it is now and as it could be in the future.

Key Social Media Journals

Chinese Journal of Communication (https://www.tandfonline.com/toc/rcjc20/current)

Convergence: The International Journal of Research into New Media Technologies (https://journals.sagepub.com/home/con)

Data + society (https://datasociety.net/)

First Monday (https://firstmonday.org/ojs/index.php/fm/index)

Mobile Media and Communication (https://journals.sagepub.com/home/mmc)

New Media and Society (https://journals.sagepub.com/home/nms)

Social media + society (https://uk.sagepub.com/en-gb/eur/journal/social-media-society)

Television and New Media (https://journals.sagepub.com/home/tvn)

Key Social Media Research Centres

Centre for Analysis of Social Media, Demos (https://www.demos.co.uk/research-area/centre-for-analysis-of-social-media/)

Digital Culture at King's College (http://www.kcl.ac.uk/artshums/ahri/centres/Digicult/Homepage.aspx)

Digital Methods Initiative, University of Amsterdam (https://wiki.digitalmethods.net/Dmi/DmiAbout)

GESIS, Leibniz Institute for the Social Sciences (http://www.gesis.org/en/home/)

Institute of Network Cultures, Hogeschool van Amsterdam (http://networkcultures.org/)

Microsoft's Social Media Collective (https://www.microsoft.com/en-us/research/group/social-media-collective/)

#NSMNSS – New Social Media or New Social Science (http://nsmnss.blogspot.co.uk/)

Oxford Internet Institute, Social Data Science (https://www.oii.ox.ac.uk/research/social-data-science/)

Queensland University of Technology (QUT), Social Media Research Group (http://socialmedia.qut.edu.au/) and Digital Media Research Centre (https://research.qut.edu.au/dmrc/)

Social Media Lab, Ryerson University (http://socialmedialab.ca/)

Social Media Research Centre, University of Westminster, MA in Social Media (https://www.westminster.ac.uk/news/2015/new-book-christian-fuchs%E2%80%99-%E2%80%9Cculture-and-economy-in-the-age-of-social-media%E2%80%9D)

Visual Social Media Lab, Sheffield University (http://visualsocialmedialab.org/)

PART I

WHAT ARE SOCIAL MEDIA AND WHERE DO THEY COME FROM?

1

THE SOCIAL MEDIA LANDSCAPE

Chapter Overview

Introduction	4
Data and Surveillance	5
Cambridge Analytica	6
China's social credit systems	8
Community and Connection	11
Pokémon Go	12
Memes	16
Conclusion	19
Further Reading and Key Resources	20

Chapter Objectives

- Introduce game-changing cases making up the social media landscape
- Identify key themes relevant to social media
  - Data and surveillance: Cambridge Analytica and China's social credit systems
  - Community and connection: Pokémon Go and memes
- Critically assess individual cases and their relationship to the broader social landscape

Introduction

Social media are not just about connection, but also about the circulation of information and communication, sometimes at lightning speeds. Fake news and disinformation are rampant, leading some to refer to the state of pandemic misinformation as an infodemic (see Donovan and Wardle 2020; Gruzd and Mai 2020). The rise of deepfakes, images and videos using AI technology to swap faces or even create people who don't exist at all threatens public trust and the public good. Social media invite new kinds of interaction, impacting on friendship and family groups, as well as reconfiguring public engagement through influencers, memes, viral media, algorithms and bots. Each of these also morphs and changes, from influencers to micro or even nano-influencers, and from memes to meme factories and troll armies (e.g. Abidin 2020). In addition, the normalization of social media metrics, how many likes, views, shares, follows we get, shapes how people perceive and negotiate belonging (see Rogers 2018b). All of these innovations make up a dynamic and shifting social media landscape, making it difficult to work out what is going on and how to make sense of it.

The purpose of this chapter is to provide a focused look at these changes, and introduce game-changing cases which have impacted on how we think about and understand social media. To pick the most relevant cases, I have chosen examples that are cross-platform and widely recognized, and that raise questions about the purpose and meaning of social media. This whole book addresses current and emerging issues across the social media landscape, cases that indirectly and directly illustrate social media power and capture tensions between individual agency and infrastructures, as well as weaving together both commercialism and community. Subsequent chapters address specific platforms as well as cross-cutting themes, particularly in Part III on everyday life, with chapters on selfies (Chapter 7), privacy and dataveillance (Chapter 8), social screens (Chapter 9), and love, intimacy and disconnection (Chapter 10). Yet this chapter focuses on cases that are too big to fit into one chapter, and are relevant, in some way, for all of the other chapters in this book. In addition, it is useful to introduce cases which are not already wrapped in a particular conceptual framing, and can be applied to different theoretical reflections as it suits the reader.

The first two cases focus on data and surveillance, including the Cambridge Analytica events and what we understand as China's social credit systems. The second theme looks at social media in terms of community and connection, and introduces Pokémon Go, Google's augmented reality game that shook popular culture in 2016, as well as memes. Pokémon Go may seem to be an unusual case for a book on social media, but it does highlight the ways in which we are social on location-based platforms, and helps drive our thinking around what are and are not social media (see Chapter 2). Finally, this chapter introduces memes, which are not platform specific but constitute a significant part of digital culture and social media content. These are all complex cases, so at the end of this chapter you will find further readings on all of these cases to help direct you to where you can learn more.

In an age increasingly defined by social media and platforms, it is impossible to capture every relevant and thought-provoking case. This chapter does not aim to be comprehensive; instead it looks to provide a strategic introduction to key issues on and off of social media. These cases illustrate the contradictory and often uneven social landscape, marked by rapid change, fierce debate and serious negative and/or positive implications.

Data and Surveillance

The 2010s have been marked by unprecedented surveillance, the scale of which was revealed by former National Security Agency (NSA) contractor and whistleblower Edward Snowden. Granted permanent residency in Russia in October 2020, Snowden was responsible for leaking 200,000-plus documents to *Guardian* journalists, proving US, UK and Australian government surveillance of citizens around the world. These documents revealed several government programs, such as PRISM, which directly incorporated big tech companies in the mass surveillance of citizens, including Microsoft, Facebook, Apple, Google, YouTube, Skype, Microsoft, Yahoo and many other telecommunications companies (Greenwald 2013, 2014). Other international mass surveillance programs included XKeyScore and Tempora. The NSA selects about 22.4 terabytes of data for review every minute, which is about 5,724 two-hour HD movies (MacAskill and Dance 2013). The NSA established a global precedent for government agencies and how they monitor and surveil citizens through social media.

At near to the same time, the 'Apple-Foxconn alliance', what Jack Qui calls 'Appconn', had become famous for mistreating its staff so badly that a wave of Chinese Apple staff committed suicide in 2010, highlighting a global IT business model based on severe worker exploitation (e.g. via resource extraction for smart phones as well as IT manufacture) (Qui 2017: 6–8). Indeed, Qui argues that Appconn best represents a 'new hegemon', and it is not just Apple or Foxconn, or China's low wages, that contribute to re-creating digital slavery, but the exploitative nature of the global platform economy (2017; cf. Zuboff 2015, 2019; China Labour Watch 2018).

These are important points. In our current landscape, datafication comes with mass surveillance, gross exploitation and the tremendous power of big tech, all of which set the background for two of the most important social media cases of the late 2010s: Cambridge Analytica and China's social credit systems.

Cambridge Analytica (CA)

Cambridge Analytica, henceforth referred to as CA, is a strategic communications firm, self-described as 'a data driven political consulting and commercial marketing firm'. CA is part of SCL (formerly Strategic Communications Laboratory, then called the 'SCL Group'), and came to public attention for using personal data, primarily demographic information as well as 'likes', from 87 million Facebook accounts in 2015. These data were collected, with consent, from approximately 300,000 Amazon Turk workers and Qualtrics panels in 2015 through an app that claimed to test people's personalities. This app was designed by Aleksandr Kogan, a Cambridge professor working with Facebook. Kogan's app collected additional data from each user's Facebook friends (approximately 267 friends each) without consent (Venturini and Rogers 2019: 533). The app collected demographic data and likes in order to make personality predictions about users which were then used for both the Leave.EU and Trump political campaigns in 2016, amongst many other uses (Cadwalladr 2018; Kogan 2018; UK Parliament 2019).

Widely reported in the media as another major 'social media scandal' (e.g. Chang 2018; Confessore 2018; Wong 2019b), the Cambridge Analytica events revealed Facebook's business model is about **collecting user data** and profiting from those data, rather than about connecting people. Based on Facebook's apparent data harvesting, the UK Parliament conducted an 18-month investigation into CA and social media. Based on this, their final report, *Disinformation and Fake News*, found that Facebook offered 'friend permissions' to app developers, allowing those developers to access personal information from users' Facebook 'friends'. This also involved whitelisting or priority access to these kinds of 'friend' data, only for the highest paying developers from 2015. Finally, developers were granted full access to 'lookalike audiences', i.e. audiences mirroring certain demographics or interests shared with the developers' target audience (UK Parliament 2019, based on court case documents for Six4Three vs Facebook on anti-competition and privacy violations).

The parliamentary report found that, contrary to Facebook's claims, these kinds of data-selling practices were not only commonplace, but also integral to Facebook's business model:

> We consider that data transfer for value is Facebook's business model and that Mark Zuckerberg's statement that 'we've never sold anyone's data' is simply untrue. (UK Parliament 2019: 134)

Although directly related to Facebook, the UK Parliament's findings apply to many social media platforms and the 'complex web' of actors involved not only in the Cambridge Analytica events, but also in datafication processes across the web, social and mobile ecosystems. Dr Emma Briant (2018), a propaganda researcher and expert on SCL Group, argues that this case is about much more than one company, and about much more than privacy invasions or data harvesting:

> It's a story about how a network of companies was developed which enabled
> *wide deployment of propaganda tools* – based on propaganda techniques that were
> researched and designed for use as weapons in war zones – on citizens in democratic
> elections. (Emphasis added)

Bearing these two points about CA's broader implications in mind, the most essential points of this case begin with a very brief background.

In terms of politics, CA was founded in deeply political circumstances. For example, Steve Bannon, well known for his far right and extremist politics, was the former Vice President of Cambridge Analytica (2014–2016) as well as the chief executive and chief White House strategist for Donald Trump (2016–2017), and founding member and former executive chairman of Breitbart News ('the platform of the alt-right', 2012–2018) (Cadwalladr 2018, 2019; Osborne 2018). Christopher Wylie, one of the key whistleblowers in the Cambridge Analytica revelations, reported directly to Steve Bannon during his employment at CA – and he claims that he built Bannon's 'psychological warfare machine' (Cadwalladr 2018).

Briant (2018) has also documented the extremist tactics used by CA and its multiple affiliates in political campaigns, such as 'racist and violent video content designed to drive fear and intimidate voters in fragile states' as well as in the US and UK. Cambridge Analytica was not unique in building these kinds of campaigns. It was one company in a complex web of companies and actors, where it is clear that harvested data – from Facebook, from Republican databases, and many other sources – were used by CA (and others) in both Donald Trump's election campaign and Leave.EU campaigns (UK Parliament 2019: 140–47).

While some claim that the quality of Facebook data was too low to be meaningfully analysed (e.g. Venturini and Rogers 2019), Kogan himself notes that not much data are needed to make personality and voting predictions:

> [Former colleagues had] already developed a model to make predictions from likes, and I had experience using the Facebook login app from my previous. This idea of predicting personality from page likes became the foundation of the project that I did with SCL. (Kogan 2018)

In addition, the quality of information has little to do with the fact that these kinds of data are collected, without consent, sold, and used to manipulate political votes and sentiment.

Notably, the public and political attention focused on Cambridge Analytica has many important implications. The first of these is that Facebook has been under investigation by both the US and UK parliaments, and has been fined £500,000 by the Information Commissioner's Office in the UK (ICO 2018) and $5 billion USD by the Federal Trade Commission (FTC) in the US (FTC 2019). While this may seem a hefty fine, when the exchange rate is accounted for and the two fines are combined, they account for 0.03% of Facebook's 2019 total revenue (Facebook fourth-quarter 2019 report).

The ICO has also found that current UK electoral law is not fit for a digital age and has called for radical reform of 'electoral communications laws and rules on overseas involvement in UK elections' (UK Parliament 2019). The ICO has also called for the creation of a powerful new independent regulator to oversee a new 'Compulsory Code of Ethics for tech companies' (UK Parliament 2019). These proposals have been further explored in the Online Harms white paper, which 'sets out the government's plans for a world-leading package of measures to keep UK users safe online' (UK Government 2019). In what seems like a final development, CA and SCL filed for insolvency and shut in early 2018.

Thus, while it seems the CA revelations have sparked serious changes to Facebook's practices and the regulation of tech, data and political practice, many questions remain about the effectiveness of such proposals. For starters, both CA and the SCL Group have a parent company, Emerdata, which continues to conduct business and is run by the same players as CA and the SCL Group. Indeed, the UK Parliament's final report on 'Fake News and Disinformation' states:

> Senior individuals involved in SCL and Cambridge Analytica appear to have moved onto new corporate vehicles ... We recommended that the National Crime Agency, if it is not already, should investigate the connections between the company SCL Elections Ltd and Emerdata Ltd. (2019: 337–338; cf. Dwilson 2019; Siegelman 2018)

Some of the actions taken by Facebook, like their controversial 'pivot to privacy' (discussed in Chapter 8), may appear to be a serious attempt to address its horrendous privacy record, yet it continues aggressive data collection and harvesting as standard practice (Lapowsky and Thompson 2019; Sujon 2019a, 2019c; Wong 2019a, Wong 2019b; Zuckerberg 2019).

China's social credit systems (SCS)

Credit, the process of securing money or resources in exchange for repayment, often with interest, at a later date, takes many forms:

> From traditional reciprocal gift exchanges to the present digital credit scoring systems, the credit rating is seen to reflect an individual's character, traits, and morality. Because of credit, a subject's economic life is inseparable from his or her social life. (Chong 2019: 291)

Credit scoring and rating systems share many features with China's social credit systems, all of which calculate a score indicating how much of a risk it is to give a person credit, such as a mortgage, a loan or a credit card. Social credit incorporates social and civic data with financial information to develop 'social credit scores' for citizens. In China, these systems involve government coordination with private companies to create a proposed national 'centralized data infrastructure' to do just this (Liang et al. 2018). Wong and Dobson (2019), two internet researchers from Curtin University, argue that although the nationalization of social credit is unique to China, credit scores, ratings systems and even loyalty schemes operate on similar principles (e.g. FICO, Schufa, Affirm, Lodex). While China's social credit systems have received a lot of attention, they are part of a broader global trend merging social and financial data – and these are lucrative new markets for social platforms and big tech (see O'Dwyer 2019; Swartz 2020). The next section introduces the global players and the Chinese context.

Baidu, Alibabi, Tencent and Xiaomi (BATX) are considered the Eastern hemisphere's power platforms, and are often compared to Google, Amazon, Facebook and Apple (GAFA) for their size and dominance in the 'global platform economy' (Barwise 2018, see ch. 5; Kloet et al. 2019: 2; Van Dijck et al. 2018: 164). China is also tech savvy, featuring the world's largest national 'internet user base' (Kent et al. 2017: 2) and 'achieving global leadership in 5G, AI and quantum computing' among other innovative digital technologies (Shi-Kupfer and Ohlberg 2019). De Seta (2015) refers to the Chinese context as 'post-digital', which refers to a state where apps and the internet are deeply embedded in everyday life. WeChat and WeChatPay have 'become the most popular mobile application[s] in China today' and are often reported as the next Facebook or Google, particularly as the 'leading model of innovative products' (Plantin and de Seta 2019: 2). Indeed, social platforms in China are significant, but they are only one part of the Chinese digital infrastructure and ecosystem (Chong 2019; de Seta 2015; Plantin and de Seta 2019).

Within this dynamic digital environment, China is also known for its authoritarian post-socialist political state, one that many argue is marked by increasing private ownership (Fuchs 2017: 257–61) and a move towards 'excessive liberalization rather than democratiza-tion' (Han 2018: see ch. 1). It is also shaped by the 'collapse of communist political systems in Eastern Europe', and a long record of human rights abuses (e.g. the Tiananmen democracy movement, see Wang and Minzner 2015; and mistreatment of 13 million Muslim minorities such as the Uighurs and Kazakhs; as well as a long record of censorship and arbitrary detention, see Amnesty 2019; Human Rights Watch 2019). In terms of the digital environment, the 'Great Firewall' started as a 'large-scale infrastructure project' in the 1990s and is made up of:

> … social media regulations, IP blacklists, keyword filters, data gateways, and human censors, [and] is regularly invoked to explain online surveillance and internet censorship in China (Tsui, 2007). The Great Firewall is perhaps the most well-known example of Chinese ICT infrastructure. (Plantin and de Seta 2019: 8)

Thus, on the one hand, many experts in Chinese media note a longstanding tradition of state surveillance, social control and monitoring. On the other hand, many point to the immense difficulty in exercising control over the internet due to digital complexity and fragmentation, factors that complicate both China's social credit systems, which are pilots, and their national integration (e.g. Cassiano 2019; Han 2018; Ohlberg 2019). Deploying a centralized SCS by 2020, as has been the plan, means developing an infrastructure synthesizing platform, economic and social data, as well as 'distinct but interconnected processes of data collection, data aggregation, and data analytics' (Liang et al. 2018).

What this means is that discussions of 'China's social credit system' often conflate existing smaller pilot projects with plans for a nationally centralized and state governed one, due to deploy in 2020. The reality is that 'there is no single, nationally coordinated system' and smaller social credit systems work very differently (Ohlberg, as cited in Kobie 2019; cf. Creemers 2018). Indeed, the SCS involves many currently decentralized projects, which are often presented in western media as a single coordinated and national system.

Bearing all of this in mind – China's position as a global tech innovator, including the dominant role of BATX in the global platform economy, its long record of human rights abuses and the rise of social media – there are two major mobile payment systems, which use voluntary social credit systems. These two payment systems are both bigger than Paypal and have prompted some to note that China is leading the way towards a 'cashless society' (Ipsos Mori 2017). Both of these 'platform based systems' (Chong 2019: 1) currently offer opt-in social credit systems:

- The WeChat Payment Score, launched in 2014 and part of WeChat Pay, Tencent; and
- Sesame or Zhima credit, launched in 2015, which is a feature of Alipay, formerly an Alibaba affiliate and now a subsidiary of Ant Financial.

Gladys Chong argues that 'credit' is indispensable 'in today's post-socialist consumption driven China' (2019: 2). Sesame credit generates a social score based on five factors, i.e. 'credit history; behaviour and preference; fulfillment capacity; identity characteristics; and social relationships' – all of which are used to predict risk and trustworthiness, based on a range of sources including government information:

> Because of the platform's close connection and cooperation with state authorities, data are collected from reliable and authoritative sources, such as the Public Security Ministry, the Taxation Office, and legal financial institutes. Its reliability is then translated into both economic and political value. (Chong 2019: 5–6)

According to Chong (2019: 6), who conducted ethnographic research with 39 Sesame Credit users, her informants were assigned credit scores ranging from 350 (very low) to 950 (very high). A 'good' although average score is approximately 600–650 (Koetse 2018). Those with credit scores of 750 or more were given a number of social privileges such as:

- access to dedicated priority check-in and security services at the Beijing Airport;
- being allowed to apply for foreign visas without providing documentation;
- receiving waivers on deposits for transport rentals and hotel rooms;
- being granted higher credit limits. (Chong 2019: 6; cf. Koetse 2018)

Indeed, Chong relays that her informants confirm connections between Sesame Credit and real estate companies. Any potential clients of rental platforms (like Ziroom) must submit their Sesame Credit score along with their applications.

Those with high scores may be released from paying deposits and be placed on red or reward lists, while those with lower scores may be denied properties along with other social rights (Chong 2019: 6–7). For example, social credit scores have been linked with blacklists, preventing 17.5 million purchases of plane tickets and 5.5 million train journeys (Moran 2019). Others have reported the use of blacklists as a form of 'public shaming', experienced by those who have had their mobile greeting messages changed so that all incoming callers hear that the person they are calling has been blacklisted (Moran 2019). While current coverage focuses on individuals, companies are also subject to these social credit systems, and both 'red' (rewards) and 'black' (punishments) lists are in place (Ohlberg 2019: 23–24).

'Nosedive', an episode of *Black Mirror* (Season 3, episode 1), tells the story of Lacie Pound's rise and fall in a speculative vision of a society where the number of likes you get directly corresponds to your social status – including your ability to travel, to rent property and to smoothly interact with others. This dark fiction touches a nerve with many viewers, by directly tapping into today's like economy. This particular episode, along with Orwell's *Nineteen Eighty-Four*, are often compared to China's new 'social credit system' introduced above. Many researchers caution against a totalizing view, as currently only plans exist for *one* nationally coordinated social credit system, and the current state of affairs shows a complicated and 'highly localized' set of pilot systems (Ohlberg 2019: 25; cf. Han 2018; Kobie 2019; Liang et al. 2018). Others compare these social credit systems to an advanced loyalty scheme, pointing to existing western practices around calculating credit ratings based on character traits (e.g. age, marital status), trade experience and 'moral attributes (e.g. honesty and punctuality)' (Chong 2019: 5). While there may be similarities, it is worth noting China's political history and the implications of scoring people based on algorithmic calculations linking their social behaviour, credit, social status.

Community and Connection

We all tell stories about who we are, and through telling these stories, we connect with others and affirm our own sense of self. For human beings, this is our modus operandi. It is how we survive – through expression and social connection.
(Papacharissi 2018: 1)

As Papacharissi opens in the quote above, 'we all tell stories' and 'connect with others'. Digital tools and social media are among the most dominant contemporary places for us to tell our stories, even if 'the narratives we produce [can be] connective, but not always connected' (Papacharissi 2018: 9). From its earliest inception, the internet has been driven by a vision of 'connection', linking people so that they can communicate, and as such there are almost countless cases to choose from. Wikipedia, for example, aims to create a reality where 'every single person on the planet is given free access to the sum of all human knowledge' (Jimmy

Wales, Wikipedia co-founder, interview with Tippet 2016). This site has been widely documented as one of the greatest examples of collective intelligence and collaborative work. Many have held up the collective rather than capitalistic orientation of Wikipedia, finding it exemplifies: collective intelligence and a radical democracy (Fuchs 2017; Shirky 2009); a new kind of networked fourth estate (Benkler 2006); the democratic and participatory potential of digital media (Jemielniak 2014; Lih 2009; Reagle 2010); and the power of open systems and open knowledge (Tkacz 2015). Wikipedia is just one of the Wikimedia Foundation's (https://wiki mediafoundation.org/) many ambitious not-for-profit projects aiming to promote 'free knowledge'.

Similar to Wikimedia and Wikipedia's 'alternative' approach to social technologies, 'alternative social media' share a similar not-for-profit logic. Following in the footsteps of alternative media (e.g. community radio, citizens' media, underground newspapers, Indymedia), alternative social media are any social media that 'challenge ... actual concentrations of media power' in terms of production, organization and audiences (Couldry and Curran 2003, as cited in Gehl 2015). Indeed Robert Gehl (2015) provides a useful overview of alternative social media, including sites like TOR (an onion browser that anonymizes users' locations and IP addresses), Diaspora* (an open source and decentralized social network project that is independently owned and operated by its users) and Mastodon (a Twitter-like micro-blog, based on an open-source platform that users can build, design and develop), among others. All of these provide different user experiences based on a collective orientation, rather than one driven by profit like with corporate social media. Many have argued that this orientation fosters a very different social experience that enables user rather than platform control, opening up 'a world beyond Facebook' and shaped by a more people-oriented sociality (e.g. Gehl 2015, 2018; Lovink and Rasch 2013; Zulli et al. 2020).

We might also consider the many heart-warming tales of social media users finding long lost friends and family, mobilizing life-saving support in times of personal crisis or disaster, and we could even turn to the many examples of protest and social movements (e.g. #BlackLivesMatter, #MeToo, #IdleNoMore) to find vibrant instances of community building, connection and collective organizing (see Chapter 6; Tufecki 2017b; also Highfield 2016; Lingel 2017). All of these cases are worth thinking through, yet they are all well documented elsewhere. Next, this chapter provides two cases, first on Pokémon Go and then on memes. Both of these cases illustrate what Picone et al. refer to as 'small acts of engagement' (2019, as discussed in Chapter 3). For these reasons, both memes and Pokémon Go provide an interesting insight into social connection and community building in everyday life. Each case provides a closer look at how users engage social technologies to share, shape, engage, play and tell their own stories.

Pokémon Go

Pokémon Go is a mobile gaming phenomenon that shook popular culture in 2016, enabling users to connect with others in surprising ways. Pokémon Go players were able to play and explore their own stories and experiences within the much bigger story of Pokémon.

In terms of its origins, Pokémon Go made its first public appearance as 'the Pokémon Challenge' on April Fool's Day, 2014 (https://youtu.be/4YMD6xELI_k). The challenge placed virtual Pokémon on Google Maps, daring users to catch as many as they could. The winner would be rewarded with a job at Google as 'Pokémon Master' (Statt 2014). While many claim this was one of Google's many 'April Fool's jokes' (Hern 2016; Statt 2014), this may have been more of a PR trick than anything else, particularly given Google's underground success with Ingress, an augmented reality game developed by Niantic, one of their subsidiaries (https://www.ingress.com/).

Regardless of Google's motivation, the response to the challenge was overwhelming, leading to a formal partnership between Niantic, Pokémon Company and Nintendo announced in 2015, followed by the launch of Pokémon Go in July 2016 (Shamsian 2016; Webster, 2017). From there, the game exploded. People downloaded the app, and hit the streets with their phones in hand, leading them through an augmented overlay of the city, so they could catch virtual Pokémon. Within days of its 2015 launch, it had become a global phenomenon, with daily use outstripping daily traffic on Facebook, Twitter and Tinder (Bogle 2016; Isbister 2016; O'Neill 2016). The game had been downloaded more than 1 billion times between its launch and 2019 (Webster 2019). (See Figure 1.1.)

Figure 1.1   Pokémon Go! Game play in Helsinki, Finland

Source: photograph by David Grandmougin on Unsplash

In terms of social media, Pokémon Go may not be a perfect fit for widely accepted criteria (see Chapter 2), yet it raises interesting questions about how we define social media, and provides a fascinating example of the convergence between industries (Google and Nintendo), platforms (augmented reality, mobile phones, gaming consoles and apps) and emerging digital socialities. In addition, Pokémon Go and social media share a similar haptic (touch-based) and connective user experience, shaped not only by the smartphone interface, but also by sociable apps – apps that enable interaction, exchange and connection (Apperley and Moore 2018; Hjorth and Richardson 2017). Thus, Pokémon Go is an important example for those interested in social media because it provides insight into the life of one social technology, developed by a powerful platform and for engaging millions of people in play. To fully understand the Pokémon Go phenomenon, it is important to look more closely at: the game's meaning and transmedia history; its wildly popular public response; and Google's stake in the game.

Pokémon has a much longer history as a popular children's story and game, one that enrolled kids in imaginative world making. Created by Satoshi Tajiri in 1996, Pokémon is Japanese slang for 'pocket monsters', and although it began its public life as an interactive game on Nintendo's Game Boy, it evolved into a booming media franchise, featuring a TV series (launched in 1996), trading cards, digital games, films, merchandise, events, apps and more (https://www.pokemon.com/us/about-pokemon/). The game is based on Tajiri's love of insect collecting, a passion which is clearly translated into Tajiri's colourful Pokémon world where trainers (the players) capture and collect wild 'pocket monsters' for training, trade, battling and sharing. Notably, all of the 'monsters' grow best under their trainers' *caring* guidance, emphasizing pro-social interactions (Bainbridge 2014: 402). Thus, the central story of learning to know and value Pokémon is deeply inspiring to children and young people.

This is not all. Pokémon also encourages children to develop intense literacies. For example, Giddings (2017) argues that the franchise's imaginative power is its key strength. Any Pokémon fan or 'any parent whose children are or have been fans of Pokémon' will remember the intensity of collecting (cards, toys, merchandise, etc.) and the rich knowledge fans develop of each Pokémon (its strengths, weaknesses, points), expressed in 'the constant chatter' of interactive game play (Giddings 2017: 60–61; see also Bainbridge 2014: 400; Henthorn et al. 2019: 6). Certainly, 'interactivity' and intense sociality have always been 'a major part of the game design' across platforms and across generations (Bainbridge 2014: 402).

Pokémon's longer history may provide some indication of its 2016 success. As Henthorn et al. (2019) argue, Pokémon Go's enthusiastic public response was:

> Fueled by a mix of nostalgia, curiosity, and simply having something to do while enjoying the summer months, players took to the outdoors in hopes of finding their favorite Pokémon. And they did so in unprecedented numbers (Henthorn et al. 2019: 7; on nostalgia, cf. Keogh 2017).

Reports of the game increasing people's physical and mental well-being also began flooding social media. For example, Clem Bastow commented on 'the beauty of the game', claiming she had 'already':

> … helped strangers find local gyms and Pokéstops, or informed them of a Psyduck infestation nearby. In fact, far from causing Pokémon-related clashes, the game seems to be bringing people together. (July 11, five days after Pokémon Go's launch on July 6, 2016)

Others reported that going outside to catch Pokémon meant they were walking more, noting improved mental health and benefiting from increased exercise (e.g. Donovan 2016; Isbister 2016; Saker and Evans 2018). Indeed, Larissa Hjorth and Jordi Jiminez (2019) report on early findings from their mobile gaming research, noting that Pokémon Go enabled respondents to deeply engage mundane places in their neighbourhoods, inspiring new experiences and perspectives. Additionally, respondents developed social connections with new people and with those whom they were already familiar with. Hjorth and Jiminez (2019) relay the story of one 67-year-old grandmother, Sofia, who used Pokémon Go with her young grandson, rediscovering niche locations and finding new ways to spend time with family. Indeed, Sofia said the game made her 'feel fit and socially engaged in her community. And she became an outstandingly super-cool grandmother in the eyes of her grandson, Diego.' Hjorth and Jiminez argue that Sofia's story is only one of many other similar stories where the game helped players discover a revived sense of the world (cf. Chamary 2018; Henthorn et al. 2019; O'Neill 2016). Social workers in Sofia's home town, Badalona, recommend Pokémon Go to improve health, well-being and, most of all, one's sense of connection to others (Hjorth and Jiminez 2019).

Yet, when we look at Niantic, Google's former subsidiary, and Google's role in the creation of Pokémon Go, we see a very different role. John Hanke, founder and CEO of Niantic, began his career developing a digital map of the world, which Google bought and rebranded as Google Earth in 2004. Thus, Hanke brings with him tremendous knowledge of mapping, as well as years of Google geo data (https://nianticlabs.com/). While still a subsidiary of Google, Niantic developed and launched Ingress, another alternate reality game using smartphones to navigate an augmented reality overlay of the world. Similar to Pokémon Go, Ingress players wandered their cities making real-life connections with other players, and providing real-time, real-place information of those cities (Shamsian 2016). Pokémon Go builds directly on Ingress-generated data on specific places. Pokestops and gyms, all the places where players gather to stock up on Pokémon and interact with others, are built directly on top of the most popular places in Ingress (Bogle 2016).

As a result, Niantic can sell advertising and access to these geo-located hotspots, generating revenue from 'retailers and fast-food restaurants' hoping to boost sales and traffic (Jin 2017: 57). In addition, as Shoshanna Zuboff notes, Pokémon Go (and Ingress before it) generates masses of personal data, providing a data collecting 'prototype' where big tech can develop what she calls a 'behavioural-futures-market' (2019: 341). From this perspective, Pokémon Go may very well connect players in new and interesting ways, but it also enables big tech to capitalize on the personal and locational data generated by players.

Next, we turn to memes, introducing what they are and why they are meaningful for understanding social media.

Memes

The final case in this chapter concentrates on a much more granular and bottom-up phenomenon, i.e. memes. Memes sit between personal expression and public communication, providing important insights on everyday digital connection across social platforms, digital sites and everyday life. Although commonplace, and widely understood, it is worth defining exactly what they mean, before exploring them further:

meme (mēm)

N. A unit of cultural information, such as a cultural practice or idea, that is transmitted verbally or by repeated action from one mind to another (Free Dictionary, https://www.thefreedictionary.com/meme)

A meme is basically an idea that is easily transferable from one mind to another. Think "catchphrases." Memes are created when a large group of users come to identify with a particular image or slogan (4Chan FAQ, http://www.4chan.org/faq#meme)

A unit of human cultural transmission analogous to the gene. (Dawkins 1976)

Of all of these definitions of 'meme', the one most often cited by media and cultural researchers is the last one, developed by evolutionary biologist and atheist Richard Dawkins. The term meme is grounded in the notion of 'cultural evolution' and the idea that culture can be transmitted and replicated, much like genetic material. The etymology of the word comes from the Greek word *mimēma*, meaning 'that which is imitated', and is often linked to 'mimic' or 'mimicry'. According to one leading cultural theorist and meme researcher, Limor Shifman, the genetic analogy has been pushed too far, and 'seeking cultural equivalents for all principal evolutionary genetic concepts' compromises our understanding of culture (Alvarez, 2004: 25, as cited in Shifman 2013: 366). Memes work quite differently to genes, and as a result the genetic metaphor can reduce culture to biology, which unnecessarily 'narrows and simplifies complex human behaviors' (Shifman 2013: 366).

Bennett and Segerberg take a different position, arguing that a meme is 'a symbolic packet that travels easily across large and diverse populations because it is easy to imitate, adapt personally and share widely with others' (2013: 37–38, 2012). Based on social movement and large-scale mobilizing research, Bennett and Segerberg argue that memes are *'network building and bridging units of social information*' as they have seen in: Put People First March; the Arab Spring; the Indignados (the indignant); and Occupy (Bennett and Segerberg 2012: 745). Taking a related angle, Shifman proposes approaching memes as '*a prism for understanding certain aspects of contemporary culture*' (2013: 363, emphasis added; 2014).

Like Pokémon Go, memes are not confined to one social media platform, and instead illustrate flow across social apps, sites, technologies and platforms. In this way, memes are an important part not only of people's personal experience, and the stories we tell, but are also crucial aspects for connecting people across social media, and across time and space. This section introduces the origins of memes, and examines the intensely individual and social aspect of memes (cf. Milner 2016; Shifman 2013).

Digital memes can be traced back to the first use of the emoticon on September 19, 1982. At this time text-based bulletin boards were widely used, and because these boards were visually limited, very few emotional cues could be easily communicated, leading to 'flame wars'. Flame wars were highly emotive or abusive exchanges. Professor Scott E. Fahlman proposed a sideways smiley face as a way to indicate emotion (see Figure 1.2).

From: Scott E. Fahlman <Fahlman at Cmu-20c>

I propose the following character sequence for joke markers:

:-)

Read it sideways. Actually, it is probably more economical to mark things that are NOT jokes, given current trends. For this, use

:-(

Figure 1.2 The first emoticon

Source: Fahlman http://www.cs.cmu.edu/~sef/sefSmiley.htm, cf. Deffree (2018); Baer (2015)

Kate Miltner (2014) examines LOL (laugh out loud) cats, a proto-meme of the early 2000s, arguing that her research shows 'how seemingly trivial pieces of media – pictures of cats with captions – can act as meaningful conduits for intricate social relations'. LOLcats is an interesting example of early meme culture (see Figure 1.3), and features a standard meme layout (image macros overlaid with text). LOLcats generally feature cute pictures of cats, captioned using 'lolspeak', a kind of grammatically incorrect language often removing all linking verbs (e.g. 'am', 'is', 'are') Miltner argues that 'lolspeak' 'is the lingua franca of the I Can Has Cheezburger comment boards', and is about demonstrating who is (or is not) a part of the LOLcat community.

'I can has cheezburger' was at the heart of the LOLcat community, and it not only grew in popularity but also came to be a 'web empire' soon after the Cheezburger Network was founded in 2007. The network bought up 53 other social humour sites such as Fail blog and KnowYourMeme (Wortham 2010), becoming 'a multi-million dollar media empire and was ranked 28 on the Wall Street Journal's top 50 venture capital-backed companies' (Ehrlich

Figure 1.3 'Lolspeak: I furst language born of I intertubes'

Source: Miltner (2014)

2013. At its peak, the site generated a massive fan base and considerable traffic, including a 'readership of 16.5 million people who share more than 500,000 pictures and videos a month, and those same folks view 375 million pages and 110 million videos a month as well' (Ehrlich 2013). Cheezeburger, Inc., based in Seattle, was purchased in 2016 by a media company called Literally Media based in Tel Aviv (Cook 2016).

Although memes and social humour can be profitable, the point for most people is not about making money, or even about acknowledging authorship. Instead, memes are about 'the inherent fun' and 'being able to share something with someone else' (MemeGeek CS, male 27, as cited by Miltner 2014). Miltner, whose early work examined the LOLcat community, notes that LOLcat users, like contemporary meme consumers now, are most interested in meaningful social connections:

> Fundamentally, people engaged with LOLCats for their own entertainment and to make meaningful connections with others, whether on a dyadic or a communal level. (Miltner 2014)

Thus, memes are a cultural shorthand – an abbreviated symbolic system – used for personal expression and social connection. Yet, memes also act as a cultural shorthand for participatory culture (see Chapter 6), and are one of the foundations of social technologies, making up 'public conversations' (Milner 2016). While many theorists have noted the dualistic nature of memes, as both intensely, individually personal and as well as intensely social, even public – Milner frames memes as 'aggregate texts' that 'are significant as individual strands in vast tapestries of public conversations' (2016: 2, 4). Memes have come a long way from LOLcats, but even in their early days, they have always been about connection and shared culture as well as humour.

Conclusion

The four cases presented in this chapter surface big tensions between data, surveillance, community and connection. These tensions are a part of every social media experience, and sit at the heart of the logic driving social media from both platform and user perspectives. These four cases provide important insights into the contours of the social media landscape, even if that landscape is made up of many more platforms, apps, cases, longstanding and emerging trends.

Cambridge Analytica reveal social media as data extraction and collection platforms, which drive greater user surveillance and push the 'social platforms' into ever expanding sectors and markets. These personal data have been used for political manipulation and expose serious flaws with the regulation of public information and misinformation. China's social credit systems, only part of a crowded global market of social payments and social credit scoring, show a move towards the nationalization of social and financial data which has far-reaching consequences not only for human rights, but also for the public role of social media. Both of these cases expose the importance of social media, particularly those platforms that are part of the GAFA and BATX empires, as *public infrastructures* shaping the political, economic and social dimensions of everyday life. These issues, and the changing roles of data and surveillance in our lives, intersect with every aspect of the social media landscape.

Yet social media are also about human connection. Pokémon Go, a social gaming platform, illustrates the sometimes surprising ways that social media can bring people together. Pokémon Go players found community where they were not expecting it, including the strengthening of existing bonds and the discovery of new ones. Building upon Google's gaming predecessors like Ingress, Pokémon Go was able to capitalize on massive amounts of user and geo-data, but in ways that evoke feelings of connection and togetherness. Similarly, memes, the lingua franca of the internet, allow people to easily express themselves and participate in public conversations. In these ways, memes are fundamentally connective, easily linking people across platforms, through shared ideas, experiences and feelings. These multiple, platformed points of connection are also central to the logic of social media.

In closing, this chapter introduces readers to the social media landscape through four cases which surface pervasive tensions within each case, and across the sector more broadly. Within this dynamic landscape and within each social platform, there are many additional tensions, yet data and connection, surveillance and community are at the heart of all of them. Each of these cases (Cambridge Analytica, China's social credit systems, Pokémon Go and memes) provide an important foundation for making sense of social media, as well as their current impact and future consequences.

Further Reading and Key Resources: Data and surveillance

Cambridge Analytica (CA)

The Great Hack (2019) https://www.thegreathack.com/, film by Amir, K.; Noujaim, J. (Directors), Netflix.

The Cambridge Analytica Files, *Guardian*. https://www.theguardian.com/news/series/cambridge-analytica-files

Cadwalladr, C. (2019) Facebook's role in Brexit — and the threat to democracy, TED, April. https://www.ted.com/talks/carole_cadwalladr_facebook_s_role_in_brexit_and_the_threat_to_democracy/transcript?language=en

UK Government (2019) Online Harms White Paper, Gov.UK, April 8. https://www.gov.uk/government/consultations/online-harms-white-paper

Kogan, A. (2018) Written evidence submitted by Aleksandr Kogan, text submitted to the The Digital, Culture, Media and Sport Committee of the UK Parliament. https://www.parliament.uk/documents/commons-committees/culture-media-and-sport/Written-evidenceAleksandr-Kogan.pdf

UK Parliament (2019) Disinformation and 'fake news': Final Report, Feb. https://publications.parliament.uk/pa/cm201719/cmselect/cmcumeds/1791/179102.htm

Zuckerberg, M. (2018) 'I want to share an update on the Cambridge Analytica situation …', Facebook, March 21. https://www.facebook.com/zuck/posts/10104712037900071

China's social credit systems (SCS)

Chong, G. P. L. (2019) Cashless China: securitization of everyday life through Alipay's social credit system—Sesame Credit, *Chinese Journal of Communication*. DOI: 10.1080/17544750.2019.1583261

De Seta, G. (2015) Postdigital Wangluo: the Internet in Chinese everyday life, *Anthropology Now*, 7 (3), pp. 106–117. DOI: 10.1080/19428200.2015.1103621

Han, R. (2018) *Contesting Cyberspace in China: Online Expression and Authoritarian Resilience*. Columbia University Press.

Kloet, J. D.; Poell, T.; Guohua, Z.; Fai, C. (2019) The platformization of Chinese society: infrastructure, governance, and practice, *Chinese Journal of Communication*. DOI: 10.1080/17544750.2019.1644008

O'Dwyer, R. 2019. The bank of Facebook, Institute of Network Cultures, June 19. https://networkcultures.org/blog/2019/06/19/rachel-o-dwyer-the-bank-of-facebook/

Ohlberg, M. (2019) China's social credit system: what you should know and how you can prepare, American Chamber Shanghai – *Insight Magazine*, January/February, pp. 23–25. https://www.amcham-shanghai.org/sites/default/files/2019-01/AmCham_InsightMagazine_JanFeb_2019.pdf#page=23

Swartz, L. (2020) *New Money: How Payment Became Social Media*. Yale University Press.

Further Reading and Key Resources: Community and connection

Pokémon Go

'Google Maps: Pokémon Challenge' (2014), https://youtu.be/4YMD6xELI_k

Niantic Labs, https://nianticlabs.com/

The Pokémon Company, https://www.pokemon.com

Bainbridge, J. (2014). 'It is a Pokémon world': the Pokémon franchise and the environment, *International Journal of Cultural Studies*, 17 (4), pp. 399–414. https://doi.org/10.1177/1367877913501240

Giddings, S. (2017) Pokémon GO as distributed imagination, *Mobile Media & Communication*, 5 (1), pp. 59–62. https://doi.org/10.1177/2050157916677866

Henthorn, J.; Kulak, A.; Purzycki, K.; Vie, S. (Eds.) (2019) *The Pokémon Go Phenomenon: Essays on Public Play in Contested Spaces*. McFarland.

Jin, D. Y. (2017) Critical interpretation of the Pokémon GO phenomenon: the intensification of new capitalism and free labor, *Mobile Media & Communication*, 5 (1), pp. 55–58. https://doi.org/10.1177/2050157916677306

Memes

Meme Generator, http://memegenerator.net/

Know Your Meme, http://knowyourmeme.com/

Miltner, K. M. (2014) There's no place for lulz on LOLCats: the role of genre, gender and group identity in the interpretation and enjoyment of an internet meme, *First Monday*, 19 (8), August 4. URL: http://firstmonday.org/ojs/index.php/fm/article/view/5391/4103

Miltner, R. M. (2016) *The World Made Meme*. The MIT Press.

Phillips, W.; Milner, R. A. (2017) *The Ambivalent Internet: Mischief, Oddity and Ambivalence Online*. Polity.

Shifman, L. (2014) *Memes in Digital Culture*. Wiley.

Shifman, L. (2013) Memes in a digital world: reconciling with a conceptual troublemaker, *Journal of Computer Mediated Communication*, 18 (3), pp. 362–77. http://onlinelibrary.wiley.com/doi/10.1111/jcc4.12013/full

THE HISTORICAL ORIGINS
OF SOCIAL MEDIA

Chapter Overview

Introduction   24
Life Cycles of Social Media as Products, Technologies and Knowledge   27
Four Stages of Social Media   28
    Stage 1: Prehistory (1980s–1990s)   29
    Stage 2: Early development (1990s–2006)   34
    Stage 3: Consolidation and growth (2007–2012)   44
    Stage 4: Maturation (2013–present)   49
Conclusion: What Next?   54
Questions and Activities   56
Further Reading   56

╶Chapter Objectives╶

- Gain an understanding of the origins and development of social media
- Understand the rich historical context related to the emergence of social media
- Map the technological and conceptual development of social media in chronological order
- Provoke thoughtful analysis of social media and their broader digital landscape
- Identify unique features of social media compared with other networked media

Introduction

Almost everyone knows what social media are and can easily identify what kind of sites are and are not social media. However, despite this familiarity, there has been a long search for a definition, one that clearly cuts through the constant change and widespread ubiquity of social media. While social media and networked technologies have evolved, social media scholarship has also become a field of its own, bringing together a wide range of multi-disciplinary scholars and researchers from diverse fields such as media, sociology, education, computer science, web science, cultural studies, science and technology studies, human computer interaction, computer-mediated communication, information science, humanities and many others. The range of methods, tools and disciplinary lineages leads to vast differences in approach, as well as understandings of social media. In addition, platforms are growing, overlapping and converging with different industries, as we can see with social video, film and television (e.g. YouTube Red, Facebook Watch, IGTV and Snapchat's Bitmoji TV). Promotional media are now the territory of influencers and memes, and blur the ways ordinary people and professionals use social media for self-promotion and self-branding. Some of these tactics and features may be shared by those who use social media for creating community and connecting with others, but the differences in interpretation and meaning make it difficult to make sense of a field in churn.

These are the grounds for the current debate and for the contestation around what we mean by 'social media'.

One of the lessons I have learned as a scholar of media and communications is that history is often neglected in the face of new technologies and exciting innovations. This same historical forgetfulness often accompanies thinking on social media, not only by focusing on what is novel, but also on how we contextualize social media within a longer cycle of social and technological development. This chapter closely examines the evolution of social media as networked technologies and as a field, mapping forty years of change in the process. This has been no easy feat. However, this chapter provides an original framework for making sense of a complex territory, primarily from a media and communications and social sciences perspective. Given the wide range of approaches and of definitions, it looks at social technologies as an inclusive term for not only social media sites, but also for the tools, sites, practices and devices which were integral to shaping what social media are today.

This framework is drawn from models of the life cycles of technology, knowledge and products, all of which share a longitudinal approach and account for change over time. In addition, as I have learned by visiting Facebook, Twitter and Google offices, most social media and tech companies organize themselves into 'product teams', responsible for developing and managing specific features. For example, the 'like' button (or 'reactions' on Facebook) is just one product team. Other product teams include the 'newsfeed', 'camera', 'filters', 'updates' and many others. Each product has a team of people working on it, often led by a product manager, who is responsible for leading the team and overseeing the product's development, as well as working with the company's other product managers. This is important. It means that although we think of each social media platform as one entity, they are complex organizations geared towards making and profiting from successful products. As a result, the product life cycle is an important model for understanding how social media change and develop over time. However, they are not just single products, they are multiple products within complex technologies linked with and involving systems of knowledge.

Based on the life cycle model for products, knowledge and technologies, this chapter proposes that social media have developed over four stages: prehistory (1980s–1990s), early development (1990s–2006), consolidation and growth (2007–2012), and maturation and a more critical turn (2013–present). Over these four stages, social media have moved from single-sited web spaces only accessible by often fixed computers, to multi-sited, cross-platform spaces spread across the web and accessible from most people's pockets. In each of these stages, social media, and how we think of them, have changed. Social media are no longer what they once were, but their roots are important, and knowing these origins help us understand what they are today. This chapter is about those origins and how they have shaped social media, and this will help us know where they are going tomorrow.

Social media studies has also developed alongside the development of social media. Looking to the origins of social media shows that there has been a gap between these technologies and related scholarship. For example, although SixDegrees (1997) may be one of the first recognizable social media sites, the term 'social network sites' only emerged in the news in 2003, and was not widely used by researchers until 2007 (boyd and Ellison). Yet, despite these gaps, both the technologies and the scholarship follow similar patterns of development. As such, these four stages of social media development also apply to the interdisciplinary roots and cognate work on early social media, as well as their explosive rise as they begin to consolidate as a field. Mapping the field over these four stages illustrates that it has taken time to make sense of and understand these technologies and their social, cultural and political impact. Finally, this is a retrospective project, one that reveals a shifting nomenclature for 'social media', which can make it difficult to pin down a definitive and overarching description. For example, in the late 1990s and early 2000s, names like peer-to-peer, groupware and social software were used before social network sites, so even the term 'social media' took time to take root. While this chapter illustrates the birth of a field, the field (and the technologies) did not arrive from a blank space, where devices and practices went from anti-social to suddenly social ones. Instead, social media, as a set of technologies and as a field of scholarship, build upon and bring together many technologies and many fields.

While writing this chapter, it has become clear that definitions of social media change at every stage. It is very difficult to work through this scholarship without noting these changes. However, having reviewed all of these definitions, one of the most useful comes from Jean Burgess, Alice Marwick and Thomas Poell, in their introduction for *The SAGE Handbook of Social Media* (2018). In this authoritative work on social media, the authors recognize what they call the '*social media paradigm* – a distinctive moment in the history of media and communications shaped by the dominance of social media technologies' (2018: 1, emphasis added). Burgess et al. further elaborate what they include as social media and social media technologies:

> By social media technologies, we mean those digital platforms, services and apps built around the convergence of content sharing, public communication, and interpersonal connection. (2018: 1)

While this may be a useful definition of social media, this breadth can make it difficult to define what social media are and thus what are *not* social media. In addition, this definition does not account for the networked nature of social media, and while 'interpersonal connection' could include affordances, this is less apparent than in the preceding body of work on social media. The advantage, however, is that this broad definition provides considerable flexibility which better accommodates a rapidly changing set of technologies within a rapidly growing field. Bearing this definition of social media in mind, it is clear that social media share a number of unique features. Social media:

- are networked and embedded, within internet and/or mobile networks;
- incorporate user-generated content;
- engage platformed sociality (e.g. profiles, shares, lists); enable interpersonal connections (e.g. comments, likes, messaging);
- are forms of 'polymedia' and complex products or products systems;
- are public, albeit in widely variable ways;
- are interactive;
- are increasingly massive in terms of audiences and as technologies.

While this chapter does not address the many debates and issues associated with the use and development of social media, such as privacy, ownership, narcissism, bullying, algorithms, big data, bias, among many others, it does provide a framework for better understanding these debates, many of which are addressed in the chapters that follow. This chapter aims to provide a comprehensive overview of the conceptual development of social media, as technologies and as a field of study.

Life Cycles of Social Media as Products, Technologies and Knowledge

Many have acknowledged how difficult it is to pin down social media, internet and networked technologies because of their constant and rapid change, making them moving targets. As Nancy Baym suggests, 'trying to list specific types of digital media is frustrating at best. Between this writing and your reading there will be new developments, and things popular as I write will drop from vogue' (2015a: 14). This certainly applies to what I am writing now. However, bearing this caveat in mind, it is worth thinking through these technological and nominal changes in terms of *life cycles*. While this approach is not widely used in social science literature, variations are used in other disciplines. For example, the product life cycle has been very influential for marketing and business (e.g. Levitt 1969; Rink and Swan 1979), while the technology life cycle is used for foresight and future studies, as well as for some approaches to media, science and technology studies (e.g. Jin 2017; Kurzweil 1992; Lehman-Welzig and Cohen-Avigdor 2004; cf. the knowledge life cycle, Birkinshaw and Sheehan 2002). Although there are many differences between and across these life cycles, they point to some consistency around the ways in which products and technologies develop over time, and this helps contextualize innovation and change. (See Table 2.1 for a comparison of these stages across the product, technology and knowledge life cycles.)

Table 2.1 Overview of shared stages across different models for the life cycles of products, technology and knowledge

	Cyclical models			
Stages	Product life cycle (e.g. Levitt 1969)	Technology life cycle (e.g. Kurzweil 1992; Lehman-Welzig and Cohen Avigdor 2004; Sontog 2001)	Knowledge life cycle (e.g. Birkinshaw and Sheehan 2002)	Cycle of technological change (e.g. Anderson 1988; Uusitalo 2014)
1	Development	Precursor, invention and development	Creation	Ferment
2	Growth	Growth	Mobilization	Substitution
3	Maturity	Maturity	Diffusion	Era of dominant design
		False pretenders/defence		
4	Decline/ Saturation	Obsolescence/adaption/ convergence	Commodification	Incremental changes to dominant design

These models provide a useful framework for making sense of change, not only in terms of one innovation, but also for how that innovation compares to others over time. This is an important contribution, one that allows us to make sense of change, and position new technologies within a broader cycle, rather than continually beginning from where a new technology begins – a point that is often immersed in hype and excitement. While each model is distinct, they all share stages which cycle through:

- creation,
- development,
- maturity, and
- decline/obsolescence or saturation/adaption/convergence.

These stages are extremely valuable for understanding the birth and growth of social media. While these cycles have been critiqued for being too broad, too difficult to apply to specific technologies and too hard to measure at each stage, they do give an account of change and life stage, both of which are missing from many accounts of social media (for critiques, see Dhalla and Yuspeh 1976; Jin 2017; Rink and Swan 1979; Taylor and Taylor 2012).

In terms of research and scholarship, there are also cycles. Barry Wellman offers a helpful cycle for framing 'the three ages of internet studies' (2004; cf. Lievrouw and Livingstone 2006). The first age was the transformative era of internet studies, dominated by excitable claims about the positive or negative impact of the internet (Wellman 2004: 124–25). The second age was marked by 'systematic documentation of users and uses', while the third was marked by a transition from documentation to analysis (2004: 125–27). Wellman's three ages provide a conceptual frame which maps predominant themes in different generations of internet scholarship.

This chapter draws inspiration from both the ages of internet studies and the cyclical approaches to products, technology and knowledge, proposing that there are four stages to the development of social technologies, which correspond to the development of social media scholarship. The four stages, detailed in the next section, include: pre-history and ferment (1980s–1990s); early development (1990s–2006); growth and consolidation (2007–2012); maturation and a more critical turn (2013–present).

Four Stages of Social Media

It is quite impossible to include every detail in the development of social technologies, so any history of social media will risk being incomplete. This one is no different. However, each stage aims to capture key moments in the technical and scholarly development of social media, providing an overview of how they emerged as technologies, as a field, and also in relation to parallel or related concepts. In order to balance both breadth and depth, the focus is quite narrowly on 'social media', as they gained traction and cultural currency distinct from digital or internet based technologies (cf. Danet 1995; Goffman 1959; Jenkins 2006; Scholz 2013; Terranova 2004).

Choices have been made around what to include in order to make sense of a vast amount of material. There is also some overlap within and between stages, as it is at times difficult to isolate a precise technological moment and its impact across fields of study. Thus, within each stage, I have included three dimensions: dominant social technologies, key works and related or parallel fields of study as summarized in Table 2.2 (cf. Baym 2006; Lievrouw and Livingstone 2006). Each of these dimensions is indicative of what was happening during each time period, although at times the technological and conceptual do not always fit easily with each other. This conceptualization focuses on understanding social media broadly, identifying commonalities rather than differences, and the many tensions and absences that come along with innovation and social technologies. These stages of social media, as presented here, provide a snapshot of the development of social media as a field, through a select overview of influential work and concepts. (See Table 2.2 for an overview of the social technologies, key concepts and scholars, and parallel concepts and fields central to each stage.)

The purpose of this detailed historical overview is to provide evidence that social media did not arrive out of a blank space. Instead, social media build upon longer histories of networked media. This detailed look at the stages of social media provides a counter-narrative to the presentism that so often accompanies accounts of social media, as well providing a theoretically informed trajectory accounting for change.

Stage 1: Pre-history and ferment of social media (1980s–1990s)

The history of social media begins much earlier with the history of the internet and participatory media, including MUDs (multi-user domains), MMPORGs (massive multiplayer online role-playing games), virtual and online communities, list serves, newsgroups, email and blogs, among many others. These kinds of digital tools grew in popularity in the late 1980s and 1990s, and began shifting the boundaries of more traditional interaction in new and interesting configurations, raising questions about their impact on communication, community, group formation and social organization. At the same time, new interdisciplinary genres of research such as computer-mediated communication (CMC), computer-mediated and communication work (CMCW), computer-supported cooperative work (CSCW), human–computer interaction (HCI) and internet studies, among others, also grew. One marker of this was the 1992 launch of the journal *Computer Supported Cooperative Work* (*CSCW*). In its inaugural editorial, the characteristics of the emerging field were marked by interdisciplinarity, fluidity, and many 'new sociotechnical phenomena' including:

> … large scale systems, new cooperative technologies, new possibilities afforded by networks and distributed computing technologies – and a number of very old ones, such as the nature of cooperation and conflict. (Editorial 1992: 1)

The field itself was defined as 'a complex field of research', involving 'some kind of combination of computing and social science' often 'referring to such disparate notions as groupware,

Table 2.2 Four stages of social media: Social technologies, key scholars, related concepts and parallel fields

	Stage 1: Prehistory & ferment (1980s–1990s)	Stage 2: Early development (1990s–2006)	Stage 3: Growth and consolidation (2007–2012)	Stage 4: Maturation and the critical turn (2013–present)
Social technologies	ARPANET Usenet (1979) BBSs (1980s) The WELL (1985) Email (1973/1990s)	Groupware (1990s) World Wide Web (1993), Peer-to-peer networks (1999) Social software (1990s-2000s) SNSs (e.g. SixDegrees 1997, MySpace 2003, Facebook 2004, Twitter 2006), Blogging (Blogger 1998)	Platforms and mobility, iPhone (2007), VKontakte (2007), Facebook Connect, AirBnB (2008), Whatsapp, Uber (2009), WeChat (Weixin) (2010), Instagram and Snapchat (2011)	Massification - massive users and global industry (e.g. GAFA - Google, Amazon, Facebook, Apple) Extension of platforms Increased platformization Copycat features (e.g. Instagram 'reels', as TikTok copy) Policy and regulation reviews
Key concepts and scholars	Virtual communities (Rheingold 1993; Hauben & Hauben 1997; Hafner 1997) Internet (Abbate 2000; Stevenson 2018; Brügger 2018) Public communication (Abbate 2000; Delwiche 2018) *Computer Supported Collaborative Work* (Launched in 1992)	Network society (Castells 1996; Wellman 1997, 2004; Terranova 2004; Benkler 2006) Web 2.0 (O'Reilly 2005) Participatory culture (Shirky 2001; Davies 2003; Jenkins 2006; Jenkins, Ito, boyd 2015) New media (boyd 2004, 2006; Lievrouw and Livingstone 2006; Silverstone 1999) *Association of Internet Researchers* (AoIR, founded in 1999)	Social Networks Sites (boyd and Ellison 2007; Beer 2008; Lovink 2009; Papacharissi 2011; Siapera 2012; Mandiberg 2012) Polymedia (Madianou and Miller 2012, ethnography, Miller 2009) Produser (Bruns 2008) Platforms (Gillespie 2010) First mention of social network sites in Pew (2007) and Ofcom (2008)	Social media entertainment (Cunningham and Craig 2019) Platform sociality and connective media (Van Dijck, Poell, de Waal 2018; Van Dijck 2013) Capitalist critique, corporate and alternative social media (Fuchs 2014, 2017; Sandoval 2014; Gehl 2015) Platformization (Gerlitz and Helmond 2013; Helmond 2015; Bucher and Helmond 2017) Redefining social media (Ellison and boyd 2013; Carr and Hayes 2015; Baym 2015a, 2015b; Humphreys 2016)

	Stage 1: Prehistory & ferment (1980s–1990s)	Stage 2: Early development (1990s–2006)	Stage 3: Growth and consolidation (2007–2012)	Stage 4: Maturation and the critical turn (2013–present)
		Journal of Computer Mediated Communication (Launched in 1995)		Dedicated scholarship (Burgess, Marwick and Poell 2018; Sloan and Quan-Haase 2017)
		New Media & Society (Launched in 1999)		*Social Media + Society* (Launched in 2015)
Parallel concepts and fields	Social networks and social capital (Bourdieu 1986; Granovetter 1973)	'New media' studies	Debates emerge about legal dimensions, privacy, openness, freedom, community, offline/online dichotomy, political participation, etc.	Data colonialism and rise of the 'social quantification sector' (Couldry and Mejias 2019)
	Symbolic interactionism (Goffman 1990)	Computer-mediated communication (CMC)		Surveillance capitalism (Zuboff 2015, 2019)
		Science and technology studies (STS)	Networked self (Cohen 2012; Papacharissi 2011)	Critical race studies of technology (e.g. Benjamin 2019a, 2019b; Brock 2020; McIlwain 2020; Noble 2018)
	Community (Tonnies)	Information and communication technology (ICTs)	User-generated content (UGC)	Platform capitalism (Srnicek 2017)
	Development of human–computer interaction, computer Sciences and cognate fields	Actor network theory (ANT)		Sharing culture and economy (John 2012, 2016; Sundararajan 2016)
		Convergence culture		Mediatization (Couldry and Hepp 2016)
		Internet studies		
		Social sciences more broadly (political economy, anthropology, psychology)		

collaboration technology, coordination science, articulation work, organisational computing and so forth' (Editorial 1992: 1). As explained in this and the next section, all of these technologies are social technologies although they were not described using these terms at the time.

Early virtual communities: Usenet, the WELL and Afronet

Perhaps the most notable examples of this prehistory come from the vibrant grassroots communities of the early internet, as seen in Usenet (established in 1979) and the Whole Earth 'Lectronic Link (the WELL, established in 1985; see Hafner 1997; Rheingold 1993; Stevenson 2018). Both Usenet and the WELL were communities built on 'message based group communication applications' or bulletin board systems (BBS), where members used relay chat (a kind of early Internet Relay Chat (IRC) similar to instant messaging) to join conferences, post on message boards, and/or write to mailing lists to interact and communicate with each other (Bidgoli 2006: 98). There were many BBSs around at this time, including PLATO, and these also illustrate the vibrant sociality of online communities (e.g. see Jones and Latzko-Toth on PLATO 2017; see Delwiche 2018 for a history of BBSs; see McLelland et al. 2018 for a non-western history of social media).

Usenet was both a community and social technology, built by dedicated users of UNIX, a multi-user computer operating system still in use today. The name was intended to reflect the user-oriented and UNIX based ethos of the site. Ronda and Michael Hauben, passionate Usenet pioneers, argue that today's internet owes much of its development to the hard work and dedication of this online community of early adopters and network builders. In terms of its purpose, Usenet allowed users to connect to the internet using a UNIX based 'public conferencing network ... via physical networks like the Internet', and was notably *much* cheaper than using ARPANET for sharing messages and files (Hauben and Hauben 1998: 40). Perhaps bearing the most resemblance to Reddit, Usenet was also interest driven, providing a public access network for Unix users seeking technical and social support. Users shared interests, stories, events, information, whatever they wanted via public newsgroups, not unlike the social news sites and community forums in existence today (Hauben and Hauben 1998).

The WELL, one of the most famous 'virtual communities' and home to many early internet pioneers, was built upon a dial-up bulletin board system (cf. Delwiche 2018). For Howard Rheingold, a notable figure and author in early internet history, the WELL was a place of intense social connection, and community users logged in to share personal experiences, get support, offer advice and, most important of all, to connect to a community (cf. Hafner 1997). Still active today (https://www.well.com/), the WELL has been described as wholly consuming, often involving genuine and 'heart-to-heart' connections between geographically distant people (Rheingold 1993).

While both of these sites, like early internet culture, were predominantly white and male, reflecting the demographics of power which continue to dominate Silicon Valley and technology sectors today, there are also accounts of 'Black software'. Charlton

D. McIlwain offers a powerful counter-narrative, documenting the work of Black software designers and activists, responsible for creating AfroLink and Afronet, usenet sites by and for Black people (2020).

Socio-technical systems: Browsers, computer-mediated communication and public communication

What Usenet, the WELL and Afronet show us is that social technologies did not suddenly appear. Instead, social media are deeply embedded within internet technologies and are what many refer to as *socio-technical* systems. As Janet Abbate suggests, such technologies are related to social behaviours and the early logic of internetworking which grew over decades of investment and passionate commitment:

> In the 1990s the Internet emerged as a public communication medium and there were countless commentaries on its social impacts and implications. To the novice user, the Internet seemed to be an overnight sensation – a recent addition to the world of popular computing. The reality was different. In addition, to the two decades of work that had gone into packet switching networks, it took serious transformations over the course of the 1980s and 1990s to turn the Internet into a popular form of public communication. (Abbate 2000: 181)

Part of the serious transformations in the late 1980s and 1990s included major innovations, such as Tim Berners-Lee's World Wide Web, first appearing at CERN in 1989, followed by a number of web-browsers in the early 1990s (e.g. Erwise, Mosaic, Netscape Navigator, Internet Explorer). These content innovations made the internet more easily accessible and usable to ordinary people, marking the transition of the internet as a network accessible by enthusiasts, scientists, military and other technically proficient individuals to enable a widespread form of *public communication*.

In terms of parallel concepts and related fields, many links between computer and social sciences were developing, as seen in human–computer interaction (HCI) and social network theory (originally based in sociology and anthropology and intended to understand how people are connected along networks of interaction, like kinship networks). Mark Granovetter's widely cited (1973) work on 'the strength of weak ties' is one such example of early social network theory, and established that weak links are more important than strong ties for influence, diffusion and mobility. This line of inquiry is also closely related to Pierre Bourdieu's influential (1986) work on social and cultural capital, which effectively theorizes the ways in which social connections and things like educational qualifications can be converted into economic capital. Social capital continues to inspire social media research and wider thinking on the role of networks. In addition, symbolic interactionism, a theoretical frame for understanding the symbolic dimension of human interaction, although originating in the 1950s and 1960s, has been tremendously influential in CSCW, and later in CMC. Indeed, symbolic interactionism still provides a basis for understanding the presentation of self in everyday life and informs much thinking on social media (e.g. Brake 2014; Goffman 1990 [1959]; see also Chapter 7). All of these cognate concepts make up a range of parallel fields from across the social sciences contributing to the vibrant pre-history and *fermentation* of early social media-like technologies, patterns of interaction, and conceptual and intellectual foundations.

Looking at the history of early online communities highlights several things, namely that early networked technologies are deeply social, that these technologies are *embedded* within other technologies and involve systems for *public communication*. Similarly, social media have taken time to become what they are and have important historical precedents. This history is not just technical, it also involves an intellectual lineage which brings together a wide range of thinking across disciplines. Virtual communities, presentation of self, social capital, social networks, internet and public communication all raise important issues about the nature of sociality and continue to influence social media research and scholarship. As we will see in the next section, there are many more social media-like examples, even though the language of connection associated with social media was not yet present.

Stage 2: Early development: From groupware, peer-to-peer networks and social software to social network sites (1990s–2006)

The early 1990s saw intense internet and internet-content development. As the early internet matured and became more widely accessible, more developers began building user-friendly interfaces and tools for enthusiasts with wide-ranging social uses, quickly building appeal for the general public. While the tools and technologies may only seem a small part of this moment, they were profoundly shaping the grounds for internet mediated human interaction. Those tools and technologies were in a rapid state of development, yet their social value and purpose were still in flux. At this time, technologists, scholars, researchers and the public were searching for the right kind of language to describe and understand the new social capacities of the internet and of the networked software built alongside it. This section maps some of the main trends arising in this period.

World Wide Web and networks

One of the big changers at the beginning of this period was the release of the World Wide Web between 1989 and 1993, and the launch of many web browsers quickly following this. In addition, there were also many 'social' applications used for communicating, collaborating and connecting with others. In this section, we look at groupware, peer-to-peer networks, social software and social networks sites (SNSs), demonstrating the virtual explosion of 'social' tools in the field. Thus, while the kinds of available social technologies were growing in the hundreds, there was also a quest to find the appropriate terms and concepts to name social technologies. Many influential researchers, like Barry Wellman (2004), Manuel Castells (1996), Tiziana Terranova (2004) and Yochai Benkler (2006), focused on *networks* as a kind of general catch-all for the capacities of the internet and social technologies at that time. Terranova, for example, explains her book on *Network Culture* as:

> ... an attempt to give a name to, and further our understanding of, a global culture as it unfolds across a multiplicity of communication channels but within a single informational milieu. (2004: 1)

Benkler (2006) also tries to examine and capture the profound changes brought on by the 'networked information economy' and its impact on the capacity for collective and individual action, as well as the information economy more broadly. The term 'network' plays an important conceptual and technical role in the development of social media. The networked tools developing at this time have also been described as manifesting the participatory ethos of Web 2.0 (2005) and participatory culture (Jenkins 2006; Jenkins et al. 2015): both of these are hugely influential concepts for understanding social technologies and the new cultural era they enable (see also Chapter 6). All of these conceptual approaches were developing in this period of early development.

The tools and technologies in use during this stage include: groupware (e.g. email, list serves, conferencing systems and even computer networks); blogging (e.g. Open Diary, Blogger); peer-to-peer networks (e.g. Napster); social software (e.g. any software supporting collaboration including social media, and tools for group communication); and, importantly, social network sites (e.g. Six Degrees (1997), Blogger (1998), Friendster (2002), MySpace (2003) and Facebook (2004), among many others). At the end of this period, Web 2.0 became a popular term for making sense of the more interactive technical aspects of these sites as a whole. Each of these is addressed below.

Groupware

Merging computing and communications technologies, *groupware* was a term widely used in the 1990s and early 2000s to refer to any often *work*-oriented software tools used for group based interactions (Ellis et al. 1991). Scholars researching groupware were largely interdisciplinary and often built cross-disciplinary partnerships, most visibly in the field of CSCW (computer supported and collaborative work), which was just establishing itself in the early 1990s (e.g. Greenberg, 1991; Hughes et al. 1991; Schmidt and Bannon 1992; plus the launch of the CSCW journal in 1992). Some of these specific tools include IBM Lotus Notes (1989), email and mailing lists, electronic meeting rooms, computer and video conferencing, online calendars, intelligent agents and collaborative database software, among others. Although the first ARPA-based email was developed in the 1970s, it was not until 1993 that the first webmail services were released (e.g. AOL, Hotmail, Yahoo!). This later date for the public release of webmail services followed the launch of the World Wide Web in 1991, and shows how important some aspects of 'groupware' are, beyond work-based groups.

Groupware promised to radicalize hierarchies, transform working relationships and maximize productivity (Sproull and Kiesler 1991, as cited in Brown 2000) – all features championed by Web 2.0 and participatory culture. However, by the late 1990s and early 2000s, more critical analysis began to find evidence to the contrary. For example, in an ethnography of Lotus Notes, Barry Brown (2000) argues that this collaborative email and database software better enabled routine organizational work, rather than prompting any radical transformation. Similarly, based on longitudinal research, Kelly and Jones argue that without a shared community and social support for software systems, groupware consistently fails (2001; cf. Udell 1999). Although the term groupware continued to circulate, it has declined in popularity from the early 2000s and is not in use for current collaborative and work-based software applications like G Suite, One Note, Slack or others (Driskell and Salas 2006; Lukosh and Sümmer 2006).

Blogging

In the realm of popular culture, web logs, or what came to be known as blogging, hit a critical point around 1999. Rebecca Blood (2000), one of the first bloggers, maps the shift from blogs as sites requiring coding skill pre-1999, and the move towards much more user-friendly and popular interfaces post-1999. Jill Walker Rettberg (2014) also documents this history, noting that the landscape went from only a few sites, to many different services such as Open Diary (1998), Blogger (1999), Metafilter (1999), Pitas (1999), Groksoup (1999) and Edit-this-page, among others (1999) (see also Blood 2000). Although these tools show that there was considerable demand for these services, it is also worth noting the cultural context. First, blogs marked a shift from personal websites as a finalized and polished text, to an ongoing and updateable site meant to publish someone's life or interests as they happened (Rettberg 2014: 7). This is an important shift, one that is clearly linked to the nascent logic of social media. Second, blogging became popular, moving from a niche hobby for the technically skilled to a practice that anyone interested in writing could take up. As an example of this popularity, Technorati, a blog search engine, launched in 2002, allowed different bloggers to find and connect with each other much more easily. By 2004, Technorati had tracked over 3 million blogs, up from 100,000 in 2003 (2014: 12). This goes to show that blogging was dynamic and vibrant, enabling all sorts of users to engage in increasingly user-friendly forms of public communication.

Peer-to-peer file sharing

In terms of *peer-to-peer file sharing*, perhaps the most famous was Napster (1999), a free software program anyone could download and use to share personal music files, linking many millions of users' personal MP3 collections with those of many millions of others. The software allowed users to search a network made up of people's personal music collections, by artist or song title. Napster was particularly popular in colleges, gaining over 80 million users by mid-2000, and pushing university servers to their absolute capacity (Lessig 2005: 67). At the same time that Napster was released, CD burners and high-speed file sharing were also popular, making it easy to download and copy files to rewritable CDs. Yet much more was going on than just these easy-to-use technologies. For example, Mary Madden (2009) claims that:

> Napster arrived at a time when tightly controlled access to new music was still the norm. While online radio stations were starting to flourish, music lovers were becoming disillusioned with the homogenizing effects of terrestrial radio consolidation ...

As such, Napster did not just provide a new service, it fundamentally opened up a huge range of easily accessible artists and genres where users could easily navigate the artists and songs they loved, as well as exploring new material. For ordinary people, this provided unprecedented access to music, disrupting the control of established industry and copyright holders – as well as demonstrating the *social value of networks*. Lawrence Lessig argues that fair use and circulation of content is not only a major force in every sector of the creative industries, but also that Napster drove the popularization of the internet:

> The appeal of file-sharing music was the crack cocaine of the Internet's growth. It drove demand for access to the Internet more powerfully than any other single application. It was the Internet's killer app ... [and] it no doubt was the application that drove demand for bandwidth. (Lessig, 2005: 296)

Despite the ways Napster drove popular take-up of the internet, and even trained people to download and navigate software on networks (Madden 2009), copyright holders blamed lost profits on Napster and took legal action. The same year that Napster launched, the RIAA (the Recording Industry Association of America) saw this kind of peer-to-peer file sharing as stealing directly from music industry profits and filed a lawsuit against Napster in 1999, followed by a legal action from Metallica drummer, Lars Ulrich, in 2000 (Alderman, 2001). Although this forced Napster to file for bankruptcy in 2001, many other music file-sharing and peer-to-peer networks followed Napster's lead and quickly hit the market, e.g. Kaaza, LimeWire, Gnutella, and many other free programs. Even proprietary giants wanted in, so software like Windows Media Player and iTunes were released. However, these only allowed users to rip and burn their own CDs and share other electronic music files. It was not until 2003 that Apple released the iTunes store, which made it possible to deflect some of the demand for music back into a copyright-controlled and profitable music service, somewhere between file sharing, file playing and the early monetization of shareable content.

While this battle between community and commodity and between ownership and innovation has been expressed in many ways and is addressed throughout this book (see Chapters 4, 6 and 9), Napster also demonstrates a kind of popular 'groupware'. In this instance, Napster and other peer-to-peer sharing programs were not used for collaboration or communication, but they were used to coordinate resources and files, seriously disrupting established hierarchies in the music industry in the process.

Social software and social network sites (SNSs)

In the next stage we have social software, which overlaps with the rise of social network sites (SNSs) at this time. Social software marks an expansion of the work-oriented collaborative tools associated with groupware, and when marketed as something brand new, also embarked on a kind of historical erasure characteristic of new media when they are new (cf. on the telephone see Fischer 1992; Martin 1991; Marvin 1988). In addition, fields like computer-mediated communication (CMC) and CSCW were also expanding, focusing more on interpersonal relations and personal communication. This expansion marked a shift towards defining social technologies in line with the social media paradigm that was so dominant in the early twenty-first century. At the same time, internet-enabled sites used specifically for social interaction were also developing in the mid- to late 1990s. danah boyd, established technology and social media scholar, holds that social software are in fact distinct from previous internet technologies in three ways: 'in the way that the technologies are designed ... in the way that participation spreads, and ... in the way that people behave' (boyd 2006b).

Using MySpace as an example, boyd argues that MySpace's site design process, which involved rapid development and public release of the site without usability testing or the usual product development process, highlights a new design process; one that sidestepped traditional processes and directly engaged user feedback. In other words, MySpace released its site long before it would have been approved by and signed off by engineers, marketing, or other developers. Despite being full of bugs and inconsistencies, MySpace appealed to users, apologizing for problems and responding quickly and directly to user needs. In terms of the 'way participation spreads', MySpace, Friendster, Flickr and other 'social software' started organically, building a small and dedicated user base through site developers' friends, and friends of friends. boyd notes that this is significant as it marks a shift away from interest-based and context-specific connections to more broadly socially oriented connections. As such, users may end up interacting across contexts and as a result specific online norms shift and are blurred. Finally, boyd argues that social software mark the emergence of *ego-based networks* – a significant development in social technologies and one of the first characteristics of social media.

Other social network sites were built on this primarily ego-based model, and new online sites helped people build up their personal connections for social interaction. The earliest of these include interactive websites like classmates.com, a site intended to connect former primary and secondary school classmates, and match.com, the first online dating site. Social network sites also referred to interactive online games, like early MUDS (multi-user domains) and MMOGs (massive multiplayer online games) such as EverQuest and World of Warcraft, games which share a long history of collaboration dating to the earliest use of games as a social space (Morris 2003; Siapera 2012: 221).

All of these genres of social technology demonstrate a vast range of terms and tools, but also show the growth of a kind of social ethos, later captured in the meaning of Web 2.0 and participatory culture. Many other social network sites launched in the late 1990s, like LiveJournal, Asian Avenue and BlackPlanet among others, and continued to develop in the early 2000s, including CyWorld, LunarStorm, Ryze, Tribe.net, LinkedIn, Friendster, MySpace and many others. The rapid development and take-up of these sites point to the rise of social media as a widespread genre of sites well before Facebook in 2004 and YouTube in 2005. (See Table 2.3 which documents the largest of these sites.)

Table 2.3 Overview of early social network sites (SNSs) and social media (1990s–2006)

Year of launch	SNS/Social media	Brief description
1995	Classmates.com	Connects high school alumni with each other, and provides online yearbooks, facilitates reunions, based in the US and owned by People Connect (classmates.com).
	Match.com	One of the first online dating sites, worldwide and under IAC (https://uk.match.com/).
1997	SixDegrees	Included profile pages, friends' lists and school affiliations, created by Andrew Weinreich, owned by MacroView, closed in 2001.
	AOL Instant Messenger	Instant messaging service, owned by AOL, closed in 2017 (Constine 2017)
1998	Blogger	Blogging platform allowing users to create, post and share content, developed by Prya labs and bought by Google in 2003 (https://www.blogger.com/about/?r=2)
	Friends United	A profile-based site, allowing users to link to long-lost friends, classmates and family, and to send messages and/ or share photos, closed in 2016
1999	Yahoo! Messenger	Supported by advertisements, Yahoo! Messenger is a free instant messaging service allowing users to chat, send pictures and other content, owned by Yahoo! (https://messenger.yahoo.com/)
	MSN Messenger	An instant messaging service, also known as Windows live, owned and developed by Microsoft. Discontinued in 2013, at which point users were encouraged to migrate to Skype
	Asian Avenue	A US-based social networking site for American Asians, featuring chat rooms, profiles, friends' lists, now AsianAve, owned and operated by Community Connect and InteractiveOne (http://www.asianave.com/)

(Continued)

Table 2.3 (Continued)

Year of launch	SNS/Social media	Brief description
	BlackPlanet	A social networking site and online community, featuring jobs, dating, profiles, friends' lists, group and private chats, along with many other features, owned by Interactive One (http://www.blackplanet.com)
	LunarStorm	A Swedish social networking site, launched in the UK in 2007 and discontinued in 2010, owned by Lunarworks
	LiveJournal	A Russian-based and international 'community publishing platform, wilfully blurring the lines between blogging and social networking', open source and non-proprietary (https://www.livejournal.com/about/)
	Tencent QQ (originally OCIQ)	Instant messaging service by Chinese platform Tencent, the first of many social services (https://www.tencent.com/en-us/system.html)
	Napster	A popular free to download peer-to-peer file-sharing service, used to search and share MP3 music files, founded by Sean Parker and Shawn Fanning, acquired by Rhapsody in 2011 (http://gb.napster.com/)
2001	Ryze	A social network for businesses and professional development, includes a home page and messaging features (https://ryze.com/faq.php)
2002	Friendster	'An online community that connects people through networks of friends for dating or making new friends', discontinued in 2015 (2004 screenshot, from Internet Archive, as cited in McMillan 2013)
2003	Couchsurfing	'A global community of 14 million people in more than 200,000 cities who share their life, their world, their journey. Couchsurfing connects travellers with a global network of people' (http://www.couchsurfing.com/about/about-us/)*
	LinkedIn	A professional social network site using profiles, messaging and job search to 'connect the world's professionals to make them more productive and successful' (https://press.linkedin.com/about-linkedin)
	MySpace	One of the most popular profile-based social network sites prior to Facebook, included top friends, messaging, song players and html personalization (https://myspace.com/)
	Hi5	A massive social network for members wanting to meet new people through social games and dating, purchased by the Meet Group in 2014 (https://secure.hi5.com/)
	Last.FM	A profile-based, music and taste sharing site, linking 'your favourite music services and join up listening, watching and sharing to connect your musical world' (https://www.last.fm/)

Year of launch	SNS/Social media	Brief description
	Skype	Sometimes referred to as a web conferencing service, Skype is a video chat service allowing users to message, share files and interact, purchased by Microsoft in 2011 (https://www.skype.com)
	Xing	'Xing is the leading online business network with 13 million members in German-speaking countries', members set up profiles and to connect, job search and seek professional advice (www.xing.com/en)
	Plenty of Fish	The largest free online and profile-based dating site (https://www.pof.com/)
	Second Life	A virtual community where users can create, interact, share and participate in an online community, part of Linden Labs (http://secondlife.com/#)
2004	Orkut	A Google operated social network and community, most popular in Brazil before being discontinued in 2014 (http://www.orkut.com/index.html)
	Dogster	An information-rich site for dog lovers, including community forums for social networking (http://www.dogster.com/, sister site is Catster, www.catster.com/)
	Flickr	One of the largest and original photo and video sharing communities, purchased by Yahoo! in 2005 (https://www.flickr.com/)
	ASmallWorld	'One of the first social networks, ASW combined the traditions of a country club with the power of a digital platform to connect people both online and more importantly, in real life' (https://www.asmallworld.com/)
	Facebook (Harvard only)	Starting off as a Harvard-only profile-based social network, Facebook is now the largest ad-based social media platform, incorporating many products and services (www.facebook.com)
	Digg	Once considered the 'front page of the internet', Digg is a popular social news site, using 'data and social signals to power a user-influenced, editorially-controlled content portal' (http://digg.com/)
	OkCupid	A free, profile-based and ad-supported online dating site, claiming to use 'algorithm magic to find people you'll actually like', whose parent company is match.com (https://www.okcupid.com/()
	World of Warcraft	Computer-based massively multiplayer online role playing game (MMORPG), well known for its rapid development into a global online community (http://eu.blizzard.com/en-gb/games/wow/)

(Continued)

Table 2.3 (Continued)

Year of launch	SNS/Social media	Brief description
2005	Bebo	Originally a social networking site, Bebo is now a community-based streaming service linking with Twitch, Spotify, StreamLabs and more (www.bebo.com)
	YouTube	With the tagline 'Broadcast Yourself', YouTube is a video-sharing site, allowing users to create their own channels, create original content and watch shared content (youtube.com)
	Reddit	'Come for the cats, stay for the empathy', Reddit describes itself as 'the front page of the internet', and is a social news aggregator and online community where users can share, vote on and discuss any Reddit content (www.reddit.com)
	Qzone	A Chinese social networking site created by Tencent, where users can blog, share photos, watch videos and listen to music (qzone.qq.com/)
2006	Twitter	A micro-blogging site, where users can follow others, share content and participate in public conversations (twitter.com)
	VKontakte (VK)	A Russian-based social network site, often compared to Facebook, where users can set up profiles, share content and connect with others (https://vk.com)

Source: adapted from boyd and Ellison (2007); Anon (2009); Associated Press (2012); CBS News (2014); Tencent QQ (2017); Titcomb (2017). *According to boyd and Ellison, Couchsurfing launched in 2003; however, the Couchsurfing website claims it launched in 2004: all links were accurate at the time of writing (August 2020)

For social media, this was a critical time, and many social media scholars attribute this period as the beginning of social media as we know them.

One of the challenges around mapping the emergence of SNSs is the significant gap between the appearance of SNSs as sites and the relatively late use of the term 'social network site' as a category for social, interactive web-based sites. For example, although classmates.com appeared in 1995 and SixDegrees was launched in 1997, a Lexis-Nexis search of hundreds of world news sources reveals that 'social network site' was not used in the news until 2003. Instead, these early network sites were often classed as groupware or social software, and were described as a kind of *personal technology* that could help users more easily connect to the internet (e.g. Haddad et al. 1997; Snider 1997).

Web 2.0 and participatory media

As the internet matured, the number of software and application programmes focused on making connectivity usable, interesting, and widely accessible reached a critical point. Even without the SNS label, all of the technical developments and terminologies outlined so far were coalescing around a social and interactive logic increasingly focused on individuals and their personal connections – which helps explain the explosive power of Web 2.0 (O'Reilly 2005) and participatory culture (Jenkins 2006; Jenkins et al. 2015). These terms were not explaining a new phenomenon per se. Instead, Web 2.0 and participatory culture provided a vocabulary for all the 'new' digital tools in use and embodied a social ethos.

Thus, for the last part of this section, we look more closely at Web 2.0 and participatory culture. Widely associated with Tim O'Reilly, Web 2.0 is not just a particular set of tools, but also captures a cultural shift from the web-as-providing-single-services to the web-as-providing-a-platform for many functions and many users. This shift is also apparent in blogs, with peer-to-peer file sharing, and with social software. O'Reilly (2005, 2009) describes Web 2.0 as a shift towards better harnessing the collective through 'network effects' and collective intelligence:

> From Google and Amazon to Wikipedia, eBay, and craigslist, we saw that the value was facilitated by the software, but was co-created by and for the community of connected users. Since then, powerful new platforms like YouTube, Facebook, and Twitter have demonstrated that same insight in new ways. Web 2.0 is all about harnessing collective intelligence. (O'Reilly 2009)

In a similar vein, participatory culture is a term which is also intended to capture a widespread cultural and technological shift, away from a consumer-oriented culture marked by expensive barriers to civic expression and cultural production, towards a bottom-up, collaborative culture with 'relatively low barriers' to civic expression and cultural production (Jenkins 2006; Jenkins et al. 2016; see Chapter 6). Both of these terms, Web 2.0 and participatory culture, aim to capture the myriad technological, cultural and communicative changes coalescing around social technologies. So, at the beginning of this period, scholars and researchers were focusing more on the *network* and its many social, cultural, political and economic implications (e.g. Benkler 2006; Castells 1996; Terranova 2004; Wellman 1996, 2004). And by the end of this period, researchers built further upon network scholarship, incorporating traditions from computer-mediated communication, online communities, to better understand shifts in individual and social patterns of connection and interaction.

Yet despite this active scholarship and as reviewed above, there were different communities using different languages and tools, from groupware, peer-to-peer networks, social software and social network sites. While all of these may have shared the networked sociality of 'new' internet-enabled sites, they did so with different terms and different foundations. These differences point to a shared preoccupation with the social capacities of network technologies along with the use of many different vocabularies. In effect, this period of early development shows a disjointed field that comes together more coherently in the next stage of consolidation and growth (2007–2012).

Stage 3: Consolidation and growth (2007–2012)

In this period, social media and SNSs were growing exponentially, and with this proliferation, numbers of users were also growing pointing to the *massification* of both audiences and of social media sites, which were also consolidating as a distinct industry. This massive growth was also influenced by the release of the iPhone in 2007, popularizing the smart phone and making social media and social network sites *mobile* and much more publicly usable. As an example of this massive growth, Facebook had 58 million monthly active users in December 2007 – a number which would make up *only 5%* of Facebook's active monthly users of over 1 billion in October 2012 (Facebook 2017; Sedghi 2014). Facebook was one of the fastest-growing social media platforms at this time, and although many other social media sites were also on the rise, none of them demonstrated this rapid growth quite as well as Facebook.

The rise of 'social networks'

Despite this massive growth, a gap between the technical growth and scholarship continued to persist. For example, major national research centres did not use the term 'social network' until 2006 (Pew Internet Research, a US-based independent think-tank and research organization) and 2008 (Ofcom, the UK's telecommunications regulatory body also responsible for annual research on media use). In terms of broader scholarship and public coverage, a year-by-year analysis of the number of peer-reviewed publications and newspaper articles on 'social media' also shows rapid growth (see Figure 2.1).

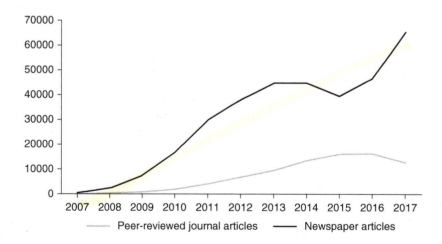

Figure 2.1   Number of peer-reviewed academic publications and newspaper articles using the exact term 'social media', 2007–2017

Source: compiled in December 2017 from: ABI Complete, ProQuest, Taylor & Francis, Sage, ACM Digital Library, SpringLink, IEEE Conference and Journal Publications, JSTOR, Wiley Online Library, arXiv, EBSCO databases.

Figure 2.1 also illustrates two additional features about the rise of social media (cf. Foote et al. 2018: 114). First, perhaps unsurprisingly, public coverage of social media significantly outstrips scholarship and shows different frequency patterns (e.g. dipping in 2015 and increasing by just over 25% in 2017).

Second, the number of peer-reviewed academic publications increased 36 times from the 187 articles published in 2007 to the 6,854 published in 2012. The number of newspaper articles would increase 91 times in the same period. The growth slowed in the subsequent period where the number of peer-reviewed publications roughly doubled in quantity from 2012 to 2016, peaking at 16,223. Based on data from Google trends, Richard Rogers (2018a: 92) documents a similar trajectory and increase from 2005 to 2015 in Google searches for 'social media'. Rogers notes that searches for the term 'Web 2.0' began to decline in 2007, when it fell below the number of searches for 'social media' and then appears to all but dwindle out. Similarly, Google searches for 'social media' massively outnumber searches for 'social network sites' which also appear to be dwindling (Rogers 2018a: 92–93).

Although widely varied, many scholars in this period focused on defining and mapping social media, as well as identifying their growth, their patterns of use and their impact (e.g. Cho and Tomkins 2007; Lenhart and Madden 2007; Ofcom 2008; Thatcher 2007). The differences between social software, Web 2.0, social network sites, social bookmarking sites and other innovations were often blurred, sparking many first attempts to identify, consolidate and understand what these social technologies were and how they were being used. As David Beer (2008) suggests, 'there is a pressing need to classify [social sites] in order to work toward a more descriptive analysis'. This pressing need to classify and define *what* social media are, what they include or exclude, continues as many offer contrasting definitions of social media well into stage 4 (e.g. Burgess et al. 2018; Carr and Hayes 2015; Fuchs 2017; McCay-Peet and Quan-Haase 2017; Van Dijck 2013).

However, specifically focusing on social media as distinct from the internet and coming primarily from media and media-related fields, it is possible to see a general distinction between very narrow or very broad definitions.

On the narrow side of the spectrum, danah boyd and Nicole Ellison's (2007) seminal article defining social network sites and the state of scholarship on the topic is an important starting point. boyd and Ellison were among the first to offer a precise definition and documentation of SNSs, and as a result they are also among the most widely cited:

> We define social network sites as web-based services that allow individuals to (1) construct a public or semi-public *profile* within a bounded system, (2) articulate a *list* of other users with whom they share a connection, and (3) view and *traverse* their list of connections and those made by others within the system. The nature and nomenclature of these connections may vary from site to site (emphasis added).

Thus, boyd and Ellison's definition identifies a user-oriented definition based on behaviours, including profiles, friends' lists, and traversing or moving and looking through profiles and friend lists as the unique properties of SNSs. Helpfully, boyd and Ellison provided a brief overview of scholarship primarily coming from the field of computer-mediated communication (CMC). They emphasize the integrated nature of networked media and highlight the importance of CMC in providing a foundation for an increasingly multidisciplinary field. The precision of this definition makes it possible to define which sites may be *social* in nature, but are not exactly social networks. For example, the following sites and services would not be included as SNSs on their own: instant messaging, blogging, MOOGs and MMPORGs, video chat and video sharing, non-profile-based social news sites like Digg and Reddit, among many others (cf. Carr and Hayes 2015).

David Beer (2008), writing directly in response to boyd and Ellison, argues that their definition of SNSs is still too broad, opening up too many points of overlap between very different kinds of sites enabling friending, sharing, profiles and commenting for example. For Beer, Web 2.0 or user-generated content (UGC) work better as an overall genre for the many kinds of sites related to SNSs. Beer argues that reconceptualizing SNS as a broader category detracts from existing terms, like Web 2.0 and UGC, as well as the specific differences across SNS sites. A typology of different sites would help establish some order in the chaos of change. As Beer (2008) states, we need 'some clarity to the terminology' in order to better understand vast differences between sites which 'service so many different agendas'.

From social networks to social media

On the other end of the scale, however, many other scholars take a contrary view, arguing that the meaning of social networks and social media should be understood much more broadly (e.g. Mandiberg 2012; Papacharissi 2011; Shirky 2008; Siapera 2012). For example, Clay Shirky, like Michael Mandiberg (2012), brings many disparate terms for similar tools together as 'variations on a theme':

> These communication tools have been given many names, all variations on a theme: 'social software', 'social media', 'social computing', and so on. Though there are some distinctions between these labels, the core idea is the same: we are living in the middle of a remarkable increase in our ability to share, to cooperate, with one another and to take collective action, all outside the framework of traditional institutional institutions and organizations. (Shirky 2008: 20–21)

For Shirky, the emphasis is on the ways social tools increase and enable social (whether individual or collective) action *outside* traditions and institutions. This sentiment resonates with participatory culture (popularized by Henry Jenkins 2006, 2009a) and the rise of the 'prod-user' or empowered producer-users who are as busy making content as they are consuming it, marking a shift away from transmission technologies with a one-way flow of content from producers to users (Bruns 2008, discussed further in Chapter 6). While Shirky is well known for his optimistic view of technology, often focusing on the best cases and celebrating their potential, he is also one of many scholars searching for the commonalities across social technologies including Web 2.0, UGC and social media. Indeed, this perspective requires a broad view of social media as both a kind of mass media for creators and a socially transformative technology.

The differences between broad and narrow definitions of social media reflect two contrasting tendencies often working in tandem – the tendency to group together to understand commonalities and deep change and the tendency to break apart to understand social media's unique differences and specific characteristics. The problem with the latter approach is that the rapid pace of change and constant proliferation of social media makes it very difficult to identify and understand fleeting differences versus those that are more lasting and meaningful. In addition, a lot of the research taking place in this stage focused on kinds of users and patterns of use rather than on defining the sites themselves (Lenhart and Madden 2007; Ofcom 2008).

The idea of *affordances*, discussed further in Chapter 4, and the numerous links between technologies and the possible behaviours they enable, runs counter to working out a typology (e.g. Baym 2015a, 2015b; Bene 2017; Bucher and Helmond 2018; Norman 2013 [1988]). This is an important and influential concept. In essence, affordances refer to design principles, and how certain actions are made more possible or more difficult based on the design (Bucher and Helmond 2018: 236). In terms of social media, we can understand affordances as what is made possible through platform features. For example, YouTube users can like or dislike content they view. Other platforms like Instagram and Twitter don't have a 'dislike' feature, and as a result, users are discouraged from sharing these kinds of reactions. Affordances take many different forms, and it is worth thinking through the affordances particular to social platforms.

Although arguably a feature of Web 2.0 (O'Reilly 2005), two important transitions were also occurring in 2007/2008, both involving the consolidation of social media as sites and as industries. The first of these transitions is marked by the transition from more or less single sites to *platforms*, and the second is the rise of *mobile and apps* (Facebook 2007a, 2007b, 2008a; YouTube 2006–2008 as discussed in Gillespie 2010; Helmond 2015). These transitions were sparked by the launch of the Facebook platform and by the launch of the iPhone.

In terms of the Facebook platform, Facebook launched its 'platform for developers of social applications [apps]' (May 2007a) and Facebook's 'platform for mobile' (October 2007b). These changed the way developers worked with social media, and set data precedents across the social media ecosystem. Developers are the people interested in building social applications or web features for their own sites, and with the Facebook platform, they could now capitalize on Facebook's user base by tailoring their own sites or products to the Facebook platform. As Mark Zuckerberg explained, 'any developer can build an application that is as integrated into the site's information flow and connections of relationships as Facebook's own applications' (Facebook 2007a).

This effectively positioned Facebook as an important technical, informational and social platform (Gillespie 2010). This position was solidified in 2008 with the launch of Facebook

Connect – a single sign-on service allowing users to use their Facebook details to log in to other sites (2008a; see also 'platformization' in Chapter 5). Facebook Connect meant developers could take advantage of Facebook's copious user data, as well as providing 'deep integration' across the web. The iPhone, of course, shifted a great deal of networked media from computers to smart phones, impacting on the social media landscape and patterns of use.

From single sites and polymedia to platforms

All of these factors consolidated social media as platforms of power, linking large networks of users with developers, advertisers and a range of other partners (see also the 2001–2007 internet platform interoperability era in Korea; Jin 2017). These changes mark a serious shift from social media as 'early' towards their consolidation and continued growth. At the beginning of this period scholarship on 'social media' was just beginning to overtake 'Web 2.0', focusing on SNSs primarily in terms of users and uses. There is also a more critical turn at the end of this period, noting social media as by-products 'of business management strategies' and marketing speak, designed to titillate, trivialize, and waste people's time rather than enable a deeper social or community connection – a turn which becomes much more pronounced in stage 4 (Lovink 2011: 6; cf. Morozov 2012; Scholz 2008; Zimmer 2008).

Also, nearer to the end of this stage, Madianou and Miller (2012) were among those scholars more critically looking at social media, and who proposed the concept of *polymedia*, which is a theory of media as 'an integrated structure of affordances' through which each medium is defined by its relation to other media (2012: 171,173). In essence, polymedia points to the increasing complexity of social media as media environments and not just single sites, often incorporating multiple communicative forms, such as messaging, video, news, links and photos. These features become meaningful through the interplay between users, medium and their affordances. Following on from the 2006–2008 launch of the platform in YouTube and Facebook, the concept of polymedia helps explain some of the rising complexity of social media, as well as the move away from single purpose sites to multi-functional, personal and networked media.

Zizi Papacharissi (2011) bases her definition of social media on the key features identified by boyd and Ellison (2007) – profiles, connections or friends lists, and the ability to view those lists. However, Papacharissi includes a Goffmanesque interpretation of social media where profiles and friend connections are understood as front stage presentations of self, 'used to authenticate identity and introduce the self' (2011: 304–5). In addition, Papacharissi draws from the 'liquid self' (Bauman 2000, 2005), Giddens' idea of reflexivity (1991), everyday life (De Certeau 2011 [1984]) and convergence culture (Buckingham 2008; Jenkins 2006) to better explain the networked self. Papacharissi provides a historically informed and theoretically rich analysis of social media, noting continuities and differences in patterns of human connection on and off of social media.

Despite these more critical analyses of social media, many equated SNSs with social media more broadly, maintaining an emphasis on profiles, connections or lists, and the ability to browse and follow those lists (e.g. Papacharissi 2011: 304–5; also Mandiberg 2012). This equivalence between SNS and social media became less frequent at the end of stage 3, and as the field grew.

In sum, this period is marked by rapid growth, as well as the consolidation of social media through major developments like the launch of the platform, and the convergences brought on by the integration of mobile networks and launch of apps. Despite the breadth of approaches and observations outlined in this section, social media were becoming increasingly widespread, pervasive, intensive and disruptive of established media as well as social norms. In this period, researchers were coming to terms with *what* social media are, as well as how they might shape and impact those that use them. boyd and Ellison provided an important definition of SNSs, and in doing so also set the agenda for this emerging field of study. However, the consolidation of social media from specific sites to platforms also marks an expansion of these sites across the web and across the global market, as they became powerful global players. Scholarship was also flourishing, moving beyond descriptive work and towards more critical accounts. Certainly, critiques of marketization, commodification and 'platformization' point to a widening of social media definitions beyond use and users, a theme taken up more frequently and consistently in stage 4.

Stage 4: Maturation and a more critical turn (2013–present)

The fourth stage marks continued growth and also a maturing of social technologies as established sites and massive networks, as social technologies, as platforms and as a market. This is also the most prolific stage in terms of the quantity of research and published work on social media, as indicated by the rise in academic articles and news articles in Figure 2.1. The rise of dedicated scholarship, including historical analysis and a general emphasis on more critical and nuanced work, formalized the study of social media as its own interdisciplinary field. Although the body of work in this field is growing exponentially, this section focuses on key thinkers informing how we think of social media, as well as key themes within this scholarship. Based on the select scholarship presented here, the last section draws out key points from across the four stages.

Massification

Like the exponential increase of academic work, social media sites continue to grow. For example, Facebook reached 2.7 billion monthly active users in August 2020 (Clement 2020). Many other popular social media sites also continue to grow their user base, as shown in Figure 2.2 which illustrates the rise in millions of worldwide monthly active users on Facebook, Snapchat, Instagram, WhatsApp, WeChat and TikTok (launched in 2016).

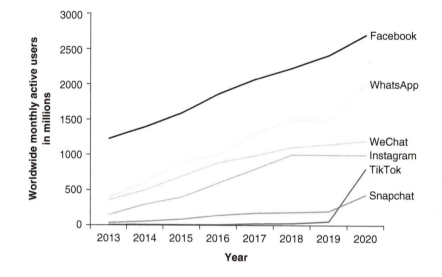

Figure 2.2   The rise in millions of worldwide monthly active users on Facebook, WhatsApp, WeChat, Instagram, Snapchat and TikTok

Source: data compiled from statista.com, Wikipedia and Verge.com, no updated data for WhatsApp in 2018 and 2019, and no data for Instagram 2019 and 2020

Notably, Facebook in combination with WhatsApp and Instagram, has the largest user base by far. When these numbers of users are combined, Facebook, WhatsApp and Instagram have a total of almost 5.7 billion monthly active users. As an additional explanation of the kind of economic power of these platforms, Facebook and Google were set to surpass the global advertising revenue made from traditional media in June 2020 for the first time (Barker 2020). This means that Google, Facebook and Alibaba are 'predicted to account for more than half of the $530 billion global advertising industry, up from 20% of the global advertising revenue in 2017' (Barker 2020; Bond 2017; Kollowee 2017). These are significant numbers, pointing to phenomenal growth and the establishment of big social media as global players.

The social media marketplace has become increasingly crowded and continues to be dominated by Facebook and the big established sites, making it much harder for new sites to enter the market and compete with those more established sites (like Mastodon.social; see McHugh 2017; Rogers 2018a: 92). Users become tied to these established sites through the long-term accumulation of both personalized user-generated content and their personally curated networks, which are very difficult if not impossible to move to other sites – what some have referred to as 'lock-in' strategies (e.g. Barwise 2018). In this way, social media sites provide 'architectures of participation' which thicken over time, contributing to users' attachments to those sites as well as to those sites' continued economic and symbolic power (Peterson 2008). Chapter 3 takes up these issues of power more fully. In terms of the current social landscape, we see a global system with two geographic centres of power, the US and global big tech companies – Google, Amazon, Facebook and Apple (GAFA), and China with Baidu, Alibaba, Tencent and Xiaomi (BATX) (see platform empires in Chapter 5).

The birth of a field and dedicated scholarship

In terms of scholarship, social media continues to grow as a field, and is an increasingly central focal point for many researchers from a wide range of fields. Based on a SCOPUS analysis, Foote et al. identify the top eight disciplines producing the most publications on 'social media' as: software, medicine, library and information science, information systems, human–computer interaction, education, computer science and communications (Foote et al. 2018: 114). Rogers' (2018a) also documents the decline of Web 2.0 and the rise of social media in Google searches. Web 2.0, social network sites and other related concepts coalesce from many disparate parts into the field of social media (cf. McCay-Peet and Quan-Haase 2018; Foote et al. 2018; Rogers 2018a). In this sense, while the terminologies change, there is a longer conceptual lineage for this scholarship, and social media scholars need to reformulate aligned concepts in order to better understand social technologies over time and as they change. Thus, 'big' social media companies like Facebook and WeChat, and their contenders, have consolidated, expanding across the web as platforms and as sites of economic concentration and symbolic power.

Although there are many more sites and works than can usefully be discussed here, there are a few noteworthy themes emerging during this fourth stage that define social media as a recognizable field of its own, as well as furthering definitions of social media. Very broadly, these include: developing histories, the emergence of a body of dedicated scholarship and, most importantly, a broader turn to more critical work beyond use and users, each addressed in turn below.

Scholars and popular media have begun developing *histories* of social media and their affiliated networked technologies, as documented in the first two stages of social media. These histories both extend the meaning of social media as rich and overlapping social technologies with embedded networked capacities. As Thomas Streeter argues, this work situates social media as 'structures of feeling' incorporating a whole range of social technologies prior to the launch of SixDegrees and SNSs (Williams, cited by Streeter 2017; Abbate 2017; Brügger 2015; Delwiche 2018; Hartley 2018; Jones and Latzko-Toth 2017; McLelland et al. 2018; Stevenson 2018). In addition, a new journal called *Internet Histories: Digital Technology, Culture, Society* pulls together a whole range of scholarship focused on documenting and examining the often recent history of networked technologies. While not exclusively addressing social media, social media feature prominently and are central to the journal's content and scope.

In addition, the fourth stage sees the emergence of *dedicated* scholarship, indicating that although the field is still growing, it has also begun maturing and developing coordinated methods, frameworks and scholarship networks. Although some of the first international research centres and networks studying social media were established prior to this period (e.g. the Social Media Lab in Toronto), these centres become increasingly international and numerous from 2013 (e.g. see the list of 'select research centres' at the close of Chapter 1). Launching in 2015, the journal *Social Media + Society* is committed 'to advancing the understanding of social media and its impact on societies past, present and future' (http://journals.sagepub.com/home/sms#). In addition, there is a boom in new social media degree programmes, as well as many specialist short courses for a wide range of students and practitioners (e.g. QUT MOOC on social media on Future Learn as well as numerous undergrad and postgrad courses, MA in Digital Social Media at University of Southern California, MA in Social Media at University of Westminster, among many others). Finally, in addition to the publication of many specialist articles and books, numerous high-quality edited reference books featuring leading experts have been published between 2014 and 2018 (e.g. Burgess et al. 2018; Hunsinger and Senft 2014; Sloan and Quan-Haase 2017).

As such, scholarship at the beginning of the fourth stage deepens analysis of users and uses to also include context, and moves towards affordances and platforms. Ellison and boyd (2013) update their earlier work, redefining SNSs and emphasizing a shift towards *media-centric* rather than profile-based sites, which are still made of user-generated content, and public lists of connections that can be viewed and 'traversed by others' – although traversing is much less important than in 2007. Like Madianou and Miller's concept of polymedia, Ellison and boyd note that SNSs are increasingly *fluid and asymmetrical* (2013; cf. Miekle and Young, 2012; Postill and Pink 2012), as well as implementing great nuance in contexts of use (e.g. boyd 2014; Marwick 2013). Many more scholars also develop critical accounts of social media, seriously engaging politics, industry and ideology (e.g. Albarran 2013; Fuchs 2014, 2017; Gerlitz and Helmond 2013; Helmond 2015; Sandoval 2014; Taylor 2014; Van Dijck 2013; Weller et al. 2014; on Google and the logic of data accumulation, Highfield 2016; Srnicek 2017; Tufecki 2017b; Vaidhyanathan, 2018; Zuboff 2015).

Towards a critical turn

Within this growing and multi-disciplinary scholarship, many continue to debate what social media actually mean. Social media scholarship thus shifts from a focus on social media as sites of social interaction more characteristic of stage 3, to a focus on platforms for social interaction, advertising and power. José Van Dijck's (2013) work, for example, argues that social media are better conceptualized as *connective media* because there are so many ideologically laden associations with the word 'social', such as 'likes', 'follows', 'friends', 'community' – all terms whose meanings have been co-opted by social media (2013: 14–15; cf. Gerlitz and Helmond 2013). These sites no longer act as mere conduits for delivering content or services, but are instead providing a platform which shapes everyday life and carves out enclaves of platform specific social behaviour. Van Dijck refers to this process as '*platformed sociality*' (2013: 5, emphasis added), arguing that 'the online ecosystem is embedded in a larger sociocultural and political-economic content where it is inevitably molded by historical circumstances' (Van Dijck 2013: 9; see also Bucher 2018b). At stake in the struggle to understand connective media are 'new norms for sociality and values' played out through the 'ongoing clash between user tactics and platform strategies' (Van Dijck 2013: 20).

Alice Marwick (2013) also extends analysis of users and uses by conducting an ethnography of social media companies in Silicon Valley, and found that rather than enabling more democratic participation, social media were used to train people in '*social entrepreneurship*' (emphasis added). For Marwick, respondents informally learned a whole range of entrepreneurial techniques just by using social media, including self-promotion, branding and circulating very specific kinds of content geared towards generating the greatest number of likes, shares, retweets and comments (2013: 276). The most successful social entrepreneurs became part of the 'digital elite', yet Marwick observes that in contrast to the meritocratic basis for this elite, they tend to follow existing hierarchies:

> Digital elitism does not reconfigure power; it entrenches it. It provides justification for enormous gaps between rich and poor, for huge differences between average people and highly sought-after engineers who are paid large starting salaries and showered with benefits. It idealizes a 'better class of rich people'. (2013: 275)

Marwick's argument repositions social media from a tool or use-oriented frame to a sociocultural frame, where social media articulate an individualized and entrepreneurial logic (cf. Abidin 2018; Duffy 2017; Neff 2012).

More recently and reiterating themes emerging at the end of stage 3 (e.g. Madianou and Miller 2012; cf. Van Dijck 2013), social media are defined as much more than an instrumental set of technical features, but also must include the social affordances bundled up within social technologies. For example, Taina Bucher argues that:

> the social in social media is not a fact but a doing. The social is constantly performed and enacted by humans and non-humans alike. Social network sites, it seems, are less about the already articulated networks, as boyd and Ellison originally suggested. (Bucher 2015)

Bucher points to a shift from social networking sites to social media as a framework for the *social*, merging network with behaviours and the process of *doing*, and this reshapes how we are able to understand 'the social' (see Chapter 4). In this vein, Shoshanna Zuboff (2019) and both Nick Couldry and Ulisses Mejias (2019a, 2019b) advanced their respective works on surveillance capitalism and data colonialism. These theories position social media as major players in the next stage of capitalism. These researchers are theorizing the impact of platform empires, such as Google, Amazon, Facebook and Apple (GAFA), who 'make up a new economic order that claims human experience as free raw material from hidden commercial practices of extraction, prediction and sales' (Zuboff 2019: 8; cf. Couldry and Mejias 2019a,

2019b). While Zuboff bases her research in the US and on American platform empires, Couldry and Mejias expand their scope more globally, and place the role of social media in the US and the East, including Baidu, Alibaba and Tencent (BAT), as giants in the 'social quantification sector' (2019a: xiv ff.; also see Chapter 5). These are both important works, providing critical analysis of the social media within the contemporary media ecosystem (see also Chapter 3 and 4).

Another crucial area of research has developed in the latter part of this stage: critical race studies of social media. This important area of research brings to light the extent of racism in social media and digital cultures. For example, Safiyah Noble (2018) identifies racism in Google search algorithms, where searches for 'Black girls' give pornographic and hypersexualized results. Ruha Benjamin (2019a, 2019b) edited and wrote two books on race and technology, both of which provide crucial critiques of the ways in which race and technology intersect. Charlton McIlwain documents and maps the absence of Black contributions in the established histories of networked software. McIlwain (2020) writes a rich counter-narrative, documenting Black software history and its impact on how we understand technology. André Brock (2020) provides a thought-provoking account of the ways social and networked technologies provide space for Black culture to come together on Twitter. All of these are crucial accounts of race and social technologies, pointing to a new era of critical scholarship.

In sum, the fourth stage of social media shows continued growth, but also a centring of social media as industries, and also of social media as a field of study. It is clear that social media is increasingly platformed and, in the same breath, increasingly subject to a new era of critical scholarship. The move towards a more critical turn marks a shift from a focus on description to analysis. This is an important shift, one with already important contributions but with much more work remaining to be done, although social media continue to be complex, multiple, integrated, and involve a broader feeling of belonging as well as increased surveillance and datafication (see Chapter 8).

Conclusion: What Next?

The purpose of this lengthy chapter has been to introduce the reader not only to social media, but also to the rich prehistory shaping social technologies and social media as we know them today. This chronological development provides a deep snapshot of what social media means and where they have come from over forty years of networked history. Social media did not suddenly emerge in 1997 with SixDegrees, but much earlier with the socially networked technologies of the internet, virtual communities and mediated interaction. This longer history shows that the terms and descriptions used to describe social technologies are slippery and context specific. Within this chronology, there are also many tales of battles between regulation and openness, between commodification and community, and between ownership and innovation. These battles are especially important, and continue in various ways throughout many more social technologies – a point explored more fully in the chapters to come.

This chapter has mapped the development of social media as a broad category of diverse social technologies over four stages beginning with its prehistory in the 1980s to the current stage of maturation from 2013 to the present. Social technologies continue to proliferate and social media has become a distinct field of study, yet while documenting the development of both of these over these four stages, little focus has been paid to documenting specific genres of social media. Instead, this chapter is about understanding what social media are, by writing their history in relation to other internet-based and networked technologies. Given the rate of change in and across social media sites, it is especially difficult to classify social media sites by type, particularly as many sites become increasingly complex, integrating functions and features within their sites. It is clear that social media increasingly involves multiple products and technologies, and these require similarly complex and multiple theories and concepts. While there has been a gap between the developments of social technologies and how we make sense of them, there is also a growing field dedicated to making sense of these technologies.

Ownership also has an impact. Many social media sites have complex partnerships and may be subsidiaries of powerful corporations (e.g. Google or Microsoft), which makes it harder to define the boundaries around specific social sites. In this way, Facebook, YouTube (Google) and Skype (Microsoft), for example, share many *platform* features because of their size, scale and cross-functionality than these sites share with smaller sites. This has implications for how we understand new players on the field. For example, how do you class Google which has many social applications, like Google Plus, Blogger, Duo, Google Meet, G Suite, Google docs, plus more, with up and coming players like TikTok or Triller?

Snapchat, in contrast, more easily fits with classic understandings of social media, but is also expanding its features and functionality, such as augmented reality, technological devices (Snap glasses) and filters, among others. In addition, Snapchat has no profiles, no lists of friends or connections, and messages primarily support interpersonal connection. Before the introduction of 'my story', a feature which allows users to share and consume content publicly, Snapchat also has not always been public, demonstrating although social media sites might start off with one or more of these features, this is subject to change. This example supports Baym's (2015a) point that when it comes to social media, the ground upon which we are standing is shifting, and these technologies change quickly and frequently, as well as more slowly over time.

In terms of the four stages of social media, where do we go next? There is still much critical work to be done, so although we may find ourselves in a more critical turn, we are only at the beginning. In a historic moment, US Congress brought Mark Zuckerberg (Facebook), Sundar Pichai (Google), Tim Cook (Apple) and Jeff Bezos (Amazon) for an antitrust hearing, examining the online dominance of these companies (July 29, 2020). In this hearing, tech company CEOs were questioned on platform dominance including closing down competition, strangling the market and gross profiteering from user data. This points to an important space for policy and regulation to play a role in the next steps in social media's maturation and development. Related to this, Uusitalo (2014) and Anderson (1988) point to 'incremental changes to dominant design' as part of the fourth stage. When looking back at the last forty years of networked technologies, where they have come from, and how we have understood them, it is possible to make the argument that this is what we have seen – many incremental changes to networks. It is also possible to make the argument that the breaking up of big tech can open up new vistas for social diversity and the four stages can begin again.

Questions and Activities

1   What do early precedents of social media like groupware, peer-to-peer networks and social software tell us about social media?
2   Activity: Based on your own interests, pick a social media platform and identify a) when it was launched, b) who founded it and who owns it, c) how it makes money and d) who the users are. Prepare a short presentation on your platform and share with the class. Compare notes. What do you see that is the same and different across social media platforms?
3   What do we learn about social media by applying a life cycle model? Evaluate the four stages of social media presented here. Based on this, what do you think is the next step in the development of social media?
4   Issue for debate: Can Netflix, Uber, WhatsApp be considered social media in a broad sense of the term? Explain your answer.

Further Reading

Burgess, Jean; Marwick, Alice; Poell, Thomas. 2018. Editors' introduction, in *The SAGE Handbook of Social Media*. Sage.

Ellison, Nicole B.; boyd, danah. 2013. Sociality through social network sites, in William Dutton (Ed.), *The Oxford Handbook of Internet Studies*. Oxford University Press. http://www.danah. org/papers/2013/SocialityThruSNS-preprint.pdf

Papacharissi, Zizi. 2015. 'We have always been social', *Social Media + Society,* 1 (1). http://journals.sagepub.com/doi/full/10.1177/2056305115581185#articleCitation DownloadContainer, DOI: https://doi.org/10.1177/2056305115581185

3

POWER AND IDEOLOGY

Chapter Overview

Introduction	58
Power: The Basics	59
Marx, capitalism and ideology	60
Forms of power	62
Power/knowledge	64
Media and symbolic power	67
The Ideology of Connection: From the Culture Industries to Platform Empires	69
The culture industries	70
The audience commodity	71
Platform empires: Every click is capital	73
The ideology of connection	75
Critiques: The Active Audience Tradition and 'Small Acts of Engagement' (SAOE)	76
Conclusion: Ambivalent Cultures and the Power of Connection	79
Questions and Activities	80
Further Reading	80

―――――――┌─Chapter Objectives─┐―――――――――――――――――――――――――――

- Introduce power and important concepts used to make sense of power, such as ideology, power/knowledge and symbolic power
- Contextualize current approaches to power in relation to their longer histories in media and communication studies
- Unpack social media's 'ideology of connection'
- Make sense of key critiques drawing from the active audience tradition

Introduction

The purpose of this chapter is not to provide a comprehensive account of the great body of work on power. Instead this chapter aims to outline important conceptual foundations that help to understand power, and its application to social media.

Media are cultural technologies and processes enabling the production and circulation of meaning. What we see and hear through media can shape our social expectations of what is right and wrong – of who is accepted and who is not. Nick Stevenson and David Morley connect media content with cultural citizenship, meaning that what and who we see through media can legitimate or change social exclusions, validate group identities, represent entire nationalities and connect us to or disconnect us from others (e.g. Miller 2007; Morley 2001; Stevenson 2003a, 2003b). Media reflect and represent our worlds, facilitate self-identification and self-expression, and support cultural, social, political belonging and exclusion. In the twentieth century, professionally produced media – newspapers, television and radio broadcasting – dominated this cultural sphere. The shift towards digital and social media also meant a significant transformation not only in content, but also in content production, forms of public interaction, and contingent frames for self and group identification.

So here are the key questions: What power do social media have? Why are some social media platforms so powerful? How do they empower some and disempower others? How do they shape our lives and interactions? Where are we, as users and as citizens, in social media?

There are many answers to these questions, and many different approaches to what power is and how it works in relation to social media. Yet the goal of this chapter is not to provide a systematic account of this body of work. Instead the goal is to introduce a conceptual foundation to think through power in the twenty-first century. These basics include Marx, capitalism, ideology, Foucault's power/knowledge and symbolic power – all essential concepts. The next section introduces the ideology of connection, mapping the import of critical work on the cultural industries (Adorno and Horkheimer 2005 [1944]), the audience commodity (Smythe 1981) in the development of current thinking on surveillance capitalism

(Zuboff 2019), data colonialism (Couldry and Mejias 2019a, 2019b) and platform societies (Van Dijck et al. 2018). Finally, this chapter draws from the active audiences tradition (Brundson and Morley 1978; Du Gay 1997; Hall 1999; Livingstone 2019) to introduce critiques of top-down workings of power in light of user empowerment and agency. Current work on 'small acts of engagement' (SAOE) illustrates these principles as well as showing that power is not monolithic or unidirectional.

Although this chapter aims to simplify and untangle the complexity of power, it is important to remember that power is always plural, always complex and often works in what may seem to be oppositional ways. As Nick Couldry (2012) suggests:

> … domination is plural; it possesses an economic dimension but always also a symbolic dimension, what Boltanski calls 'the field of determining what is' (*le champ de détermination de ce qui est*). This lends particular importance in social analysis to 'the instruments for totalizing and representing what is, or at least what's given as relevant for the collective': they are the institutions that shape 'how things stand with what is' (*ce qu'il en est de ce qui est*).

Power: The Basics

Given the vast body of work dedicated to theorizing power, this section provides an overview of basic concepts that have been used in many disciplines to unpack and make sense of the workings of power. This section is intended to be short and introductory, providing a basis for exploring these concepts further, as well as for their application to real world situations whether they are digital or not.

It is important to note that although we often think of power in terms of domination or hard coercion, power can also be soft, and as present in the quiet and boring moments as it is in the loud displays. We might see power most clearly when we think of extremism and violence, but it is also there in the choices we make when we uphold or reject social norms, regardless of whether those norms are good or bad. Power does involve exploitation, force, coercion and domination, but as we shall see throughout this chapter, it also involves much softer and intangible elements that may be harder to see. As Des Freedman (2014) rightly argues, power is always contradictory.

Earlier understandings of power tend to focus on a wide range of strategies of control and influence. This approach to power is often based on Weber's framing of power as the power of A over B and can be made visible through influence, force, coercion and/or control. Max Weber, a key sociological theorist, argues that power is the capacity to influence others, to exercise one's will over another (Weber 1995 [1922]: 38). Many have critiqued this as negative and one-dimensional (see Lukes 2005 [1974]), particularly in relation to the 'puzzle of media power' (Freedman 2014: 11; see also Couldry and Curran 2003; Curran 2006; Trivundža et al. 2017).

Marx, capitalism and ideology

Perhaps one of the most influential and revolutionary thinkers in terms of power is Karl Marx, inspiring generations of thinkers and activists, as well as generating copious texts which directly or indirectly take up, critique, update and/or amend his work. Indeed, Marx and his many colleagues inspired critiques of economic power and capitalism, leading to a well-developed field loosely defined as the political economy of the media (e.g. Williams 2005 [1980]). Although Marx's work and the related literature are too vast to cover in any depth here (Marx and Engel's writings have been reported to exceed 114 volumes in one archive; see Fang 2018), 'Marxism' provides at least two key points fundamental to broader understandings of power: capitalism and ideology. At the beginning of *The Communist Manifesto*, originally published in 1848, Marx and Engels write:

> The history of all hitherto existing society is the history of class struggles. Freeman and slave, patrician and plebeian, lord and serf ... in a word, oppressor and oppressed, stood in constant opposition to one another, carried on ... a now open fight, a fight that each time ended in either revolutionary reconstitution of society at large, or in the common ruin of the contending classes. (Marx and Engels 1998 [1888]: 4)

While *The Communist Manifesto* may have been written in 'the springtime of socialist thought' (McLellan 1998: xvi), the above quotation highlights the heart of these two key points. First, capitalism is a polarized socio-economic system designed to accumulate commodities at the expense of wage labourers (proletariat), and for the profit of the bourgeoisie (owners of the means of production). Class, one's social and economic status, is a collective rather than personal condition under capitalism (Marx and Engels 1988 [1888]: 19), and necessarily involves exploitation of the poor by the ruling class, resulting in economic and political inequality, and perpetual class struggle between the two. Thus, all social relations from the private realm (family, romance, friendship, etc.) to the public (politics, art, community etc.), involve conflict between the ruling power and those who are ruled over.

Although this is only a very brief summary, there are two points that are absolutely central for understanding power. First, that Marxist thinking identifies capitalism as a system marked by dominant forms of power – that of the ruling class (and those that own the means of production) who are able to dominate others through a system of economic exploitation. Thus, economics (the base) determines all else, including all 'legal, educational, artistic, and political activities' and all social relations (the 'superstructure', Marx 1859, cited in Jones 2006: 28). Second, capitalism is *ideological*. Ideology, another widely used concept, refers to the system or 'set of ideas' arising from a particular group, which for Marx and Engels refers to class (Williams 2015 [1976]: 110). This 'set of ideas' comes from multiple sources such as history, family, education, 'dominant symbolic sources', media – to name but a few (Thompson 1995: 210). Thus ideological beliefs around class differences are often naturalized, in that such differences are justified by inherent personal characteristics and that disparities in wealth are part of the social order. Indeed, the process of coming to class consciousness involves identifying these belief systems and unpicking them from the 'natural' order.

In terms of power, Marxist thinking prioritizes economics as determining social action, because those who have the most resources make the rules (ruling classes), and that those who make the rules set up a system of beliefs that support and maintain this system (ideology). Notably, political economists of media in the Marxist traditions see the media as tools of the ruling classes and are therefore the instruments of capitalist ideologies. While these concepts are important and have generated tremendous volumes of work, there are also critiques of this work. For example, please see Box 3.1 on Kimberle Crenshaw's influential concept of *intersectionality* for a contrasting view of power and ideology.

Box 3.1 Intersectionality and Kimberlé Crenshaw

Intersectionality, a term attributed to American legal professor Kimberlé Crenshaw (1989, 1991; cf. Grzanka 2014: xiv), refers to a serious limitation of Marxist and feminist thinking – both of which conceptualize power along the 'single-axis framework' of class, sexism or racism (Crenshaw 1989: 139). Crenshaw takes issue with this one-dimensional axis of power because it excludes the 'multidimensionality of Black women's experience' which is often at the *intersection* of classed, raced and gendered systems of power and oppression (1989: 139).

Beginning with the legal system, Crenshaw details how anti-discrimination law (1989), domestic violence and rape law (1991), as well as feminist and anti-racist thinking, open up deeply problematic frameworks which end up erasing Black women and perpetuating 'patterns of subordination' (1991: 1249). For Crenshaw, intersectionality best describes 'the location of women of color both within overlapping systems of subordination and at the margins of feminism and antiracism' (1991: 1265). To illustrate this often unintentional problematic, she draws from many examples, including first-hand experience at battered women's shelters. She finds serious legal absences that further victimize immigrant and/or women of colour experiencing abuse because legal frameworks reinforce their dependence on their abusers and deny support services to non-English-speaking victims (e.g. the marriage fraud provisions of the Immigration and Nationality Act, 1991: 1245–1249). In addition, Crenshaw highlights objections around the release of LAPD domestic violence statistics from within Black communities because such statistics would support negative and violent racial stereotypes, as well as positioning domestic violence as a 'minority problem' and potentially undermining support and policy work supporting victims (1991: 1252–53).

These examples illustrate what Crenshaw refers to as political and structural intersectionality. These are only two of many examples showing how women of colour are

(Continued)

further marginalized. By being at the intersection of multiple exclusionary and often competing legal or regulatory systems, women may be subjected to systems dealing with race (but not gender or class) or gender (but not race or class) or class (but not race or gender). She argues that:

> the violence that many women experience is often shaped by other dimensions of their identities, such as race and class. Moreover, ignoring difference within groups contributes to tension among groups. (Crenshaw 1991: 1242)

The concept of intersectionality problematizes whiteness in the development of social, political and cultural critique and in the systemic perpetuation of inequality. Intersectionality demands a rethinking of single-axis dimensions of power in order to 'better acknowledge and ground the differences among us' in multiple and intersecting systems of power (Crenshaw 1991: 1299).

For further work on intersectionality, see Cho, S.; Crenshaw, K.; McCall, L. (2013) Toward a field of intersectionality studies: theory, application, praxis, *Signs: Journal of Women in Culture and Society*, 38 (4), pp. 785–819.

Brief biography

Kimberlé Crenshaw is a founding thinker on both intersectionality and critical race theory (CRT), using her knowledge and expertise to contribute to civil rights and Black feminist legal theory, and to found the African American Policy Forum (AAPF). Crenshaw has served as the UN Rapporteur for the United Nations' Expert Group on Gender and Race Discrimination for the United Nations' conference on racism. She has authored many books and articles, all of which promote gender and racial inclusivity, two of which include *Black Girls Matter: Pushed Out, Overpoliced and Underprotected* (2014) and *Say Her Name: Resisting Police Brutality Against Black Women* (2015).

Forms of power

Many position power and culture as more than just economics or extensions of economics, opening up new ways to think about power (Hall 1980; Williams 2005 [1980]; for Gramsci on hegemony, see Jones 2006). As such, power can also be amorphous and ubiquitous, making it difficult to pin down. John Thompson (1995) helps resolve this slipperiness when he suggests that power is organized around different kinds of resources, which can concentrate or extend power. This is a helpful framework, one that makes it more possible to unpack the workings of power (e.g. Curran 2006; Freedman 2014; cf. Fuchs 2017: 92–98). Thus, Thompson argues that these forms of power tend to be clustered around economic, political, coercive, and/or cultural/symbolic resources, even if they are also overlapping (e.g. economic power is also political and/or symbolic, coercive power can be cultural and/or economic; Thompson 1995: 12–18). Those with many more resources at their disposal are able to potentially magnify their actions and impact on others (Thompson 1995: 13). As shown in Table 3.1, these 'forms of power' are clearly grouped according to different resources, explained further below, which may be more difficult to tease out in real life scenarios.

Table 3.1 'Forms of power'

Type of power	Primary resources (and institutional forms)
Economic	Material, financial, or other quantifiable and measurable values (e.g. commercial or corporate enterprises, financial markets)
Political	Authority, and actions involving coordination and regulation (e.g. government, state, municipality)
Coercive	Force and threat (e.g. military, prison, law enforcement)
Cultural or symbolic	Meaning, status, reputation (e.g. media, education, churches)

Source: adapted from Thompson (1995: 17)

Economic power is acquired through the accumulation or allocation of material resources. Although economic power is often understood in terms of wealth, it is not just about money or financial resources, but can also include any kind of resource whose value can be determined and exchanged. In this sense, economic power in a social media age might include the number of followers an Instagram account has and the use of this number in negotiating the value of that account holder's posts or in their potential reach, as is often the case for influencers. (For more on influencers and power, see Box 7.2 on influencer Essena O'Neill.)

Thompson takes a relatively narrow view of political power, one that relates politics to formal state or governance actions. While many would contest this, arguing that 'small p' politics exist in the civic and public realm as much as they do in political institutions, political power, for Thompson, is about authority and regulation. Thus, 'political power' refers to those resources that can be used to command or encourage obedience from others, regardless of whether that compliant behaviour is demanded, manipulated, encouraged or inspired.

Coercive power involves all of those resources and activities used to directly or indirectly force others to obey, act or think in accordance with the source of coercion. Thompson uses the military as a key example of how threat and/or physical force (augmented by weapons, techniques, tactics or other sources) can be used to get others to act in particular ways (1995: 15–16). While coercion and political power may often go hand in hand, coercion is a particular type of action that can be hard or soft, direct or indirect, physical or psychological.

Finally, cultural or symbolic power is of central importance for those concerned with media, social media and everyday life. Symbolic power refers to a wide range of resources used to express, inform and communicate meaning. Thompson defines symbolic power as a 'fundamental feature of social life' involving the 'capacity to intervene in the course of events, to influence the actions of others and indeed to create events, by means of the production and transmission of symbolic forms' (1995: 16–17). Thompson designates this dimension of power to the media and cultural industries, to educational and religious institutions and to all of those actors primarily concerned with the production and circulation of information and meaning. This is indeed a broad and especially important dimension for social media, one that includes many intangible expressions of power, such as reputation, status, cultural knowledge and innovation, and is also centred around media where symbolic power is often concentrated.

Some critique these forms of power as indistinct, somewhat arbitrarily confining media and culture to the symbolic realm when indeed it should be overarching (e.g. Freedman 2014: 9–10; Fuchs 2017: 92–95). For example, why is symbolic power distinct from the other forms when both often go hand in hand? Think of the control over information Rupert Murdoch or Mark Zuckerberg exercise through News Corp or Facebook (including all of their subsidiaries) – both clearly demonstrating an overlap between economic and symbolic power. Thus, while critics may be technically correct in pointing to the limitations of this framework, the point is to break through some of this complexity and understand power in its multiplicities. Thompson's framework effectively illustrates the multiple dimensions of power, breaking down a broad and difficult concept in more easily identifiable clusters, even if each of these contains elements of other forms of power. We will return to these dimensions and the distinctions between them in the sections below. Next, we introduce influential conceptions of power, such as Michel Foucault's ideas of power as productive.

Power/knowledge

In contrast to conceptions of power as reductive and often negative (only observable through visible consequences), Michel Foucault argues that power is both positive and constructive. It is as much about making as it is about taking, albeit in multiple, inseparable and deeply interacting systems, processes and actions. For example, Foucault famously states:

> Power is everywhere; not because it embraces everything, but because it comes from everywhere. (1980: 93)

Unlike Thompson and Weber, Foucault does not attempt to break down power into smaller chunks so that we can better understand where it is and how it works. Instead, Foucault positions power as broad, complex and pervasive. He argues that *power is productive*, and has written many books mapping the genealogy of power through systems (e.g. *The Order of Things*, 1970; *Discipline and Punish: The Birth of the Prison*, 1977; *The History of Sexuality*, Volumes 1–3, 1976–84). In all of these works, Foucault analyses the historical development of whole systems of thought. In the *History of Sexuality*, for example, he challenges historical understandings of Victorian sexual attitudes as prudish and prohibitive, arguing that a commonly understood 'repressive hypothesis' ignores the army of people writing, talking about and professionalizing sexual discourse in this era (1980: Part Two).

Foucault argues that rather than seeing attitudes towards sex and sexuality as the out-come of repressive power wielded by churches, Victorian authorities and a prudish mentality, we must see power as something that is productive and processual – as the nexus between 'pleasure/power/knowledge' which can produce silence as well as incitement (1980: 11–12). Foucault examines the detailed development of a coordinated sexual morality that vastly multiplied who talked about sex, creating systems to document and classify perversions, immoral acts and indecencies – all in minute detail. Based on this analysis, he documents a Victorian explosion of *discourse* (any verbal accounts or written works) including the development of an 'encyclopedic' knowledge on sex and sexuality. It seems that rather than the silencing of sex and sexuality, the Victorian era saw quite the opposite.

Foucault points to the emergence of 'the homosexual' as an illustration of both productive power, and as one part of the explosion of discourse around sex. Prior to the nineteenth century, there was no word and indeed no concept for a person who had a sexual preference for other people of their own gender – and indeed there were no words for many kinds of sexual behaviours which came to be classed as perversions, deviances and abnormalities. Instead, Foucault argues:

> Homosexuality appeared as one of the forms of sexuality when it was transposed from the practice of sodomy onto a kind of interior androgyny, a hermaphrodism of the soul. The sodomite had been a temporary aberration; the homosexual was now a species. (1980: 43)

In this way, knowledge produces a subject whose identity is shaped by public knowledge, and by discourse, and this is an interiorization of discourse. As a homosexual himself, Foucault was not trying to pinpoint the birth of a particular sexual orientation and identity; rather, he was trying to map the ways in which social practices constructed systems of thought which also *produced identities and ways of being in the world*. For Foucault, this is one example of many illustrating how *'power produces knowledge'* and knowledge produces our perceptions and experiences of the world (Foucault 2012 [1977]: 76, emphasis added). Foucault goes on to say that 'there is no power relation without the correlative constitution of a field of knowledge' (Foucault 2012 [1977]: 76). Here is a wonderful example of the way knowledge constructs not only ways of being, but also ways of interacting with the world.

This point echoes throughout Foucault's many works, such as *Discipline and Punish* which examines not only 'the birth of the prison' but also the birth of socialization – of soft power – via institutional systems as seen in education, in bureaucracy and in the military. It is in this book that he so clearly articulates what 'productive power' means:

> We must cease once and for all to describe the effects of power in negative terms: it 'excludes', it 'represses', it 'censors', it 'abstracts', it 'masks', it 'conceals'. In fact, power produces; it produces reality; *it produces domains of objects and rituals of truth* (Foucault 2012 [1977]: 491–92, emphasis added)

Foucault's work has been hugely influential, informing the way many thinkers understand power, and his name is often used to signpost these ideas of power as productive. These are particularly important points for how we understand media as well as surveillance (see Chapter 8). (See Box 3.2 for an overview of Taina Bucher's work on *programmed sociality*, which applies Foucauldian power to algorithms.)

Box 3.2 Programmed sociality: From Foucault to Bucher

Drawing from Foucault's concept of power as 'exercised, relational and productive', Taina Bucher defines *algorithmic power* as an 'ensemble of strategies' which 'helps to produce certain forms of acting and knowing' (2018: 3). Crucially, Bucher argues that algorithms do not *have* or *exercise* power, but they increasingly automate the curation and collection of vast amounts of information for machine and human use.

As an example of 'relational and productive' algorithmic power, Bucher focuses on friendship on Facebook as an example, noting that friend-to-friend connections are:

- multiple – involving connections between people, algorithms, platforms and third parties;
- nodal – do not need to be between two humans, but can be between a person and a thing (e.g. movies, books, businesses, organizations, places), each of which is a node in a network;
- organized by 'set', which are 'powerful classification devices based on demographic information, attributes of connections, frequency of interaction and other factors' (Bucher 2018: 10);
- productive – 'making up' categories to define certain kinds of people, such as a 'top friend' – someone who is algorithmically identified as someone a user may share all kinds of content with (e.g. photos, other connections, game-play, instant messaging);
- ranked – friends, products, people you may know – everything made visible to users on Facebook through news feeds, recommendations, stories, memories, and other features are algorithmically sorted.

Bucher argues that each of these 'computational friendship' points are numerically scored, and then 'used to feed rankings or enhance predictions' for maximizing advertising revenues and time spent on the platform (Bucher 2018: 11). For Bucher, all of this demonstrates how friendship algorithms are about an 'equation geared towards maximizing engagement with the platform', rather than connecting friends. She proposes the term 'programmed sociality' to capture this process, as well as the role of algorithms and computational infrastructures in setting the 'conditions of possibility for sociality in digital media' (2018: 12). It is in these ways that Bucher supports her argument that:

> Algorithms do not merely *have* power and politics; they are fundamentally pro-
> ductive of new ways of ordering the world. Importantly, algorithms do not work
> on their own but need to be understood as part of a much wider network of rela-
> tions and practices … [they are] entangled, multiple, and eventful. (2018: 20)

In a study on the Israeli data analytics industry, Dan Kotliar, a visiting researcher at Stanford University, illustrates Bucher's point. Kotliar (2020) examines how people in the data
industry work with user-analytic algorithms, finding that although algorithms generate data
clusters about users, *people* must translate and group these clusters according to more
understandable social categories. In this way, algorithms program social relations and
how it is those social relations are shared and understood by those working in analytics.

So far, we have seen big differences in theoretical understandings of power, ranging from
the economic ideology of capitalism, power as multiple and overlapping, and now power as
productive. Yet, where does this leave us for understanding power in relation to media? Do
media *have* power or *direct* power? Do media require their own specific formulations of
power (e.g. symbolic power) or are they part and parcel of all dimensions of power? In order
to address these questions, the next section focuses on symbolic power and its relationship
to media.

Media and symbolic power

Building upon Thompson's view of power as multi-dimensional (e.g. economic, political,
coercive and symbolic), many media scholars have focused on symbolic power as the key to
understanding media power. Nick Couldry, for example, has been researching and thinking
through this complex relationship between media and power throughout his long career,
including in his first book, where he defines symbolic power as:

> … the media's 'power of constructing reality' (Bourdieu 1991: 166) in a general
> sense. Each programme, text or image, of course, has its particular way of
> maintaining your belief (that it is a true representation of the facts or a convincing
> fiction). But I am interested in something more general … the *media's status as
> sources of social knowledge*. (2000: 4, emphasis added)

For Couldry, even in his early conceptions of symbolic power, the media are central
resources for the public and private construction of meaning. Couldry argues that 'media
power' specifically refers to the collection and concentration of *symbolic resources* used to
create texts (e.g. images, stories, songs, words, ideas) that shape our sense of who we are,

where we are and of who others are – and the ways in which we are able to communicate these senses.

Many other theorists and scholars frame this relationship in terms of representation and the media's role in reflecting or constructing 'shared meanings or shared conceptual maps' (Hall 2012 [1997]: 18, 1980; see also Chouliaraki 2006, 2013; Noble 2018; Ong 2015; Orgad 2012; Thumim 2012). In this instance, absences and invisibility are as important as what is made visible in and through media.

Beginning with any kind of inequality, we can see patterns of visibility and invisibility not only for who is represented within media content, but also in who makes media content – all of which has an impact on our symbolic understanding of the world. For example, researchers from USC Annenberg have been mapping inequality in top Hollywood films from 2007. Although they note an increase in films with a female lead in 2018, these films make only 40% of top Hollywood films (up a remarkable 8% from 2017; see Smith et al. 2018). Their annual monitoring reports on representation in Hollywood film document the dominance of white characters – making up 70.7% of all leading characters – and the under-representation of women, Black, Hispanic, Asian, lesbian, gay, bisexual and trans characters (Annenberg Inclusion Initiative 2019; Smith et al. 2018).

Another example applies to Google Search's algorithmic racism, which Safiyah Noble painstakingly documents, revealing a long history of racial profiling and the over-sexualization of Black girls and women. Noble shares the story of searching for things to do on Google with her young step-daughter and nieces, using the search term 'Black girls'. The first result was 'HotBlackPussy.com', proving an algorithm linking 'Black girls' or 'Black women' with sexualized and racialized web content (2018: 3–4). Noble documents a wide range of similar cases, demonstrating a deeply ingrained racism and the perpetuation of damaging stereotypes 'fundamental to the operating system of the web' (2018: 10). Others like Lilie Chouliaraki have examined the impact of how suffering is represented in the news and media, culminating in a 'humanitarian imagination' limited by incomplete and culturally repetitive stereotypes of distant others (2013, 2006; cf. Ong 2015; Orgad 2012). Many – too many to introduce here – have examined and thought deeply about the ways media content shapes not only what we know, but also what we think about ourselves and others.

Couldry situates these kinds of incidents as distinct aspects of media and symbolic power. According to Couldry:

> … all forms of power work in a dispersed way, but symbolic power impacts upon wider society more pervasively than other forms of power (such as economic power) because the *concentration of society's symbolic resources affects not just what we do but our ability to describe whatever 'goes on'*. (Couldry 2012: 233–34, emphasis added)

Smith et al., Noble and Chouliaraki provide key examples of how pervasive representations of inequality – in film, in digital media and in news for example – shape perceptions of the world and impact on people's everyday lives. These are only a few illustrations of *symbolic power*, often working beyond our conscious awareness, which makes it much harder to unpack the ways media intersect with our knowledge and understanding of the world.

So far, this chapter has introduced some of the key conceptual foundations for understanding power: ideology, forms of power, power/knowledge and symbolic power. Media help shape our view of the world, ourselves and the people within it. All of these concepts are important for thinking through power in a social media age. Bearing this in mind, the next sections introduce the trajectories of power through the development of what are often understood as two very different schools of thought – those focused on money and economics, and those focused on people's agency through reception, participation and engagement.

The Ideology of Connection: From the Culture Industries to Platform Empires

This section contextualizes contemporary thinking on the ways in which social media are not only powerful but also have transformed our socio-economic systems and our media landscapes (cf. Livingstone 2019). For much of the current work being done on social media, there are intellectual precedents focusing on other kinds of media. For example, Adorno and Horkheimer write about film and music in 1940s America, and Dallas Smythe writes about broadcast television – all early articulations of the culture industries. By beginning with these bodies of work, I hope to trace the roots of critical work on the current moment including important work, such as 'surveillance capitalism' (Zuboff 2019), 'data colonialism' (Couldry and Mejias 2019a, 2019b), 'platform capitalism' (Srnicek 2017) and 'the platform society' (Van Dijck 2013; Van Dijck et al. 2018).

This tracing exercise shows that while there are continuities, there are also significant distinctions. One of the first continuities is a focus on unpicking the workings of media and cultural industries to reveal an underlying ideology. The pursuit of greater profits and the trickery of advertising is shared from the culture industries to platform empires, or the combined work of Srnicek, Zuboff, Couldry and Mejias. Taken together, this body of work makes clear 'the ideology of connection' driving social media and platform expansion.

These approaches make loose correspondences between political economy and top-down, structure orientations, as well as between cultural or audience studies orientations and agency, reception, and everyday orientations. However, these disciplinary correspondences and their distinctions and alignments are not absolute. Each offers insight which helps us better make sense of social media and their relationship to power. Generally, those approaches mostly aligned with the political economy of social media tend to focus on structural or top-down issues, such as patterns of ownership, technological or company infrastructures, intellectual property, labour, profits and business models. Those approaches mostly aligned with active audiences, interpretivism and participatory culture tend towards a more agency-oriented and bottom-up perspective. Each of these approaches are critical, sometimes of the other, yet they also provide complementary although often contrasting accounts of power and social media.

The culture industries

As founding members of the Frankfurt School, Theodore Adorno and Max Horkheimer, two of the first 'critical theorists', escaped the rise of fascism in Germany under Hitler's growing totalitarianism and entered into 'free' America in the 1930s and 1940s (Wolin 2019; cf. Bernstein 1991). Adorno and Horkheimer were immediately struck by the parallels between the two states and horrified by the overwhelming power of capitalism in American popular culture, including what they saw as a commodified sense of free will. Some have critiqued these thinkers for an elite view of culture, and for underestimating individual agency, yet their critique of mass media as industries in the business of producing and commodifying culture is important.

In *Enlightenment as Mass Deception,* Adorno and Horkheimer argue that film, television and music *are in the business of disguising economic coercion as cultural expression.* There are three main components to this argument: mass media is about the business of entertainment; entertainment disguises the extension of work; and freedom of choice is illusory.

Beginning with the first of these points, Adorno and Horkheimer argue that the culture industries are deceptive because they claim to do one thing – amuse, entertain, titillate, offer an escape from everyday life – and yet do something entirely different; they sell culture and lifestyle in a way that transforms everyday life into economic relations. For example, Adorno and Horkheimer explain: 'The culture industry remains the entertainment business. Its control of consumers is mediated by entertainment and its hold will not be broken by outright dictate ...' or force, but by the soft power of seduction and promise (Horkheimer and Adorno 2002 [1948]: 108). This dynamic results in what Adorno and Horkheimer call a

> *paradoxical commodity.* So completely is it subject to the law of exchange that it is no longer exchanged; it is so blindly consumed in use that it can no longer be used. Therefore it amalgamates with advertising. The more meaningless the latter seems to be under a monopoly, the more omnipotent it becomes. The motives are markedly economic. (2005 [1944], emphasis added)

Here, culture is something produced by an army of professionals and consumed by individual audience members who are mostly unaware or unengaged with their collectivity as an audience. With this positionality comes not only a particular consumer-oriented lifestyle where values can be bought and sold, but also a broader ideology enshrining the way the world works and the consumer's position within it, including class, gender and relational norms. The culture industries not only promote a consumer lifestyle, they also 'reproduce a mental state' and capitalist ideology equating social values with products and behaviours (Adorno and Horkheimer 2005 [1944]). For Adorno and Horkheimer, mass media does not only work as the entertainment business, but also in popularizing and normalizing an advanced capitalist and class-oriented ideology.

Part of this capitalist ideology includes what Adorno and Horkheimer argue is about further deception, such as the disguising of 'amusement [as] … the prolongation of work' (2005 [1944]). They first argue that ordinary people are unable to resist the allure of the culture industries, and the 'off-duty worker can experience nothing but after images of the work process itself' (Horkheimer and Adorno 2002 [1948]: 109). In this way, entertainment is determined by the culture industries and is fundamentally about 'the withering of imagination' so that consumers believe 'the illusion that the world outside is a seamless extension of the one' perpetuated through film, sound, art, music – and the culture industries. As Horkheimer and Adorno state:

> The whole world is passed through the filter of the culture industry. The familiar experience of the moviegoer, who perceives the street outside as a continuation of the film [s]he has just left, because the film seeks to reproduce the world of everyday perception has become the guideline of production. (2002 [1948]: 99)

Related to this, workers now engage in consumer behaviour, which is a kind of labour that not only perpetuates capitalism, but which also instils capitalist ideology in those consumers.

Finally, Adorno and Horkehimer argue that the 'freedom to choose an ideology … proves to be freedom to choose what is always the same' (2005 [1944]). Here, they are referring to how all 'mass culture under monopoly is identical', and although it may 'leave the body free [it] sets to work directly on the soul' (Horkheimer and Adorno 2002 [1948]: 93, 105). By this they mean that although the culture industries present entertainment as optional, and as containing what seems like an infinite number of stories to choose from, all the options are the same, thinly disguised as choice, and underpinned by the totalizing logic of capitalism.

Although writing about mass culture, there are striking similarities between what Adorno and Horkheimer understood as 'the culture industries' and the social platforms of today – particularly in that economic relations are disguised as social relations – a point illustrated by the data-harvesting work social media platforms are built upon, as illustrated in the Cambridge Analytica case discussed in Chapter 1.

The audience commodity

Dallas Smythe (1907–1992), one of the founding thinkers shaping the political economy of communications as a discipline, focused on the complex work of advertisers and television in the 1970s–80s. Like Adorno and Horkheimer, Smythe was inspired by Marxist thinking, and argued that television's real product was not entertainment or information content, but instead it was advertising. The real product of television was consumers, neatly packaged as popular audiences. In this sense, all of the 'content' produced by professionals and which ordinary users watched on television was actually only filler for the real content – advertisements. Network producers and broadcasters were obsessed with the best ways to sell audience attention to advertisers, all quantifiable through the metrics of ratings and numbers of viewers. As Smythe argues:

> In economic terms, the *audience commodity is a nondurable producer's good* which is bought and used in the marketing of the advertiser's product. The work which audience members perform for the advertiser to whom they have been sold is learning to buy goods and to spend their income accordingly. (Smythe 1981: 243, emphasis added)

For Smythe, the driving principle behind all television production is the commodification and monetization of audience attention and their income expenditures. Like Adorno and Horkheimer, Smythe focuses on the fundamental deception of the culture industries. This work marked the beginning of a new phase of television, and also of a new approach to the analysis of media industries – the political economy of media – which focused on ownership, profits, wages and the behind the scenes work of media professionals. At the same time, professionals became skilled in quantifying audiences, carving them up into demographic and socio-economic categories so that advertisers and media professionals could more easily buy and sell audience attention. Smythe argues:

> ... as collectivities these audiences are commodities. As commodities they are dealt with in markets by producers and buyers (the latter being advertisers). Such markets establish prices in the familiar mode of monopoly capitalism. (Smythe 1981: 234)

Thus, in terms of research, the idea of the 'audience commodity' marked an important contribution to the political economy of media and communications, as well as marking a departure away from a focus on texts, meaning and the content of media. In terms of new ways of doing media business, Smythe (1981: 251) argued that this era of television and the emergence of the audience commodity marked 'a qualitatively new major social institution', one that mobilized a whole network of professionals, jostling to gain traction in new markets.

These two bodies of work point to a continuity from Marxist thinking on capitalism and ideology to work on the culture industries and the audience commodity. While there are many distinctions between these ideas and current work, the next section outlines important continuities between these early ideas and not only current work, but also current media institutions. Indeed, it is clear that articulating media or platform power in terms of economics follows a trajectory around capitalism, ideology and domination – both in media and cultural analysis, and in the everyday lives of platform users and consumers.

Platform empires: Every click is capital

Bringing together current work on platform, surveillance and data capitalism, it seems that there has been a shift from the culture industries to platform empires, as the size, scale and scope of platforms extend beyond mega corporations, beyond national boundaries and into extensive spheres of action (see Chapter 5). Thus while Facebook, for example, purports to 'build community', they are also building a complex advertising and behavioural surveillance machine (Zuboff 2019). See their mission statement:

> Facebook's mission is to give people the power to build community and bring the world closer together. (Facebook mission statement, July 2019. https://newsroom. fb.com/company-info/)

Following the critical turn identified in Chapter 2, *The Four Stages of Social Media*, there has been an explosion of work drawing attention to the sheer size of social platforms (see Chapter 5, on platform empires: GAFA and BATX). This poses challenges around the relationship between data harvesting and profit-making, which are systematically marketed to users as reconfigured social relations. There is a long and growing list of authors who may approach 'this problem' of social media, each wrestling with what social media really do. Of this long list, Nick Srnicek (*Platform Capitalism*, 2017), Shoshanna Zuboff (*The Age of Surveillance Capitalism*, 2019), and Nick Couldry and Ulisses Mejias (on data colonialism, 2019a, 2019b) best articulate how social media are fundamentally deceptive companies, advancing a new stage of capitalism. While there are many other voices and arguments worthy of considering, it is these arguments that best capture the economic and global dynamics of social media, along with the cultural moment they represent. (See also Bucher 2018a; Vaidyanathan 2018.)

Despite the many differences and distinctions, these authors share some fundamental arguments, including the role of platforms in developing new business models based on data extraction and commodification, the massive growth of global platform oligopolies and oligopsonies, and in marking the emergence of a new stage of capitalism.

First, unpicking the economics of social media reveals the complex platform infrastructures involved in economic exchange (Srnieck 2017), surveillance (Zuboff 2019) and colonialism (Couldry and Mejias 2019a, 2019b; see also Chapter 5). These authors demonstrate platforms designed to surveil users and datafy every click, browse or view in order to better serve advertisers and generate profits. All of these authors point to a new kind of business model, one that drives big social media companies and the digital environment. Couldry and Mejias situate social media as major actors in the 'social quantification sector' which incorporates social media, fitness trackers, education (e.g. educational technologies, behavioural monitoring, quantified learning), fertility and reproductive trackers, behavioural economics, purchasing patterns, targeted advertising, and on and on and on. Indeed, they argue that social quantification has permeated every aspect of the economy, and is increasingly driven not only by data collection and commodification, but also by the battle over new resources and the commodification of human life.

For Nick Srnicek, platform capitalism is not only about specific platforms, but also about the ways that platforms have developed anti-competitive tactics and generated their own walled-off ecosystems:

> Platforms also seek to build up ecosystems of goods and services that close off competitors: apps that only work with Android, services that require Facebook logins ... All these dynamics turn platforms into monopolies with centralised control over increasingly vast numbers of users and the data they generate. We can get a sense of how significant these monopolies already are by looking at how they consolidate ad revenue: in 2016 Facebook, Google and Alibaba alone will take half of the world's digital advertising. In the United States, Facebook and Google receive 76% of online advertising revenue and are taking 85 % of every new advertising dollars. (Srnicek 2017: 96)

Srnicek points to the role of platforms in the global economy, and their dominance in advertising often engaging anti-competitive behaviour as has been evidenced in the sharing economy (and beyond typical definitions of social media such as Uber, Airbnb and Google, as well as Facebook, Instagram and other social media).

Shoshana Zuboff points to a new logic of accumulation based on human data extraction and the emergence of totalizing 'behavioural futures markets' (Zuboff 2019). Like Zuboff, Couldry and Mejias also highlight such markets as a new stage of capitalism, although they go one step further, arguing that this market is historically grounded in the British and Spanish colonial empires (2019a, 2019b). Drawing from a more global rather than Zuboff's mostly American-based perspective, Couldry and Mejias argue that while what they call the 'historical colonialism' of earlier centuries focused on the extraction of natural resources (land, oil, coal, etc.), this stage of data colonialism aims to capitalize on new data frontiers. This means that every online click, like, view, link or digital movement is subject to vast and coordinated systems of data collection, data manipulation and monetization (see also Box 3.2). For Couldry and Mejias, data colonialism is not a metaphor, but a literal description of economic and social processes:

> Just as historical colonialism over the long-run provided the essential preconditions for the emergence of industrial capitalism, so over time, we can expect that data colonialism will provide the preconditions for a new stage of capitalism that as yet we can barely imagine, but for which the appropriation of human life through data will be central. (Couldry and Mejias 2019b)

Thus, while Zuboff concentrates on the role of surveillance in the 'new economic order', Couldry and Mejias bring the transformation of social relations into 'data relations' to the fore:

> Through what we call 'data relations' (new types of human relations which enable the extraction of data for commodification), social life all over the globe becomes an 'open' resource for extraction that is somehow 'just there' for capital. These global flows of data are as expansive as historic colonialism's appropriation of land, resources, and bodies, although the epicenter has somewhat shifted. Data colonialism involves not one pole of colonial power ('the West'), but at least two: the United States and China. (Couldry and Mejias 2019b)

Indeed, it is not just GAFA and BATX (see 'Platform Empires' in Chapter 5) which raise concerns about the function and impact of big tech. The sheer size of these platforms has precedents in the nineteenth- and twentieth-century big oil companies, which then raised massive concerns about the impact of corporate power on 'political liberty, individual opportunity, and democracy' (Moore and Tambini 2018: 1–2) – concerns which continue to resonate today.

Platform capitalism, surveillance capitalism, data colonialism and even 'the platform society' (Van Dijck et al. 2018) all aim to capture the big structural and social changes brought about by social platforms within digital environments. We can conclude that these changes are both intensive and extensive, incorporating an economic ideology – the 'ideology of connection', as discussed further below – into social, political and cultural realities (Couldry and Mejias 2019a).

Arguably, we have seen a shift from platform capitalism and the functioning of platforms within a reconfigured 'sharing' economy to the emergence of global 'platform empires', i.e. extensive spheres of activity controlled by 'big' companies that extend across the web, apps, and throughout digital ecosystems. As we will see in Chapter 5, GAFA and BATX make up every level of 'the stack', literally constructing the undersea cables that circulate the flows of digital information across space and time, as well as the web territories that sit on top of our web and app systems – making up the sites we visit and the activities we engage in. The authors we have looked at in this chapter so far – from Marx to Zuboff – further understanding about how the economics of dominant media subsume social relations for profit, thereby masking the real workings of media and platform industries.

The ideology of connection

One of the themes emerging from the chapter on power is that we find ourselves in a cultural moment where social media articulate the ideology of connection. Perhaps this first became visible in 'friend collecting', where Friendster users took pleasure in amassing large groups of 'friends' to boost their friend metrics and publicly display their friendships (boyd 2006a; boyd and Ellison 2007). More recently, the covert collection of personal data to create 'shadow profiles' of people on and off of social media has been documented, as demonstrated through features like 'People You May Know' (PYMK) (see Chapter 8). These practices are the consequence of a connection-at-any-cost logic, driving the motives of social media platforms. One of Facebook's vice presidents, Andrew Bosworth, explained that their deep belief in 'connecting people' drove 'all the questionable contact importing practices' associated with these features (2016, cited in Mac et al. 2018).

Similarly, the like, favourite or equivalent button on Facebook, Twitter, Instagram, TikTok and other digital platforms from Amazon to email has been linked to pro-social behaviours, making positive interactions easy and convenient in line with the platform's motives (Fuchs 2017; Van Dijck 2013). Other platforms like YouTube, Reddit and Imgur also have a dislike or downvote feature, which may not fit with these 'pro-social' platform affordances, but they still promote the ideology of connection. As further discussed in Chapter 4, like buttons generate shareable data that are used to to generate and monetize social media clicks.

Shareable information and time spent on platforms are profitable, as illustrated in Box 3.2 on programmed sociality, and the quality of that information or time is irrelevant. Thus, misinformation, trolling and extremisms are as, if not more, profitable across social media platforms as high-quality information. Indeed, sensational and negative content generates much more virality than 'good' content, so there is an economic justification for many platforms' slow responses to hate and trolling (see also Chapter 9; Phillips 2018; Phillips and Milner 2021).

Finally, the ideology of connection reflects all the elements of power discussed in the section on 'the basics'. First the ideology of connection promotes the extension of classroom, and the belief systems of the dominant tech classes. Bundled up in 'connection' is all of the promise of new technologies, and buying into this connective logic also carries these connotations. In other words, using and knowing social media and 'displays of connection' carry symbolic currency which can be exchanged for status and influence – both important in the digital reputation economy (Gandini 2016; Hearn 2010). The ideology of connection is also productive, requiring certain design choices in platforms and content leading to specific behavioural affordances. On a deeper level, connection metrics have provided new ways to make sense of ourselves, our society and of others. As Foucault's description of the link between 'homosexual' and an interiorized identity, influencer and connection metrics provide new identity categories where people interiorize the ideology of connection.

The next section turns to the active audience tradition for important critiques of ideological structures.

Critiques: The Active Audience Tradition and 'Small Acts of Engagement' (SAOE)

Even in the face of platform domination, there are many heartfelt stories of long-lost connections being restored via social media, and stories of villages coming together to recover stolen property (Shirky 2008), as well as amazing stories of people facing seriously dire situations and using social and digital media to literally save lives (Rainie and Wellman 2012). There are stories of social movements who have used social media to articulate and share collective struggles, making those struggles visible, effecting real social change – as seen in social movements such as #MeToo, #BlackLivesMatter and #everdaysexism (see also Taylor and Gessen 2011; Tufecki 2017a). How do all these experiences fit in with the rise of pervasive global platforms which dominate our online and offline experiences and the ways in which we are able to interact with others?

In order to answer this question, it is important to think beyond economic and ideological infrastructures and turn to people's everyday lives which make up the fabric of cultural life. As Du Gay argues, 'excessive focus on production and the economic has the effect of shutting down the analysis of culture' (1997: 84, as cited in Livingstone 2019). Understanding everyday life involves an entirely different set of tools and focus on different kinds of evidence. Rather than concentrating on money and its economic and ideological circulation, we turn to those approaches that focus more on agencies and on *people*, often drawing from an interpretivist frame and one that aims to unpack the rich and complex tapestry of the seemingly mundane, the everyday and the ordinary (see also de Certeau 2011 [1984]).

Audience or reception studies focus on how people make sense of cultural stories and the media they use. This kind of research often falls between questions of meaning (what is it, where does it come from?) and questions of interpretation (why do people interpret stories and experience things differently?; see Livingstone 1998). This approach to media has blurred across different kinds of media, and is increasingly shaped by convergence and the digital. Yet despite twenty-first-century changes, it is within this frame of looking at the moments between text and audience, and between interpretation and meaning making, that the idea of people as *agents of meaning* came to be in the work on active audiences. This now well-established tradition broke with fixed ideas of meaning as a linear transmission from producer to audience, and opened up a whole line of questioning around individual and cultural agency.

Stuart Hall theorized that people are active in their interpretations, and while every interpretation is part of predetermined meaning structures, shaped by and made of shared ideological positionings, people are also not passive recipients of meaning. Instead, people and collective groupings of audiences actively interpret complex meanings and negotiate all the elements of media: technical infrastructures, relations of production, frameworks of knowledge with meaning structures around content (Hall 1999: 510).

Part of Hall's legacy to media and communications studies is the gift of active audiences – a broad accounting for the 'culture of the everyday' increasingly marked by a shift 'away from the moment of textual interpretation [as was dominant in the 1960s and 1970s] and towards the contextualisation of that moment [in the 1980s and 1990s]' (Livingstone 1998). This legacy lives on, influencing ethnographic and critical work challenging the presumption of *fixed meaning* set by dominant infrastructures and the ruling elite – although ideology and the 'ruling elite' are often present. Certainly, Hall's work has been tremendously influential, inspiring the Birmingham Centre for Contemporary Cultural Studies (CCCS) (e.g. Brundson and Morley 1978; CCCS 1982; Gilroy 1987) and many others to take up the question of what people do with media.

Those most inspired by the interpretivist and active audience traditions fiercely object to the 'monolithic accounts of power that tend to downplay or exclude audiences' (Livingstone 2019: 171), raising questions about positioning people as unthinking and disengaged – 'unknowingly datafied, commodified, surveyed, or polarized' (Picone et al. 2019: 11). The active audience tradition has much to offer along this line of critique, producing decades of evidence showing that people, as users, as publics, as networks, or as 'audiences, are not so gullible as popularly feared, precisely because they are neither homogeneous nor unthinking' (Livingstone 2019: 174).

Drawing from the rich history of audience and reception studies, Ike Picone and his colleagues propose a new concept for all of those 'small' behaviours so characteristic of social media, such as 'liking, sharing, and commenting' (Picone et al. 2019). For these researchers these simple, normalized and everyday behaviours are 'small acts of engagement' (SAOE) which reveal human agency rather than just algorithmic tricks to generate and exploit human data for economic gain. Although SAOE are 'intentionally more casual' than 'convergence culture or produsage', they are intentionally more meaningful for the construction and expression of identity, for connection and for collective action (Picone et al. 2019: 1–2). Picone and colleagues argue that rethinking SAOE in terms of everyday life provides a 'microlevel analytical lens' for understanding how often taken for granted and everyday functions of social technologies work on an aggregate level – a level that accounts for the social rather than economic life of data (Picone et al. 2019: 11–12).

While Picone et al. raise critiques about how we think of social technologies and platforms as monoliths, they also aim to situate SAOE as both resistant and productive of meaning rather than only as datafiable content:

> Talking about SAOE thus reconnects theories on productive audiences with the concerns of the everyday and forces us to consider the empowerment of audiences in terms not only of content production but also identity building and personal resistance—practices, indeed, much more connected with the ways audiences deal with interpreting messages than the ways producers make content. (Picone et al. 2019: 15)

As such, there are several points to reiterate in relation to how power works in social media through the lens of SAOE, i.e. that people are active agents, value and meaning do not always fit dominant economic frames, and, finally, meaning is multiple and contested. Others call for embracing the ambivalence of the internet and life online as a starting point, not only to understand power, but also to better reflect the chaos and messiness of life. Whitney Phillips and Ryan Milner, for example, describe the internet as:

> ... simultaneously antagonistic and social, creative and disruptive, humorous and barbed ... [the internet and] countless other examples that permeate contemporary online participation, are too unwieldy, too variable across specific cases, to be essentialized as this as opposed to that. (Phillips and Milner 2017: 10)

Phillips and Milner describe the 'ambivalent internet', focusing not on the economics of the internet as socio-political structure or on users' interpretations of their online experiences, but on digital culture as 'folkloric expression' that is both constitutive of online culture (e.g. memes and 'internet ugly' aesthetics) as well as the cultural literacies required to participate within such cultures (2017: 96–97, 112).

Regardless of how we might sum up the meaning of 'commenting, liking and sharing', it is crucial to note that while meaning is and will always be contested, the audience tradition aims to problematize established paradigms. SAOE carry on this tradition, offering a thoughtful analysis of 'small acts', and in the process opening up room for new insights by focusing on interpretation and meaning, and unpacking often taken-for-granted behaviours.

Conclusion: Ambivalent Cultures and the Power of Connection

So far in this chapter, we have introduced some important concepts for understanding power, as well as outlining the historical roots for critical accounts of power and social media. This includes breaking down thinking on power to influential concepts, including Marx, capitalism and ideology, as well as economic, political, coercive and symbolic forms of power (Thompson 1995), power as productive (Foucault 1972, 1975, 1976, 1984, 1986), and the specifics of media and symbolic power. These concepts are helpful for making sense of power, and can be applied to many different contexts.

From here, we traced a critical tradition from Adorno and Horkheimer's culture industries, through to Dallas Smythe's work on the audience commodity, and current work on platform empires. These theories share a focus on ideology, media and unpicking the ideological underpinnings for taken-for-granted media systems. There is a strong lineage between these theories. Presenting them together provides the historical context for understanding both the development of media technologies and critical thinking about those technologies. The shared focus on power is striking and, when taken together, point to an ideological shift around a connective logic. While this is an important contribution for understanding the social media ecosystem, there are other perspectives, like those critiques coming from active audience and reception studies that also provide important insights. From these researchers, we are reminded that power is not monolithic, and there is power in agency and small acts of engagement.

The ambivalence of digital culture and social media – as simultaneously lived experiences and as broader data structures transforming every click into capital – is tangible. It is this ambivalence that makes it a challenge to bring the conceptual trajectories of power around money and agency together, whether that is specifically related to social media or more broadly related to the world. Indeed, this is an ongoing challenge, one that renders any single approach incomplete. Yes, economic and structural power is real. Those working on understanding the complexities of these structures have peeled off the utopic veneer, exposing the ideology of connection and the 'misdirection' and deception of *social* technologies. At the same time, people are active in their own lives, making sense of their connections with the tools and interpretative frames available to them – in ways that are original and surprising. SAOE are an excellent example of how a significant aspect of social technologies, such as the like button, is not just a powerful tool for platform empires (generating data, linking social territories across the web and devices, creating new frontiers of affective data as measurable and visible). The like button is also an expression of connection and identification, and for users it may also be an act of engagement, one that requires enough investment to be meaningful without serious effort. Meanwhile, trolling misinformation and public displays of connection all illustrate the shift towards an 'ideology of connection'.

Questions and Activities

1. Drawing from Thompson's forms of power, describe what kinds of power best explain influencers?

2. Foucault describes power as productive. What does he mean by this? Select an example related to social media as an illustration of your response.

3. Review the 'ideology of connection'. Does this concept relate to your own experience of social media? Explain.

4. With a partner, review and discuss your response to the chapter. What made sense? What raised further questions? Where do you position yourself in relation to these trajectories?

5. The purpose of this chapter is to introduce major approaches to power. In order to better assess these concepts and their conceptual roots, apply them to an example (e.g. a social media platform or app). What do you find? Share your findings and discuss with the class:
   i   The audience commodity
   ii   Platform empires
   iii Small acts of engagement

Further Reading

Adorno, M.; Horkheimer, T. 2005 [1944]. The culture industry: enlightenment as mass deception, trans. Andy Blunden, *Dialectic of Enlightenment*. https://www.marxists.org/reference/archive/adorno/1944/culture-industry.htm

Bucher, T. 2018. Introduction: programmed sociality, in *If...Then: Algorithmic Power and Politics*. Oxford University Press.

Couldry, N.; Mejias, U. A. 2019b. Data colonialism: rethinking big data's relation to the contemporary subject, *Television & New Media*, 20 (4), pp. 336–49. DOI: 10.1177/1527476418796632

Picone, I.; Kleut, J.; Pavlíčková, T.; Romic, B.; Hartley, J. M.; De Ridder, S. 2019. Small acts of engagement: reconnecting productive audience practices with everyday agency, *New Media & Society*. DOI: 10.1177/1461444819837569

PART II

SOCIALITY AND SOCIAL TECHNOLOGIES

4

UNDERSTANDING THE 'SOCIAL' IN SOCIAL MEDIA

Chapter Overview

Introduction	86
Defining 'the Social'	87
The social according to social media: Twitter, Instagram, Facebook, Snapchat and YouTube	89
Unpacking the social: Structure and agency	92
Infrastructures of everyday life: From structuration to deep mediatization	94
Affordances and Tactics of Belonging	98
The 'like' button: Metrics in the like economy	100
New vernaculars and literacies	101
Conclusion: Social Solidarities and the Public Good	103
Questions and Activities	104
Further Reading	105

┌─ Chapter Objectives ───

- Introduce key debates and challenges related to the meaning of the 'social'
- Analyse and unpack the social in social media
- Understand key theoretical concepts involving media and technology
- Engage a sociologically informed approach to the 'social'

Introduction

The purpose of this chapter is to understand what it means to be social in an age of hyper-connection and social media. This chapter will outline what is at stake in the interplay between human interaction and connection technologies. Beginning with how social technologies shape so many experiences of togetherness, co-presence and connection, this chapter examines what it means to be 'social' in the face of a pervasive ideology of connection.

The current moment marks a global reconciliation with the tensions between public health and social life: on physical and embodied terms (COVID-19 pandemic), on the socio-political level (Black Lives Matter and global protests against a racialized pandemic), the environmental (climate change, floods, wildfires and global protests) and the economic (e.g. Brexit). The COVID-19 pandemic means we have to rethink physical health, particularly as those who are the most economically vulnerable are as important to public health. The new front lines in the pandemic are in public services such as food, health and education sectors, all of which are low paid and lack worker protections, yet are fundamental for society to function. This public reckoning has meant that people around the world have shared similar circumstances of fear, uncertainty, various kinds of lockdown, school closures, working from home or job losses – all in real time. As such, this moment is both intensely personal and intensely public. These issues are social and systemic, operating at the institutional and global level, as well as at the affective, intimate and individual levels. But they are not either/or, they are simultaneous. There is a kind of behavioural scrutiny, seeking out health infringements. Are you wearing a mask? Was that a microaggression? There is a genuine examination of the links between social structures and everyday life. There is a stretching from the micro to the macro – which also mirrors the ways in which social and digital media scale up and amplify social relations.

Questioning what it means to be social is more important than ever, and the stakes are high. Social media promises connection, and this is a balm to those who are isolated, socially distanced and lonely. Yet, what does this mean in an age of powerful social platforms who compromise the public good at every turn? Of course, the intersections between social media and everyday life are numerous and densely interwoven, making it very difficult to easily make sense of how social media are or are not social. To address this challenge, this chapter first looks at the best ways to define the social, drawing from primarily socio-logical and media approaches to the social. From here, we turn to social media platforms themselves to determine how exactly they are picturing the social.

In keeping with 'the ideology of connection' (see Chapter 3), social platforms present 'the social' in positive terms based on number of connections. To help make sense of what this means for social relations, I then introduce a longstanding model from sociology which aims to make sense of the relationship between social structures and individual agency. While this is a useful starting point, it does not explain changing social relations. For that, I turn to structuration theory and deep mediatization, both of which provide accounts for the intersections between infrastructure, for example, and individual behav-iours. It is clear that social media have quickly become the infrastructures of everyday life, and this means that there are particular affordances associated with these platforms. These affordances show specific tactics of belonging, such as the like button, metrics, new ver-naculars and literacies, all of which impact on social relations. Finally, one of the absences in social media platforms and their articulations of the social is the social or public good. In light of the 2020 crises of public health (pandemic, systemic racism, climate chaos, etc.), it is more important than ever to move beyond connection towards genuine social good and publicly oriented social solidarities.

Defining 'the Social'

To begin, the meaning of the terms 'social' and 'society' have been debated well before the advent of classical sociology. At one extreme, there are those like former UK Prime Minister Margaret Thatcher who deny the existence of a collective 'society', arguing instead that there are only individuals who make up groups. On the other side, many argue that society and the social occur as something greater than the individual, made up through the collec-tive ethos of groups. While the nuanced differences of these terms in social theory and classical sociology are not the focus here, it is important to unpack what 'the social' actually means. For example, the etymology of the word 'social' shows a historical trajectory marked by shifts in meaning:

social (adj.)

late 15c., "devoted to or relating to home life;" 1560s as "living with others," from Middle French social (14c.) and directly from Latin socialis "of companionship, of allies; united, living with others; of marriage, conjugal," from socius "companion, ally," probably originally "follower," from PIE *sokw-yo-, suffixed form of root *sekw-(1) "to follow." Compare Old English secg, Old Norse seggr "companion," which seem to have been formed on the same notion). (https://www.etymonline.com/word/social)

Breaking this down and according to the historical origins of the word, the social related to 'home life' and as 'living with others' in the fifteenth century. The Latin root '*socialis*' refers to a wide range of terms inferring some kind of companionship or alliances. Given the prevalence of 'following' in the social media landscape, the root '*sekw*' meaning 'to follow' is especially notable. However, in the sixteenth century, being 'social' began to mean 'friendliness' and 'geniality', and later as referring more to 'fashionable society' in the late nineteenth century.

Common definitions in current dictionaries tend to focus on the social as a positive attribute of connection between affiliative or friendly others (e.g. the Merriam-Webster dictionary, Oxford Dictionary, Cambridge Dictionary). Although the dictionary provides some clarity, it is important to remember that the concept of the 'social' is indeed broad and often considered to be fuzzy. For example, the social can mean something very specific, like a gathering or a particular orientation towards others. As Couldry and Van Dijck (2015) argue:

> The word 'social' is our necessary term for thinking about the complex interdependencies out of which human life really is made and the claims to represent that interdependent reality made from particular positions of power.

These complex interdependencies point to the ways that 'the social is always double in character: both form of meaning *and* built environment' (Couldry and Hepp 2017: 3). This doubleness illustrates some of the difficulty in understanding the social – as it comes as much from the ties that connect us to each other as from the structures shaping those ties. Sociologists have long questioned this double nature in terms of free will and society, or agency and structure, a framework which goes a long way for simplifying the complexity of these interdependencies, as I will discuss further below.

Ferdinand Tonnies, German social theorist and philosopher, defines the social as a 'consciousness of belonging together and the affirmation of mutual dependence' (Tonnies 1988, as cited in Fuchs 2014: 40). This is also important, as a sense of 'belonging' is one of the building blocks of community, social relations and meaningful interactions with others. Taina Bucher extends this notion further, emphasizing that the social is a *group process* and is 'similar to a community which emerges from interaction and exchange' (Bucher 2015). For Bucher, the social comes from social action, from *doing* rather than being. Georg Simmel, another founding sociologist, turns to the German distinction between *gesellschaft*, a form of sociality defined by a collective society made up those bonded through purpose, and *gemeinschaft*, where sociality is made up of community (family and personal connections):

> It is nevertheless not without significance that in many, perhaps in all, European languages, the word 'society' (Gesellschaft) indicates literally 'togetherness'. The political, economic, the society held together by some purpose is nevertheless, always 'society'. (Simmel 1987 [1949/1950]: 122)

We could also turn to John Thompson, British sociologist, who traced the impact of early electronic media and the 'the creation of new forms of action and interaction [and] new kinds of social relationships' (1995: 4). Or Benedict Anderson (2006), political scientist, who mapped the rise of print capitalism with the emergence of nation-based 'imagined communities'. Or we could turn to Jürgen Habermas, leading German sociologist, whose work on the 'public sphere' generated decades of thinking about how publics are formed, and why they are important. Each of these theorists approach the 'social' very differently, yet they are also driven by questions about how humans come together, and to some degree the role of media in shaping how we interact with others.

Yet with inclusion there is always exclusion. Sociology may be built upon an intellectual tradition of unpacking and making sense of how inequalities become a part of the social, but there is much more work to be done. The other side of 'togetherness' is exclusion, and part of the 'social' is the erasure of difference and inequality, exacerbated by the pro-social rhetoric of platforms. For example, a lot of recently published evidence establishes the sexism and racism of algorithms (Noble 2018) and social technologies (Benjamin 2019a, 2019b). Eubanks (2018) writes about the ways platforms and digital technologies use sorting algorithms which 'profile, police and punish the poor' more than those who are wealthy and privileged. From another angle, there is longstanding critical work addressing the privileging of white, male perspectives in science and technology, and this recent work reinvigorates these foundations (e.g. Cockburn 1997; Haraway 1988; Keller 1983; Nakamura and Chow-White 2011; Nakamura et al. 2000). Although this work points to the forthcoming end of 'the myth of neutral platform', much more needs to be done to dismantle the systemic bias(es) in both social infrastructures and behaviours (Gillespie 2018a).

This brief look helps us identify *what* the social means. Yet one of the broader questions facing us today is what do togetherness, shared values, common norms, group processes, interaction and exchange mean in an age of social media? This is a critical question. Arguably, all of the ways in which ideas and experiences of the social exist today are in some ways shaped by the social technologies making up everyday life through complex processes of *mediatization*, discussed further below. Indeed, failing to think through how social relations are shaped by and through social technologies and platforms means missing out on collective affordances (discussed further below). The next section looks at how social media platforms envision 'the social'.

The social according to social media: Twitter, Instagram, Facebook, Snapchat and YouTube

The story we are told about social media by social platforms is that they are social because they connect people. They connect people from all over the world, make it easy to share photos and information, and thus help create shared culture and global communities. However, as we have learned in the chapters so far, they do a lot more than connect people. This section looks at the ways social media platforms describe themselves in their public facing 'about' or 'what is' pages. Although End User Licence Agreements (EULAs) and the terms and conditions (or statement of rights and responsibilities as Facebook has started calling them) are likely to change, these pages are the 'face' of these platforms, offering carefully crafted statements. Perhaps unsurprisingly, none of the major platforms use the word 'social' or 'society'. (See Table 4.1 for an overview of the ways social media platforms define themselves for 2018–2019.)

Table 4.1 How social media platforms present themselves in their 'About' pages and what this means for understanding the social

Platform	Mission/About us	Source
Twitter	'Twitter is: What's happening in the world right now and what people are talking about right now.' … '**Join the conversation**'	'About us': https://about.twitter.com/en_us.html (15.08.2018) and https://about.twitter.com/en_gb.html (20.09.2019)
Instagram	'a **community** of more than 1 billion who capture and **share** the world's moments on the service…. Since the beginning, Kevin [Systrom, founder] has focused on simplicity and inspiring creativity through solving problems with thoughtful product design. As a result, Instagram has become the **home** for visual storytelling for everyone from celebrities, newsrooms and brands, to teens, musicians and anyone with a creative passion.'	Excerpt from 'About us': https://www.instagram.com/about/us/ (15.08.2018)
Facebook	'Facebook helps you **connect** and **share** with the people in your life'	'Home': https://www.facebook.com/ (15.08.2018)
	'Facebook's mission is to give people the power to build **community** and bring the world closer **together**'	Facebook's 'About' section: https://www.facebook.com/pg/facebook/about (15.08.2018 and 20.09.2019)
Snapchat	'Snap Inc. is a camera company. We believe that reinventing the camera represents our greatest opportunity to improve the way people live and **communicate**. We contribute to human progress by empowering people to **express** themselves, live in the moment, learn about the **world** and have fun **together**'	'Company Profile': https://www.snap.com/en-GB/ (15.08.2018 and 20.09.2019)
YouTube	'YouTube. Our mission is to give everyone a **voice** and show them the world. We believe that everyone deserves to have a voice, and that the **world is a better place** when we listen, **share** and build **community** through our stories'	'About': https://www.youtube.com/yt/about (15.08.2018 and 20.09.2019)

The most powerful and often repeated words in these public-facing statements include 'world', 'people', 'community' and 'share', along with many words related to expression such as 'connect', 'communicate' and 'voice'. In these statements, social media companies position themselves as providing social spaces – equating platform spaces with 'the world'. In addition, these companies also claim to provide the means for intensely personal forms of social engagement, via 'voice', 'sharing' and 'expression' – all with a highly pro-social rhetoric. (See Figure 4.1 for a word cloud depicting the most frequently occurring words in these statements.)

Figure 4.1 Word cloud showing the most frequently occurring words on Twitter, Instagram, Facebook, Snapchat and YouTube in their 'about us' and 'what is' pages (September 2019)

This brief analysis supports a growing body of critiques around the ideology of connection. Social platforms present a positively oriented view of the 'social' and of the role of the platform in achieving that vision. While the above segments from mission statements and other public-facing pages may seem to be merely idealistic, they are much more than just an optimistic view of the 'social'. As van Dijck argues, 'Sociality is not simply "rendered technological" by moving to an online space [or social platform]; rather, coded structures are profoundly altering the nature of our connections, creations, and interactions' (as cited by Gillespie 2018a: 22). Social platforms are reconfiguring the social as platform-enabled connection, from which they are about to generate and extract data. It is this rhetoric which has led researchers to call out social media for misdirection (Zuboff 2019), data colonialism (Couldry and Mejias 2019) and exploitative connectivity (Van Dijck 2015). Indeed, these statements illustrate the logics of a connective ideology which must be critiqued and dismantled.

Indeed, part of the 'coded structures' at work here includes the structures in place to surveill and dataveill (see Chapter 8) social media users, and those in their networks. Thus the mechanisms for social connection are also 'the global architectures' of social media and key surveillance capitalists (Zuboff 2015: 75). Lina Dencik (2018), data activist, also unveils the working of 'connection' to reveal sophisticated data analytics. These point to a broader shift in what it means to be social. Van Dijck (2015) argues that:

> During the first decade of social networks (2004–2014), the word 'social' gradually shifted its connotative gravity from 'connectedness of human users' to 'automated connectivity of platforms'—automated through algorithms, data flows, interfaces, and business models.

Van Dijck raises a central issue, but this third party kind of exploitative connectivity is only one aspect of the many ways social media have impacted on our experience and understanding of the social. Algorithmic sociality (see Chapter 3) is associated with an *erosion* of human connection, worn down by sticky platforms designed to monetize interaction with the platform above all else. Thus, when Mark Zuckerberg made a vow 'to make everything social' in 2010, he did not mean more togetherness. Instead, he was talking about moving 'social traffic onto a networked infrastructure where it becomes traceable, calculable, and ultimately manipulatable for profit', marking yet another deceptive articulation of 'the social' (Couldry and Van Dijck 2015).

There are a number of gaps around how we think of the social, how social media platforms define and present it to us, and the ways 'connection' works as double speak for orchestrated data exploitation. This is an important point. However, the layers of misdirection and deep integration of social media in everyday life make it especially challenging to critically account for the social today. In the next section I introduce 'structure and agency', a model which is especially helpful in the first stages of social analysis.

Unpacking the social: Structure and agency

Understanding the social in social media is a difficult challenge. While the ideology of connection is at play, there are also billions of users whose experiences of and with social media may tell us much more about what it means to be social. Part of this fuzziness is because the social is an amalgamation of many, intersecting and sometimes counterposing aspects of life. For example, when you think about why you do or do not use social media, is this only your decision? Or are other factors like the dominance of social media in how we communicate with others also at play here? To take this example further, you may choose to use social media, but you are only able to make that choice because there are specific communicative structures in place. Behaviours, individual choice and infrastructures are deeply entangled:

> Clearly, the explosion in social media usage rests on a deeper infrastructural change led by profound political-economic investment: the expansion in richer nations (and in many poorer ones) of pervasive access to high-speed internet access, increasingly via mobile phones and other mobile devices. (Couldry et al. 2018: 5)

While only a simple example, thinking through the factors contributing to the conditions for individual choices, such as the choice to use social media or not, illustrates how complex it can be to work out the origins of social action. There is a deep tension between self and society, between individuals and structures, and between free will and set systems. Thus the structure and agency model is really important for making sure your thinking does not start by favouring the individual over the structure, or the structure over the individual. In the current moment, mid-way through 2020, there is an intense scrutiny of this relationship with, for example, systemic racism. Are microaggressions individual acts? Or are they embedded within inherited systems? The scrutiny inspired by the global protests against racialized violence is an important moment where this tension needs to be accounted for. In an age of social media, understanding structures and agencies provides a framework which helps make sense of complexity, as well as moving beyond the screen, opening up underlying structures.

Social structures shape and constrain social actions or agency and vice versa. Breaking down the social into these conceptual components, structure and agency, helps us make sense of what society is and where social action comes from. Structure most often refers to the material conditions of society, such as social norms and institutions, like the family or education, and is composed of systems, beliefs, political-economic systems (e.g. communism or capitalism), nation states, government structures, material conditions (e.g. urban or rural architectures), resources, and so on. In contrast, the 'agent' is the individual or person and can refer to free will, preferences, individual choices – all the factors making up the agency of actors in social situations. (See Figure 4.2 for a visual representation.)

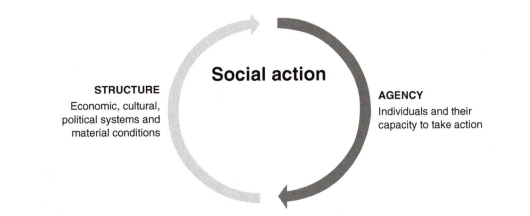

Figure 4.2 Representing social action through structure and agency

Although simplified, this illustration demonstrates the dualism of social action, at once structural and agentic. In the case of social media, we might think of 'structure' as the platform itself, the technical infrastructures, regulatory frameworks and small materialities such as social buttons (e.g. the like or reaction buttons), comment boxes, and status updates, tweets or posts. All of these provide a structural frame, which create particular affordances (discussed further below), and directly or indirectly shaping behaviours. Based on my own research on Facebook (Sujon et al. 2018), the ideology of connection, and research in the field, social media are increasingly the infrastructures of and for our everyday lives. The next section looks at how we can understand the interplay between structure and agency in social media.

Infrastructures of everyday life: From structuration to deep mediatization

Technologies and social platforms are not neutral (Gillespie 2018a). They are built by people who have been enculturated with particular social and culture systems, and they are embedded within social life. As Roger Silverstone, one of the major contributors to media studies in the UK, cogently stated:

> Technology, it can be seen, does not come naked. It does not come neutral. Nor, indeed does it come simply or straightforwardly. For technology arrives, dramatically ... [or] stealthily perhaps ... carrying on its back a burden of social, economic and political implications, and carrying in its baggage *bundles of material and symbolic string which tie those who use it into systems of social relations and cultural meanings* which are as disguised and unwelcome sometimes as they are obvious and welcome. (1994: 79; emphasis added)

Silverstone explains some of the complexity embedded in the media and communication technologies we use to connect with others or to store and share information. These technologies involve socio-technical systems made up of 'bundles of material and symbolic string' and which carry real-word resources. These 'bundles of string' are a metaphor for the interaction between the structural or infrastructural and individual agency. This metaphor also works to capture what Anthony Giddens, famous English sociologist, means by 'structuration' (1984, 1986). For Giddens, structuration is about the close relationship between structures and actions.

Although structure and agency began their conceptual life as dualistic concepts, there are many more aiming to account for social action and socio-technical change (see Sovacool and Hess (2017) for a meta-analysis of 96 of these theories). Yet, Anthony Giddens' theory of structuration, 'an unlovely term at best' (1984: xvi), provides a useful although somewhat historical starting point. In his most extensive work on structuration, he states that 'all social systems, no matter how grand or far-flung, both express and are expressed in the routines of daily social' life (1984: 36). By this, Giddens means that structure and agency are mutually constitutive rather than mutually exclusive entities. Instead of 'structures' as indelibly distinct from human action, *agency* and everyday routines, these human dimensions ground and reiterate structural rules, resources and material conditions. Ira Cohen, a professor specializing in social action, elaborates:

> Structural circumstances provide the means to reproduce social practices, but when social practices are reproduced they perpetuate the structure, making it a social reality in a new historical moment. (Cohen 2006a: 16)

Thus, Giddens' theory of structuration fundamentally rejects an 'ontological dualism' between structure and agency (Cohen 2006b). Legal structures, for example, consist of a whole series of agents – judges, lawyers, members of parliament, police, citizens and non-citizens – all of whom interpret and uphold the law through adherence to and interaction with legal structures in the course of their everyday actions. Even romantic partnerships enact legal and social structures. For heterosexual unions, the choice to co-habitate or marry is one shaped by legal structures and the dense network of people involved in formalizing marriage. For homosexuals, the battle to legalize same-sex marriage has been fierce, resulting in legalization in the UK (excluding Northern Ireland) in 2014 – a big step towards civil rights and civic legitimization. The international #BlackLivesMatter movement has brought global attention to endemic racism and police brutality – all of which are enacted through practices like racial profiling, and established norms in police culture (Freelon et al. 2016). In these ways, individual actions instantiate visible and invisible social structures. There can be great variation around how people adhere to or break the law, as well as how police choose (or choose not) to intervene. In this way, no institution or social structure can exist on its own without agents enacting that structure's rules and procedures. As Christian Fuchs (2014: 37) argues, media and other social structures 'enable and constrain human activities' connecting 'technological structures and human agency'.

Therefore structuration, the mutual reciprocity between structure and agency, is an important concept and one that has generated much further work and discussion. Indeed, many other approaches and theories have emerged which also aim to critically unpack social action, focusing on the close connections between structure and agency in media, positioning media as *socio-technical systems*. Giddens' theory of structuration marks a broader constructivist turn within the social sciences, particularly in studies of media, communications, and science and technology. (For a compelling example, see Box 4.1 on gendered technologies.)

Box 4.1 Gendered technologies: Social or individual?

Take a moment to consider the technologies you use. Do technologies have a gender? Are some technologies for boys and men and others for girls and women? Or are all technologies neutral and without any gender, appropriate for everyone, regardless of where they are on the gender spectrum? Compare your first perceptions of a microwave or other white good and a smart phone. Is there one that you consider more 'technological' than the other? Why or why not?

While these questions may seem subjective and based on individual perspectives of technologies, science and technology scholars have long considered the deep relationship between gender and technology, and it is indeed reflective of the tensions between structure and agency. Indeed, many have documented the complex ways that a widespread devaluation of the domestic realm influences largely male technology designers, sales people, marketing and advertising teams, even consumers in their perceptions and categorizations of technologies.

Cynthia Cockburn, a feminist researcher and writer, takes up these questions arguing that technologies are highly gendered:

A house, a household, housework and home life: this is not the scenario that is spontaneously evoked by the word technology. It is possible to watch one television programme after another devoted to 'the new technologies,' or 'our technological society,' and to read articles predicting our 'technological future,' without being offered much insight into the technology of the domestic indoors. 'Technology' is popularly represented, rather, as environmental nemesis or salvation. It is microchip and Internet. It is transport and mobility – interplanetary and intercity. If home is mentioned at all in technological scenarios it is most likely to be in connection with the penetration of the business world into the home, as in 'homeworking' by computer-link to the office. *Technology is anything but housework.* (Cockburn 1997: 361; emphasis added)

White goods like fridges, washing machines, microwaves and other domestic technologies, have often been attributed less glamour and less excitement, especially compared to 'brown goods' – those high-end entertainment technologies often associated with the 'cutting-edge'. Brown goods, according to Cockburn's European research (1994, as discussed in 1997), are often given more attention by designers, considered a higher value by production and sales teams, and illustrate a 'mutual shaping process' between 'existing unequal relations' and technological innovations (Cockburn 1997: 362).

This gendering of technologies has a long historical precedent. For example, the telephone was also highly gendered as Michèle Martin documents. Martin finds that the exclusively female work of telephone operators and the more general denigration of 'chatty' female telephone users wasting valuable time by being social both had a direct impact on the development of Canadian telephony (1991, cf. Fischer 1992; Marvin 1988). In addition, women's contributions to the development of computing were often marginalized. For example, Ada Lovelace's brilliant work on the first plans for a general purpose computer was minimized until recently (Hammerman and Russell 2016). In addition, it is only historical analysis that shows women's pioneering role in e-communities like Plato (Korn 2016), and their work has been all but erased from ENIAC, 'America's first electronic computer' (Light 1999). These are only a few of many examples of the highly gendered nature of public perceptions of technology. As a result, women are often excluded from certain kinds of technologies and tech communities, and their scientific and technological contributions can be minimized.

Cockburn conducted the research described above in the 1990s. While some may think that a lot has changed since then, and it has, many scholars still argue that gender relations and gendered perceptions of technologies remain unequal. For example, Kylie Jarrett (2016) argues that much of the affective labour making social media platforms 'sticky' and hence profitable is conducted by women and is central to the invisible political economies of the commercial web. Brooke Erin Duffy (2017), in a thorough analysis of the rising fashion influencer industry, finds that the majority of influencers are unable to sustain themselves, and is part of a broader feminizing of the social industry and digital labour. Zoe Glatt, based on an ethnography of YouTubers, finds that even successful influencers face increased precariousness due to YouTube's algorithmic uncertainties – a situation further complicated by gender differences (as discussed in Stokel-Walker 2018).

While the theory of structuration can be used to explain many complex social phenomena, including moving the debate beyond the social dualism of structure/agency, it does not quite account for the specifics of rapidly changing technologies and their impact on social behaviours – and also on potential social behaviours. Mediatization provides a more up-to-date and media specific account of the relationship between social life and media structures:

> Mediatization is a concept to encompass the changes brought by media into every aspect of our lives. It goes beyond the conventional textual analysis, production economic-politics and audiences' studies. (Niea et al. 2014: 362)

Developed as a concept intended to make sense of the rise of media and its intertwining impact on society and culture, mediatization is also a paradigm for media and communication research (Livingstone and Lunt 2014). Noting the limits of media centrism and determinism, the mediatization paradigm takes account not only of media history, but also of the role of *mediated* information, knowledge, culture and communication and their impact on social life. Livingstone and Lunt note three phases of mediatization: cultural evolution; the institutional corporatization of the media sector; and the radical transformation of our socio-technical systems and infrastructures (2014: 705).

For some mediatization is not only a paradigm for understanding the social, but also an ongoing process of reappropriating 'the social' as 'a site of new economic value' within social media (Mejias 2013, as cited in Couldry and Van Dijck 2015: 1). In this sense, understanding mediatization as a process means recognizing it as a 'dialectic', a kind of ongoing negotiation, between infrastructures and practices (Couldry and Van Dijck 2015: 1–2). As Couldry and Van Dijck argue, 'the institutions we have come to call "media" have been involved for over a century in providing an infrastructure for social life' (2015: 2), reaching a point of acceleration:

> Where every element of social process and social life is composed of elements that have already been mediated. This shifts the question of media's 'influence' on the social into a higher-dimensional problem. (Couldry 2017)

Couldry and Hepp argue that while 'the mediation of everything' (Livingstone 2009) once accounted for these broad shifts in the infrastructures of social life, it is no longer enough to explain the massive shifts in the meaning and practice(s) of 'the social'. Take for example, the shift from face-to-face to screened communication (e.g. phones, screens, apps, platforms) as the nucleus of our daily social lives. Following this intensification of mediation, Couldry and Hepp propose 'deep mediatization' as a framework for understanding the multiple and mediated interdependencies interwoven in the 'construction of the social world [as it] becomes implicated in our uses of media' (2017: 33).

Deep mediatization, like structuration, provides useful conceptual frameworks for understanding 'the social' in social media, not just at the screen interfaces, but also as a broader organizing principle for understanding the interplay between communication, interaction and the social order. While structuration enables a close look at the multiple interactions between structures and agencies, deep mediatization extends these principles. According to these theoretical framings, social media are made up of structural and agentic elements, each of which are in a constant process of mutual constitution – a simple way to describe Giddens' theory of structuration. Deep mediatization, on the other hand, argues that media, and social media in this case, make up the infrastructures of our everyday lives, and in this process rewrite the social. One of the ways we can see this re-writing is through affordances, described further below, and their mediation of changing social relations. Affordances are introduced as a behavioural articulation of mediatization, one that helps explain the social through new tactics of belonging: likes and metrics, literacies, and solidarities and the public good.

Affordances and Tactics of Belonging

Social media have introduced new tactics of belonging, which shift social relations towards mediated indicators of value and affinity. By 'tactics of belonging', I mean the primary mechanisms people use to figure out and negotiate the conditions of and for belonging.

As the infrastructures of our everyday lives, social media frame how, when and where a significant proportion of social life takes place. While affordances, an important concept relevant to every chapter in this book, explain the links between technologies and social action, thinking about how they relate to belonging means positioning those affordances within the broader context of social life. In other words, affordances are key for making sense of our interaction and relationships with social technologies, but we also must account for how those links are understood and negotiated as social. After defining affordances, we look at how specific affordances, such as the like buttons, metrics, new languages and literacies make up new kinds of social relations.

Near the beginning of their conceptual life, 'affordances' largely applied to design and human–computer interaction (HCI), and having gained popularity, are now a central principle in user experience (UX) design, as well as media and technology studies. Affordances refer to the ways that material features or objects enable or even demand particular kinds of behaviours. Don Norman, professor and director of the University of California San Diego's design lab, explains:

> *Affordances exist even if they are not visible.* For designers, their visibility is critical: visible affordances provide strong clues to the operations of things. A flat plate mounted on a door affords pushing. Knobs afford turning, pushing, and pulling. Slots are for inserting things into. Balls are for throwing or bouncing. *Perceived affordances help people figure out what actions are possible* without the need for labels or instructions … Many people find affordances difficult to understand because *they are relationships, not properties,* (Norman 2013 [1988]: 13; emphasis added)

This concept gives a name to the many ways that human action is made more or less possible in relation to the design of the tools, structures, technologies and sites around us, sometimes regardless of whether we use them. For example, the message-length restrictions on different platforms enable different kinds of communication. Twitter, like other micro-blogging sites, has a limit of 280 characters, which means users must fit their message to the style and length *afforded* by the platform. In contrast, Instagram is a primarily visual platform where photos and stories are afforded. Blogging, on the other hand, can be long-form and affords a different style of content and thinking. Affordances also help understand and articulate the social processes shaped by all sorts of material constraints and the structural designs for who will use a tool and how they might use it. Norman elaborates further when he says, '*Affordances represent the possibilities in the world for how an agent (a person, animal, or machine) can interact with something. Some affordances are perceivable, others are invisible*' (2013 [1988]: 18, emphasis added).

When Norman first applied the affordance concept to design, he was doing so for professional designers, artists, and those thinking about how to make things in ways that would be sensible to people who used them. However, this concept has been widely taken up by interdisciplinary scholars and researchers interested in media, technology and social relations. As another example, think of the link between the pathways people take and existing roads. Roads make possible particular routes and particular kinds or travel, and those routes shape how people can navigate the spaces around them. Affordances are about the relationship between structural design and human activities:

> Thus, the concept of affordances is attractive for communication researchers because it suggests that neither materiality (e.g., an object) nor a constructivist view (e.g., human agency) are sufficient to explain technology use (Leonardi & Barley, 2008), and advocates focusing on relational actions that occur among people and technologies. (Evans et al. 2016)

In media and technology studies, affordances have had a big impact in making sense of social media, including on content moderation (Gillespie 2018), everyday life (Humphreys 2018), personal connections (Baym 2015), and algorithms and social media platforms (Bucher and Helmond 2015). In the next section, we look at the kinds of affordances related to the like button.

The 'like' button: Metrics in the like economy

'Like' or 'reactions' buttons provide an interesting case study of affordances. Many scholars have written about 'social buttons' and those social media features where users can 'like', favourite, up or down vote, or share their reactions. Like buttons, as discussed in Chapter 5, are also a major part of social media metrics, what Richard Rogers calls 'vanity metrics' (2018).

In 2016, Facebook extended its like button to include five additional emojis as well as the like button – love, haha, wow, sad and angry – called Facebook reactions (Facebook 2016). For many users, these buttons help individuals express their views and reactions to content, and can often feel like a very personal act. Yet the like button is also a product designed to collect user information within and across platforms, as well as from across the web. Gerlitz and Helmond claim the widespread use of these kinds of buttons creates flows of personal data and web metrics across platforms culminating in a 'like economy' where *the social is of particular economic value*' (2013: 1349; emphasis added). Christian Fuchs takes this monetization further, arguing that the like economy promotes a *like ideology*, creating an 'affirmative atmosphere' supporting particular kinds of positive user engagement that promote traffic and are unlikely to threaten advertisers or other vested interests (2014: 160–61).

Van Dijck examines Facebook's like button, particularly in relation to cross-platform data-sharing. Over 350,000 people installed the like button in the first three months following its launch in 2010 (Van Dijck 2013: 49). Yet Facebook reactions massively increased use, as they were shared over 800 million *times a day* in their first year of existence (Keating 2017; Russell 2017). Van Dijck argues that the like button, similar to the reactions buttons, collects user data:

… including IP addresses, [and] are automatically routed back to Facebook. In fact, Facebook records any user's presence on a site with a Like button, including non-members and logged out users; a Like box allows Facebook to trace how many users and which of their friends have pushed the button. The visible part of the interface calls attention to user-to-user interaction, suggesting that information stays within the first meaning of sharing [person-to-person, rather than person-to-platform]. However, invisible algorithms and protocols execute the programmed social task of "liking." Personal data are turned into public connections, as the Like function is ubiquitously dispersed to many items on the Internet. (2013: 49)

It seems almost every platform has a version of the like button. Twitter, Instagram, Tumblr, for example, also have a like feature. YouTube, like many news forums, provides the option of liking or disliking, which is similar to the up and down voting on Reddit and Imgur and so on. Each of these features generates user metrics which other users rely on to make sense of their content, sometimes validating what is good, what is interesting and what gets people's attention. These buttons also generate metrics which people must become literate in understanding. Indeed, the numbers of views, likes, followers or subscribers are often used to gauge how popular or important a user or a piece of content might be. Ji Won Kim (2018), for example, finds that metrics increased how believable Twitter content was, and the higher the metrics, the more likely users were to believe, retweet and comment on that content. Johannes Paßmann and Cornelius Schubert (2020) find that users on MemeEconomy use 'liking' to develop and define their tastes. Metrics, in this case, are used to perform, display and negotiate these tastes with others in the forum.

These buttons have become part of common vernaculars, enabling users to quickly express and share their views, and to navigate the views of others. Social media affordances like these mean that users must develop new literacies to engage the often platform specific affordances and the common vernaculars of those social media platforms, discussed further in the next section.

New vernaculars and literacies

One of the recurring themes in detailed accounts of social media platforms or genres of content is *vernacular*, the everyday language spoken by ordinary people. In an interview with Henry Jenkins (2007), Jean Burgess defines vernacular creativity as:

… everyday creative practices like storytelling, family photographing, scrapbooking, journaling and so on that pre-exist the digital age and yet are co-evolving with digital technologies and networks in really interesting ways.

This concept has informed much of Burgess's ongoing work, including her YouTube research with Joshua Green (see Chapter 9). While Burgess, later with Green, focuses on creative practices, many have identified the language(s) people develop to use particular platforms or content. Thus, when we are thinking about what is social about social media, the abundance of everyday and platform-local languages is important. For example, these everyday languages develop around the visual and cultural aesthetics of selfies, the folkloric vernaculars of memes, and visual creativity on YouTube – and each of these also means that users must develop new technical literacies.

For example, as discussed in Chapter 7, selfies involve complex visual aesthetics, communicating particular aspects of one's personal life with the everyday language of digital culture. Annette Markham argues that this language is not just outward facing, but also frames how selfie makers see themselves, affording users to 'write ourselves into being' (2013, as cited in Rettberg 2014: 13). Others draw from a longer visual language around photography, self-portraiture and the broader context of digital visual communication from memes to videos.

Figure 4.3 Tier 3 meme, illustrating the everyday vernacular of memes

Source: Creator unknown, Imgur, https://imgur.com/gallery/RFYuzWP

Memes, discussed in Chapter 1, also provide a fascinating case of everyday vernaculars, requiring new literacies. Meme researchers have observed that memes *are* a kind of language. When asked about memes, one of Kate Mitner's interviewees stated, 'this is our language, these are our shared cultural reference points' (CS, 27, male, as cited by Mitner 2014). In addition, Whitney Phillips and Ryan Milner, both widely published on memes and internet culture, argue that 'decoding humour ... requires a set of broader cultural literacies' (2017: 112). (See Figure 4.3 for an illustration of meme literacies.)

In his book on memes, Milner points out that memes are the 'lingua franca of digitally mediated participation, a common tongue allowing geographically dispersed participants to connect and share' (2016: 7). For example, the 'Tier 3' meme makes light of the complexity of memes, particularly in light of the ways they are deeply embedded within internet culture, often requiring multiple cross-references. In addition, memes also are 'polyvocal' and allow users to engage in public conversations (2016: 111). This is a compelling argument, one that identifies the importance of everyday language internet culture.

Conclusion: Social Solidarities and the Public Good

This chapter raises questions about how we think of and understand the social, particularly in relation to the rise of social media and the expansion of social technologies into almost every aspect of the lives of 3.48 billion social media users (Kemp 2019). Understanding the social in an age of social media matters for many reasons. First, global platform power threatens the fabric of social life by 'hollowing out the social' in favour of monetizable data extraction (Couldry and Mejias 2019: 115; see Chapter 2). The monopolistic tendencies and colonizing power of social platforms also threaten the quality of political life, where disinformation, misinformation and xenophobia reign *because they are profitable*. Many researchers and media thinkers continue to raise these concerns (e.g. Srnicek 2017; Vaidhyanathan 2018; Zuboff 2019). As Van Dijck argues, we must urgently challenge what it means to be social when platform power outstrips national systems, and thereby re-writes the rules of the system:

> Online sociality increasingly eludes national societal structures, which are traditionally cemented entirely in (public and private) institutions. Despite Facebook's 'social rhetoric' of connectedness and openness, the undercurrents of global information flows are increasingly and uniformly channeled through the bottled water systems that they themselves commission. (Van Dijck 2015: para 4)

It seems that there is no longer a question about the social being overtaken and rewritten by the aggressive creep of the ideology of connection, made clear in the 'about us' and 'what is' pages where they define themselves as being about the 'world', 'people', 'community' and 'sharing'. Yet, the obsession with data means that the ideology of connection does not account for the *quality* of or *meaning* for connection. Social value is evaluated on the number and frequency of connections, meaning that highly connected malevolent influencers, trolls, widely shared misinformation and rumours that get a lot of likes are valuable to platforms. No distinction is made between what is good or bad, and this is a problem. The numerous public health crises of 2020, such as the pandemic, systemic racism and climate chaos, point to the importance of moving beyond connection and building real solidarities oriented towards the social and public good. Connection is no longer an effective indicator of social relations.

This chapter has provided a road map of concepts which help us make sense of the incredible complexity of social life and how they are related to social media. I have introduced important concepts like the tensions between structure and agency, long positioned as binary between society and self, between social systems and free will. This model is especially useful to begin thinking about the social, to help push past either or thinking. From here, I introduced several concepts which aim to problematize the relations between structure and agency (structuration), and media and social life (deep mediatization). What they show is that social media do shape our experience of the social, and these are illustrated through affordances, which work as new tactics of belonging.

It is not just the economic and political threats to social structures which make understanding the social so urgent. It is also about the platform opportunities and affordances which call for attention. Now, more than ever, we are able to coordinate global movements, develop and maintain affiliative connections across space and time, and re-write the historical limits of social interaction. Yet, these capacities sit within particular social economics of the social technologies making up the infrastructures of our everyday lives. To reach the true potential of 'the social', we must also nurture and protect the ties that bind us together.

Questions and Activities

1   Why does the 'social' matter?
2   Social media are the infrastructures of our everyday lives. Reflect and discuss how this does (or does not) apply to your own life.
3   Social media metrics, such as the number of likes, shares, views, etc., are increasingly important indicators of status and belonging. What do you think of Instagram's decision to limit these metrics?
4   Using a social media app or platform as an example, explain what kind of affordances you think are unique to that platform. Discuss.

Further Reading

Couldry, N.; Hepp, A. 2017. *The Mediated Construction of Reality*. Polity.

Couldry, N. Van Dijck, J. 2015. Researching social media as if the social mattered, *Social Media + Society*, September 30. https://doi.org/10.1177/2056305115604174

Jarret, K. 2016. *Feminism, Labour and Digital Media: The Digital Housewife*. Routledge.

Noble, S.U. 2018. *Algorithms of Oppression: How Search Engines Reinforce Racism*. New York University Press.

Van Dijck, J. 2015. After connectivity: the era of connectication, *Social Media + Society*, May. https://doi.org/10.1177/2056305115578873

5

MATERIAL INFRASTRUCTURES AND PLATFORMIZATION

Chapter Overview

Introduction	108
Embedded Technologies and Overlapping Networks	109
Early Internet History and Internet Infrastructures	110
The 'stack' and global megastructures	113
Telephony and mobile social media	118
Platformization: Extending social media across the web	120
Platform Empires and the Social Landscape: GAFA and BATX	122
Conclusion: Social Media and Shifting Infrastructures	124
Questions and Activities	125
Further Reading	125

Chapter Objectives

- Introduce the relationship between internet and social media
- Demonstrate the embeddedness of social media and social technologies within the internet
- Provide an overview of internet infrastructures
- Visualize the impact of social media on the internet

Introduction

Most people take an instrumental view of the technologies they rely on to communicate and interact with those around them. When I want to speak to my family who live thousands of kilometres away from me, or interact with people in my field who I may not know, or organize a birthday party, I generally go to the nearest and easiest means of communication, without even thinking about how these communication forms work. This is not unusual. Film and television audiences, book readers, radio listeners, music fans and consumers of all kinds probably do exactly the same, and have done for a long time. Indeed, it is common in many media sectors, like theatre or television for example, to purposely conceal the complex processes of production, making everything taking place 'behind the scenes' invisible and well hidden behind the screen that separates the audience from those setting the stage or otherwise making media. Although the processes of production are different, social media function in a similar way, except rather than a curtain there is some kind of screen separating social media users from the platform work being done to create and maintain most social media sites. Most users do not ever need to think about the material infrastructures or software systems and developments making a like, share, message or comment possible. This chapter aims to move beyond the screen separating most of us from the complex material infrastructure of social media, the internet and mobile networks, so that we can take a closer look.

This chapter opens up the vibrant materialities of social media, including an overview of early internet history and internet infrastructures in order to develop a better working knowledge and visualization of how the internet works and how social media fit within these complex structures. Thinking about social media and the materialities of connection is important, and challenging. It is difficult to envision invisible and hidden structures, and it is even more difficult to imagine how those structures work. And yet, it is also important to ask questions and understand how these networks – that many of use every day – work. This chapter takes up this issue, asking, for example: What do social media infrastructures look like? How do social media and the internet fit together? And finally, are social media changing the web and the internet? And if they are, what is changing and how?

The material infrastructure of social technologies matter. Laura DeNardis says that 'these arrangements of technical architecture are also arrangements of power', and indeed they are

(2012: 720). They are arrangements of power because technologies do not arrive without value or prejudice (see Chapter 3). At the heart of the infrastructures that so many of us rely on every day are fundamental debates between regulation and openness, between public and private interests, between economic growth and innovation (von Schewick 2010). All of these issues play out not only in policy and regulation, but also in the material realities of where infrastructures go, what they are made out of and who is responsible for them. Many scholars researching the infrastructures of internet or mobile networks are struck by the often large and very wired warehouse or bunker-like spaces hosting the servers and cables responsible for circulating our 'signal traffic', i.e. all of the electronic messages we receive and send (Parks and Starosielski 2015).

Indeed, the first part of this chapter examines the embedded nature of social media and internet technologies, tracing the ways they overlap with the social technologies of today. From here, I turn to the early history of the internet, outlining the revolutionary and anti-hierarchical visions inspiring the construction of the internet. Yet tensions between public and private play out in the movements around who built and maintained the internet as it shifted responsibility from ARPA to the National Science Foundation, and then to private, profit-seeking buyers. All of these conditions matter. As DeNardis goes on to say:

> … architecture is not external to politics and culture but, rather, deeply embeds the values and policy decisions that ultimately structure how we access information, how innovation will proceed, and how we exercise individual freedom online. (DeNardis 2010)

With these issues in mind, we introduce 'the stack', a layered architecture of the internet, to understand how the internet works and how it connects the physical nuts and bolts making up the material structures to the seamless flow of content. The undersea submarine cables making up the physical layer of the internet make up a global megastructure, which is in part owned by global social powers like Facebook and Google. In order to understand how exactly social media fit into this global megastructure, two concurrent developments are introduced: the rapid growth of the mobile web and mobile social media including the importance of apps, and platformization (briefly introduced in Chapter 1). Based on this overview and exploration of internet infrastructures and social technologies, this chapter concludes with observations on how social media fit within the web and the internet.

Embedded Technologies and Overlapping Networks

Social technologies work as *socio-technical* systems – linking broader social patterns with specific technical tools or structures. Socio-technical systems illustrate the breadth of thinking around participatory kinds of media, long before 'social media' entered the popular vernacular. Many histories of social media begin with Web 2.0, a term popularized by Tim O'Reilly in 2005 and intended to capture the next generation of interactive and dynamic web capabilities. Although Web 2.0 is widely documented elsewhere (e.g. boyd and Ellison 2007; Fuchs 2017; Hinton and Hjorth 2013; Mandiberg 2012), it is important because it marks a shift from static websites to dynamic platforms, as seen in the shift from websites to blogs, from double click ads to Google's Adwords, and from MP3s to peer-to-peer file sharing, among others. Although social media broadly reflect the ethos of Web 2.0, it actually has much deeper roots directly connected with the early internet as a 'network of networks' (see Chapter 2).

Indeed, as Barry Wellman, one of the internet's most pioneering network scholars, suggested in 1997:

> When a computer network connects people, it is a social network. Just as a computer network is a set of machines connected by a set of cables, a social network is a set of people (or organizations or other social entities) connected by a set of socially meaningful relationships. (1997: 179)

Wellman, like many others, demonstrates the *overlap between the internet and web-based software with early social media*. This overlap renders social media simultaneously unique and is characteristic of other media technologies, when they were new (e.g. Lievrouw and Livingstone 2006; Marvin 1990). As the technologies we know and use today, social media are uniquely hybrid, embedded and are made of networks of networks within networks. Again, this is not necessarily new. As Marshall McLuhan famously claimed, 'the content of a medium is always another medium' (1964: 8), so as the printing press contains the written word and the telephone contains the wired infrastructure of the telegraph, social media contains the wired network of the internet. Like the many communication technologies preceding them, social media build upon the network infrastructures of the internet and the connective potential of these infrastructures. In order to understand just how overlapping and embedded social media are, and the implications of this embeddedness, the next section addresses early internet history and internet infrastructures.

Early Internet History and Internet Infrastructures

Infrastructure studies emphasize the importance of understanding how the internet works and how it is structured, and how exactly social media are related to the internet (e.g. Hunsinger 2014; Plantin et al. 2016; Sandvig 2013). As the internet provides the technical and physical foundation for social network sites and social media platforms, understanding the basic workings of the internet means better understanding social media. As Parks and Starosielski suggest, media infrastructures converge and coordinate 'broadcasting cable, satellite, internet, and mobile telephone systems' (2015: 1). Focusing on the infrastructural networks prioritizes the materialities and 'processes of distribution' taking place behind the screen, rather than the 'screened entertainment' where content, 'textual interpretation' and production have long dominated research agendas in media and communications (Parks and Starosielski 2015: 5; cf. Sandvig 2013).

In addition, understanding the internet infrastructure helps visualize how social media physically overlap and converge with the internet. Thus part of the purpose of this chapter is to situate social media within the broader digital environment, technically and culturally. Finally, the historical insights gained by looking at the early history of the internet and its infrastructure make it possible to identify what social media have changed over time, fitting within and increasingly shaping the digital environment more broadly.

The early internet began as the ARPANET, a military-funded project to create a robust communication network that could withstand attack in the 1960s, growing from zero to 15 nodes (independent hosts) across the US by 1971 (Abbate 2000: 44–45). In the 1980s, ARPANET was increasingly paralleled by the growth of the National Science Foundation's internetwork (NSFNET), which extended publicly funded networks, making the internet much more widely available and accessible (Abbate 2000: 191). Over the 1980s, and by investing hundreds of millions of dollars in the NSFNET to extend regional networks linking supercomputing centres through high-speed data cables, the National Science Foundation publicly subsidized *the internet backbone* (Abbate 2000: 191–93). At this time, these networks were seen as radical democratic technologies, which would enable citizens to share knowledge freely and enable innovation on unprecedented levels. Yet the NSFNET networks were sold off to private investors and commercial buyers beginning in the late 1980s, becoming fully privatized by the mid-1990s. This story of public investment followed by privatization is familiar and continues to play out on public infrastructures (e.g. privatization of railroads, trains, health services). Nevertheless, the new internet service providers (ISPs) extended the internet beyond science and research communities into the early adopting majority (Abbate 2000: 198). Within this brief history of the internet's development, there is also an often untold history of longstanding battles between the conflicting logics of freedom and ownership, of open and closed standards, as often expressed in the technical and infrastructural specifications of networks.

For example, as many have documented, the internet has long been understood as radically transforming power from top-down, hierarchical systems to flat, non-hierarchical systems where everyone can access information and share their own voice. This revolutionary potential is both social and technical. Paul Baran, the man responsible for inventing TCP/IP (Transmission Control Protocol/Internet Protocol), was an important figure in internet history. TCP/IP provided a model for packet switching, which enabled the transmission of information over networks, and is the basis for the internet as we know it. In addition to this, Baran also modelled the internet's communication network structure, illustrating the radical and non-hierarchical potential of a decentralized communicative structure (see Figure 5.1).

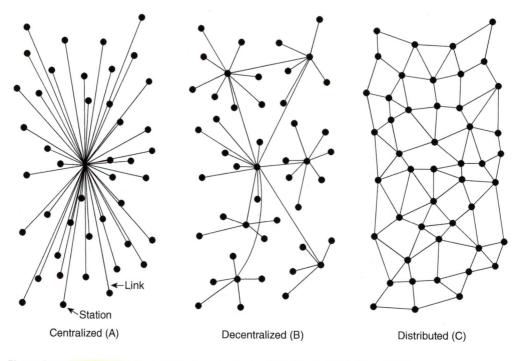

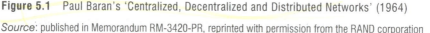

Centralized (A)   Decentralized (B)   Distributed (C)

Figure 5.1 Paul Baran's 'Centralized, Decentralized and Distributed Networks' (1964)

Source: published in Memorandum RM-3420-PR, reprinted with permission from the RAND corporation

Notably, Baran's centralized communication network (A) shows one dominant centre of power, often in the form of a hierarchy, as would be seen in the military, or in a monarchy, or in a celebrity network. This kind of communication network is also referred to as 'star' network, in light of the power the central node holds for the rest of the network. Decentralized models, as seen in (B) and (C), break down this hierarchy and central control, sharing power across the network, albeit sometimes in clusters as seen in the tree like structure of (B), rather than evenly across the network, as shown in the distributed (C) network. For (B), each cluster would exercise autonomy across a flatter, rather than hierarchical network, and would likely be seen in the way teams work together on a larger project or issue. Distributed or mesh networks, as seen in (C), depict the ideal communication and network of the internet. Each node has as much importance and centrality to the rest of the nodes in the network, making a flat, distributed and non-hierarchical network.

In these senses, power and control are distributed across the network, rather than in clusters or in hierarchies. Here, the communication flow in grassroots networks serves as an example. The internet is inspired by the idea of the distributed network, where each node is a network connecting to other networks, flattening power hierarchies and facilitating individual and collective empowerment (Baran 1864; Hu 2015: 5–6). Indeed, this ethos of flattening power hierarchies and democratizing access and control is pervasive, even if this is mythic and overstated in practice. Baran provides an important demonstration of how infrastructures are important. The networked infrastructure of the early internet repositions the flow of information and communication, and for many internet pioneers fundamentally re-writes the circuits of power.

Another important concept for understanding the internet is 'the stack' – a longstanding model of how each node within an internet-mediated network is connected, and ultimately a model of how the internet works (see also Bratton 2015). From the early days of the 1960s and 1970s internet, ARPANET and NSFNET were conceptualized as a stack of 'layers', with each layer responsible for specific functions and yet capable of interacting with other layers – referred to as *interoperability*. The early internet was made of a network of networks, where each network used different rules for processing data and/or protocols. This meant the early internet looked more like a version of the clustered and decentralized model, except each cluster was unable to connect to other clusters because the use of different protocols prevented connecting to a different network. In part, this lack of interoperability was built in the early internet which was designed for 'survivability', where the communication infrastructure would still work even if parts of it were destroyed, unlike telephone, railroad or telegraph networks where one attack would disable the flow across the entire network. It took decades for the internet to become a mainstream network of networks, largely because different computers and networks had many different networking and routing specifications, as well as different networking protocols, meaning networks were not always compatible.

The 'stack' and global megastructures

In the late 1970s, this problem was resolved. The Open Systems Interconnection (OSI) model standardized the 'layers' of the internet, well before the requirements of the internet and networking were fully understood. The OSI model bears a strong resemblance to the internet protocol (IP) model, which combined with packet switching (TCP) is more widely used (TCP/IP). The OSI model, composed of seven rather than five layers, is still often used in training, research, and by those developing network infrastructures. Both of these 'layered architecture' models allow developers and users to discuss and work with 'well-defined, specific layers' with specific functions, and to 'come together in a large and complex system' (Kursoe and Ross 2013: 49; see also Cath et al. 2017: 6). In addition, conceptualizing the internet as a 'stacked' set of physical layers from the network cables carrying data to the packet switching protocols allowing data to transfer between layers and reach other computers is a useful visual map. Other scholars have developed a less technical model of the internet 'stack' in order to communicate the layered architecture of the internet to different disciplinary audiences, like policy makers, social scientists and the general public. (See Figure 5.2 for a side-by-side visualization of these models.)

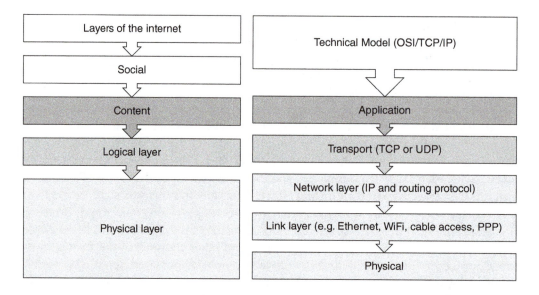

Figure 5.2 'The stack': Models of the layered architecture of the internet, comparing Lessig (2001) and Cath et al. (2017) 'layers of the internet' with the technical models of OSI/TCP/IP

Corrine Cath et al. (2017) extend Lawrence Lessig's (2001) layered architecture of the internet by adding the 'social' dimension at the top level. By this, Cath et al. are referring to 'the people that build, use and regulate, and interact with the internet' (2017: 17). For Lessig and Cath et al., the *content* layer is the layer most people are familiar with and includes all the stuff that comes up on our screens. Specifically, the content layer includes:

> … websites, social media, blogs, news sites, video and audio content, and virtually all the content that is exchanged by users … including the newest multimedia developments like the Internet of things (IOT) and Virtual Reality (VR). (Cath et al. 2017: 17)

The *application* layer corresponds almost identically, including 'http, SMTP, FTP, URLs, browsers, search engines', etc. (Kursoe and Ross 2013: 50). The *logical* layer, also referred to as the 'code layer' (Lessig 2001) and the *transport* layer by others, includes 'sets of protocols enabling the internet to function' such as TCP/IP, the domain name system (DNS), hardware, WiFi standards and host-to-host communication (Cath 2017: 17; Kursoe and Ross 2013: 51).

Cath et al. and Lessig define the *physical* layer in a fairly straightforward way, suggesting that this layer is both complex and multi-layered, including a 'physical technology through which data packets travel', and also the networks of cable, cellular towers and data centres through which the internet is structured and electronic messages circulate (Cath 2017: 18). Kursoe and Ross, following standard visualizations of the layered architecture of the internet, describe three distinct layers which correspond with the physical layer. These distinct layers include the '*network* layer' (e.g. IP and routing protocol), the '*link* layer' (e.g. ethernet, WiFi, cable access), and the '*physical* layer' (e.g. 'the actual transmission medium' such as the fibre optic cables, copper wire and coaxial cables) (Kursoe and Ross 2013: 51–53).

The layered architecture of the internet is important for at least two reasons. First, without digressing too much into technical detail, this model helps explain what the internet looks like. The stack models provide a visual representation of the layered nature of the internet which differentiates each level of the internet by functionality. The bottom layer, made up of physical artefacts, such as the actual tubes, cables, data servers, wires and cables connecting computers to networks, enables the flow of data through networks. It is this layer which provides the physical architecture of the net and includes the undersea cables connecting the internet across the globe (Starosielski 2015). In contrast, the top application or content layer is where we find the World Wide Web (www), software applications and platforms (e.g. email programmes, websites, blogs, browsers, social media sites; cf. Hunsinger 2014; Van Dijck 2013: 6–9). Thus, 99% of web content and services are added on only to the top of the internet, sitting on top of this layered stack. For most people, most of the time, this top layer is as far into the internet as they need to go, and most ordinary users only ever interact with or think about the very top layer of the internet. Yet thinking through the stack as a whole and linking content, packet switching, network and link protocols with physical architectures is complex.

The second reason the stack model is important is because it provides a set of standards to coordinate how each layer works together in order to connect networks to the networks, and to connect individual computers to the internet. Therefore, coordinating internationally agreed standards, as done with the OSI, allows the internet to work and makes it possible for international, national and local variability to seamlessly integrate networks into other networks from across the globe. This seamless integration creates a kind of global 'megastructure' for the world's dominant communication networks, and also links many different and physically complicated 'systems of different genres of computation' (Bratton 2016). This megastructure is composed of the physical, logical, content and social layers making up the 'stack'.

The submarine cable map in Figure 5.3 shows the stylized geography of the undersea data cables making up the physical infrastructure of the internet and all 'transoceanic digital communications' including some television (Starosielski 2015: 1). Originally built by telecoms, major investors now include Facebook, Google and Amazon among other big tech and social companies (TeleGeography 2017). While most people may not consider the physical infrastructure of the internet or social media, the bottom layer of the stack is the foundation for all kinds of electronic communication, and is often the grounds for important battles over control and power of those communications and connections.

The 'stack' is both an infrastructural model for a global system linking networks of networks, which would otherwise not be able to connect, and a powerful metaphor for 'a new governing architecture' (Bratton 2016). Another way of understanding this 'governing architecture' is that it has global currency across all the layers of internet networks, providing a

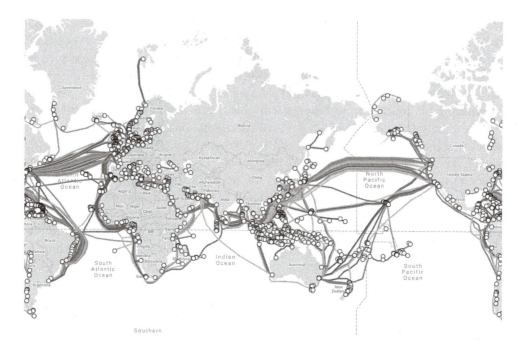

Figure 5.3   Submarine cable map

Source: created and updated by TeleGeography (August 10, 2020), interactive version at https://www.submarinecablemap.com/. Reprinted with permission from TeleGeography.

common language for all those working in and on developing internet and computer networking infrastructures. For ordinary people who do not work or think about the technicalities of computer networks, 'the stack' is an invisible and important infrastructure for many daily life activities.

In terms of importance, those who regulate, monitor and control the global megastructure wield a lot of power. (See Box 5.1 explaining how this works and why infrastructure matters use 'net neutrality' as an example.)

Box 5.1   Why infrastructure matters? The case of net neutrality

Widely considered a foundation of the open internet, net neutrality refers to the idea that the internet should act as a neutral network, and no preferential treatment should be accorded to any particular kinds of content, internet service providers (ISPs) or organizations using the internet. The net neutrality principle means that the Federal Communications Commission (FCC) and US government have been responsible for ISP regulations preventing differential access to the internet through faster service for those that can afford it, and slower access for those who cannot. Without net neutrality regulations, ISPs and broadband providers are free to charge or slow down service to companies, like Netflix, Skype, WhatsApp or Wikileaks, for any reason.

Net neutrality has been fiercely debated since the early 2000s and a number of cases demonstrate the importance of this principle for a free and open internet (Dunham 2016; Jordan 2007). For example, US-based network company Comcast throttled download speeds for Netflix content, deterring Netflix consumers from using the service and threatening Netflix's place in the market (AP 2014; Shu 2014). Others have expressed concern over the slowing down of video and messaging services like Skype and WhatsApp, because ISPs may want to restrict competition and encourage users to use ISPs' own services (Sulleyman 2017). Finally, without net neutrality, ISPs and broadband providers have the power to limit internet services based on political disagreements with a service as was the case with WikiLeaks (DeNardis 2010, 2012).

With net neutrality in place, ISPs and broadband providers must treat all internet content neutrally, regardless of its content, its owner, or its place in the competitive market. The FCC repealed net neutrality on December 14, 2017, despite a concerted effort by those advocating for a free internet through active campaigning and great protest.

Net neutrality is important, linking regulation and control of the internet infrastructure with many social and political implications – for democracy, for innovation, and for everyday users. For advocates of a free internet, an open internet infrastructure has serious implications for both political participation and democracy. FCC's chairman, Ajit Pai, has former affiliations with Verizon, one of the US's largest telecommunications companies and ISPs which supports the repeal of net neutrality and stands to reap many benefits as a result (Murphy 2017). The FCC's repeal of net neutrality has global consequences in part because the technology companies responsible for much of global internet infrastructure are concentrated in the US and this has far-reaching implications for internet freedom (Hu 2015; Starosielski 2015a: 54).

So far, the early history of the internet helps explain the vision and infrastructure making up the layered architecture of the internet, from the physical to content layers. However, the top content and social layers are also important. As illustrated in Chapter 2, particularly over the first two stages of social media, there were many communicative and interpersonal programs in use from the very beginning of the ARPANET (c.f. Baym 2015: 15–16). Nancy Baym comments on a crucial development in the internet, namely the launch of the World Wide Web (WWW) in 1989 as led by Tim Berners-Lee at CERN, which:

> … heralded a shift from communication that was purely text-based to multi-media communication, and gave rise to many new forms of mediated communication… these include web boards, blogs, wikis, social network sites, video and photo sharing sites, and graphically intensive virtual worlds. (2015: 17)

Although many of these social technologies are introduced in Chapter 2, it is important to note that the public launch of the WWW effectively served as the OSI/ICP/TP protocol for the content layer of the stack. In other words, the WWW provided a common platform for internet users, site developers, content makers and internet enthusiasts to interact with the internet network. In the same way that TCP/IP developed protocols allowing many different networks to share common physical and networked connections, the WWW developed a common platform for content. Groupware may have been a powerful set of tools and for enabling business-sized groups to take advantage of networked capacities, but the WWW extended the scope and scale of these networked capacities across the globe. As well, all of the impressive number of 'new forms of mediated communication' fit at the top level of the stack, comprising a small part of the internet and a massive part of the WWW.

A brief historical scan of the development of internet infrastructures, including the layered architecture of the 'stack' and the launch of the WWW, provides a basic overview of how the internet works and what it looks like. Following Wellman's observation, the internet itself may also be a *social network*, but it is one that with a complex multi-layered architecture including a global wired infrastructure of cables and data centres, as well as a dynamic and ever-changing 'content' layer. In theory, and at least in the early days, social media follow the open and distributed network structures of the internet, and these are the structures that shaped the development, implementation and use of social media. However, although briefly mentioned in Chapter 1, there were two parallel shifts occurring which also had a tremendous impact on the size, scale, scope and impact of social media: the rise of mobile media and platformization, each of which is addressed in turn below.

Telephony and mobile social media

As discussed in Chapter 2, the first iPhone launched in January 2007, followed by the first Android phone in November 2008 (Arthur 2012). From this point, 4.77 billion people or 62.9% of the global population had mobile phones in 2016, and they reported forecasts of over five billion people using mobile phones in 2019 (Statista 2017a). Ran Wei (2013) claims the mobile phone is one of the 'fastest diffusing communication technologies' across the globe, a fact which seems undeniable given its rapid growth. Many have referred to the monumental impact of the iPhone as the 'iPhone moment', marking the beginning of the smartphone era (Hjorth et al. 2012; Miller 2014).

Lee Humphreys (2013) describes the global impact of mobiles:

> For many in the developed world, our internet use started out on a computer and moved to a mobile phone; however, globally, more people will be accessing the internet through a mobile device than through a desktop or laptop computer. When people access the internet with their phones, unsurprisingly, they often use social media.

In addition, Wei (2013) argues that the mobile phone enables a strong sense of 'connected presence' between users, mediating a sense of closeness more than any other communication technology. The rise of mobile social media is closely tied to camera phones and the convenience of easily taking and sharing images or videos across networks (Goggin 2014; Hjorth and Hendry 2015; Humphreys 2013).

However, mobile media have had an impact on far more than just interpersonal connections. For the purposes of this chapter, it is also important to understand how mobile infrastructures fit with social media, and the implications of both mobile social media and the rise of app culture that comes with pervasive mobile use and the convergence of telephone and internet networks.

Goggin describes mobile and telephone networks as based on 'circuit switched fixed line telecommunications networks' as merging with internet and wireless networks, but also including a whole range of networks from radio and broadcasting to satellite, private and ad hoc networks of private companies and grassroots organizations (2011: 3). All of these networks paint a complex picture of our network infrastructures. In a letter explaining the mobile system, Portnoy and Gillula (2017) from the Electronic Frontier Foundation (EFF) describe the Public Switched Telephone Network (PSTS), or what is also known as the Plain Old Telephone Service (POTS), as interconnected with the internet 'at the network level'. And although these systems are complex, they are integrated and 'unified' for interoperability, as demonstrated through voice or video over internet protocol (VoIP) and other services (Portnoy and Gillula 2017).

Like content on the WWW and social media, some aspects of these systems continually change. For example, mobile apps, popularized through Apple's AppStore and Google's Play Store, are as much on the rise as mobile social media and are changing how people use those social media. As a result, the flow of data across the internet and mobile networks is also changing. Daubs and Manzerolle (2016) explain this change as transforming the web from an open platform to a kind of walled garden:

> The 'app' – a stand-alone, self-contained software application – is rapidly becoming the organizing logic of the internet. This logic is visible both in the development of key native app platforms such as iOS and Android and, despite residual notions of Hypertext Mark-Up Language (HTML) as an open format, in the transformation of the Web into a 'platform for applications'. (Anthes 2012: 6, as cited in Daubs and Manzerolle 2016: 53)

In this sense, the WWW has enabled developers, internet users, web browsers, social media enthusiasts and others to browse the web, in a potentially infinite pattern. However, apps limit access to the web, bringing content and links into the app – or walled garden – and effectively keeping users in the app rather than enabling free movement across the web. Going back to Paul Baran's communication networks, the app economy would best fit with the centralized model, where the central node is controlled or limited by the app in use.

Goggin (2014: 1076) discusses Facebook's mobile strategy, launched for developers in 2007, as one aiming for 'seamless integration' in order to 'replace the internet', and involving developing mobile photography via Instagram and mobile games via Zynga (Facebook 2007). As Goggin concludes:

> ... it is not by accident that mobile Facebook now unfolds as the majority world, the 'global south' and the titans of China and India, not to mention the rise of Latin America, Africa and other regions, become the forces to be reckoned with, in the fully fledged achievement of global mobile media (Goggin, 2011) – but also in the new directions remodelling the Internet. (2014: 1081)

Thus the convergences between mobile phones, the rise of apps, telephone networks and social media lead to a whole new articulation of social media as mobile, and as a central platform for the internet (see the controversies around Facebook's *Free Basics*; Bosch et al. 2020; Moore and Tambini 2018; Nothias 2020). Returning to Paul Baran's models of network communication (see Figure 5.1, on p. 112) shows that between apps and mobile strategies, social media begin to resemble more centralized networks characteristic of twentieth-century media and communications systems. The next section introduces platformization, and the extension of social media across the web.

Platformization: Extending social media across the web

So far this chapter has been grounded in critical infrastructure studies, following a line of inquiry based on making the invisible visible, in order to better understand the functionality and structural logics of the internet, mobile networks and social media (e.g. Parks and Starosielski 2015; Starosielski 2015, 2015a). However, a major contribution to understanding social media comes from platform studies (Gerlitz and Helmond 2013; Gillespie 2010; Helmond 2015) – both relatively new fields of study. Following the critical work of Plantin et al. (2016), great value can be gained from combining the two approaches, particularly as bit tech and mega-corporations, like Google and Facebook for example, are stakeholders at all levels, exhibiting characteristics of both platforms and infrastructures. It is an important component for both linking and separating the web and social media. Platformization, taking place at the same time as mobile social, refers to:

> The rise of the platform as the dominant infrastructural and economic model of the social web and the consequences of the expansion of social media platforms into other spaces online. Central to this is the offer of APIs [Application Processing Interfaces], which turn social network sites into social media platforms. (Helmond 2015: 5)

As briefly mentioned in Chapter 2, platformization was a parallel shift occurring alongside the rise of mobile social media and apps – both taking place at the beginning of the growth and consolidation stage, what I have called stage 3 between 2007 and 2012. For Helmond, one of the key features of platformization is access to the API, which is 'an interface provided by an application that lets users interact with or respond to data or service requests from another application' (Murugesan 2007, as cited in Helmond 2015: 4). In other words, the API makes a site *programmable*, which is 'at the core of the shift from social network *sites* to social media *platforms*' (Helmond 2015: 4, emphasis in original). This is an important development, one that repositions social media from single sites sitting on top of the layered architecture of the internet to 'parasite networks' funneling control and data through the platform rather than the full network (personal communication, Plantin 2017).

In addition to providing a dominant infrastructural and economic model, platformization involves an invisible and visible transition for many social media sites. Platformization extended social media beyond the boundaries of their own sites, embedding each social site across and through the web. Helmond maps these transitions for a number of sites from the early to mid-2000s, including Flickr in 2004, YouTube in 2005, and Last.fm, Twitter and Facebook in 2006. Platformization was visible through the use of *social plug-ins* such as like buttons, share buttons, comment boxes, embedded posts or content, as well as Facebook Connect (now called Facebook Login). (See Box 5.2 for a further explanation of Facebook Connect.) Social plug-ins are widget-like features that can be added on to a social site, such as Facebook's 'like' button, which will then 'set up a two-way data channel … in which data flows' between the sites using the plug-in (Helmond 2015: 7). Elsewhere, Gerlitz and Helmond argue that these plug-ins make up a 'like economy' which not only transforms social behaviour, such as 'likes', into 'valuable consumer data' and metrics, but also transforms the web into social converter for 'data mining and circulation' (2013: 1349, 1358). Indeed, these are signs of the ideology of connection driving social media platformization.

Box 5.2   Facebook Connect and platformization

Facebook Connect, piloted in 2007 and publicly launched on December 4, 2008, is a single sign-on service allowing users to use their Facebook login and password to access other apps and websites without making a new account. For developers, those making or managing apps and websites, Facebook Connect provided access to Facebook's *API*, including access to user behavioural analytics and data in order to *personalize* content, increase engagement, and maximize content distribution (Facebook Newsroom 2008). Facebook Connect is only one of many developer tools, similar to the like button, share button, embedded posts, comment box, reactions and

(Continued)

other social plug-ins which facilitate developer access to Facebook's API and allow user data collection. See below for Facebook's official announcement:

December 4, 2008 – Facebook® today announced the ability for any Website to implement Facebook Connect [now Facebook Login], a service designed to make it easy for its more than 130 million active users to combine their Facebook experience with any participating Website, desktop application or mobile device. Following several months of testing, Facebook Connect is now available to all interested third parties through a self-service application on Facebook Platform, at: http://developers.facebook.com/connect.php (Facebook Newsroom 2008)

Facebook Connect was rebranded as 'Facebook Login', and Facebook's 2013 press release announcing this change also promised that any apps using the service must 'separately ask you for permission to post back to Facebook' (Facebook Newsroom 2013). This rebranding suggests privacy concerns around the misuse of data collected via Facebook Connect resulted in a re-working of this product in line with consumer demand.

Platform Empires and the Social Landscape: GAFA and BATX

Platforms share an increasingly pervasive business model – one based on buying out the competition, closing off social ecosystems and building platform monopolies (see also Couldry and Mejias 2019a, 2019b; Srnicek 2017; Van Dijck et al. 2018). Facebook, for example, has bought out Instagram (2012), WhatsApp (2014), Oculus VR, facial recognition companies Faciometrics and Grokstyle (2019), a Blockchain tech startup called Chainspace (2019) and, following TikTok's spike in popularity, has released an Instagram knock-off called 'Reels' (2020). All of these acquisitions and knock-off features highlight Facebook's plans to expand its platform, by buying out competition and gaining high-level market intelligence in the process of investing in new tech markets, a common practice for big tech (see Reiff 2019). 'Big' social platforms also employ sophisticated corporate social responsibility departments that are responsible for developing seemingly charitable international projects which also effectively colonize global digital space. Free basics, one of Facebook's global programmes offering free internet only via Facebook (e.g. Facebook Lite and the Aquila drone) to developing countries, is an excellent example of this (Couldry and Mejias 2019a, 2019b; Solon 2017; Willems 2017). Similarly, Google for Education, a loss-leading and not-for-profit arm of Google, offers free educational products to educators, schools, students and to those in the educational sector which provides market access to the highly profitable edtech sector (Singer 2017; Sujon 2019a; Van Dijck et al. 2018).

Yet the current global social landscape is dominated by the rise of two clusters of 'platform empires': GAFA (Google, Amazon, Facebook and Apple) in the west, and BATX (Baidu, Alibabba, Tencent and Xiaom) in the east. These platform empires generate more profits than many countries and are often referred to as the planet's biggest firms. In addition, they invest in and control the digital communications infrastructures making up global networks, maintaining control to other players in the market. As Van Dijk et al. argue:

> … the unbridled growth of the Big Five's [GAFA and Microsoft] infrastructural platforms has left very little room for competitors to penetrate the core of the US-based ecosystem. Virtually all platforms outside of the Big Five constellation are dependent on the ecosystem's infrastructural information services. For instance, Airbnb embeds Google Maps as a standard feature in its interface; it also incorporates Facebook's and Google's identification services to "clear" hosts and guests. The Big Five profit most from the bourgeoning development of sectoral platforms and millions of websites and apps integrated with their basic services, enabling the collection of user data throughout the Web and app ecosystem. Digital disruptors like Spotify and Netflix are dependent upon the Big Five's infrastructure: Spotify's services run on Google Cloud, while Netflix relies on Amazon Web Services. (2018: 15)

Synchronized with this infrastructural business model is the development of monopsonies, similar to a monopoly (a market dominated by one seller), but instead referring to users and establishing 'markets with only one buyer' (Couldry and Mejias 2019a). Platforms do this by embedding user-generated content, such as contacts, communities, comments and shared moments, in non-transferable platform-specific formats. Patrick Barwise refers to the difficulty of leaving a platform because of users' personal investments in that platform, i.e. *switching costs*. The more users lose when they leave a platform, the higher the switching costs, and the stronger the platform's 'lock-in' strategy, both of which are used to prevent users from leaving (Barwise 2018: 29–30; cf. Peterson 2008).

We can see *monopsonies* in action through the ongoing struggles between 'new' alternative social media and 'big' corporate social players that dominate the digital landscape (Moore and Tambini 2018). Often 'new' and alternative social media emerge amidst great press expectations, followed by a virtual disappearance into oblivion, a phenomenon Zulli et al. (2020) refer to as the 'killer hype cycle'. While Zulli et al. focus on Mastodon as the 'new Twitter', and its promise to enable users to more meaningfully participate and a social platform they make, Mastodon is only one of many examples: there is also Triller, the new YouTube; Vero, once hoped to be the 'new' Instagram (BBC 2018; Newton 2018); Ello as the 'new' Facebook or Instagram (Caralucci 2014; Kim 2014; on replacing Instagram, see Zeller 2018); and Minds as the once 'new' anti-Facebook (Makauch and Pearson 2019; Matsakis 2018). Most of these alternative social media provide a fundamentally different social business model – one that is not driven by advertising or for-profit motives at all costs, as is the case with corporate social media (see Gehl 2015, 2018). In contrast, these alternative social media enable a more user-oriented kind of sociality, one that may require users to develop some tech skills, but in the process also allows those users to make meaningful decisions about the look and quality of their social sites (Gehl 2015, 2018; Zulli et al. 2020).

In sum, platformization is an important process transforming the purpose and function of social media sites. However, platformization is only visible from a computational lens, closely trained on the platform and data infrastructures of social media.

Conclusion: Social Media and Shifting Infrastructures

Christian Sandvig (2015) outlines the ways social media extend the culture industries, repackaging consumer culture rather than replacing them with new participatory structures:

> Social media appear to remove the bottleneck of the mass media system, allowing everyone to aspire to celebrity, or at least popularity. However, despite these appearances, social media have also now evolved into an elaborate system that selects social products and makes them popular based on obscure determinations of economic value. Social media platforms filter, censor, control, and train – and they may do so without the user's awareness.

Jean-Christophe Plantin et al., Helmond, Sandvig and Gillespie move beyond the screened interface of social media, furthering understanding of how social media function as platform infrastuctures. Based on a careful analysis of how both a platform and infrastructure analysis apply to the open web, Google Maps and Facebook, Plantin et al. argue that there are a number of shared characteristics. These include: embeddedness, a degree of invisibility, extensibility and broad coverage. In addition, Plantin et al.'s analysis shows that each approach provides an important and complementary lens for understanding these complex structures. Indeed, based on their analysis they argue that they found a 'platformization of infrastructures' or the extension of infrastructures across specific platforms (Plantin et al. 2016: 14).

In terms of 'the stack', social media may have first developed as small sites sitting on top of the content layer. However, as big tech and social media converge, they have had an impact on both ends of the layered architectures of the internet – including the internet infrastructure and the content layer of the web. As investors and major stakeholders in the material internet infrastructure of wired connections and undersea cables, social media have become global megastructures, and new players on the market are forced to increasingly rely on corporate giants like Facebook and Google. Here we see the largest social media platforms building, extending, shaping the physical layers of the internet as well as the content layers.

Telephone networks, the mobile web and mobile apps carve up and recentralize communicative networks. Platformization means social media sites extend their layered architectures, creating both 'parasite networks' and top-heavy layers, and as such the stack layers are infiltrated at every level.

From an infrastructural perspective, the Cloud, the Internet of Things (IoT) and social VR should only occupy the top content layer of the stack. Yet as this chapter has shown, the size and scope and interconnectedness of social media platforms are important, impacting on the material infrastructures of social media and networked technologies.

Questions and Activities

1 Activity: Draw a picture of the internet and then a picture of where you see social media in relation to the internet. What does this tell you about the internet and social media? What do you learn from visualizing the internet?
2 How does understanding the infrastructures of the internet help you understand social media?
3 What is a platform? Are all social media sites platforms? Explain.

Further Reading

Electronic Frontier Foundation. https://www.eff.org/

Helmond, A. 2015. The platformization of the web: making web data platform ready, *Social Media + Society,* September 30. http://journals.sagepub.com/doi/full/10.1177/2056305115603080, DOI: https://doi.org/10.1177/2056305115603080

Lessig, L. 2005. *Free Culture: How Big Media Uses Technology and the Law to Lock Down Culture.* Penguin. http://www.free-culture.cc/freecontent/

Plantin, J.C.; Lagoze, C.; Edwards, P. N.; Sandvig, C. 2016. Infrastructure studies meet platform studies in the age of Google and Facebook, *New Media and Society,* August 4. DOI: https://doi.org/10.1177/1461444816661553

Starosielski, N. 2015. *The Undersea Network.* Duke University Press.

PARTICIPATION, CULTURE AND PROTEST

Chapter Overview

Introduction: Media and the Long Promise of Public Participation	128
Thinking Through the Meaning of Participation	130
Participatory culture and creative agency	133
Participation and Play	135
The Participatory Turn in Culture and Politics	136
PostSecret	139
We're Not Really Strangers (WNRS)	140
2011 Egyptian revolution	142
Black Lives Matter	147
Conclusion: Making Sense of Participatory Culture	150
Questions and Activities	151
Further Reading	152

- Introduce the concepts of participation and participatory culture
- Better understand current thinking and debates on public participation and participatory culture, including debates around 'free labour' and 'the cute cat theory'
- Identify key elements of participation in four cases (PostSecret, We're Not Really Strangers, the 2011 Egyptian revolution and Black Lives Matter)

Introduction: Media and the Long Promise of Public Participation

Media are often understood as a mirror and a window, reflecting the world's hopes and anxieties as well as helping us see what is going on around us. One of the great hopes bundled up in new technologies is the promise of greater public participation, wider social inclusion and new levels of democratization. These are long promises, reappearing throughout history and often pinned to new and changing technologies. For example, Myron Gilmore, a renaissance scholar, argues that the introduction of movable type and other printing technologies opened 'new horizons' in the fourteenth and fifteenth centuries:

> The invention and development of printing with movable type brought about the most radical transformation in the conditions of intellectual life in the history of western civilization. It opened new horizons in education and in the communication of ideas. Its effects were sooner or later felt in every department of human activity. (Gilmore, cited in Eisenstein 1980: 28)

These kinds of optimistic hopes are also bundled up in early electronic technologies, promising tremendous potential to expand who can be included in the circulation of ideas through education and communication. In 1884, for example, the telephone was described as the 'youngest and most wonderful development of the means of communication', characterizing a 'high speed tool of civilization ... the symbol of natural efficiency and co-operation' (Casson, cited in Martin 1991: 3). In 1922, the radio was predicted to open up 'new vistas for democracy, education and personal enrichment ... like a gigantic school ... [with] a greater student body than all our universities put together' (Radio Broadcast in Alexander and Pal 1998: 1).

Later in the twentieth century, 'small media' like telephones, Xerox photocopies and home-recorded tape cassettes played a huge role in communicating information which could enable dissent as well as inspire new ideas. Dhiraj Murthy, associate professor and social media researcher, contextualizes Twitter's revolutionary impact in the 2011 Arab Uprising as one of the latest developments in a long history of communicating protest, political unrest and social change. For example, Ayotollah Khomeini, leader of the 1979

Iranian revolution, recorded his political philosophies on tape cassettes which were heard, re-recorded and shared by thousands of people, mobilizing the population and leading to the successful overthrow of the Shah of Iran (Mowlana 1979: 111, cited by Murthy 2013: 99). Like these other communication technologies, newer social technologies enable the flow of ideas across bigger spaces, faster and with greater ease. Murthy argues that Twitter is one of these (2013: 100).

All of these technologies reflected promises to enhance human connection, and the capacity to communicate across the harsh barriers of geographic distance and social status, saving people the time and effort required to speak – and listen – to those who might have otherwise gone unheard. These are only a few examples of the ways in which communication technologies have enabled niche communities to come together and for cultural and political participation. And there are many more. For example, riot girl, punk and, more recently, pussy riot have embraced a participatory ethos using zines, radio and music for political expression and activism, bringing together (sometimes global) communities in the process (e.g. Bryant 2014; Schilt 2003).

While 'participatory media' are far from new, Henry Jenkins' work on 'participatory culture' – lauded for its prescience and critiqued for its optimism and political reductionism – is important. Jenkins, who coined the term in 1992, helped provide a sharper vocabulary for making sense of a cultural moment where 'participation' reached a tipping point. As briefly discussed in Chapter 3, 'participatory culture' refers to a widespread increase in people's capacity for action in public life, for engagement with experts and authorities, as well as for collective connections (Jenkins 2006, 2009a; see also Chapter 1; cf. Baym 2018; Massanari 2015; Phillips and Milner 2017; Zuckerman 2015, etc.). It is worth noting that the 'participatory' ethos goes by many names (e.g. Web 2.0, media, user-generated content, social technologies, immersive or interactive media), and this is a likely sign of the growth of participatory media (Mandiberg 2012: 1–2).

Although the participatory turn is often aligned with the rise of social technologies and digital media, participation is not only about technologies. It is also about readiness and the capacity to participate, which are as much cultural as they are technological. Thus while digital media may appear to move hopes for greater social inclusion and democratization from a promise to a reality, it is an uneven process, one often shaped by gross social and economic inequalities. As Jenkins has come to argue in response to critiques, participation is an ideal to strive for, and we find ourselves in 'a *more* participatory culture' (Jenkins et al. 2016: 22, emphasis added; cf. Jenkins, in Jenkins and Carpentier 2013: 266).

This chapter examines the meaning of participation in relation to social technologies and the broader cultural moment related to the blurring of production and consumption in creative labour, as seen in popular culture (PostSecret and We Were Never Really Strangers) and social movements (Egyptian revolution 2011 and Black Lives Matter). In addition, this chapter also introduces debates around 'free labour' associated with the blurring of consumption and production associated with social media. Politics and culture also become blurred in the media environment, and the 'cute cat theory' is introduced to better contextualize how popular culture and political mobilization contribute to social and political action. This chapter then examines participation and participatory culture, providing conceptual tools for making sense of their complexities in the context of networked media and social technologies.

Thinking Through the Meaning of Participation

As Darin Barney, political theorist and technology specialist, and his colleagues argue, 'participation is not a quality added to some other thing or activity, not one hailing process among others, *but a condition that is constitutive of the social itself*' (2016: x, emphasis added). Indeed, fully understanding participation means incorporating power (see Chapter 3) and the many ways we can make sense of the 'social' (see Chapter 4). Understanding participation means understanding how people are able to come together, in singular and collective formations, as well as what they are able to do in those formations. This applies to individual and collective agency, and is about people's '*capability of doing things*' (Giddens 1984: 9, emphasis added). In this way, participation necessarily implies agency as the individual capacity to do things, across local, collective and sometimes public levels.

Bucy and Gregson (2001: 358) define 'media participation' as any format, venue, programme that enables discussions or interaction with others, including 'net activism', donating, or any kind of effort 'which may contribute to the psychological feeling of being engaged'. Nico Carpentier (2011), a prolific thinker on media and power, calls for a much more critical take on participation. For example, drawing from a long line of political theorists, Carpentier makes an important distinction between maximal and minimal forms of participation based in part on who controls the process and outcome. For example, television programmes with live audiences may appear to be participatory, but as the network producers control how and when audiences participate, as well as the overall production, Carpentier argues this is only minimalist participation. Maximalist forms of participation occur where 'the power relations [between] media professionals and non-privileged groups are balanced', in contrast to minimalist forms of participation, where 'media professionals [rather than amateur or ordinary person] retain strong control over process and outcome' (2016: 84; cf. Carpentier 2011: 69). In other words, maximal or full participation must also include 'equal decision making powers' made visible in both production processes and procedures, as well as any material or symbolic outcomes. On the other end of the spectrum, Carpentier argues minimalist forms of participation do not involve decision making, although they might include representation and involvement. This spectrum between maximalist and minimalist forms of participation builds on the distinction between content participation (mostly representation) and structural participation (representation + decision making powers), which is a useful way to distinguish between superficial and meaningful participation (2011: 68–69).

Digital and social media have blurred the lines between those who make media and those who consume media, and this has raised numerous debates about what makes meaningful participation, especially regarding the line between user exploitation and expression. (See Box 6.1 for a synopsis of these debates.)

Box 6.1 — Debating user-generated content: Free labour or creative agency?

User-generated content (UGC), a term for any kind of content created by internet and digital media users, reconfigured the relationship between professional content makers and amateur creators. While social media platforms like YouTube and Facebook were especially adept at monetizing this content, many creators, like the fandoms that Henry Jenkins wrote about (1992, 2006), embraced UGC as a new creative outlet for their passions (see also Hjorth and Hinton 2019).

For Axel Bruns (2008), UGC on digital sites like YouTube, Flickr, Wikipedia and The Sims show the erasure of boundaries between producers and consumers, as consumers become content producers. In other words, the rise of user-generated content disrupts cycles of cultural production from the more linear model characteristic of the twentieth century (see Figure 6.1), to a hybrid model where the 'produser' is both consumer and producer in the digital age (see Figure 6.2)

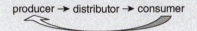

Figure 6.1 Industrial production value chain

Source: Bruns (2008)

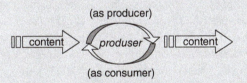

Figure 6.2 Produser as hybrid producer/consumer in individual UGC value chain

Source: Bruns (2008)

While both of these models simplify the value chain, they illustrate a shift not only in the interactions between producers and consumers, but also in the economics of cultural production. As Trebor Scholz (2013) has argued, digital networks are both 'playground and factory'. It is at this point that the debate about labour and participation gets fierce.

On one side, most often attributed to Jenkins, many creative producers, like fans, do what they do in opposition to corporate culture, namely aiming for non-commercial activities in the creative industries (2006, 2013 with Carpentier; see also Hills 2002). Creativity is powerful, connective and affords the freedom of agency as well as a profound feeling of engagement with others (e.g. Banet-Weiser et al. 2014; Frieling and Grays 2008; Gauntlett 2011; Massaneri 2015).

(Continued)

Yet, for many others, the blurring of boundaries between consumers and producers means that some people get paid and others do not, and some people make profits from the work of others. Instead of a radical break with commercialism, we see new kinds of immaterial or 'free labour' in many digital forms (e.g. chat, moderation, web design, multimedia content, content curation, friend or follower connections, views, clicks, likes) (Fuchs 2017; Jarrett 2016; Scholz 2013; Terranova 2000, 2013). Looking at the ways in which users have been exploited, and creative work is increasingly precarious *and* expropriated for commercial gain, opens up serious critiques of participatory culture as a 'mutation' rather than a break from the 'widespread cultural and economic logic' of advanced capitalism (Terranova 2000: 54). Indeed, as radical labour theorist Tiziana Terranova argues:

> The Internet does not automatically turn every user into an active producer, and every worker into a creative subject. The process whereby production and consumption are reconfigured within the category of free labor signals the unfolding of a different (rather than completely new) logic of value … [and] the provision of "free labor," as we will see later, is a fundamental moment in the creation of value in the digital economies. (2000: 35–36)

Terranova does contextualize the free labour phenomenon within a longer history, noting that people have long committed their 'free' time and energy to the styles, fashions, music, stories and other subcultural vestiges before they become co-opted by popular culture and drive profit margins of the cultural industries. Yet Terranova also notes that free labour has become 'common business sense', mirrored by a similar rise in 'voluntary work, unpaid work, underpaid work and a growing gap' between the precarious and the wealthy (2013: 52). Many have spoken of an upwards trend in precarious labour, such as the aspirational and mostly unpaid labour of fashion influencers (Duffy 2017), the underpaid work of Amazon Turk workers (Aytes 2013), fandoms as free publicity (De Kosnik 2013), the underpaid contract work of content moderators across all social platforms (Gillespie 2018a), as well as across the creative sectors more broadly (Jarrett 2016). Indeed, some have gone so far as to classify genres of labour (e.g. 'natural labour of sociality', 'wage labour', 'free labour' and 'labour of struggle'; Qui 2018), thereby illustrating that the exploitation and empowerment or creativity and free labour frameworks aren't quite enough to explain 'participation'.

In an ambitious project to document 'social media entertainment' (SME) as an emerging 'proto-industry', Stuart Cunningham and David Craig (2019) interviewed approximately 50 content creators, along with many others within SME. Based on this extensive research and listening to creators themselves, they argue that 'creator labour' as a broad category for creative work and expression is 'both empowered and precarious' (Cunningham and Craig 2019: 65). While they don't resolve the debate around value, labour and creative agency with one definitive answer, they do provide a way forward that balances the tensions around participation and participatory labour, including the dynamics of professional and amateur creators working within a competitive landscape encouraging both entrepreneurialism and precarity.

Along with the debates on 'free' labour, the differences between minimal and maximalist participation are helpful foundations for making sense of the meaning of participation.

Nancy Baym, leading internet scholar, like others before her, picks up on the wide breadth of participation, posing the question: 'participation in what?' For Baym, part of the term's complexity is that it also presumes:

> ... participation in *something*, and when we take for granted what it is that people are participating in without identifying or interrogating it, we find ourselves talking in terms of media and fans rather than culture and life ... People have always been participating; that's how culture continues. (Baym in Banet-Weiser et al. 2014: 1079–1080; cf. Jenkins and Carpentier 2013: 272–74)

Thus, participation is incomplete without a broader context. While some may try to fix participation to a broader something like politics, culture, capitalism or community, for example, its conceptual flexibility is important, and also frequently controversial. Key debates aim to get at the heart of what participation means whether we are seeing the expansion of people's creative potential or the greater capitalist exploitation. These debates position participation very differently, and are introduced below.

Participatory culture and creative agency

From status updates to blogging, it is easier than it has ever been to create and share content with those we know and those we don't. Both Pokémon Go and memes, introduced in Chapter 1, highlight the contradictory nature of community participation, each of which is addressed in turn below. Many players revelled in the engaging and interactive feel of Pokémon Go, which helped them forge new affinities and impromptu collectivities. Pokémon Go may not have involved creation of content, but it did inspire a 'feeling of being engaged' and connected with others, which are important aspects enabling a more participatory culture (Bucy and Gregson 2001; Hjorth and Jiminez 2019; Hjorth and Richardson 2017). Yet others question if this kind of participation is meaningful, regardless of enthusiastic user reports, because Pokémon Go is owned by a major tech giant (Google) that profits from the data generated by players who have no say in what happens to those data.

Memes and other 'small acts of engagement' (see Chapter 1 and 3), on the other hand, require very low investment from users, are easily circulated across platforms and carry rich cultural meanings. For most users, memes are about relatability and symbolic connection to others rather than individual ownership of content. Despite the folkloric role of memes in enabling 'public conversations' (Phillips and Milner 2017), they can also be used to attract users to sites (e.g. Reddit, Imgur, Facebook, Twitter, KnowYourMeme, I Can Haz Cheezeburger). In addition, as Crystal Abidin has found, meme factories coordinate meme production as a kind of 'strategic calculation to obtain virality or activate a call to arms' (2020: 2). As a result of these kinds of monetization, memes incorporate a commodifying logic rather as well as their folkloric roots and community building capacities (see Bucher 2018b, discussed in Chapter 4). Both memes and Pokémon Go raise longstanding questions around what participation actually means, especially in relation to community, agency and the changing nature of creative labour.

In both cases, there is greater potential for creative production and it is this potential which is at the heart of 'participatory culture'. As a *media* term, participatory culture is distinct from the public sphere[1] (Habermas et al. 1974 [1964]; Lunt and Livingstone 2013) and public or citizen media (c.f. Carpentier 2011: 17; Glasser 1999; Voakes 2004). Participatory culture more accurately captures users' active engagement with television and media texts and what this means for public engagement than any of these other concepts (Jenkins 1992). In my view, participatory culture corresponds closely with the active audience tradition, especially as Jenkins wanted to counter dominant accounts of fans as passive spectators and consumers, with evidence that media consumers are also active agents (Jenkins 1992, 2006, 2009a). For Jenkins, this does not exclude accounts of fans as consumers (Hills 2002; Sandvoss 2005) or as creators, both of whom are subject to the neoliberal logic of entrepreneurialism (e.g. Cunningham and Craig 2019: 77–79; Duffy 2017).

The concept of participatory culture has been hugely influential in media, communications, and cultural studies, particularly from the mid-2000s, and does capture a cultural shift in how we understand systems of cultural production and changing relationships to and with media. Prior to this moment in media studies, Carpentier (2016) argues that there have been two major disciplinary approaches to participation. The first of these is the sociological approach, which tends to be much broader, uses a broad definition of participation (e.g. media consumption, fandoms, audience interpretation) and is more often taken up in media, cultural studies and reception studies (2016: 71). The second approach draws from political science and political communication, and tends to be more restrictive, offering a narrower definition of participation directly related to political or governing processes and decision-making powers (Carpentier 2016: 71–72; see also Bucy and Gregson 2001).

The logic of 'participatory culture' also draws from a broad range of scholarship. For example, David Gauntlett, well known for his work on creativity and digital cultures, notes that we have shifted from a 'sit-back-and-be-told culture' defined by the television and the factory of the twentieth century to a 'making-and-doing' culture defined by the creativity afforded through craft and digital tools in the twenty-first century (2010, 2011). Lawrence Lessig, a Harvard law professor and long-time advocate of free information, argues that the twentieth century brought in a proprietary 'read only' culture shaped by the introduction of recorded music in 1906 (2008: 24–28) and exacerbated by broadcast and mass technologies. This proprietary, 'read only' culture meant that cultural artefacts like TV programmes, books and records could not be easily adapted, yet all of these were displaced by the shift to 'read write' technologies

---

1 The public sphere, coined by Habermas in 1964, is 'a realm of our social life in which something approaching public opinion can be formed. Access is guaranteed to all citizens. A portion of the public sphere *comes into being in every conversation in which private individuals assemble to form a public body*' (Habermas et al. 1974 [1964]: 49). Focusing more on the formation of public opinion, Habermas's work provided a historical account of the transformation of the public, from a representation of absolute authority (e.g. the king's body) to the collective sharing of information enabling the formation of rational public opinions. For more on the public sphere, see Calhoun (1992); Curran (1991); Fraser (1990); Lunt and Livingstone (2013).

like writable CDs, home video taping and other digital technologies enabling users to record their contributions (2008: 28–33). For Lessig, 'read write' technologies marked a profound cultural shift, where amateurs could more easily create, remix, mash up and share their creations – all of which are crucial elements for an enriched public life. The free flow of ideas and participatory interaction in and through music, art, literature, information, news, public critique and social interaction, promise to nourish a rich public life based on the participation of many – without which, Lessig argues, the commons and public culture may starve.

Jenkins, Gauntlett and Lessig look at the massification of creative agency as an important cultural shift, one that prioritizes human agency in the intersections between culture, technologies and social action. For these thinkers, people are more able to do the things that matter to them via digital and social media. As Trebor Scholz argues, 'the internet has become a simple-to-join, anyone-can-play system' opening up new vistas for engagement and exploitation (2013: 1). This is not to say that this approach 'ignore[s] ownership, capitalism and class' (Fuchs 2017: 68); rather it tends to focus on how media technologies can be used creatively and playfully to shape individual experiences and enrich cultures.

At the same time, many others have wrestled with the implications of user-generated content on platforms that enable peer production and individual creativity – thus providing greater opportunities for ordinary people to contribute to and profit from cultural production. Despite this openness, there are still issues around diversity and homogeneity. For example, although there may be increased opportunities for more people to become cultural producers, early adopters tend to be 'disproportionately white, male, middle class and college educated' (Jenkins 2006: 23) – as reflected in the top creators on social media (see Chapter 9), and the overwhelming whiteness of big tech (e.g. Google's infamous 'anti-diversity' memo; Molteni and Rogers 2017). For Jenkins, fan and creator cultures can also provide deep insights into cultural innovations and help 'define the public culture of the future' (2006: 24). In many ways, social media have also enabled greater diversity facilitating spaces for self-expression, identity building and community formation. Take, for example, the ways drag communities have come together on Facebook (Lingel 2017), and the formation of what André Brock (2020) calls 'Black Twitter', where Black identity is discursively shared and constituted.

All of these factors contribute to the complexity of 'participation', and it is important to understand that participation can be equally empowering and exploitative. It is certain that the participatory turn has reshaped cultural production in ways we are still coming to terms with (e.g. see 'social media entertainment' in Cunningham and Craig 2019; or 'meme factories' in Abidin 2020). As we know from Chapters 1 and 2, the social media landscape is dominated by big players who are able to easily profit from and exploit others, but this does not exclude agency, creativity or playful engagement.

Participation and Play

Play is a crucial factor for understanding participatory culture, and social media engagement as well as media cultures more broadly. Play has always been important, but its role in engaging people in their relationships with media is louder than ever. Roger Silverstone, preeminent and founding British media scholar, describes the connections between media, play and participation:

> Play is central, so it seems, to media experience ... Play involves ... *mutual participation* ... [and] enables the exploration of the tissue boundary between fantasy and reality, between the real and the imagined, between the self and other. In play we have a licence to explore both our selves and our society. In play *we investigate culture but we also create it.* (1999: 63–64, emphasis added)

Silverstone beautifully articulates the centrality of play for our media experiences, and also articulates the role of play as a foundation from which we engage others, texts, ideas and 'the tissue boundary between fantasy and reality', between self and society. Silverstone's point, that play is a fundamental factor for the exploration and creation of culture, resonates with Jenkins' work on fan cultures. In particular, it is *play* that inspires affective and symbolic connection through the creation, circulation and consumption of digital and cultural artefacts.

Many others have also examined the importance of play. For example, Milner argues that 'mimetic media are a lingua franca for digitally mediated participation' (2016: 7). Phillips and Milner (2017) also examine the role of identity play as a crucial factor in the generation and exchange of memes. For Hjorth and Hinton (2019: 61), play is 'inherently paradoxical' as it is about both 'resistance and submission, reactive and unimaginative experiences'. Adrienne Massanari argues that play is the 'primary mode by which Reddit culture is enacted' at first engaging users before enrolling them through a sense of shared interests and enjoyment (2015: 22). In my own work on Google Cardboard, play disrupts routines and sometimes social expectations, inspiring new insights and a sense of affinity with others (Sujon 2019a). Jenkins, of course, positions play as the basis for learning and skill development, as well political engagement and social connection (Jenkins 2006: 23). All of these scholars situate play as a central factor in mediated experience, one that both entices and exhilarates, and most importantly mobilizes participation and engagement through and across culture, politics, community and sociality. Through select case studies, the next section looks more closely at the participatory turn.

The Participatory Turn in Culture and Politics

Many have moved beyond the idea of one 'participatory culture', repositioning it as a participatory turn (e.g. Couldry and Jenkins 2014) or condition (e.g. Barney et al. 2016). As previously introduced in Chapter 3, Henry Jenkins' original concept of 'participatory culture' refers to a decrease in barriers for artistic and civic expression. This concept has matured from this early conceptualization, and the next section incorporates examples from popular culture and wide ranging political protests – both of which illustrate public participation and community building. While this section does differentiate between culture and politics, some, like Ethan Zuckerman, media scholar and activist, would argue that culture and politics are intimately connected on social media. (See Box 6.2 on the 'cute cat theory', which furthers this argument.)

Box 6.2 Cute cat theory

One particularly interesting theory of the ways participatory technologies are opening up 'new space for political discourse', as well as weaving play and politics in compelling ways, is Ethan Zuckerman's 'cute cat theory' of political activism (2015 [2013]). Zuckerman, an inspiring public intellectual who is the Director for MIT's Center for Civic Media and co-founder of media advocacy group 'Global Voices', argues that the cute cat theory shows that 'Internet tools designed to let ordinary consumers publish non-political content are often useful for activists' because they are robust, popular and difficult to censor (2015 [2013]).

In other words, ordinary tools like Facebook, Twitter or Daily Motion (a French video-sharing site) are strong enough to withstand millions (if not billions) of users, many of whom are posting, sharing, clicking on and viewing whatever sparks their interests, including bits of popular culture like cute cat videos. As we can see in cases like the Tunisian use of Daily Motion to challenge the Ben Ali government (ca. 2004–2007), or in attempts to resist censorship on Chinese social media sites like Weibo, activists use popular sites to communicate and share info. Tunisian and Chinese governments reacted to protest by shutting down popular sites like Daily Motion, Twitter and Weibo (Zuckerman 2015 [2013]; see also Murthy 2013), which led to two unintended consequences. First, it radicalized the majority of non-activists who were more interested in sharing cute cat videos and who were all of a sudden unable to post cute cats or popular content. Second, it encouraged people to skill up their digital communications knowledge, such as learning how to use VPNs and seeking out creative ways to code and circumvent censors, internet blackouts or site blockages (Zuckerman 2015 [2013]; Murthy 2013). Both of these consequences politicized the population, ultimately widening political information networks, and empowering the population in unforeseen ways. Zuckerman argues that humour and participation are important in these processes:

> Examining the successful use of consumer tools for activism in Tunisia and China suggests that resilience to censorship may be a less important benefit than the *ability to leverage participation, remix and humor to spread activist content to wide audiences.* (2015 [2013], emphasis added).

In essence, Zuckerman's cute cat theory points to a blurring between play, popular culture and politics, suggesting that the circulation of cute cats on digital platforms is a good thermometer for the strength and potential efficacy of political networks. While the cute cat theory points to ways in which popular culture and politics are connected, participatory culture is often addressed in either/or terms so Zuckerman's theory is an excellent reminder to consider the ways both culture and politics are connected.

Perhaps by drawing from some of the most enthusiastic groups on digital social media, the roots of participatory culture are necessarily optimistic. From early accounts tracing the global circulation of proto-memes (e.g. 'Bert is Evil') and many amazing accounts of dedicated fans using digital media in innovative and fascinating ways, Jenkins explores some of the most inspiring aspects of participatory culture. It is important to recognize this optimism and look at the potential of digital culture, bearing in mind that technologies are not a quick fix and that the long promises of participation and democratization are overblown. In other words, social media, *on their own*, will never enable or disable greater participation, instead requiring active support and engagement. However, it is worth taking a closer look at participation 'as a governing concept' for digital culture (Jenkins 2006: 169; Jenkins and Carpentier 2013; Jenkins et al. 2016). While this concept may have roots in fandoms, there are many other illustrations, such as through the reshaping of pathways from amateur to celebrity (Abidin 2018; Cunningham and Craig 2019; Duffy 2017), mobile media and art (Hjorth and Hinton 2019), or alternative social media like Mastodon (Gehl 2015; Zulli et al. 2020; see also Chapter 3).

There are also times where participation involves low-level activities, like the creation or even just circulation of memes, clicks, likes, views and shares, for example. These can be about enacting popular culture or can be acts of resistance and political expression. Small acts of engagement (see Chapter 3) enabling people to connect to and participate in larger social movements or political actions. For example, from early Zapatista communiques shared on BBSs in the early 1990s up to the Extinction Rebellion protests of 2018–2020, networked and social media have become essential for social and political movements. And there are many more examples, such as #everydaysexism, #Occupy, #TahirSquare, #UmbrellaRevolution, #Ferguson, #ICantBreathe, #MeToo, #IdleNoMore, #HongKong, #SayHerName, and so on (see Jackson et al. 2020). Networked and social media are impacting on how people connect, how they communicate and how they mobilize. Some argue that politics and social movements are more personalized than they have ever been, with a noticeable blurring between formal and everyday political spheres (Gerbaudo 2017: 136; Highfield 2016).

This chapter considers four examples from across a spectrum of genres. The first of these is Frank Warren's community art project called PostSecret, the second is Koreen Odiney's card game and social media accounts We're Not Really Strangers (WNRS). These two examples are both community-oriented projects, as well as privately owned American enterprises. Both aim to connect people and, in the process, surface serious experiences of troubling loneliness and struggles with mental health. Both have also surged in popularity, quickly becoming globally networked in a relatively short period of time. Both manifest the tensions between community and commercialism, so characteristic of social media. The next two cases focus more directly on political protest and social movements. The first of these is the Egyptian revolution of 2011, which although well documented, established important precedents for how we can understand social media and political mobilization. The fourth case, Black Lives Matter, began in the US and has evolved into a sustained and global movement. Both of these provide important illustrations of how social media can help make dissent visible, enabling solidarities and mobilizing political change. Both are also powerful examples of networked participation.

PostSecret

PostSecret (see Figure 6.3) describes itself as 'an ongoing community mail art project, created by Frank Warren, in which people mail their secrets anonymously on a homemade postcard' (https://post--secret-blog.tumblr.com/).

Figure 6.3 'PostSecret' home page

Source: https://postsecret.com/, January 5, 2020, reprinted with permission from Frank Warren

PostSecret began in 2004, when Frank Warren distributed 300 postcards to strangers by leaving them around his neighbourhood, in coffee shops, and by handing them to those passing by (Warren 2012). Those postcards, like the one in Figure 6.3, invited people to participate in a community art project by mailing in a secret, any kind of secret, on a post-card. Not only did Warren receive many responses, from many locations, but the postcards also included rich kinds of content and a great variety of secrets. From PostSecret's humble beginnings, it has grown as a community and now has a notable media presence. The PostSecret blog has had over 800 million visitors, their Facebook page has over 1.6 million likes, on Twitter they have 463.8 thousand followers, with nearly the same on Instagram (January 2020). In addition, Warren has a YouTube channel with almost ten thousand subscribers, featuring many videos of events, exhibits, postcard montages of secrets people have anonymously sent in, all with hundreds of thousands of views. Warren has also published six PostSecret books, launched two apps and spoken at hundreds of live events, which many participants describe as life-saving moments of acceptance and belonging.

The secrets people send in are a particular kind of user-generated content: part confession, part soulful expression and part identity play. PostSecret is a compelling case of networked community for a number of reasons. First, it crowdsources *anonymous* user-generated content, capturing the logic of participatory media across analog and digital media. In this way, it was a leader in terms of anonymous social media, inspiring a number of apps and services whose unique selling point (USP) is (or was) anonymous exchange (e.g. Whisper 2012–, Ask.FM 2010–, YikYak 2014–2017). Second, PostSecret illustrates a global networked community, one that is both on and offline, traversing many platforms with transmedia content (e.g. blog, website, Tumblr, Facebook, YouTube, Twitter, Instagram, Reddit, books, live events, art exhibits). Notably, and in line with the age of this community, PostSecret has migrated online along with its members rather than originating there. Third, although Warren does generate income from the publication and circulation of user-generated secrets, all of PostSecret's social media sites are advertising free. In this way, Warren aims to honour and maintain PostSecret's community ethos and protect users' data.

In 2011, Warren launched a PostSecret iPhone app, which cost $1.99 to download, and which quickly leapt to the top of the US best-selling app list. Yet despite this success, the app was plagued with bullying, pornography and violent threats. While abuse is a problem for all social media platforms, it has been particularly prevalent in anonymous apps (e.g. Kik, Ask. FM, Whisper and PostSecret), even leading to the closure of location-based anonymous app YikYak in 2017 (Kobie 2016; Safranova 2017). Warren attributes the downfall of the PostSecret app to deliberate trolling, naming Tiger Text, the 'app for spies and cheaters' (now called TigerConnect), as the primary perpetrator, which meant the PostSecret community was 'no longer a safe place to share secrets' (2014: 36; cf. Schaffer 2014; see also VanderMay 2014).

Despite this setback PostSecret is a highly successful and participatory community, providing an outlet for millions of people to share, read, engage and create 'secrets'. Many of the hundreds and thousands of secrets posted to Warren and shared online tell painful stories of depression, isolation and other struggles with mental health. In response to this, Warren and his PostSecret community have raised over $1 million dollars for suicide prevention, and community members have set up the largest international suicide prevention wiki (Golbeck 2014). PostSecret is not just a forum for anonymous public participation, it is also a safe space for personal expression.

We're Not Really Strangers (WNRS)

Beginning as a kind of photographic diary, former model Koreen Odiney began We're Not Really Strangers around 2016 (Witte 2018). Odiney describes WNRS's overall aims as 'To empower meaningful connections. To make us feel less alone. To broaden our empathy. To reconnect with us with ourselves' (Furlong-Mitchell 2019). These aims are achieved through an Instagram community, and a purpose-driven card game, that sits at the centre of what Odiney also sees as a movement, and a community (https://www.werenotreallystrangers.com/).

The WNRS Instagram account features a mix of photos of cards, signs, windows, and the sides of buildings with uplifting and self-affirming slogans photoshopped onto them. For example, the slogans say things like 'Stop dropping hints, speak your truth' and 'You can mute people in real life too. It's called boundaries' (2020). Thus, WNRS captures a particular urban visual aesthetic interspersed with encouraging images assuring people to be clear, strong and true. In this way, WNRS aims to build a supportive community where people share what it means to be genuine in a difficult world.

Odiney aims to reinvigorate human connection by providing a series of questions on WNRS cards featuring probing questions. Odiney claims to have developed these questions based on hundreds of street interviews, which led her to believe that anyone could develop a connection with anyone else, even strangers. Thus, the WNRS cards feature carefully crafted questions intended to prompt intimate and meaningful exchange. (See Figure 6.4 for an example of some of the cards.)

Figure 6.4 We're Not Really Strangers – a sample of the cards

Source: reprinted with permission from WNRS, 2020

WNRS is a younger and fairly small case, yet it is also growing. Two million followers on Instagram, 79 thousand followers on Twitter and 4.65 thousand followers on Facebook (August 2020). In addition to growing its online community, WNRS has also partnered with Bumble. For Odiney, Bumble focuses on building all kinds of relationships rather than just romantic ones. This can be seen in some of Bumble's other projects such as 'Bumble BFF, its friend-finding platform, and Bumble Bizz, for professional networking' all of which align with WNRS's key aims (Chavez 2019). As Odiney states, 'one connection can change the course of your life and I know that Bumble facilitates millions of new connections every week' (Chavez 2019).

Yet aside from its collaboration with Bumble, WNRS is not entirely unique, as a number of other similar games are appearing on the market, such as Uncurated, Big Talk, SoCards, We Connect Cards and Known Project – all games that 'are often pitched as antidotes to loneliness and isolation and facilitators of self-discovery and personal growth' (DeShong

2020).[2] WNRS brings together an online community interested in human connection and meaningful interaction. Odiney, an Instagram model herself, may just be trying to expand her brand and monetize a profitable online trend. Yet she often shares personal stories about her own struggles with anxiety and depression, offering an outlet and platform for those who relate. Thus, even if Odiney is motivated by capitalizing on her community, many have benefited from her openness, and the intimate connections enabled through WNRS.

2011 Egyptian revolution

For many social movements, Twitter appears to be especially central, perhaps because it is one of the easier platforms to collect data from, explaining why it is one of the dominant social media sites in the literature. (See Box 6.3 for an overview of Twitter as a platform.)

Box 6.3 Introducing Twitter

Founded in March 2006 by Jack Dorsey, Evan Williams, Biz Stone and Noah Glass, Twitter was built on a 'new media coding culture', SMS communications, dispatch enthusiasm and radio scanners, and its first iteration began as 'Twttr' – a short communication service intended to be used by friends in urban settings (Rogers 2014: x). Dorsey refers to Twitter's early history as part of a broader set of 'squawk media' technologies found in the culture of bicycle couriers, truck drivers, emergency services, police, fire trucks and citizen band radio, yet also 'a new medium in itself, [as] a public instant messaging system' (Rogers 2014: x). Indeed, Jack Dorsey's first ever Tweet (see Figure 6.5 below) refers to 'Twttr':

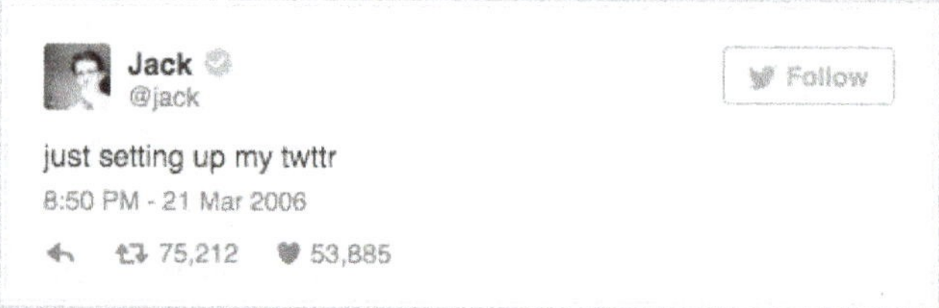

Jack ☑
@jack

Follow

just setting up my twttr
8:50 PM - 21 Mar 2006

↩ ↻ 75,212 ♥ 53,885

Figure 6.5 Jack Dorsey's first tweet

Source: Connolly (2016)

---

2 It is worth noting Cards Against Humanity (CAH) is an early player in this growing market, except this game aims to provide a 'free party game for horrible people'. CAH launched a Kickstarter campaign in 2010, raising $15,000 in 2011 and successfully launching the game, while reaching an almost cult-like status on social sites like Reddit and Imgur (Kimball 2012). Notably, Scott Thomas, one of CAH's founders, was the design director for Obama's 2008 presidential campaign (Kimball 2012). As well, CAH is widely known for investing thousands in charitable causes, such as investing in over 300 public school programmes, sponsoring college scholarships, and campaigning against Trump's 'border wall' amongst others. At the same time, CAH has also sold literal boxes of sh*t, raised $100,000 to dig a giant hole and paid to advertise a potato during the Super Bowl (Puglise 2016).

As of October 2019, Twitter has 330 million global monthly active users, almost half of which are based in the United States (Statista, https://www.statista.com/statistics/242606/number-of-active-twitter-users-in-selected-countries/). Although Twitter may be one of the smaller platforms in terms of its reach, it is influential in the social media landscape, and an increasingly important source for legacy media and journalists.

In terms of background, several of Twitter's founders have some interesting connections in the social technology landscape. For example, Evan Williams created Blogger in 1999, reaching a million users by 2003 when it was then purchased by Google (boing boing 2017; Meyer 2016). Williams went on to co-found Odeo, a podcasting platform, with fellow Googler Biz Stone, in 2004. After his work with fellow Twitter co-founders in 2006, Williams eventually founded Medium.com, a quality publishing platform launched in 2012 (Meyer 2016). Stone has also co-founded Jelly and acts as a special advisor at Pinterest. The founders of Twitter were influential in California's Silicon Valley, and have had huge entrepreneurial success in the world of big tech.

Twitter is one of the key microblogging sites, and its competitors include Jaiku, tumblr, Plurk and Squeelr, as well as alternatives like Mastodon and Gab (Murthy 2013: 8–9; Zulli et al. 2020). Like many other social media sites in the platform era, Twitter offers a series of services and has bought a number of competing apps. Some of its key services and innovations include the following:

- promoted tweets, trends, profiles (2010)
- self-service advertising (2012)
- Tweetdeck (acquisition, 2011)
- Vine (2013–2016, RIP)
- Gnip, NanoMedia, SnappyTV, TapCommerce, CardSpring (acquisition 2014)
- Promoted Video and Fabric launched, partnership with IBM (2014)
- Periscope, ZipDial, Niche, TellApart (acquisition 2015)
- launched direct messages, promoted video, highlights, moments, hearts, Twitter brand hub, polls (2015) (source: https://about.twitter.com/company/press/milestones, January 2020).

Twitter generates profits via advertising, and aims to clearly mark advertising content through promoted tweets, promoted accounts and promoted trends along with sophisticated business and advertising support (https://business.twitter.com/en/solutions/twitter-ads.html, January 2020).

While Twitter provides one of many sites for networked publics, it has also developed a number of features based on user innovations, such as both the @ and # features. The @ feature allows users to directly tag other users, whether they are known to that user or not. The # feature allows users to join in public conversation around any topics, trends, events or other things people might be discussing. Many have commented on Twitter's unique propensity for information sharing, in that it provides 'an awareness system that allows for immediate, fast and widespread dissemination of information' (Ausserhoffer and Mareider 2013: 306).

The Arab Spring consisted of a wide range of anti-government movements across the Middle East in 2010–2011, including the: Jasmine Revolution (Tunisia), the Egypt Uprising of 2011, the Yemen Uprising of 2011–12, the Libya Revolt of 2011 and the Syria Uprising of 2011–12 (Editors of Encyclopedia Britannica 2019a, 2019b). These movements have come to be synonymous with the social media revolution, as Paolo Gerbaudo, leading political sociologist specializing in digital activism, explains below:

> With the explosion of the Arab Spring in the early months of 2011, pundits, journalists, and academics competed in coining expressions such as 'Twitter revolution', 'Wiki-revolution' and 'Revolution 2.0' to emphasise the nexus between digital media and protest—a signature of contemporary movements. (2017: 135)

Even while all of these movements may have shared social media as a shared space mobilizing and for communicating with Western media, they involve many different countries with different political contexts and historical circumstances. Focusing only on the case of Egypt, there are many competing accounts and details which make it difficult to turn to one overall account. As a starting point, and to provide some context, see Box 6.4: Brief Timeline of the Egyptian Revolution, which presents a widely agreed upon overview of key moments.

Box 6.4   Brief timeline of the Egyptian revolution

- **June 6, 2010:** Khaled Said dies after brutal police beating in police custody. Pictures of Said were shared widely on the internet. Wael Ghonim created a Facebook Page shortly after Said's death in Said's honour, called 'We are all Khaled Said'.
- **December 17, 2010**: After being fined and having his vegetable cart taken by police, Mohammed Bouazizi, sets himself ablaze in protest of police brutality, injustice and corruption in Sidi Bouzid, Tunisia. The incident is widely publicized, spurring many into action and sparking widespread protests across the Arab region. Bouazizi dies.
- **January 14, 2011**: Tunisian president Zine El Abidine Ben Ali resigns and flees to Saudi Arabia.
- **January 25, 2011**: The first coordinated mass protests are held in Tahrir Square in Cairo, Egypt. 12,000 were arrested.
- **January 28, 2011**: Mubarak government issues five-day internet blackout.
- **February 2011**: Millions of protestors in several predominantly Muslim countries stage the 'Days of Rage' protests to oppose authoritarian governments and push for democratic reforms.

- **February 11, 2011**: Egypt's president, Hosni Mubarak, in power from 1981 amidst long-standing claims of electoral rigging and government corruption, steps down and flees Egypt.
- **March 15, 2011**: Pro-democracy protests begin in Syria.

Source: adapted from Associated Press, 2012, Hosni Mubarak's Rule and Downfall, *Guardian*, June 2, https://www.theguardian.com/world/2012/jun/02/hosni-mubarak-rule-downfall-timeline; BBC News. 2019. Egypt Timeline, https://www.bbc.co.uk/news/world-africa-13315719; history.com editors 2019, https://www.history.com/topics/middle-east/arab-spring

Like the protests in Tunisia and across the Middle East, the Egyptian revolution was grounded in a much longer history of mass inequality, government corruption and police brutality. While many debate the role of the internet and social media in the protests sweeping the Arab region in the Arab Spring, it is clear that these social movements emerged from difficult historical contexts, reaching a pinnacle in 2011. Following the overthrow of both the Tunisian and Egyptian presidents in January 2011, many celebrated the role of Twitter and Facebook in this process, to the extent that one Egyptian man named his first-born daughter 'Facebook' (Memmott 2011). Gerbaudo argues that the Egyptian revolution shows a 'cyber-populist' strategy, where the mainstream appeal of Twitter and Facebook are used to politically mobilize the masses (2017: 137). In this way, social media were not used for 'internal organising, as was the case with prior movements, but as an external means of mobilisation of the citizenry' (Gerbaudo 2017: 138).

Kara Alaimo, former communicator for the United Nations and the Obama administration as well as an associate professor in media, analyses the 'We Are All Khaled' Facebook page. This page was set up to highlight and memorialize the life of a young man, Khaled Said, who was brutally beaten and murdered by police on June 6, 2010. Alaimo argues that the 'We Are All Khaled' Facebook page played an important role not only in mobilizing Egyptian youth but also in educating them about the Mubarak regime and digital activism (2015; cf. Abdulla et al. 2018). The page is one of the most popular Egyptian pages, with over 4.1 million followers. Indeed, Alaimo is among those that argue 'the revolution therefore appears to offer a powerful case study for how social media can be successfully harnessed by those attempting to promote political change' (2015: 1). Facebook, with pages that can be set up by anyone and that effectively looked the same for everyone, provided a platform that appeared equal, allowing users to 'develop a sense of equality to others' (Abdulla et al. 2018: 143). Analysis of the comments and discussion on the 'We are All Khaled' Facebook page found that the page owners asked for people's input, inviting them to participate in making sense of Mubarak's regime, as well as in how to mobilize others and organize protest actions. This kind of approach meant that the page's 75,000-plus (in 2010) Facebook users were able to develop 'more confidence in voicing their opinions, more willingness and ability to cross societal and political red lines, and a feeling that their voice mattered' (Abdulla et al. 2018: 143).

For Abdulla and her colleagues, it was not just the participatory nature of Facebook that facilitated the mass mobilization witnessed in the 2011 uprisings; it was also the 'proto-democratic nature' of Facebook communications, which:

> … helped entice active discussions on ways to fight issues of corruption, torture and police brutality and provided an unprecedented practical example of shared governance and opinion-taking, which became a model for the members to strive to apply to their country. (2018: 158)

There is another story to be told in terms of the numbers of social media users. The direct reach of Twitter and Facebook in Egypt was pretty small in 2010. Drawing from Murthy 2013, the penetration rates in Egypt for digital media were fairly low. Only 16.27% of the Egyptian population had access to the internet, 4.21 % had a Facebook account, and 0.00014% had a Twitter account making it too small to see on the chart below (see Figure 6.6). Overall, almost 80% of the Egyptian population did not use digital or social media in 2010.

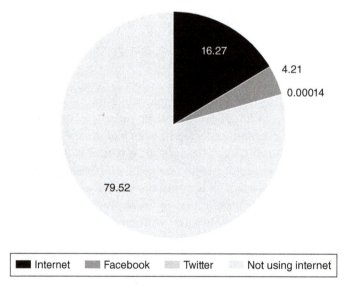

Figure 6.6 Internet, Facebook and Twitter penetration rates in Egypt, 2010

Source: based on data from Murthy 2013: 95

Although social media may have only been in use by a small percentage of the Egyptian population in 2010, both Twitter and Facebook were major sources of communication for journalists reporting on the Egyptian uprising. Aday et al. (2013) document that social media, especially Twitter, was primarily used by traditional media and 'non-MENA onlookers but less so for protesters on the ground' in the MENA region. Murthy supports this observation, arguing that the international representation of social media messages was very visible outside of Egypt, prompting the Egyptian government to respond as if both these platforms were a threat (Murthy 2013: 95). Egyptian authorities shut down the internet for five days from January 28 to February 1 in 2011. This blackout, in line with Zuckerman's cute cat theory (see Box 6.3), had a huge impact on the general population, effectively politicizing the 'non-political' and the 'business community' as well as the general population (Murthy 2013: 95). Following the government blackout, there was a tenfold increase in Twitter users by March 2011 (Murthy 2013: 97). Murthy argues that this shows that social media did not cause dissent but did extend the revolution's activist network, more easily enrolling those who became politicized post-internet blackout (see also Ethan Zuckerman's cute cat theory, Box 6.2).

Black Lives Matter

Originating in the US, #BlackLivesMatter began as a specific response to systemic racialized violence and police brutality. The hashtag has grown into a global movement, bringing together Black voices and their allies. The movement began following the long and painful accumulation of case after case of the murder of Black people, none of which were brought to justice.

Although not the first case, the murder of 17-year-old African American teen Trayvon Martin on February 26, 2012, as he tried to visit his father in Sanford Florida, began to set the stage for the movement. Returning from the shop where he had just bought candy, Martin was seen by George Zimmerman, who thought the teen looked suspicious, and fatally shot him. The 911 recording 'painted a vague, yet disturbing picture of the confrontation between Zimmerman and Martin. A cry for help, and the gunshot that followed' (Chase 2018: 1093). It was not only Martin's murder which left Black American communities reeling, but also Zimmerman's acquittal in July 2013, which outraged many, revealing systemic racism, an unfair justice system and widespread white indifference to these injustices. In addition to anger and outrage, Zimmerman's not guilty verdict also inspired Alicia Garza to write 'A Love Letter to Black People'. Garza describes what she was thinking along with the original post in her own words:

> When he [Zimmerman] was acquitted, it felt like a gut punch. And I remember sitting with friends and talking, and there was nothing to say, but we just wanted to be around each other. A lot of what I was hearing and seeing on social media

was that they were never going to charge somebody and convict somebody of killing a Black child. My thing was: I'm not satisfied with that. I'm not satisfied with the 'I told you so' and I'm not satisfied with the nihilistic 'it'll never happen' kind of thing. I was basically popping off on Facebook saying, 'Yes, I'm going to be surprised that this man was not held accountable for the murder of a child.' I was basically sending love notes to Black people and saying, 'We're enough. We are enough, and we don't deserve to die, and we don't deserve to be shot down in the streets like dogs because somebody else is fucking scared of us. And our presence is important, and we matter. Our lives matter, Black lives matter.' And Patrisse [Cullors, Garza's friend and BLM co-founder] was like, 'Oh my god, Black lives matter'. (Garza 2015)

This post inspired a series of other posts. Cullors posted on her Facebook, 'Black bodies will no longer be sacrificed for the rest of the world's enlightenment. I am done. I am so done. Trayvon, you are loved infinitely. #blacklivesmatter' (as cited by Chase 2018: 1095). The hashtag allowed these messages by Garza, Cullors and their friend Opal Tometi to be shared across Twitter, Facebook and the internet, leading towards the creation of 'a Black-centered political will and movement building project called #BlackLivesMatter' (Herstory, blacklives matter.com). Importantly, Black Lives Matter began as an inclusive movement, one which was intended to 'affirm the lives of Black queer and trans folks, disabled folks, Black-undocumented folks, folks with records, women and all Black lives along the gender spectrum' (as cited in Chase 2018: 1109).

Following the 2013 origins of #BlackLivesMatter, there were also many more instances of police murder of young Black men, including: Eric Garner, choked to death by police on July 17, 2014; teenager Michael Brown, shot by police on August 9, 2014; 12-year-old Tamir Rice, shot for carrying a toy gun in Cleveland, November 23, 2014; Walter Scott, shot in the back by a police officer, and caught on film April 4, 2015; and Philandro Castille, pulled over and shot by police while reaching for his wallet. The murder was filmed and livestreamed by Diamond Reynolds, Castille's girlfriend, on July 6, 2016. In 2020, Minneapolis resident and father of five George Floyd was murdered on May 25, 2020 by a white police officer, who knelt on his neck for 8 minutes and 46 seconds while other officers watched. The police officers were not charged with first-degree murder. Ahmaud Arbery and Breonna Taylor were also murdered in 2020, and like Floyd have yet to come to justice despite local and global attention to their deaths. The UK also has its share of police murders of Black people, as well as a long record of systemic racism (e.g. Roland Adams, Stephen Lawrence and Sara Reed, among others). Floyd's death sparked global protests against racism and police violence, turning the #BLM protests into a long-term global movement (e.g. Emejulu 2020; Page 2020).

In relation to the first five years of the BLM movement, Freelon et al. argue that these horrific incidents led to many protests across the US, as well as the introduction of many other hashtags such as #HandsUpDontShoot, #NoJusticeNoPeace, #IfTheyGunnedMeDown,

#Justice4All and, in 2020, #GeorgeFloyd, #BreonnaTaylor and #IcantBreathe – all of which frequently overlapped with #BlackLivesMatter. (See Figure 6.7 for an overview of the #BlackLivesMatter surges in Twitter use over time.)

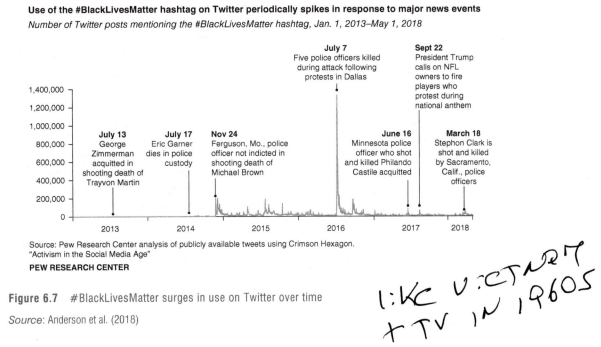

Use of the #BlackLivesMatter hashtag on Twitter periodically spikes in response to major news events
Number of Twitter posts mentioning the #BlackLivesMatter hashtag, Jan. 1, 2013–May 1, 2018

Source: Pew Research Center analysis of publicly available tweets using Crimson Hexagon. "Activism in the Social Media Age"

PEW RESEARCH CENTER

Figure 6.7   #BlackLivesMatter surges in use on Twitter over time

Source: Anderson et al. (2018)

One group of social network and activism specialists argued that while 'police violence against people of African descent is nothing new', social media and camera phones are able to amplify people's experiences, pushing 'these issues into the national spotlight like never before' (Freelon et al. 2016: 7). Freelon and his colleagues argue that 'Twitter has been the predominant hub for BLM online', but it is not the only hub as the open web and offline activism make up the broader landscape and have all contributed to the movement (Freelon 2016: 14). Freelon et al. state that the #BlackLivesMatter online network 'is clearly conducive to broadly distributing and circulating information' (2016: 16), a finding which aligns with interviewees who primarily used social media for 'education, amplification of marginalized voices, and structural police reform' (2016: 5, 35). Amidst their close analysis of the #BlackLivesMatter network, Freelon et al. find a number of important findings. First, the network is made up of those who are loosely connected which better allows the circulation of information, as well as allowing alternative voices and narratives to be heard (2016: 75). Second, Freelon and his colleagues argue that this movement shows that while 'mainstream journalism still plays a major role' in these information networks 'it is no longer alone' (2016: 78). Finally, #BlackLivesMatter successfully educated people about systemic racism and widespread police brutality, which amplified otherwise marginalized voices (2016: 79).

Conclusion: Making Sense of Participatory Culture

All of these cases demonstrate the complexity of understanding participation on and off of networked media and social technologies. More research continues to identify the power of small acts of engagement (as discussed in Chapter 2), including the act of liking as creative participation (Schonig 2020). Although not discussed here, participatory media can also enable anti-social, racist, misogynist and harmful kinds of participation. Like the general positive orientation of theories of participatory culture, the cases discussed here are also positively oriented – focusing on community, self-affirmation, protest and mobilization against injustices. Yet in terms of participation, it must be noted that it is not always positive. The decreased barriers we see in artistic expression and civic engagement also apply to anti-social behaviours like trolling, extremism and hate. Even without accounting for the kinds of content, the issue of how we make sense of participation remains. Do these cases show full or partial participation? Are those who are participating exploited by capitalist platforms or do these same platforms better allow people to create, to play and to experience a feeling of being engaged?

One of the things these cases show is an increased blurring between popular culture and political action, particularly as platforms increasingly enable communication, interaction and almost infinite kinds of participation.

There are many things to consider when it comes to understanding participation, such as the distinctions between maximalist and minimalist forms of participation, largely determined by how fully those involved can participate in decision making. Drawing largely from politics, decision making refers to the kinds of meaningful impact participants can have in decisions about the conditions of their participation in or through media, as well as for the outcome of their participation. While Carpentier prioritizes decision making as one of the essential criteria for maximalist participation, others draw attention to play, to the affective nature of connection, and to an increased creative capacity. In addition, in the contemporary platform landscape, participants' capacity for sharing in the ownership and profits generated through participation is also an important element of meaningful participation.

Yet as has been well established, the capacity for public participation and collective agency is unequal. Jenkins is one of many who makes this argument, particularly in relation to 'corporate control' of access, visibility and 'collective expression':

> Occupy did not have that same degree of access, say, to Fox News, which suggests to me a need to make distinctions between different kinds of corporate control and constraint on collective expression, (Jenkins, in Banet-Weiser et al. 2014: 1083)

All of these cases, even if unequal when compared to corporate powers, seem to exemplify the participatory turn. PostSecret and WNRS are online communities which although led by entrepreneurial founders also work towards supporting and inspiring others, and they also capitalize on the content given to them from their communities highlighting tensions between commercialism and community. In addition, those who do participate may do so for the feeling of being engaged, but they do not have any say in how the community is run, editorial decisions, or in the future of the community. For the two social movements, the stakes are different. For these participants, social media served multiple purposes – enabling the articulation of common issues so that those facing oppression and wanting change could connect, share and mobilize. For those in the Egyptian revolution and Black Lives Matter, the stakes were not about profits, but about collective movement building for making a better future.

There are many who are rightly critical of overly optimistic accounts of participation. Paolo Gerbaudo refers to 'the cult of participation', which 'conflates utopia and praxis, ends and means; the world we want to build and the ways in which we can build it' (2017: 244). Adrienne Massanari refers to 'the end of participatory culture', particularly in light of the massive privacy infringements and data exploitation of big tech like Facebook (2015: 168). Thus, while the move from 'an authoritarian and "monologic" broadcasting model to one that is more democratic and "dialogic"' has been coming for a long time, it is deeply troubled by corporate power and new frontiers of data exploitation (Lunt and Livingstone 1994: 5–6). So on the one hand, we see new spaces and new power for the public expression and circulation of marginalized voices (e.g. #Egypt, #BLM), and on the other we see that legacy media are still a crucial player for networked public participation.

Questions and Activities

1   Roundtable exercise: Identify and explore a current protest or social movement on social media. Research your selection and bring in an example of how social media is used for that protest. Be prepared to share your example in a roundtable.

2   Choose a participatory online community, and evaluate this community based on the key elements of participatory culture identified in this chapter. How does it measure up in terms of a feeling of being engaged, visibility, play, role in decision making and ownership? Discuss your findings.

3   Explore Twitter: Join Twitter, if you don't already have an account, and explore the platform. Pay attention to public figures, trending topics and/or celebrities that interest you. Share what you find and what you learn with your class.

4   Communicating concisely is a fine art. Using Twitter, write five 280-character tweets explaining your view of participatory culture. Use hashtags.

Further Reading

Black Lives Matter. https://blacklivesmatter.com/

Cunningham, S.; Craig, D. 2019. Creator labour, in *Social Media Entertainment: The New Intersection of Hollywood and Silicon Valley.* New York University Press.

Jackson, S. J.; Bailey, M.; Foucault Welles, B. 2020. Introduction: making race and gender politics on Twitter, in *#Hashtag Activism: Networks of Race and Gender Activism.* The MIT Press.

Jenkins, H. 2006. 'Worship at the altar of convergence: a new paradigm for understanding media change, in *Convergence Culture: Where Old and New Media Collide.* New York University. Press., http://faculty.georgetown.edu/irvinem/theory/Jenkins-ConvergenceCulture-Intro.pdf

Schonig, J. 2020. "Liking" as creating: on aesthetic category memes, *New Media & Society*, 22(1), pp. 26–48. https://doi.org/10.1177/1461444819855727

PART III

EVERYDAY LIFE AND SOCIAL MEDIA

7

SELFIE AND SOCIETY: SNAPCHAT AND INSTAGRAM

Chapter Overview

Introduction: The Rise of the Selfie	156
What Is a Selfie, Really?	158
Selfie Platforms	163
Instagram	163
Snapchat	166
Data Selfies	169
Filters, lenses and apps	170
Facial recognition, tagging and artificial intelligence	173
Conclusion: The Visual Logics of Selfie Culture	175
Questions and Activities	176
Further Reading	177

Chapter Objectives

- Contextualize selfies as a cultural phenomenon, practice and as an object of study
- Dispel popular myths of selfies as narcissistic
- Examine two 'selfie platforms', Instagram and Snapchat
- Introduce data selfies, particularly in relation to filters and lenses, and the role of artificial intelligence in facial recognition

Introduction: The Rise of the Selfie

Selfies appear to be one of the drivers of internet culture, and are at the heart of social media content. Selfies are a highly visible cultural phenomenon, as well as a particular genre of popular communication. Recent research suggests we are going through a 'selfie explosion', as Europeans take an average of '597 selfies of themselves a year' (Honor 2019). Declared the *Oxford English Dictionary* (*OED*) word of the year in 2013, selfies are defined as 'a photo of yourself that you take, typically with a smartphone or webcam, and usually put on social media' (*OED* 2013). *OED* chooses its words of the year based on their 'strong cultural resonance' which, in the case of the selfie, can be seen not only in the rising usage of the word, but also in the way the selfie has become a meta-genre, including sub-genres, such as a:

- helfie (a picture of one's hair);
- belfie (a picture of one's posterior);
- welfie (workout selfie);
- drelfie (drunken selfie);
- shelfie and bookshelfie (items of furniture);
- funeral selfie;
- prelfies – pregnant selfies (*OED* 2013);
- crying selfies (Heaney and Misener 2013).

Many further sub-types could also be added – selfies of people on vacation (e.g. 'beach legs', 'tiger selfies', 'travel selfies'), or in the bathroom, or making faces (e.g. the 'duck-face' selfie) – as the types of selfies across digital media are endless. The proliferation of selfie types shows that it has become deeply embedded in both the cultural vernacular and the evolving visual logics of a social media age. The selfie types briefly introduced here provide a cultural short-form for the complex ways people present themselves to others and to themselves.

Alongside the proliferating genre of selfies, popular media coverage of selfies has dramatically increased from 2013 (see Figure 7.1).

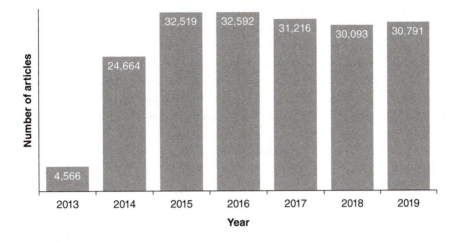

Figure 7.1   Number of global news articles in English with 'Selfie' in the headline, 2013–2019

Source: ProQuest search for 'Selfie' in newspapers, blogs and magazines in the United States, India, United Kingdom, Canada, China, Australia, Europe, Russia, Mexico, Asia, Israel, Africa, Syria and Thailand (25/01/2020)

In contrast to the *OED*'s relatively neutral definition, others tend to see the selfie as something much darker. For example, the 'crowdsourced online dictionary for slang words' *Urban Dictionary* has a very different definition of 'selfie':

> 2. The beginning of the end of intelligent civilization
>
> 3. Taking a picture of yourself like an idiot with swag. idiot 1: 'Let's take a SELFIE'; idiot 2: 'DUCK FACE #YOLO!' (https://www.urbandictionary.com/define. php?term=Selfie)

The *Urban Dictionary* definition illustrates some of the denigration selfies get, and this hate is one part of the often heated debates over what the rise of selfies means for changing social norms and the contingent impact on the social fabric.

In order to illustrate some of these changing social norms, let's consider some high-profile cases, such as Kim Kardashian, #Yolocaust and selfiegate. In this first instance, selfies have been linked to rising self-indulgence and selfishness, as most clearly highlighted through Kim Kardashian's book *Selfish*, featuring her own selfies, mostly taken for her own Instagram account. Kardashian is an American reality television and social media star, boasting 183 million followers on Instagram. German artist Shahak Shapira created a #YOLOcaust exhibit, which combined selfies posted on Facebook, Tinder, Grindr and Instagram by tourists visiting 'the Holocaust Memorial in Berlin with footage from Nazi extermination camps' (2017, https://yolocaust.de/). Juxtaposing these selfies with stark historical footage exposed an uncomfortable tension between memorializing practices around historical atrocities and 'you only live once' (YOLO) practices of Instagram. 'Selfiegate' refers to the widely circulated picture of Danish Prime Minister Helle Thorning-Schmidt snapping a selfie with then US President Barack Obama and former UK Prime Minister David Cameron, while they were at Nelson Mandela's memorial service (Miltner and Baym 2015: 1701). This selfie captured a happy moment of togetherness, which then prompted many to criticize these world leaders for making light of a memorial intended to honour the loss of one of the greatest anti-apartheid world leaders. Miltner and Baym argue that selfiegate raised questions around 'who takes selfies and under what circumstances', and it was these questions that propelled the international media to dedicate so much critical coverage to 'selfiegate' (Senft and Baym 2015: 1701).

These controversial selfies illustrate that selfies are complex, and may be highly individual, but are also reflective of broader social contexts – which make it more difficult to understand their cultural meaning. Overall, this chapter aims to provide an overview of the selfie, including an analysis of its rise and cultural relevance. As Nancy Thumim argues in a special issue on self-representation, 'the self and the digital and their articulation should remain central to explorations of power and society' (2017: 61). This chapter introduces selfies, what they are and how they have been understood, unpacking the articulation of the self as both cultural and individual. Although selfies cannot be confined to any one medium, this chapter focuses on those social technologies most associated with selfies, Instagram and Snapchat. Next, I turn to data selfies, i.e. the data imprints left behind through selfies and made especially apparent through the playful filters, lenses and apps characteristic of social media. All of these relatively banal features of selfie culture are built through facial recognition and artificial intelligence, both emerging technologies with significant social consequences, and as a result I introduce some of Facebook's work in this area, as well as the multiple intersections with selfies. In conclusion, this chapter reflects on the visual logics of social technologies and selfie culture. For the moment, however, it is worth thinking through what a selfie is and why it has come to be a cultural phenomenon.

What Is a Selfie, Really?

Everyone knows what a selfie is, yet it is worth asking what a selfie really is as thinking this through reveals many additional layers. The answer is bound up not only with the history of photography and portraiture, but also in practices of self-representation, and all of the social and cultural associations that come with these practices. In order to understand this complexity, this section draws on definitions of selfies by leading scholars, and unpacks dominant social and moral anxieties around selfies which complicate our understandings of these definitions. Finally, this section introduces two approaches to understanding selfies: Erving Goffman's presentation of self (1959) and selfies as part of an emerging language of the social media age (e.g. Tiefentale and Manovich 2018).

Many have mapped the selfie's origins with broader practices of self-representation, including self-portraiture in art, eighteenth-century diaries, and even with self-photo-taking in twentieth-century photo booths (Humphreys 2018; Rettberg 2014; Thumim 2012). Mehita Iqani and Eric Shcroeder contextualize this history in terms of the shift from elite portraits to popular photography:

> Historically, self-portraits were rare, and produced within the realm of the wealthy or celebrated. With the boom in popular photography around the turn of the twentieth century, self-portraiture proliferated, and photographic self-portraiture remains a key genre today (Doy 2005). All self-portraiture takes expressing aspects of the self as a key premise. Artists perform, gaze, reflect, and pose in self-portraits, which can be seen as both a mirror for the subject and the society in which he or she lives. Photographic self-portraits, in particular, provide an 'autobiography' of the self. (2016: 409)

These are all important precedents, showing that selfies may be one of the latest developments in a much longer history of visualizing and documenting the self. Thus, drawing from the selfie's historical roots, it is already part autobiography, part presentation of self and part self-portrait.

Katrin Tiidenberg, a leading scholar on visual culture and social media, argues that selfies refer to 'self-representational networked photographs' (Tiidenberg 2018: 21). For Tiidenberg, it is not just about a particular technology, but about the capacity for the photograph to circulate (or not) across networks. Others argue that the selfie is about the presentation and representation of the self in digital life, even if bound up in the mess of culture, so circulation is an important contribution (e.g. Humphreys 2018; Rettberg 2014).

Theresa Senft, founder of the Selfies Research Group, and Nancy Baym, leading digital scholar, argue that the selfie is an 'assemblage of non-human agents' communicating both 'immediacy and co-presence' (2015: 1589). Senft and Baym also state that the selfie is layered, at once an *object* and a *practice*. The selfie is an object because it:

> ... initiates the transmission of human feeling in the form of a relationship (between photographer and photographed, between image and filtering software, between viewer and viewed, between individuals circulating images, between users and social software architectures, etc.) (2015: 1589)

The selfie is also a practice, one that at its base includes the set of actions and postures required for taking images and (often) circulating them. On a social level, it connects the selfie-taker, photograph and viewer(s) within a network which can be 'dampened, amplified, or modified by social media censorship, social censure, misreading' or interaction through 'likes, comments, and remixes' (Senft and Baym 2015: 1589).

Therefore the selfie is both an object and a practice, yet this is not all. In addition, it also includes a *subject* – the self whose image is captured or curated in the networked photograph.

This is an important element of the selfie and a key factor in what makes it so compelling. It is this aspect that allows people to more easily inscribe themselves into their own stories, and their documentation of those stories. Take, for example, the shifting dynamics of the family photo which has moved from a more formal portrait to a more informal selfie – one that involves gendered dynamics and social conventions. For example, mothers have been more likely to 'perform the emotional work involved in curating family memory' through the taking, printing and organizing of family photos into albums and which means they may not always be included in family albums (Bresnahan 2016). Selfies allow the family photo-takers, typically mothers, to more easily include themselves in the family album. In this way, selfies as a visual form of documenting experience allow people to write their 'self into being' (Markham 2013, cited in Rettberg 2014: 13). This is a phenomenon that applies to all selfie-takers, including those that may have been excluded from visual records.

Thus, in terms of the basic elements of a selfie, it is an object, a practice, and a subject, all of which are also social and cultural. This capacity for including or writing the self into visibility is also the source for much moral anxiety. For instance, many blame selfies for the rise of narcissism, mental health risks and toxic culture (e.g. Biocalti and Passini. 2018; Halpern et al. 2016; Taylor 2020). Senft and Baym argue that selfies 'remain fundamentally ambiguous, fraught, and caught in a stubborn and morally loaded hype cycle' (2015: 1588). In their influential selfies special issue introduction, which helped define an emerging field of study, Senft and Baym do their best to challenge and unpick these deeply embedded morally loaded hype cycles. (See Figure 7.2 for a small selection of selfie headlines.)

Selfie-takers think they're cuter than they really are, study says

If you take lots of selfies then there's some bad news for you...

Hooked to selfies? You're probably unappealing

A study examined 'selfie indulgence' to reveal some shocking results

Taking selfies could make you act like a narcissistic jerk, study shows

The secret to being attractive — don't take selfies

Figure 7.2   A small selection of headlines about selfies

This critical challenge, to dispel the narcissism myth of selfies, has been taken up by others, who also question the oversimplified and reductive approaches to selfies. Katie Warfield and her colleagues are some of the researchers working in this area, arguing:

> [Many] discourses framed selfies in reductive and overly determined ways. Selfies, in this view, did not just cause bad things, but were themselves as-if fundamentally evil. Terri and Nancy's introduction (Baym & Senft, 2015) played out as a series

of discursive disruptions unraveling the knots that stitched selfies to pathology, selfies to narcissism, and selfies to gendered networked practices of self-absorption. (Warfield et al. 2016: 2)

The 'knots' stitching selfies to pathology can also be understood as a 'moral panic' – what Kirsten Drotner defines as the 'emotionally charged' reactions and debates over changing social norms often fuelled by new technologies, fears about youth culture and sensationalist media coverage (1999: 596). Drotner maps moral panics over time, beginning with eighteenth-century concerns that 'new' penny novels would 'poison the minds' of readers and up until concerns that film would promote prostitution and licentiousness (1999: 598–99, 604). Drotner argues that moral panics tend to revolve around concerns for young people's moral development, concerns which are historically repetitive and reflect conflicts between older and younger generations, and between tradition and change. Selfies are also at this intersection between youthful and established practices, both technologically and culturally.

Following Senft and Baym's call for critical thinking when evaluating claims about selfies, we must be particularly cautious about those claims that heighten hegemonic power and attack those who are already disempowered. In particular, Senft and Baym call to attention how identity markers around class, gender, race, age, sexuality, faith, etc. inform popular understandings of selfies as, for example, the territory of narcissistic young females rather than creative youth (2015: 1589–90). Mehita Iqani and Jonathan Schroeder, both media studies professors, address this in term of who has the power to make something public:

Selfies are fascinating objects not only due to their explosion within the popular culture domain, but also in terms of how they allow us to think about *modes of making public and claiming authenticity*. As well as this, selfies are an intriguing empirical object because they combine questions of subject and object, as well as questions of identity, agency, and power. (2016: 413, emphasis added)

Indeed, a number of contemporary thinkers have pointed to selfies as an emerging vernacular – communicating the everyday language of digital culture – through which people can more readily communicate the self to others. In this way selfies are part of a digital linguistics for *making the self public*. Alise Tiefentale, a photographer and cultural thinker, worked with Professor Lev Manovich to analyse *Selfie City*, a project examining 3,200 selfies from five different global cities (2015; see also http://selfiecity.net/). Tiefentale and Manovich found that there were regional similarities in how people take selfies (e.g. degree of head tilting, smiling, angles), and went on to say that:

... image making and image sharing on social media are becoming *part of general literacy*, similar to how it happened with personal computers and the internet in the 1990s. Photography is the new literacy of what Nicholas Mirzoeff (2015) calls the "global majority"— the young and urban population of the world. (Tiefentale and Manovich 2018: 170, emphasis added)

Markham may have argued that selfies help 'write ourselves into being', but Tiefentale and Manovich point to larger systems of visual language, of which selfies are only a small part of broader cultural vernacular, including memes, social videos, gifs and other social communications (see also Milner 2016; Phillips and Milner 2017).

Although covered less in this chapter, another major theoretical principle used to make sense of how people present themselves comes from Erving Goffman's theory of symbolic interactionism, particularly the ways in which people stage their presentations of self on 'front' and 'back' regions. (See Box 7.1.)

Box 7.1 Erving Goffman and the presentation of self in everyday life

Erving Goffman was a Canadian-American sociologist interested in everyday interaction, particularly in the generation and interpretation of meaning. Taking a 'dramaturgical approach', which refers to the 'craft or techniques of dramatic composition', he theorized that social interaction is based on what he calls 'front stage' and 'back stage' behaviours. For Goffman, 'the rules of politeness and decorum' mean that:

> We often find a division into back region where the performance of a routine is prepared, and front region, where the performance [behaviour or interaction] is presented. Access to these regions is controlled in order to prevent the audience [or other people] from seeing back stage and to prevent outsiders from coming into a performance that is not addressed to them. (1990 [1959]: 238)

The central tenet of his theory is that people's behaviour is not only shaped by social conventions, but also by the presence of other people. The 'front stage' refers to public or semi-public contexts, where the best version of the self is presented. Goffman uses the example of 'scenic settings' like the 'funeral cortege, the civic parade' or more informal contexts like 'the living room' (1990 [1959]: 22). On the other hand, the 'back stage', as in the theatre, is where the performance is rehearsed, where the changing rooms are located and the props are gathered for use on the front stage. By inference, the back stage is more likely to be located in the bedroom, and the preparatory spaces where people can refine their presentations of self.

While the theatrical metaphor may be limited, as even bedrooms, changing rooms and all the in-between spaces where people get ready for social interaction can also demand 'front-stage' performances, the key point is that social interaction is often rehearsed and prepared. There are big differences between private (back stage) and public (front stage) space. Goffman's work is part of a larger school of thought called symbolic interactionism, which is based on the premise that meaning not only shapes human action, but also comes from social interaction, and is subjectively interpreted by those involved (Blumer 1969: 2).

Goffman's theory of front/back stage presentation of self has often been used to make sense of how and why people use digital and social media (see for example, Baker et al. 2018; Brake 2014; Ditchfield 2019).

Selfies are indeed fascinating objects, and they reflect what we see in ourselves and how we see others. Notably, many scholars have picked up this call to disrupt and dispel common assumptions about the selfie, while also developing an advanced research agenda and international research networks to critically examine the selfie. In this section, the selfie was defined as being made up of three core elements – an object, a practice and a subject. All of these, and longer-standing practices of documenting the self, are bound up in cultural and moral anxieties. Drotner's work on moral panics helps contextualize the cyclic nature of these anxieties, and furthers the disentanglement of the selfie from these larger anxieties. Additionally, positioning the selfie as part of an emerging digital language and as involving particular modes for presenting and making the public self helps us unpack its many complexities. The next section looks at selfies across two platforms, Instagram and Snapchat.

Selfie Platforms

Of course, Instagram and Snapchat are much more than just selfie platforms, but they are also closely associated with the making and sharing of selfies. Although Instagram does have a website from which you can make posts and interact with others' posts, its primary mode of interaction, like Snapchat, is on apps for mobile phones. Both of these are also platforms in that they offer a rich array of services and other apps that live and function within the app ecosystem. Both sites are more popular amongst youth, and both have headquarters based in Silicon Valley. Their biggest proportion of users are unsurprisingly based in the United States. These are important features and mean that users' experiences and the cultural significance of the selfie, certainly on these platforms and the research based on these platforms, are grounded in a primarily youthful and American perspective. Bearing this in mind, the next two subsections introduce Instagram and Snapchat as platforms, particularly in relation to the taking, storing, sharing and liking of selfies.

Instagram

Before it was launched in October 2010 by Kevin Systrom and Mike Krieger, Instagram was first envisioned as Burbn, a location based app with check-ins for users to swap stories about their experiences with Bourbon, similar to city-guide-style app Foursquare (Leaver et al. 2020: 9). Given the heavy competition in this sector, Systrom and Krieger changed their minds, opting instead for a simpler app focused on taking and sharing photos, liking and commenting. There was plenty of competition in image-sharing sites as well, including sites like Flickr, Path, Hipstamatic, Imgur, PicPlz and Twitter-specific sites like Yfrog and Twitpic, to name but a few (Leaver et al. 2020: 10–11; see also Harbison 2010). Despite this thriving ecosystem of photo-sharing sites, Instagram quickly gained popularity, reaching over a million users by mid-December 2010, ten weeks after its launch (Harbison 2010). Instagram's success caught the eye of Facebook, who purchased the app in April 2012 for US $1 billion.

Since then, Instagram has grown into a global platform, reaching 1 billion monthly active users in January 2020. It has inspired many knock-off sites and apps, setting a global standard and visual aesthetic for image sharing. Yet Instagram's ambitions are much greater than just photo-sharing. For example, on their 'About Us' page, Instagram says 'We bring you closer to the people and things you love' (2020). True to the public logic defining Facebook, Instagram aims to *connect* people to those that matter to them. Like other platforms, Instagram has also grown from a single-sited app with a limited set of functions to a platform upon which sit many other apps and services, such as direct messaging, stories, shopping, stickers, discover, advertising, filters, emojis, Boomerang and IGTV (see Chapters 2 and 5). All of these come under Facebook's terms and conditions, meaning that 'the personal data of Instagram's users is subject to the same conditions, uses, analyses and potential misuses of any other Facebook user' (Vaidhyanathan 2018: 55).

In a book on Instagram, Tama Leaver, Tim Highfield and Crystal Abidin, all leading internet scholars, argue that:

> Instagram should best be understood as a conduit for *communication* in the increasingly vast landscape of visual social media cultures ... [It] is more than an app, more than a platform, and more than a jewel in the Facebook 'family'. Rather, Instagram is an icon and avatar for understanding and mapping visual social media cultures. (2020: 1–2, original emphasis)

Following this claim that Instagram 'is an icon and avatar' for visual social media cultures, the app does appear to represent a generation of social media users, and not just American ones. In terms of numbers, Instagram is often considered to be more popular among youth, especially compared to Facebook which many see as the platform for those in the 40+ age bracket (Selwyn and Pangrazio 2018). Based on a 2020 analysis of social media demographics, the majority of Instagram users, 116 million in total, are based in the US. Chen (2020) finds that 75% of 18–24-year-olds are Instagram users, making up the largest age group on Instagram, followed by 25–29 year olds (57% of whom are Instagram users). While there are many studies of why users like using Instagram, Alhabash and Ma argue that their respondents identified five key motivations: entertainment, convenience, medium appeal, passing time and self-expression (2017: 6–7). In my own research, I found that many people used Instagram (and Facebook) to *publicly* connect with others, meaning that friendships and posts on these platforms were intentionally visible, in contrast to the much more private kinds of interaction on Snapchat (Sujon 2018).

The meaning of this public orientation has been the source of so much controversy. Instagrammers themselves have become disillusioned with the constant spectacle and monetizing work of developing a branded self. Content that is made for public consumption can be interpreted as much less genuine than content which is not meant to be seen. (See Box 7.2 for one case which clearly raises these issues: 'What Essena O'Neill has to teach us about Instagram and authenticity.')

Box 7.2 What Essena O'Neill has to teach us about Instagram and authenticity

Essena O'Neill, an Australian teen model with over 600,000 followers on Instagram, made headlines all over the world when she suddenly announced she was quitting social media in 2015. But it wasn't just her quitting that made headlines – it was her public condemnation of social media and the 'fake' life it brought with it. In one of her last social media posts, O'Neill wrote:

Deleted over 2,000 photos here today that served no real purpose other than self-promotion. Without realizing, I've spent [the] majority of my teenage life being addicted to social media, social approval, social status and my physical appearance, (O'Neill, cited by Murray 2015).

As part of her public rejection of social media, O'Neill edited many of her Instagram posts, recaptioning selfies with a behind-the-scenes narrative explaining the costs of every photo. These costs ranged from semi-starvation to make her stomach look flat to the discomfort of taking many photos to get the perfect one – all so that she could post what she calls 'contrived perfection made to get attention' (cited in Hunt 2015). O'Neill also commented on her 'obsession' with checking and counting likes, something that shows her hunger for 'social media validation' rather than real life validation (O'Neill, cited in Hunt 2015). She also revealed paid sponsorship, where she was paid to wear certain clothes and post images on Instagram (Murray 2015).

O'Neill's experience and public castigation of Instagram and, by inference, social media culture brought a number of issues to the attention of the public. First, she was deeply disillusioned with social media and her accusations that it was fake had wide cultural resonance. Questions around what it means to be authentic on social media continue to circulate, and O'Neill was able to articulate what was superficial and inauthentic based on her experience. Second, she was one of the first to reveal that her posts had been paid for by sponsors, long before there were requirements to declare partnerships and endorsements. Indeed, the requirement to disclose sponsored content was not required by Facebook (or Instagram) until 2017 (Chacon 2017). The rules for promoting branded content and paid partnerships appear to still be taking shape (Instagram Business Team 2019). Finally, O'Neill also made the role of social media metrics, particularly her obsession with the number of likes she received, public. These are a few of the many factors that pushed her case into the public spotlight, resonating with a wider Instagram audience.

Notably, O'Neill has recently returned to the internet and social media, launching her own site (https://www.authoritywithin.com/) which takes inspiration from Karl Marx, Gilles Deleuze and other thinkers to promote a deep questioning of commodification and social media culture (Gorman 2019). While some may question her intentions, her experience as an influencer and condemnation of this culture calls out what it means to be publicly authentic and inauthentic on Instagram.

The case of Essena O'Neill raises several issues especially relevant for Instagram and selfie culture. The first of these is the role of 'likes' and what Richard Rogers calls 'vanity metrics' and the 'measurement and display of how well one is doing in the "success theater" of social media' (2018b: 450). While O'Neill may have publicly rejected these kinds of metrics, many others have embraced them, and those who are successful in generating high numbers are also more likely to be successful in financially supporting themselves. While this has led to the growing importance of influencers in internet celebrity (Abidin 2018), it has also led to new kinds of economies and converging media industries (Cunningham and Craig 2019). However, vanity metrics have also led many to question the negative impact of quantifying Instagram users' creations, selfies and photos through metrics, in ways that can cause people to experience increased anxiety and amplify mental health struggles.

Also related to the O'Neill case is the rise of a particular highly polished visual aesthetic, one that is essential to the Instagram feel (cf. Leaver et al. 2020), and is also perceived as increasing the pressure on young people to look and behave in certain ways. This pressure has been thought to compromise young people's mental health. In response to these concerns, Instagram has also begun piloting the removal of 'like' metrics, apparently to protect users' mental health (Kumparak 2019; Padilla 2019). Metrics, here, are an important part of social media, even if this particular experiment is likely an attempt to win back disillusioned and vulnerable users.

Although Instagram is often associated with selfies, a 2014 project collecting 120,000 selfies in five global cities (Bangkok, Berlin, Moscow, New York and São Paolo), found that, on average, *only 4% of Instagram photos were selfies* (Selfie City, 2014: http://selfiecity.net/). This finding suggests that our perceptions of Instagram selfies may overemphasize the numbers in reality.

Snapchat

Snapchat, although also driven by selfies, operates with an almost entirely different logic, affordances and uses than Instagram. Like Instagram, it shares a lofty social ambition to help users connect with others and visually express themselves:

> Snap Inc. is a camera company. We believe that reinventing the camera represents our greatest opportunity to improve the way people live and communicate. We contribute to human progress by empowering people to express themselves, live in the moment, learn about the world and have fun together. (Snap Inc. 2020 https://www.snap.com/en-GB)

Founded in 2011 by Evan Spiegel, Bobby Murphy and Reggie Brown, Snapchat's first iteration was under the name Picaboo, which the founders changed to Snapchat when faced with legal action from a photo-sharing company of the same name (Molloy 2017). Some tech journalists credit sexting for the birth of Snapchat, as impermanent pictures and messages better suit the exchange of nudes and personally intimate content (Gallagher 2018). Although Snapchat was not an instantaneous success, messages that automatically deleted after a short period and ephemeral content appealed to young people. Snapchat currently has 314 million active users (Clement 2019), and 73% of 18–24-year-olds are Snapchat users (Chen 2020). Snap Inc., the holding company for Snapchat, 'went public in March 2017 and was valued at more than $24bn (£18.5bn), making 27-year-old Spiegel worth more than $5bn overnight' (Molloy 2017). Snapchat is used globally but, as with Instagram, almost a third of its users are based in the US, followed by France, and then India (Chen 2020).

Snapchat is also strictly mobile. Although it does have a company website, its services cannot be accessed online. True to the platform's aims, many teens and young people have embraced it as a way to communicate with each other, whilst avoiding the watchful eyes of parents, teachers and other peers. It is in this way that Snapchat allows a private orientation, where users focus on their personal connections rather than the public-facing one driving Instagram and many other social media. It is this logic, described below by one Snapchat user, as a 'close friends thing':

> Snapchat is more of a close friends thing. You have to actually add specific people and you have to be present to add them. It's very personal. And it's the way you share a story. It's different from Facebook or Instagram … Snap is for those little things you only share with friends. (24-year-old social media diarist, cited in Sujon 2018: 3761)

The idea that Snapchat, particularly in relation to the public orientation of Instagram and Facebook, 'is more like private conversations through photos' is important, and has an impact on the kinds of selfies people create and share (survey respondent 257, age range 20–24 years, as cited in Sujon 2018: 3762). These features have helped cement Snapchat in many young people's daily media routines.

In addition to this more private orientation, Snapchat is also intensely playful. For example, in my first experience of Snapchat, I was uncertain as to why taking pictures of myself and sending them to people was at all interesting. However, the first time my 8- and 10-year-old children saw Snapchat, they were immediately enchanted. Taking pictures of themselves, applying filters, stickers, and captions was hysterical, and sharing these images with each other and with family was immensely entertaining, for all of us. It was through their playfulness that I came to understand not only Snapchat's appeal, but also how it was intended to be used (see also 'Play' in Chapter 6). (See Figure 7.3 for a selection of the author's Snapchat selfies.)

Despite the sometimes silly filters, many people find that Snapchat better enables a more authentic interaction. As Julian, a 24-year-old Snapchat user, observed, 'snapchatting, in particular, is intensely social, more interactive, safer, and more genuine than other social media' (cited in Sujon 2018: 3763).

Figure 7.3 Some of the author's Snapchat selfies

Taken on Snapchat with different filters (2020)

Another illustration of this playful aesthetic is the 'ugly selfie' trend, which may have originated on Tumblr as a 'pretty girls, ugly faces' page, and has a hashtag on Instagram (with 46K posts as of January 2020), but seems to thrive on Snapchat (see https://knowyour meme.com/memes/pretty-girls-ugly-faces). For example, Ruby, a 13-year-old Snapchat user says, 'It's fun … And it's just, like, so much work to make a good-looking selfie' (cited in Bennett 2014). In this way, the 'ugly selfie' is a radical act rejecting the beauty standards seen on Instagram. Bennett calls this 'a kind of playful slice of authenticity in an age where eve-rything seems airbrushed to perfection'. Ruby goes on to explain that, for her, sharing ugly selfies is also an act of bonding, of trust and of friendship. Indeed, 'the better the friend, the uglier the selfie' (Bennett 2014). Snapchat selfies are not about maintaining a Goffmanesqe 'front stage', but rather about sharing the back stage with selected others in an era where the front stage self is carefully crafted and constantly presented (see Box 7.1).

Katz and Schroeder (2015) offer another perspective, in their research with 214 young people in the US, UK and China, finding that respondents highlighted two aspects of Snapchat that were important to them. The first of these is 'control' of content, which was much more easily maintained on Snapchat through the ten-second expiry limit on content, especially when compared with other more permanent forms of social media content (2015: 1865). These young people also said they were particularly aware of the selfie's association with narcissism, which impacted on their view of selfies, and as they did not want to be thought of in this way, they limited how many selfies they took and who they shared them with (Katz and Schroeder 2015: 1866). Thus Snapchat meant that young people could better control who was able to see their selfies and other content, and this was much more appealing than sending their selfies out into the open where they would be indefinitely exposed to public scrutiny. Second, Katz and Schroeder argue that the exchange of Snapchat selfies is part of a 'private grammar and vocabulary' in the rich visual language particular to Snapchat (2015: 1870). For Katz and Schroeder's respondents, selfies were personal, meaningful and part of their everyday exchange.

Oren Soffer offers an interesting interpretation about Snapchat, arguing that because 'Snapchat demonstrates [a] counter-logic to the contemporary grammar of new media', Snapchat also signals a return to an oral paradigm (2016: 1). For Soffer, the ephemeral communication afforded by Snapchat resembles oral traditions rather than those shaped by text-based cultures with long-lasting records of communication. Even the name 'Snapchat' brings together 'two different cultures: that of the fixed nature of pictures (or typed text)—which catch the moment and objectify it—and the temporal, ephemeral culture of conversation' (2016: 2). Like the spoken word, Snapchats disappear into the air, and this has particularly profound implications for personal content that would otherwise belong to the elephant memory of the internet.

Data Selfies

In the days of analogue photography, the photographic object needed to be developed into an object we could hold in our hands, from the film, where images were captured as negatives. In a digital era, film no longer exists, but our digital images do leave traces, imprinting our digital environments with all the data generated and consumed in the process of making and taking photographic objects. In addition, there are many elements of the digital environment which are built for users to play with but that also capture data, including, for example, apps, filters, lenses, captions, emojis, stickers and other digital objects. Other traces include the 'vanity metrics' so often associated with selfies and digital content, things like the likes, comments, shares, views, clicks, etc. Hence the data selfie is less about the human readable image we see on Instagram or Snapchat, and more about the wide range of data collected as we navigate social media. Data selfies are about the flow of data generated through every click and translated into impressions and engagement scores, filtered by the human and non-human generation of data, and used to monitor our digital footprints. Data selfies are not just selfies; they are also the shadow of ourselves imprinted upon the platforms, devices and sites we use to represent ourselves. Therefore, the 'data selfie' includes the whole assemblage of digital objects left in traces and clicks by the subject, and used to make up the networked photograph, regardless of whether it is shared or kept private.

Data selfies are not strictly limited to networked photos of ourselves. They also include bio tracking apps that help us keep track of our fitness, diet, fertility, daily steps and so many more realms of activity – all part of what Deborah Lupton calls the 'quantified self' (2016, 2020) and Couldry and Mejias call the 'social quantification sector' (2019a, 2019b).

Following this logic, data selves could also include the cookies and behavioural tracking technologies that map what we do and, through predictive analyses, what we will do, where we'll click and who we will probably vote for. If every click is capital (see Chapter 2), then every click helps make up the data selfie of who we are online and on social media. While these issues are explored more in depth in the next chapter on surveillance and privacy (Chapter 8), this section looks at the idea of the data selfie in direct relation to the self-representational networked photograph and its digital counterparts – filters, lenses, artificial intelligence and facial recognition.

Filters, lenses and apps

Despite their popularity, social media filters and lenses are under-researched in social media and selfie literature. There is research on: the role of retro filters in contributing to a nostalgic trend on social media, celebrating lo-fi images and obsolete technologies (Caoduro 2014); the use of the #pharmacist hashtag for Instagram selfies (Hindman et al. 2017); using filters to imply personality traits (Ferwerda et al. 2016); and why Snapchat users choose to use face lenses (Rios et al. 2018). Jill Walker Rettberg, one of the few scholars seriously considering filters across a number of publications, suggests that filters can be used as 'an analytic term to understand algorithmic culture' (2014: 20). This is an important point. Filters, or lenses as Snapchat refers to them, bring together algorithms, facial recognition, and the particular selfie aesthetics of both the platform and the selfie-taker. In this sense, filters and lenses are both personal and highly platform specific, providing a forum for aesthetic expression, as well as for the algorithmic processing of that expression. Rettberg argues that Snapchat lenses 'allow us to play with our visual identity' (2017: 94), and also to:

> … similarly mark our faces as machine readable. To activate the lenses, you use the front-facing camera so you see your own face and then touch the image of your face on the screen until a biometric grid pops up on your face. You can now swipe between different lenses that apply various special effects to your face, mapping them to the grid so that the effects follow the movements of your face. (2017: 93)

Describing how people's faces are mapped using a biometric grid which both activates the Snapchat lens and allows the user to select the lens, Rettberg introduces the basic elements of facial recognition. Although selfie filters on Instagram, Messenger and Facebook work in a similar way, they are activated by selecting the camera, rather than by pressing on your own face. As well, these apps do not show the biometric grid, which obscures the ways in which their filters and lenses are facial recognition technologies.

Lenses and filters also generate numeric data which quantify faces into distances between points, or nodes, on people's faces (e.g. distance between eyes, occipital bones, size of lips, nostrils). Once a face is mapped, the quantified information can be used to fit filters to individual faces, and those facial data become the property of the platform, app, filter/lens creator and any other third parties with access to those data. Rettberg also argues that filters and lenses do much more than just generate and collect data, they also 'normalise biometrics and automated image manipulation' (2017: 94, emphasis added). This is a crucial element of both lenses and filters, highlighting that 'play', although important and enjoyable, can also have unseen and sometimes negative consequences.

Nadav Hochman links 'filters' with other things like 'tags' and 'location' data, arguing that all of these 'textual and numerical descriptions become the "DNA" of an image' (Hochman 2014: 6). Hochman's point is significant, and helps expose the 'data selfie' as a crucial imprint not only of images intended for other humans, but also that each selfie generates a machine-readable selfie. This part makes up the data selfie, and rather than being shared with other people is shared with the platform, its partners and any third parties connected to that platform.

In addition to lenses and filters, there are also a growing number of apps which allow people to change or edit their selfies. Although this is also a crowded market, some of the most popular include Airbrush, Portrait Pro, YouCam, VSCO, Fabby and Facetune (see Box 7.3). All of these apps provide easy photo-editing opportunities where people can quickly make changes to their faces and digital photos.

Box 7.3 Facetune: Photoshop for your selfies

Facetune is a user-friendly photo-editing app which promises to 'Make every selfie look amazing' (https://www.facetuneapp.com/, August 2020). Facetune claims to help its users 'perfect every photo or selfie, making each one look like it came straight out of a high-fashion magazine' (Lightricks, https://www.lightricks.com/products). Launched in 2013, Facetune 'generated about $18 million' by 2015 (Jennings 2019). By 2019, Facetune was the number 1 paid iPhone app for the second time, and had reached over 10 million downloads on Play Store (Blumenthal 2019). Lightricks, Facetune's parent company, has received millions in funding, and plans to 'double its team to 300 by the end of 2019' (Facetune Press Release 2019; Jennings 2019).

The Facetune press kit claims that the app is 'powered by the latest image-processing technologies available, including advanced AI, machine learning, and face recognition' (Facetune Press Release, 2019, https://docs.google.com/document/d/19S5ir800_waCaNdsIFRyaBDcx0LPry6KRaY-MCbdoZM/edit). While Lightrick has developed other products like Enlight Photofox, Enlight Videoleap, Quickshot and Photoloop (https://www.lightricks.com/products), Facetune Classic and Facetune 2 (launched in 2016) are the company's 'runaway hits whose digital fingerprints can be seen all over the internet: pores, lines and zits are airbrushed to oblivion, teeth whitened and waists

(Continued)

nipped' (Solon 2018). In addition to taking selfie editing to new levels, Facetune makes photo-editing very easy and very shareable. On the App Store, Facetune lists the features it has to help users:

- Perfect smiles by widening your smile and/or whitening your teeth
- Give you 'beautiful skin' by smoothing, brightening and removing any imperfections
- Emphasize your eyes, giving you a 'penetrating gaze' as well as the option to 'change your eye color' and/or remove 'red and white-eye effects'
- Provide 'hair salon' tools, including color, filling in bald spots and/or removing stray hairs
- 'Reshape facial structure', including your jaw lines, cheek bones, nose, brows, as well as enlarging or shrinking specific areas
- Apply 'vivid makeup', such as blush, eye shadow, lash extension, lipstick and intensifying colors
- Enhance photos by blurring, focusing, changing lighting, adding filters and/or special effects
- Make art including 'customizable filters'. (App store, https://www.facetuneapp.com/)

However, while Facetune makes photo-editing much more comprehensible and readily available, even to those without any Photoshop skills, it has also raised serious concerns about the easy manipulation of images and the perpetuation of unrealistic beauty standards especially for young women (Jennings 2019; Solon 2018).

Filters, lenses and apps are all increasingly central components of the visual digital environment. They are also not only sitting alongside Instagram and Snapchat filters, but are integral to how these sites work and to the production and datafication of selfies. These elements of digital photography have several implications worth noting. The first of these is that most of us pay much greater attention to the part of the networked photograph that is human readable rather than machine readable. Human readable selfies contain massive quantities of social and personal data – where we are, what we're wearing, what we look like, sometimes what we're thinking, who we're with (or not with), etc. Data selfies also contain massive quantities of information, but these are much less interesting to most of the humans in our networks, and instead are platform-facing systems that collect, process and make sense of big data to predict behaviours, and for generating profits. As Rettberg argues, 'when we post selfies online, our audience will not only be other humans. Our audience is also, and perhaps primarily, machines' (2017: 90).

All of these things – lenses, filters and face apps – are technologies which fit under the larger category of facial recognition and artificial intelligence technologies, further explored in the next section.

Facial recognition, tagging and artificial intelligence

In contrast to the relatively small coverage of filters and lenses in the research literature, there is much more on both facial recognition and artificial intelligence. Indeed, both filters and lenses are user-oriented terms for advanced facial recognition systems. Facebook, Instagram's parent company, for example, has FAIR, its artificial intelligence research department based in Paris, and which has a separate website from its other products and departments (https://ai.facebook.com/research/_). Very much like Facebook's mission statement, 'Give people the power to build community and *bring the world closer together*', their AI department promises that they are 'advancing AI to *bring the world closer together*' (emphasis added, https://ai.facebook.com/research/). Launched in 2013 (LeCun et al. 2018), Facebook's AI work began with photo tagging and facial recognition across users' uploaded photos, as described in their description of facial recognition:

> Face recognition is *used to analyze the photos and videos we think you're in on Facebook*,
> such as your profile picture and photos and videos that you've been tagged in,
> to make a unique number for you, called a template. When you turn your face
> recognition setting on, we create your template and use it to compare to other
> photos, videos and other places where the camera is used (like live video) to
> recognize if you appear in that content. Keep in mind, we don't share your template
> with anyone. (Facebook 2020, emphasis added: https://www.facebook.com/
> help/122175507864081?helpref=faq_content)

Face recognition has become a common feature of Facebook's user interface on the web and on mobile devices. True to its approach to privacy, the default setting face recognition is set to 'on'.[1]

Facebook's AI work has developed a great deal since 2013, and now includes ambitious projects like: FastMRI (using AI to quicken MRIs); memory and neural networks; self-supervised learning; text classification; language translation; and 'new benchmarks for computer vision' for which the AI team has won several awards (LeCun et al. 2018). In terms of FAIR's future, they are prioritizing 'robotics, visual reasoning, and dialogue systems', at least two of which have direct applications to Instagram, Messenger, Facebook camera and a wide range of photos including selfies. As Rettberg argues, 'machine vision is about data, not about the visual' (2017: 90), before she goes on to break down how machine vision and AI work with selfies:

> Faces become 3D grids, emotions are reduced to certain muscular movements and a
> child arriving home is simply motion in a quiet living room. These machine vision
> techniques are also easily used by humans, especially when we try to use machines
> to understand more about a phenomenon such as selfies. (Rettberg 2017: 93)

---

1 Instructions on how to turn off Facebook's facial recognition can be found here: https://www.facebook.com/help/187272841323203?helpref=faq_content (January 2020).

While the privacy concerns associated with the data generated in and through selfies are numerous, there is another quite serious element associated with machine vision and facial recognition: bias. There is a growing body of work which has identified racial, sexual, gendered, class and economic biases in algorithms, computing, and social and digital media (cf. Benjamin 2019a, 2019b; Eubanks 2018; Noble 2018). Luke Stark, a post-doctoral researcher at Microsoft, explains that the bias in facial recognition is poisonous and has toxic implications for social well-being and human flourishing more broadly:

> Facial recognition's racializing effects are so potentially toxic to our lives as social beings that its widespread use doesn't outweigh the risks. 'The future of human flourishing depends upon facial recognition technology being banned before the systems become too entrenched in our lives' Hartzog and Selinger write. 'Otherwise, people won't know what it's like to be in public without being automatically identified, profiled, and potentially exploited.' To avoid the social toxicity and racial discrimination it will bring, facial recognition technologies need to be understood for what they are: nuclear-level threats to be handled with extraordinary care. (Stark 2019: 55)

For Stark, the risks associated with facial recognition are powerful and devastating. (See Box 7.4 on Joy Buolamwini and Timnit Gerbru's fascinating and important work on algorithmic bias.)

Box 7.4 Joy Buolamwini and Timnit Gebru's work on algorithms and bias, 'Gender Shades'

Joy Buolamwini, multiple prize-winning MIT graduate researcher, is one of many critical scholars examining the disturbing intersections between race and technology. With colleague Timnit Gebru, Buolamwini has examined the many ways AI classification systems make mistakes with women and people of colour. Buolamwini and Gebru find that:

> ... darker-skinned females are the most misclassified group (with error rates of up to 34.7%). The maximum error rate for lighter-skinned males is 0.8%. The substantial disparities in the accuracy of classifying darker females, lighter females, darker males, and lighter males in gender classification systems require urgent attention if commercial companies are to build genuinely fair, transparent and accountable facial analysis algorithms. (Buolamwini and Gebru 2018: 1)

Buolamwini's research analyses the accuracy of facial classifications by IBM, Microsoft and Face++ (used by Alipay), across their AI services, finding shocking inaccuracies. In order to address these issues, Buolamwini has been the driving force behind Gender

Shades (http://gendershades.org/), The Algorithmic Justice League (https://www.ajlu-nited.org/) and most recently a new film called *Coded Bias,* directed by Shalini Kantayya (2020; https://www.sundance.org/projects/code-for-bias).

AI and facial recognition are used more widely in social technologies, as well as in the policing, insurance, monitoring and financial sectors. Bias within these technologies, and their use across multiple sectors, has human consequences, and there are serious implications to misclassification. Buolamwini documents some of these cases, which lead to false arrests and potentially fatal consequences for Black and minority people. Buol-amwini and Gebru are working hard to raise attention to these issues as well as change them. In the summer of 2020, Buolamwini's work was attributed with successfully getting IBM, Amazon and Microsoft to pause their use and development of facial recognition technology (Farley 2020).

Conclusion: The Visual Logics of Selfie Culture

The rise of the selfie also means the rise of a particular set of relationships and practices between the self, others and platforms. Within these relationships, the selfie enables specific modes of visibility, which can be public or private, often shaped by the platform and affor-dances accorded to that platform. This chapter has looked at the selfie in a social media age, but limited the exploration to two platforms. In actuality, both of these platforms involve many more apps and services than there has been room to address. For example, both Instagram and Snapchat have launched live and video channels (e.g. Instagram's IGTV and Snapchat's Bitmoji TV). In addition, the role of influencers and platform-specific celebrities is increasingly important not just for the everyday experiences of users, but also for signifi-cant shifts in audience engagements as well as the platform economy (see Abidin 2018). The point here is that there is much more to explore and think about in terms of selfies, and in relation to just two platforms.

As I have argued in this chapter, the selfie involves an object, a practice and a subject – the self in the selfie (cf. Tiidenberg 2018). In order to make sense of how these elements of the selfie are connected in a social media age, we looked at work dispelling the myth of the-selfie-as-narcissism (Senft and Baym 2015) and positioned the selfie in a longer cycle of moral panics (Drotner 1999). In addition, we approached the selfie as one part of the grow-ing global language of visual culture, widely spoken by youth cultures and the digitally networked across the world (Tiefentale and Manovich 2015, 2018). From this point we turned to the two platforms most associated with selfies, looking more closely at how those platforms developed, particularly in relation to selfies. Finally, we turned to the data selfie, the selfie shadow made up of the data traces and visual information left through the use of filters, lenses, apps, metrics and our navigation of the digitally mediated world. While selfies are an important part of this world, Instagram and Snapchat extend beyond selfie aesthetics. As Leaver and his colleagues argue, 'Instagram has become synonymous with visual design and visual culture' (2020: 191).

Yet selfies are not just about visual aesthetics, they involve the ethics of vision and visibility as well. Filters and lenses use facial recognition and artificial intelligence technologies to map faces and overlay visual information. Both of these areas are important and have significant consequences for everyday life.

Luke Stark is one of many arguing that facial recognition must be heavily regulated and whose use must be very carefully thought through, because 'it's dangerous, racializing, and has few legitimate uses' (2019: 51). Stark goes so far as to argue that 'facial recognition needs regulation and control on par with nuclear waste' in order to protect humans from excessive platform interventions and the harms associated with datafication for profit. As Jill Walker Rettberg argues, 'machine vision is changing the way we see ourselves' (2017: 90) and the selfie is a global thermometer measuring the many ways we see and represent ourselves to others.

For Goffman, the back stage referred to those areas where people prepared themselves for the front stage. While this region was not limited to the self, it was limited to people and the props and processes related to moving to the front stage. Data selfies, and the machine-readable self(ie), suggest that a new back stage region has materialized, one where only traces of the human are important for circulation and datafication. This is a significant development, particularly in relation not only to the presentation of self, but also the actualization of self-hood. Data selfies, and the technologies and processes involved in their construction, open up new territories of networked (self) representation. It is important to develop an ethics of vision and visibility to protect the self(ie) in big data territories, as well as on social platforms.

Questions and Activities

1 Select a selfie of a public figure or celebrity. What do you think the selfie is communicating? Consider the location, positioning and context. Explain and discuss.

2 What makes a good or bad selfie? Why?

3 What do you think selfies say about society?

4 Why do you take and share (or not share) selfies? Why do other people take and share selfies?

5 Trace your own data selfie on your preferred social media. What filters do you use? Who made that filter? What happens to your data? What can you learn about your own data selfie?

Further Reading

Buoalamwini, J.; Gebru, T. 2018. Gender shades: intersectional accuracy disparities in commercial gender classification, *Proceedings of Machine Learning Research*, 81, pp. 1–15. http://proceedings.mlr.press/v81/buolamwini18a/buolamwini18a.pdf, http://gendershades.org/overview.html

Katz, J. E.; Schroeder, E. Thomas. 2015. Selfies and photo messaging as visual conversation: reports from the United States, United Kingdom and China, *International Journal of Communication*, 9, pp. 1861–72. https://ijoc.org/index.php/ijoc/article/view/3180/1405

Iqani, M.; Schroeder, J. E. 2016. #selfie: digital self-portraits as commodity form and consumption practice, *Consumption Markets & Culture*, 19 (5), pp. 405–15. DOI: 10.1080/10253866.2015.1116784

Rettberg, J. Walker. 2014. Filtered reality, in *Seeing Ourselves Through Technology.* Palgrave Macmillan. https://link.springer.com/book/10.1057%2F9781137476661

Senft, T.; Baym, N. 2015. What does the selfie say? Investigating a global phenomenon, *International Journal of Communication,* 9, pp. 1588–1606. https://ijoc.org/index.php/ijoc/article/viewFile/4067/1387

PRIVACY AND DATAVEILLANCE

Chapter Overview

Introduction	180
Privacy from the Twentieth to the Twenty-First Century	181
Defining privacy: From the right to be let alone to networked privacy	184
Privacy according to social media platforms	186
Why do we need privacy rights if we have nothing to hide?	192
From Surveillance to Dataveillance	194
The panopticon, dataveillance and surveillance realism	194
Shadow profiles and 'People You May Know' (PYMK)	199
Conclusion: 'The Future Is Private'	202
Questions and Activities	203
Further Reading	204

Chapter Objectives

- Unpack privacy and dataveillance on social media
- Understand the shifting dynamics of privacy in datafication processes, and the key theoretical foundations which make sense of privacy, including an understanding of how social media platforms define and apply privacy
- Introduce privacy and the shift from surveillance to dataveillance
- Examine contemporary privacy cases related to social media, such as non-consensual image sharing, social media monitoring and police surveillance, shadow profiles and 'People You May Know' (PYMK), and current attempts to subvert dataveillance

Introduction

In an era marked by mass surveillance as revealed by Edward Snowden's revelations of collusion between governments and major social and digital media companies, mass data collection (e.g. Cambridge Analytica; see Chapter 1) and regular data breaches, it is difficult to comprehend what privacy means and why it is important. On one hand, the digital environment makes it easy and pleasurable to connect with others and navigate everyday life. On the other, cookies, digital trackers, predictive analytics and invasive data-sharing terms are de facto conditions of social media. Despite these challenges and opposing principles, the right to privacy is enshrined in the Universal Declaration of Human Rights (UDHR), and as such it is an important *universal* human right. Before taking up privacy more critically, it is necessary to start with the right to privacy, which can be found in Article 18 (freedom of belief in public or private) and Article 12 (below):

> No one shall be subjected to arbitrary interference with his privacy, family, home or correspondence, nor to attacks upon his [their] honour and reputation. Everyone has the right to the protection of the law against such interference or attacks. (UDHR 1948)

This chapter introduces the concept of privacy, outlining how it has shifted from the twentieth century to the twenty-first, outlining new articulations of privacy as social (interpersonal) or institutional (public or commercial). Yet these understandings of privacy are out of step with how it is defined by social media companies, who outline privacy and data policies which claim to put users in control but instead set up conditions for maximum dataveillance. Specific cases, such as *People You May Know* (PYMK) and shadow profiles, are considered as illustrations of both privacy invasions and the large-scale extraction of personal data for platform gain. Privacy invasions and dataveillance have become features of the social media ecosystem and this chapter provides an overview for better understanding their history, context and practices.

Privacy from the Twentieth to the Twenty-First Century

In 2014, researchers from Facebook and Cornell University conducted a 'mood manipulation' experiment with almost 700,000 unknowing Facebook users (Kramer et al. 2014). In order to manipulate users' moods, the researchers hid negative or positive content on Facebook users' news feed, recording what kind of content Facebook users posted when shown more or less negative and positive content. Kramer and his colleagues found evidence of 'emotional contagion', meaning that users were more likely to post positive content when exposed to positive content, and also more likely to post negative content when exposed to negative content (Kramer et al. 2014: 8788). However, users were not informed of the research and no measures were in place to support any users who may have been prone to or dealing with mental health issues that could have been exacerbated by the research. This Facebook research raised many ethical controversies over informed consent, harm and gross privacy misconduct.

As introduced in Chapter 1, the mood manipulation study came after Edward Snowden's 2013 mass surveillance revelations, and was only one of many other major privacy violations to come to light. Another example is Snapchat's 'Snap Map', launched in 2017, a geolocation feature so people could visually share their locations. Shortly after its launch, users found that they were sharing their locations *every time* they opened Snapchat, and not just when they were using Snap Map. This meant that Snapchat users were unknowingly sharing their exact location all the time, unnecessarily exposing users to stalking and bullying risks, which could be especially harmful for vulnerable and underage users (Deahl 2017; Solon 2017). While Snapchat came under public fire for this feature, it is one of many cases where social and technology companies employ a reactive approach to privacy, acting only when forced to through public outcry. In 2018, the Cambridge Analytica events revealed that data from 87 million Facebook accounts had been used in 2016 to create and run hyper-targeted political campaigns for the then US presidential candidate Donald Trump and for the Leave.EU's Brexit campaign. Also, in 2018, in the shadow of Facebook's publicly condemned data-sharing practices, Google quietly shut down Google+, in part because a 'bug' potentially 'exposed private data for up to 500,000 users since 2015' (Newman 2018).

These are only a few of the many privacy 'scandals' related directly to social media, and which are coming to light with greater frequency. Zeynep Tufecki (2017), brilliant internet and social movement researcher, argues that these scandals are 'features not bugs' in platforms designed to collect and monetize personal data.

While the scale and scope of these privacy invasions are unprecedented, privacy concerns are not new. For example, in the late nineteenth century, newspapers were becoming an important part of everyday life, reaching national levels of saturation, as were the photographs increasingly published alongside news. This raised concerns about what and who could be photographed, and then have their photos published in national newspapers. Two turn-of-the-century legal scholars, Samuel Warren and Louis Brandeis, were particularly concerned with what they called 'instantaneous photographs' and newspapers because both 'invaded the sacred precincts of private and domestic life' (1890: 195). At this time, developments in photographic technology meant that cameras were smaller and cheaper and more people were able to use them to take pictures. Portraits could suddenly be taken in an instant, instead of during long posed sessions, marking the beginning of 'surreptitious' photography (Warren and Brandeis 1890: 211). Warren and Brandeis argued that this new kind of photography, in tandem with the mass reach of newspapers, posed a unique challenge to existing laws. While people could legally protect themselves from libel or slander, and copyright infringements, there were no legal protections for 'private' instances captured by sly photographers or sneaky journalists. Bearing this in mind, Warren and Brandeis argued for a right to privacy as the 'right to be let alone', inspired by the prying eyes of insatiable newspaper journalists (1890: 193). Their approach to privacy has been influential, and the 'right to be let alone' has been a defining privacy principle for the twentieth century.

In the twenty-first century, new technologies and their affordances around personal information and data mean that the rules for protecting privacy do not fit the current social media ecosystem. Like 'surreptitious photography', data can be generated with every click, shared instantaneously, and permanently captured in servers from across the internet. As a result, existing rights and laws around privacy cannot account for the changing nature of personal information, global infrastructures and networked information. (See Box 8.1, 'From revenge porn to non-consensual image sharing', as an example of the poor fit between new technologies and the legal frameworks.)

Box 8.1 From revenge porn to non-consensual image sharing

Often attributed to Hunter Moore's user-generated nude photo site, 'revenge porn' is a genre of nude and explicit sexual photos shared most often by jilted exes, jealous 'friends' and anyone seeking vengeful retribution for perceived wrongs. In 2011 Moore claimed that his site was getting '30 million unique users every month, and brought in $10,000' monthly (cited in Woolf 2015). While there are no exact figures for the numbers of photos Moore hosted on his site, they were numerous and most of them were posted without consent, often appearing alongside the subject's actual name and contact details (Woolf 2015; see also Jeong 2015). One of Moore's many victims read out her devastating victim statement, detailing the consequences of these images being posted publicly, in court:

> My privacy was violated by Hunter Moore ... a guy I did not know, a total stranger. He called himself a 'professional life-ruiner,' which is exactly what he was and that's exactly what he did to me. I can't begin to express the amount of anger and pain I have built up inside of me because of this man. He completely flipped my world upside down. (Cited by Jeong 2015)

Although Moore's site is only one of many, and this is only one victim's account, these sites are commonplace, and there are many victims who are unable to get their nude photos removed. Amanda Lenhart, internet researcher, and her colleagues found that 1 in

25 Americans has been a victim of revenge porn (Lenhart et al. 2016), and others estimate that there are thousands of 'revenge porn' sites (McGlynn et al. 2017: 29).

Other examples include 'the Fappening' – the hacking and posting of 200 female celebrities' nude photos across social media and the web – within this genre, pointing to a cultural phenomenon around the non-consensual theft or hacking of private female nudes for public consumption (Eikren and Ingram-Waters 2016; Lenhart et al. 2016; McGlynn et al. 2017).

Increasingly, rather than labelling these events as 'revenge porn', researchers refer to these instances as 'non-consensual image sharing' (McGlynn et al. 2017) or 'image based sexual abuse' (Powell et al. 2018) or 'cybersexual assault' (Eikren and Ingram-Waters 2016) – any term which communicates the criminal nature of such photos. This shift in language is important and reflects the slow-moving limits of twentieth-century law. First, 'revenge porn' positions the victim as the subject of 'revenge', implying they have done something to warrant any kind abuse. Second, this term also positions the image as 'porn', something intended to titillate and sexually excite its consumers, but that is not illegal and is meant to be consumed for pleasure. Both of these framings justify positioning the victim as a 'subject of revenge', and fit with victim-blaming discourses that are especially common with sexual crimes and abuses. The laws and policies around this 'phenomenon' are expressed even in the name: 'revenge porn' is culturally sanctioned as a particular form of pornographic entertainment, whereas 'non-consensual image-sharing' is a criminal and privacy invading act.

The law has struggled to provide the language and recourse to deal with the issues around sexting and non-consensual image sharing. Some argue that privacy laws are grossly outdated and we need to rethink the legal framing to better capture these abuses and their impact on victims (Patella-Rey 2018). In the case of Hunter Moore, who was jailed for two and a half years, and fined $2000 for his crimes impacting on thousands of mostly women (Jeong 2015), there seems to be a shocking gap between privacy invasions, their human consequences and justice. As many have argued, this gap is in part due to absences in the law around social media, non-consensual image sharing and privacy protections, particularly when there is a heavy reliance on precedents and laws written in the last century.

Yet there is also progress. McGlynn and her colleagues note that there are 'new laws criminalising this practice' in:

> England and Wales, Scotland, Israel, Japan, Canada, New Zealand, Victoria
> (Australia), and in the thirty-four states in the US. Among the countries currently
> debating reform are Ireland, South Africa, Iceland and parts of Australia. (2017: 26)

Despite these steps forward, the legislative approach has been unsystematic, and is often placed in opposition to freedom of speech, in line with longstanding victim blaming practices (see Eikren and Ingram-Waters 2016; McGlynn et al. 2017). It is also important to note that non-consensual image sharing is different from consensual image sharing. 'Sexting' and sharing intimate photos are becoming a cultural norm, experienced as an important rite of passage for young people's sexual and social development, and these practices need to be legally distinct (Thomas 2018).

Defining privacy: From the right to be let alone to networked privacy

Many have fiercely debated the meaning of privacy. Daniel Solove, a world leading privacy expert, argues that this is in part because privacy is *pluralistic,* including many 'different things that do not share one element in common but that nevertheless bear a resemblance to each other' (2007: 756). For example, some might think nude photos are very personal content and should never be shared, while others might enjoy (and even monetize) such photos. Regardless of where one puts themselves on the privacy spectrum, recognizing privacy means also recognizing the power of the individual in determining what is private, even when that involves contradictions. What is private, after all, is also deeply personal.

Solove goes beyond the idea that privacy is just personal, arguing that it is also a social value, one that benefits society as much as the individual. For Solove, privacy enables people to have some reprieve from social pressures and the 'intrusiveness of others' (2007: 762). Indeed, a society without any

> privacy protection would be suffocating, and it might not be a place in which most would want to live. When protecting individual rights, we as a society decide to hold back in order to receive the benefits of creating the kinds of free zones for individuals to flourish. (Solove 2007: 762)

This is important, particularly in a networked age. For Solove, privacy is not just a right or a condition, but also a pluralistic combination of the two which both enable 'individuals to flourish' and, contingently, provides a benefit to society (cf. Cohen 2015, 2017).

Related to the complexity of privacy, Helen Nissenbaum, widely cited for her influential theory of privacy as 'contextual integrity', also sees privacy as pluralistic and as an essential condition for human life. In particular, Nissenbaum sees privacy as more than a right to 'secrecy' and 'control', instead arguing that privacy is 'a right to *appropriate* flow of personal information' (emphasis in original, Nissenbaum 2010: 127). For Nissenbaum, privacy is based on 'contextual integrity' which allows us to

> live in a world in which our expectations about the flow of personal information are, for the most part, met; expectations that are shaped not only by force of habit and convention but a general confidence in the mutual support these flows accord to key organizing principles of social life, including moral and political ones. (Nissenbaum 2010: 231)

For Nissenbaum, contextual integrity refers to the multiple ways that privacy is embedded within broader contexts – shaped by norms, values and informational flows. Yet she also argues that this does not mean privacy is an individualized condition, as it is instead shaped by social expectations and contexts. Drawing from the work of both Solove and Nissenbaum,

Julie Cohen, a legal scholar studying privacy in a networked era, argues that privacy battles – 'from nude selfies and #fail videos to leaks, hacks, and data breaches' – are actually the moral struggles of contemporary life (2017: 8). These social struggles over privacy are both 'spectacle and discipline' for the operation of 'moral and political power' (2017: 8).

Social media expert and principal researcher at Microsoft danah boyd (2012) argues that we are in an age of 'networked privacy', best characterized by the relational nature of information on social media. In order to illustrate her point, boyd argues that photos and other information on social media are like DNA. Genetic information contains personal data, not only about those who the DNA comes from, but also about entire families – mothers, fathers, siblings, grandparents, children and those children or grandchildren yet to arrive – whose information is also contained in one person's DNA. This example illustrates the networked nature of data and privacy. Although privacy is often thought of as an individual right, looking at genetic information demonstrates how deeply information connects people, groups and social contexts (boyd 2012).

It is at this point we can see a disjuncture in how privacy has been theorized – as pluralistic, as contextual and as networked – and how people negotiate privacy on social media and in digital environments. My own research finds that people value privacy, repeatedly saying that it matters and is important to them, yet they continue to use privacy-invading social networks (Sujon 2018). This points to a huge discrepancy between how many understand privacy in their everyday lives and how it is formally articulated on social media. Indeed, many people have tried to make sense of this discrepancy. One such widely cited approach is the 'privacy paradox', which suggests that people are willing to compromise their privacy and exchange their personal information for the convenience of connecting with others or using digital services.

Kate Raynes-Goldie, games designer and digital researcher, has a counter-explanation for this behavioural discrepancy. Raynes-Goldie argues that there are two kinds of privacy on social and digital media: 'social privacy' which includes friendship-oriented and reputational concerns; and 'institutional privacy', which refers to the processing of personal data generated through clicks, likes, views, etc. (2010, 2012). Mariya Stoilova and her colleagues (2019a, 2019b) further differentiate this distinction, arguing that 'social' privacy can be understood as involving interpersonal relations, and 'institutional privacy' as involving public institutions (e.g. government, health, and/or education), as well as commercial relations (e.g. platforms, advertisers, audience networks, third parties). For Raynes-Goldie and Stoilova et al., this distinction is based on different kinds of data – data that are 'given' (provided by the user) and data that are inferred (data that are analysed or profiled), discussed further below. (See Figure 8.1 for an overview of these different kinds of privacy.)

Social or interpersonal privacy relates to other people and what is visible to those who may be known or unknown. For example, social privacy could refer to privacy from (or in relation to) families, romantic interests or partners, prospective or former employers, and/or unknown people who might become known in the future. Institutional privacy, in contrast, refers to the kinds of public and private institutions that can view, collect and collate

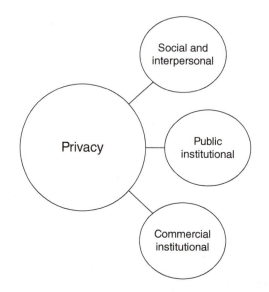

Figure 8.1 Three kinds of privacy: Social and interpersonal; public institutional; commercial institutional

Source: adapted from Raynes-Goldie 2012, 2010; Stoilova et al. 2019a, 2019b.

a person's data and personal information, without being known to the user, and without any observable interaction. Data selfies, for example, would be entirely on the commercial institutional level (see Chapter 7). Some examples of public institutions include government agencies, those in the education sector and/or health organizations. Commercial institutions would include most social media and digital platforms, big technology companies and most of the Ad Tech industry, app developers, along with many others.

These are important distinctions to make when thinking through privacy. While most people experience and understand privacy in social or interpersonal conditions, most terms and conditions address institutional privacy, often using legal terminology and language. The distinctions between social and institutional privacy show that the privacy paradox may be less about an inconsistency in people's behaviours, and more about an inconsistency in how platforms present privacy in institutional rather than social terms (Blank et al. 2014; Stoilova et al. 2019a: 7; Sujon 2018). Shoshanna Zuboff (2019) refers to this as a tremendous feat of misdirection by big tech to culturally entrench surveillance capitalism. In order to examine this claim further, the next section identifies the meaning of privacy, according to the privacy policies of key social media platforms.

Privacy according to social media platforms

Despite serious initiatives to simplify privacy policies, privacy statements are complex. The length and detail of these sites and policies can make it difficult for even privacy experts to understand and keep up with. In addition, these policies are often subject to change, and almost all platforms state that the user is responsible for being aware of any changes. For example, the privacy policies for Facebook have been reorganized, presenting a very different idea of privacy than those it presented in 2015 and 2019. In 2020, many of the same privacy policies still exist, albeit they have been reorganized in sections across different pages with new headings. For example, one of the recent changes brings the 'privacy' link straight to Facebook's 'data policy' with very little explanation of how the two are related. These kinds of perpetual changes make it more difficult to keep track of changes.

Facebook, once a single site, now has a data policy which applies to many different sites, services and apps, and has an evolving set of terms and conditions which have significantly changed over the last decade. Most notably, these include WhatsApp and Instagram. Similarly, YouTube's privacy policies refer to most of Google's products and services, and users have to work out how those policies apply to specific products, like YouTube. Many privacy statements are misleading. Although Facebook no longer makes copyright claims in its privacy pages (they are now located in its 'Terms of Service'), many user-generated content sites do make a generic claim stating that users grant the service a 'worldwide, non-exclusive, royalty-free licence' to distribute and monetize user-generated content, demonstrating a blurring between intellectual property and privacy. (See Box 8.2 for a fuller excerpt of 'Your Rights' from Twitter's terms of service. Although only an excerpt is included here, it is useful to read these terms in full, to get a sense of the terms which are fairly typical not only to social media, but also any sites with user-generated content.)

Box 8.2 'Your Rights' in Twitter's Terms of Service

By submitting, posting or displaying Content on or through the Services, **you grant us a worldwide, non-exclusive, royalty-free license (with the right to sublicense) to use, copy, reproduce, process, adapt, modify, publish, transmit, display and distribute such Content in any and all media or distribution methods now known or later developed** (for clarity, these rights include, for example, curating, transforming, and translating). This license authorizes us to make your Content available to the rest of the world and to let others do the same. **You agree that this license includes the right for Twitter to provide, promote, and improve the Services and to make Content submitted to or through the Services available to other companies, organizations or individuals for the syndication, broadcast, distribution, Retweet, promotion or publication of such Content on other media and services,** subject to our terms and conditions for such Content use. Such additional uses by Twitter, or other companies, organizations or individuals, is made with **no compensation paid to**

(Continued)

you with respect to the Content that you submit, post, transmit or otherwise make available through the Services as the use of the Services by you is hereby agreed as being sufficient compensation for the Content and grant of rights herein.

Twitter has an evolving set of rules for how ecosystem partners can interact with your Content on the Services. These rules exist to enable an open ecosystem with your rights in mind. **You understand that we may modify or adapt your Content** as it is distributed, syndicated, published, or broadcast by us and our partners and/or make changes to your Content in order to adapt the Content to different media.

You represent and warrant that you have, or have obtained, all rights, licenses, consents, permissions, power and/or authority necessary to grant the rights granted herein for any Content that you submit, post or display on or through the Services. You agree that such Content will not contain material subject to copyright or other proprietary rights, unless you have necessary permission or are otherwise legally entitled to post the material and to grant Twitter the license described above.

(*Source*: Twitter, 'Content on the Services', February 2020, emphasis added)

These terms, typical of many social media sites, highlight an important privacy issue. When platforms place personal content and individual activity on that platform in ownership or intellectual property terms, it means that privacy becomes first an economic issue rather than a rights or a human issue. This point is made apparent in social media privacy policies, where they explain what kinds of data they collect. Given the complexity of these policies, and the sheer quantity of data that social media platforms collect, Mariya Stoilova and colleagues (2019a: 7) provide a helpful categorization of the data users generate and platforms collect:

> *Data given* – the data contributed by individuals (about themselves or about others), usually knowingly, although not necessarily intentionally, during their participation online;
>
> *Data traces* – the data left, mostly unknowingly, by participation online and captured via data tracking technologies such as cookies, web beacons or device/browser fingerprinting, location data and other metadata;
>
> *Inferred data* – the data derived from analysing data given and data traces, often by algorithms (also referred to as 'profiling'), possibly combined with other data sources.

All of these terms place responsibility for the generation and use of data with the individual. As we shall see, those working on or for social media platforms need to take much more responsibility for the data integrity of their users, and for any data extraction.

Building upon Stoilova et al.'s (2019a) framework, I bring together key elements from the privacy policies of six social media platforms in Tables 8.1 and 8.2. As mentioned above, both the Google and Facebook policies apply to a wide range of platform products, many of which remain unnamed. Notably, although WhatsApp is owned by Facebook, it stands out in this review because it has its own unique policies, one of which is a declaration that it receives and shares information with 'Facebook Companies'. Twitter and Snapchat, although smaller than Google or Facebook, also make references to other products in their platform, and thus also have privacy policies which bundle many different social products together.

It is also worth noting that the privacy policies almost always begin with a statement about 'putting you in control', emphasizing user agency in controlling their content. (See the 'opening privacy statements' row in Table 8.1 below, which detail first statements made in privacy policies.)

Although these opening statements almost unanimously suggest that users have 'control', this control only refers to social privacy, and does not apply to the copious amounts of data social platforms collect from users, and share with third parties, as shown in Table 8.2 ('Data given'), across social media platforms. The information presented in this table comes from an analysis of social media privacy policies, in order to identify exactly what kinds of data social media companies claim users 'provide to us'. While 'data given' also includes data that are traced, inferred and non-consensually taken, this term appears in the privacy policies. Table 8.1 and 8.2 provide an overview of what these platforms mean by 'data given' and it is worth questioning this further.

Users are required to provide a lot of this data in order to join or set up a social media account. Facebook's 'real name policy' requires users to provide their real name and contact details. YouTube, Twitter and Snapchat allow users to use whatever name they want, but must provide a functional email and/or telephone number. WhatsApp cannot be activated without a working phone number. Thus, even the initial profile and account information requires a lot of personal information. Phone numbers are valuable data, often accurately linked to people's identities, and also containing contact lists, photo albums and other stored content which are data treasure troves. There are many other sources of personal and social information about users which social media draw from, which when taken together again shows that every click generates another piece of monetizable data.

In addition to so-called 'data given', there are also 'data traces' and 'inferred data'. Data traces include data 'unknowingly left' and picked up through cookies, beacons, geo-data and other metadata. Inferred data come from data analysis and profiling, both regularly undertaken and described in social media privacy policies. Although these distinctions are not explained in any of the privacy policies analysed here, there are clear instances of inferred data. For example, Twitter analyses your tweets, likes, views and other information to 'determine what topics you're interested in, your age, the languages you speak, and other signals'

Table 8.1 Privacy policies across social media

	YouTube	Facebook, Instagram and Messenger	WhatsApp	Twitter	Snapchat
Opening privacy statement	'When you use our services, you're trusting us with your information. We understand that this is a big responsibility and we work hard to **protect your information and put you in control**'	**'You have control over who sees what you share on Facebook'** (Privacy Basics) 'To provide the Facebook Products, we must process information about you' (Data Policy)	**'Your privacy is our priority.** Our mission is to connect the world privately by designing a product that's simple and private... **you're always in control'**	'We believe you should always know what data we collect from you and how we use it, and that **you should have meaningful control** over both'	'At Snap, we **make your privacy a priority.** We know your trust is earned every time you use Snapchat, or any of our other products – that's why we treat your information differently to most other tech companies'
Applies to...	A wide range of Google products (e.g. YouTube, Search, Maps, Chrome, Google Home, Android devices and ads)	Facebook, Instagram, Messenger and 'other products', including Oculus and WhatsApp	WhatsApp, though 'WhatsApp receives information from, and shares information with, the Facebook Companies'	'Twitter Entities' and Periscope	Snapchat and Snapchat products (Snaps, Chats, My Story, Our Story, Memories, Lenses, Bitmojis, SnapKit, Advertising, Spectacles, Scan, SnapMap)
Sources	Google Privacy Policy, https://policies.google.com/privacy?hl=en-GB&gl=uk (February 12, 2020)	Privacy Basics, https://www.facebook.com/about/basics Data policy, https://www.facebook.com/privacy/explanation Your Privacy https://www.facebook.com/help/238 3181465353337helpref=hc_global_nav (February 12, 2020)	WhatsApp Privacy, https://www.whatsapp.com/privacy (February 12, 2020)	Twitter Privacy Policy, https://twitter.com/en/privacy (February 12, 2020)	Our Privacy Principles, https://www.snap.com/en-GB/privacy/privacy-center/ (February 12, 2020)

Table 8.2 'Data given' across social media platforms according to their privacy policies (February 2020)

Data given	YouTube	Facebook, Instagram and Messenger	WhatsApp	Twitter	Snapchat
Search terms	X	X		X	
Views	X	X			X
Interaction with content	X	X		X	X
Interaction with ads	X	X		X	X
Interaction with others	X	X		X	X
Your connections	X	X	X	X	X
Voice and audio	X	X	X		X
Synced info	X	X			X
Profile info	X	X	X	X	X
Profile pictures or Bitmoji	X	X	X		X
Name	X	X	X	X	X
Birthday	X	X	X	X	X
Email	X	X	X	X	X
Phone number			X	X	X
Address book		X	X	X	X
Message content	X	X	X	X	X
Location of content	X	X	X	X	X
Things viewed through app camera		X	X		X
Uploaded content	X	X	X	X	X
Your usage of products	X	X	X		X
Frequency and duration of your activities	X	X	X	X	X
Off-platform activity	X	X			
Financial transactions	X	X	X		X
Credit or debit card info	X	X	X		X
Device info	X	X	X	X	X

(point 4, Twitter 2020). Like YouTube, Facebook and Snapchat, Twitter does this so that it can 'personalize' its services, and to match advertising to your interests, age, demographic, location, etc. In addition, most social platforms share data across their product families and with third party partners. For example, WhatsApp shares information with and from the 'Facebook Companies' (https://www.whatsapp.com/legal/#privacy-policy-information-you-and-we-share), demonstrating the extent to which data analysis and profiling extend within social platforms and beyond the social ecosystem.

In most of the classes I've taught, students are shocked and horrified when we cover privacy and data collection on social media. Although public trust in social media, particularly Facebook, may have eroded in the last few years, many are still surprised to learn just how much personal data are collected, shared and circulated by social media platforms. Most students have focused their privacy concerns on how others might perceive them, and on what we have discussed as social and interpersonal privacy. Yet institutional data collection and privacy from corporate and public institutions has become an urgent public matter, one that has tremendous significance for human flourishing and social development. Despite this, there are always some students (and some media pundits and tech billionaires) who say, 'Who cares? I've got nothing to hide. Privacy is dead anyway.' In the next section, we discuss this argument and why it is so very wrong.

Why do we need privacy rights if we have nothing to hide?

In 2010 Mark Zuckerberg said that 'the rise of social networking online means that people no longer have an expectation of privacy' (as reported in Johnson 2010). Eric Schmidt also publicly stated that privacy is only important for those who had something to hide, implying that only criminals and wrong-doers need privacy (Esguerra 2009; Metz 2009). This claim is based on the 'underlying assumption that privacy is about hiding bad things' (Solove 2007: 762). Daniel Solove, leading privacy scholar and researcher, argues that this thinking is fundamentally flawed.

Solove observes that the current data environment is marked by 'aggregation', i.e. the collection and 'combination of small bits of seemingly innocuous data' which can simultaneously decontextualize information and reveal new, at times, unexpected information (Solove 2007: 766). For example, predictive analysis and profiling mean that 'likes' can be used to identify political affiliations and intelligence (e.g. Golbeck 2013). As such, it is not just privacy that is the issue but also the changing standards of data collection and analysis. New computational methods and techniques change what it is possible to know from bits of information that may once have been discrete or meaningless. Once these bits are aggregated, this can create a much more comprehensive imprint of a person's life and habits, drastically changing what can be known about that person. For example, location data may be relatively meaningless on their own, but when combined with demographic data (age, sex, gender), they can reveal important beliefs and habits. In terms of 'having nothing to hide' privacy is not about wrong-doing.

In addition, Solove also argues that data collection by governments (or by massive global platforms) creates 'a structural problem' marked by 'a power imbalance between individuals' and powerful institutions (2007: 767). The key question in this imbalance is how much power should governments or platforms like Facebook, Google or other social media platforms have over citizens? Privacy is about protecting citizens' rights not only to be free from ever increasing data-collection practices, but also to the changing implications and applications of that data. The Cambridge Analytica events are an excellent example of this issue (see Chapter 1). Should data collected by Facebook be used to develop political campaigns to manipulate voters? The ethical and legal answer is no, yet the structural imbalances mean that little could be done to prevent such reprehensible actions.

There are two additional issues related to the nothing to hide argument. The first of these is the future – and all of the technological, policy, contextual and methodological changes that come with new developments in data analysis and collection. In terms of legal and policy contexts, information and data may be interpreted in very different ways depending on broader political contexts (as illustrated in Box 8.1, 'From revenge porn to non-consensual image sharing'). In the UK, Brexit may mean that the social media companies in the UK no longer need to comply with the EU's 'General Data Protection Regulation (GDPR), which will impact on what data can be collected, how they can be used and by whom. Although writing in 2007, Solove cogently expressed this issue, which is just as relevant now:

> The potential future uses of any piece of personal information are vast, and without limits or accountability on how that information is used, it is hard for people to assess the dangers of the data being in the government's control. (2007: 767)

Finally, there is also the problem of 'secondary use', which is when 'data obtained for one purpose' are used 'for a different unrelated purpose without the person's consent' (Solove 2007: 767). Recalling the privacy policies and terms of service reviewed earlier, this appears to be common practice (see also Chapter 1). This is a serious concern. It is not just about what a social media company might do with your data, it is also about what their partners, subsidiaries, former partners, third parties, governments or other as yet unknown actors might do with your data. All in all, secondary use of relational data now, or in the future, is serious.

In short, the argument that we don't need to prioritize privacy if we have nothing to hide may feel like an easy solution but, as I hope to have shown here, it is deeply flawed. It is flawed because privacy is not about wrong-doing or our individual preferences, and it is not just about what happens now. Developments in data collection and manipulation, like data aggregation, change what could be done with personal data and how they can be used. Changing policy and legal contexts mean that how we define data and their acceptable uses is subject to radical change. Secondary use of data is a serious matter, one that is also a basic condition of platformization. For all of these reasons, it is important to think critically about what privacy means and why it is that some people argue it is no longer important.

So far, this chapter has introduced key conceptual approaches to privacy – it is contextual and networked – and it is defined by social media site policies quite differently from how they use personal data. After the initial empowering opening privacy statements, social media platforms collect data from every user – every like, every link, every upload, every sync, sometimes off site and offline. All of these come under 'data you provide' regardless of how differently users experience or perceive these actions. Social media are built for monetizing personal data, further explained in the next section which introduces the shift from surveillance to dataveillance.

From Surveillance to Dataveillance

The word surveillance means to 'watch over', and many have theorized the ways in which technologies for 'seeing' make up and contribute to our social, economic and media systems, for surveillance and control. Some of the most influential theories in surveillance studies draw from the work of Michel Foucault (introduced in Chapter 3), particularly his work on discipline and the panopticon, an iconic symbol for modern systems of power and social control. The panopticon has inspired a great deal of work in this area, and datafication brings new kinds of pervasive surveillance, prompting an inescapable sense of 'surveillance realism' (e.g. Dencik 2018; Dencik et al. 2016). The next section briefly introduces the panopticon and the shift from surveillance to dataveillance, as well as surveillance realism as a consequence of this shift. From there, I introduce shadow profiles and 'People You May Know', two common features of social media which evidence that platforms promote an ideology of connection at the cost of user privacy.

The panopticon, dataveillance and surveillance realism

Michel Foucault's work on 'the panopticon', a prison designed in the eighteenth century by Jeremy Bentham, is one of the most widely cited examples of twentieth-century surveillance. For Foucault, the panopticon is one particular architecture symbolizing a shift in the 'anatomy' and 'micro-physics of power', which in the seventeenth century focused on disciplining the *body*. For example, Foucault offers the example of an individual being drawn and quartered, literally ripped limb from limb, as a punishment for treason, as a corporeal penal technique (1975: 3–5). In contrast, the eighteenth-century panopticon, symbolizes a shift towards disciplining the *subject* by training the mind. With the advent of the 'modern' prison, the school, the factory and even the army, 'punishment' shifted from the body onto the subject through 'discipline' and the power/knowledge nexus which focused on training and governmentality (1975: 227; see also Chapter 2). For Foucault, the panopticon was one part of a broader transition to discipline as the modus operandi of the time. (See Figure 8.2 and Bentham's plan of the panopticon, 1843 [originally 1791].)

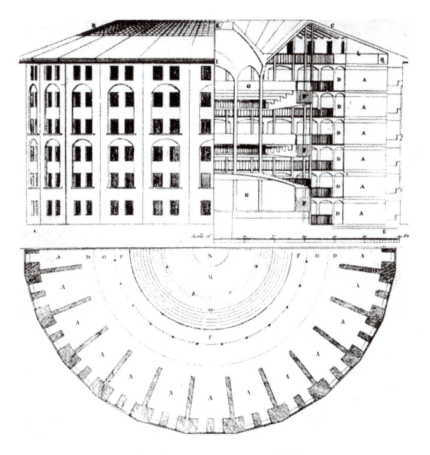

Figure 8.2   Bentham's plan of the panopticon, 1843 [originally 1791]

Source: originally from *The works of Jeremy Bentham* vol. IV, 172-3, Wikimedia Commons, public domain

The panopticon was a circular building, built around a central command tower and surrounded by enclosures for prisoners that could be clearly seen from the tower (see the cells marked A in Figure 8.2). Prisoners could not see into other enclosures, nor could they see into the tower. This model, with its asymmetrical lines of sight, was designed 'to induce in the inmate a state of conscious and permanent visibility that assures the automatic functioning of power' (Foucault 1975: 201). For Foucault, *permanent visibility* effectively replaced the manual exercise of power, where power must be physically enforced on the subject's body; instead, the prison guard became an omnipresent spectre, one that could appear at any time. In this way, the panopticon is a near perfect model for invoking the prisoner (or the student, or the soldier, or the worker) to internalize power, and govern themself in accordance with hegemonic expectations. Foucault goes on to argue that the panopticon:

> Without any physical instrument other than architecture and geometry, acts directly on individuals; it gives 'power of mind over mind'. The panoptic schema makes any apparatus of power more intense. (1975: 206)

Thus the panopticon represents an architecture of power central to the twentieth century, and with it came the birth of a new era of surveillance as a mechanism for social control.

In the twenty-first century, the panopticon has been reimagined in many different forms. For example, drawing from the mass audiences of television, there is the 'synopticon' (the surveillance of the few by the many as related to celebrity culture and television viewership; see Mathiesen 1997). Siva Vaidhyanathan, critical technology theorist, argues that Foucault overstated the power of the panopticon, and offers the idea of the 'cryptopticon', a networked surveillance structure where individuals are subject to constant surveillance by many – such as peers, platforms, advertisers, app developers, governments – often unknown and unknowable (2011: 112). Anders Albrechtslund (2008) suggests that we are in an age of something like a peer-opticon, where individuals are part of a many-to-many model or what he calls 'participatory surveillance'. These are only a few examples, among many others (see Galic et al. 2017 for a useful overview).

The networked nature of social media has had a radical impact on the central command tower model of surveillance. One such development is 'dataveillance' – 'the systematic use of personal data systems in the investigation or monitoring of the actions or communications of one or more persons' (Clarke 1998, as cited in Solove 2007: 765; cf. Galic et al. 2017). Dataveillance is not just theoretical, and not just in use for corporate profit-making. Dataveillance is the surveillance of individuals, groups and populations, through the data they inadvertently generate as they live their lives using everyday technologies such as networked and social media.

Dataveillance can have a serious and negative impact on those who are surveilled, especially those who are already marginalized and disempowered. (See Box 8.3, Police dataveillance: Social media monitoring, data harvesting and racial profiling.)

Box 8.3 Police dataveillance: Social media monitoring, data harvesting and racial profiling

In response to the rise of data-driven racial profiling, *The European Network Against Racism* published a report documenting current use of policing technologies across Europe in order to better understand the negative impact on ethnic minority and marginalised communities (Williams and Kind 2020). The report details not only a wide range of technologies used for predictive policing and racial profiling, but also the impact of using those technologies. Williams and Kind argue that such technologies are not neutral. They often use data that comes from over policed communities, fundamentally skewing the results, and leading to the mis-identification of Black people and ethnic and other minorities as high risk, as well as re-creating skewed results (2020: 6). Supporting this claim, Williams and Kind argue that:

> In England and Wales, figures indicate that Black people are more than nine times more likely to be stopped and searched by the police, a figure that increases to more than twenty times in particular areas in England and Wales. (2020: 9)

Tracing the production of police surveillance tools, Williams and Kind find that most companies have 'more in common with defence contractors than the technology sector', and that most are based in economically advanced, large arms exporting states, with the US, UK, France, Germany and Israel (2020: 14). Many of these companies have strong links with people who were previously employed in government, law enforcement and intelligence, which for Williams and Kind demonstrate a strong association with long-established discriminatory practices in policing.

In addition to policing technologies like facial recognition, automatic number plate recognition, voice identification, mobile fingerprint scanning, call detail records, IMSI catchers (mobile phone frequency catchers), body cameras and mobile phone extraction, Williams and Kind also document 'data harvesting and social media monitoring' (2020: 16–21). For these techniques, police monitor people's social media accounts in order to map their social networks and interpersonal connections, often in the attempt to show 'criminal networks and relationships for the purpose of prosecution' (2020: 18). This kind of monitoring can include private communication, closed group activity and specific interactions (2020: 18). Police can create 'fake personas', scrape or 'acquire social media information in bulk', and use keyword searches where anyone using flagged words (e.g. names, colours, clothing, groups, places) is added to criminal databases (2020: 18).

Williams and Kind argue that these techniques have a disproportionately negative impact on Black people and minorities, making it crucial to protect vulnerable groups as well as to monitor and regulate the use of these dataveillance techniques and technologies. Most social media platforms state that they will cooperate with law enforcement if there are legal requests or concerns about policy violations, the investigation, detection or prevention of fraud, and harm to individual users or to social media platforms (see 'Sources' in Table 8.1).

Dataveillance is not only a technically new kind of digital surveillance, but also involves new power (infra) structures, what Shoshana Zuboff, surveillance expert, refers to as 'the global architecture of computer mediation' and the 'distributed and largely uncontested new expression of power that I christen "Big Other"' (2015: 75). Similarly, Lina Dencik, co-founder of the data justice lab, argues that the omniscience of data analytics and always-on mass surveillance is driven by a new global power network of social media making up a new 'oligarkhia', what she describes as the:

> ... amalgam of the intelligence community, retailers, Silicon Valley, military interests, social media, the Inner Beltway, multinational corporations, midtown Manhattan, and Wall Street. This 'oligarkhia' is the product, in part, of shared interests in security (from foreign corporate espionage, cyber hacking, malevolent actors etc.) among government and technology companies, in conjunction with the rise of neoliberalism and the associated trend toward deregulation, outsourcing and privatization. (Harcourt 2015: 66, cited in Dencik 2018)

In a world where continuous and mass dataveillance is the norm, alternatives are increasingly hard to imagine. Dencik (2018) argues that we are in a state of 'surveillance realism' which is about the normalization of surveillance because 'datafication and surveillance is seen as the only legitimate response to social ills'. Ultimately, surveillance realism crushes the prospect of imagining alternatives. She observes that 'digital resignation' is a common feature where dataveillance is not only pervasive but also feels inescapable. Although she convincingly outlines the existence of surveillance realism as an 'inevitability', she also emphasizes that there is promise in resistance, and real hope in the challenge of restructuring and reimagining dataveillance. For these reasons, it is crucial to keep questioning privacy and datavelliance practices, as well as to keep imagining alternatives. (See Box 8.4, 'Subverting dataveillance on Instagram', for an example of one way young people are doing just that.)

Box 8.4 Subverting dataveillance on Instagram

Rather than expose too much of themselves on social media, some people have created what they call 'Finstas', i.e. fake Instagram accounts for their true selves, where they feel freed from the limits of Instagram's polished aesthetic (Safranova 2015). While this points to a subversion of Instagram's visual performativity, it only does so in relation to social privacy, namely their friendship groups and reputational currency. Finstas would only be shared with trusted friends (see also 'FikFoks', fake TikToks, in Longo 2020). Yet recent reports find that young people are also protecting their institutional privacy, by making it hard for Instagram's dataveillance algorithms to work properly. In this instance, a group of young people share one Instagram account not to obscure how they look to others, but so that their individual interests, friendships, networks, connections and metadata are obscured through the group (Ng 2020).

In this fascinating use of Instagram, young users are creating new collective accounts. One person might start an account, but the account name and password are shared with a group of friends, anywhere from just a few people to 20 or more (Ng 2020). Each of these people will post different kinds of content, different images, all from different locations and different devices. Group accounts on Instagram may not be welcomed by Instagram, but it is an effective tactic for protecting users' social and institutional privacy from constant platform dataveillance, from data harvesting, and even from the prying eyes of peers, acquaintances and strangers. As Ng argues, 'maybe they couldn't hide their data footprints, but they could at least leave hundreds behind to confuse trackers'.

Social media are the engines of the data economy, which drive platform empires (see Chapters 2, 3 and 5). Social media are reconfiguring the panopticon into a global power matrix, one that is networked, world spanning, multi-veillanced and also a totalizing architecture of and for dataveillance. In the next section, I introduce shadow profiles and 'People You May Know', two linked features which help to illustrate the scope and extent of dataveillance on any social media platform that recommends users to other users or offers some kind of 'discover' feature.

Shadow profiles and 'People You May Know' (PYMK)

In June 2013, Facebook quietly notified its followers that a bug had accidentally revealed 'approximately 6 million Facebook users' email addresses and/or telephone numbers'. The announcement was posted on the somewhat obscure Facebook 'notes' page, and explained that the 'bug' made personal contact information available to others who used the 'download your info' tool. While this may seem like a comparatively minor privacy invasion compared to the 87 million exposed in the Cambridge Analytica events (see Chapter 1), it was also revealing because it showed that Facebook was not only uploading users' 'contact lists or address books', but that they were also creating 'shadow profiles' of non-users with these contact details (Facebook 2013b; Hill 2018; Quodling 2018). According to Kashmir Hill (2018), this 'shadow social network' is extremely valuable, and allows Facebook (and other social platforms) to:

> ... develop a list of everyone in the world and how they were connected. Even if you don't give Facebook access to your own contact book, it can learn a lot about you by looking through other people's contact books. If Facebook sees an email address or a phone number for you in someone else's address book, it will attach it to your account as 'shadow' contact information that you can't see or access.

Although Zuckerberg has denied the existence of shadow profiles (Quodling 2018), there is a growing body of evidence which demonstrates otherwise. One of these sources of evidence is 'People You May Know' (PYMK), a feature which appears across many social media platforms under different names. PYMK reveals the existence of shadow profiles as well as the collection of personal information from other users about both users and non-users.

First, however, a little background about this feature. PYMK was launched by LinkedIn in 2006, and was described as:

> … LinkedIn's link prediction system and one of the site's most recognizable features. As the name implies, it tries to find other professionals you might know, allowing members to grow their networks. PYMK is now responsible for more than half the connections on the site and is a principal component of engagement. (LinkedIn 2012, as captured by WayBackMachine)

Indeed, shortly after PYMK's launch, LinkedIn noticed that these links 'achieved a click-through rate 30% higher than the rate obtained by other prompts to visit more pages on the site', creating millions of page views (Davenport and Patil 2012). Facebook noted PYMK's success on LinkedIn and built its own version in 2008, which has become an essential part of Facebook's massive expansion (Facebook 2008a, 2008b; Hill 2018). On Instagram, we see this feature under 'Suggestions for You'. On Twitter, we see 'Who to Follow'. On Snapchat, we can find all sorts of recommendations including possible friends under 'Discover'. On TikTok, there is the 'For You' page which makes suggestions based on your browsing behaviours (along with other data). Similarly, YouTube recommends pages and channels. Although it might have different names, the PYMK feature has become a common feature across social media platforms.

Although this feature might sound fairly innocuous, it can have serious consequences. Kashmir Hill (2016), a tech journalist who has been researching PYMK for years, interviewed a psychiatrist who reported that her clinical patients were being recommended to her as Facebook friends – and her patients reported to her that they were seeing her other patients being recommended as PYMK to them. In this particular case, the psychiatrist explained that although she was not a big Facebook user, she was in the same location during appointments, and she did have her patients' numbers in her phone, and they had hers (as described by Hill 2016). As it turns out, location data and telephone numbers are both used to generate shadow profiles.

PYMK is a feature which provides links to other people's profiles, based on common interests, emails, address book details, messages and other details on people's phones and computers – and other sources of information (Mac et al. 2018). Many users were unaware that they were 'providing' these kinds of data, and this highlights the problem of defining data as 'data given' – what many social media platforms describe as data 'you provide to us'.

Using the confidential contact information from a health practitioner, is only one of many examples of where PYMK has crossed ethical and social boundaries. Other cases include co-workers' parents being recommended as friends, people who you might follow on Instagram, but who don't follow you back (and vice versa), and people who have been on one Tinder date never to be contacted again (Franklin 2018; see Hill 2017 for more examples). Sex workers have also reported having their clients recommended to them. Kevin Kantor, a non-binary spoken-word poet, wrote a YouTube poem about the time his rapist was recommended to him as a friend (Kantor 2015). Even bigamists have been exposed because new wives have been recommended to existing wives as friends (Wasserman 2012). The anecdotes are numerous and the stakes can be brutal.

Many have speculated on how Facebook is able to connect people, and some have thought it could be location or address books, synced when uploading the app on mobile phones, or other sources. In its 'Help Centre', Facebook outlines the data sources used to generate friend suggestions for PYMK:

- Having friends in common. This is the most common reason for suggestions.
- Being in the same Facebook group or being tagged in the same photo.
- Your networks (example: your school, university or work).
- Contacts you've uploaded [or have been synced when downloading or updating the mobile app] (Facebook, PYMK 2020)

Andrew Bosworth, Facebook's Vice President of VR, has described Facebook's 'growth at all costs' mindset as one that justifies PYMK and shadow profiles, but is also ultimately damaging:

> The ugly truth is that we believe in connecting people so deeply that anything that allows us to connect more people more often is *de facto* good. It is perhaps the only area where the metrics do tell the true story as far as we are concerned ... [This justifies] *All the questionable contact importing practices*. All the subtle language that helps people stay searchable by friends. (2016, cited in Mac et al. 2018, emphasis added),

PYMK is an excellent example of 'questionable contact importing practices' and the ethically compromised tactics behind data collection, even when those data are claimed to have been 'given' by users. Shadow profiles and PYMK illustrate how privacy is implemented by social media platforms in a social media age, as well as illustrating the networked and relational nature of privacy. Shadow profiles demonstrate the shift from surveillance to dataveillance and a pervasive ideology of connection (see Chapter 3), pushed and promoted by social media.

The concluding section examines Zuckerberg's recent claim that 'the future is private', reflecting on what this means for the future of Facebook, Instagram and WhatsApp, as well as for privacy, dataveillance and the future of user rights.

Conclusion: 'The Future Is Private'

This chapter has introduced privacy as a historically situated concept and a complex networked right, important for the conditions required for human flourishing. As I have argued throughout this chapter, privacy can best be understood in terms of social or interpersonal privacy and as institutional (commercial or public) privacy. This framework is useful for making sense of how people use social media, and why they repeatedly identify privacy as important but agree to many invasive dataveillance terms. The review of social media privacy policies demonstrates that this is not just an individual contradiction in how people choose to use social media. Instead, social media platforms set out social privacy as their starting point (e.g. 'you control what others see') before shifting the terms to institutional data rights, where platforms claim ownership, intellectual property and a 'worldwide, non-exclusive, royalty-free license' to do what they want. These kinds of data-sharing practices are justified by the logic of growth and connection.

Given the sheer hypocrisy of privacy policies on social media, it is wise to be critical if not outright wary of social media's claims to protect privacy. On this note, it is worth turning to Facebook's new vision for a 'privacy-focused messaging and social networking platform' (Zuckerberg 2019). While many critics claim this comes as a desperate publicity tactic intended to save some of Facebook's damaged reputation following the Cambridge Analytica revelations, Zuckerberg claims otherwise:

> People increasingly also want to connect privately in the digital equivalent of the living room. As I think about the future of the internet, I believe a privacy-focused communications platform will become even more important than today's open platforms. *Privacy gives people the freedom to be themselves* and connect more naturally, which is why we build social networks ... Today we already see that private messaging, ephemeral stories, and small groups are by far the fastest growing areas of online communication. (2019, emphasis added)

In some respects, Zuckerberg is right. Privacy is important and associated with giving 'people the freedom to be themselves'. Many have taken this view long before Zuckerberg, emphasizing that privacy is central to 'human flourishing', as well as to the health of civil society, markets and democracy (Cohen 2017: 17, 2018). As Cohen argues, 'privacy fosters interpersonal dynamics that strengthen the social fabric', whereas the 'pervasive, networked surveillance weakens' social foundations and 'fosters intolerance and incivility' (Cohen 2017: 13). Yet social media privacy policies define privacy in ways that support the profitable dataveillance practices of social media companies. In this sense, privacy as a right or condition is perpetually compromised by the socio-legal and property framing of privacy. In Zuckerberg's vision of 'the future is private', he emphasizes the importance of 'private communication' and 'private sharing', both of which are fundamentally different from privacy as central to self-development, human flourishing and networked resilience. Zuckerberg's vision is about *privatized* communication, where private communications are a potentially lucrative revenue source, rather than about fostering human growth.

As Cohen argues, the 'networked, platform-based architectures' of social media may 'enhance the ability to form groups and share information among members, to harness the wisdom and creativity of crowds, and to coalesce in passionate, powerful mobs', but they also enable the monetization of network communications and political or extremist hyper-targeting (2009: 10). According to a great deal of social science research, like-minded groups can more easily become ideologically resistant to new ideas and new knowledge. Cohen is one of many who argue that these conditions cultivate political polarization and cement ideological beliefs (2017: 11). Solove supports this claim, pointing to how 'surveillance can create chilling effects on free speech' which in turn 'harm society because ... they reduce the range of viewpoints expressed and the degree of freedom with which to engage in political activity' (2007: 765; cf. Zuboff 2015: 82).

It would seem we are in dangerous and dark times. The erosion of privacy and the rise of dataveillance contribute to these social harms, and it is more important than ever to take stock, be aware and be critical of these issues. Drawing from the wise words of Lina Dencik (2018), it is time to 'expand the limits of our imagination and reassert the possibilities of another world, another way of organizing society'.

Questions and Activities

1   Unlock your phone and exchange with a neighbour. Why is this a good or a bad idea? What might you learn about the other person? Does it make a difference if you know or are friends with this person? Explore and discuss.

2   Pick a social media platform and read the privacy or data policy. What do you discover? Is the policy about social or institutional privacy? What does this mean for users' privacy?

3   Drawing from 'Box 8.3: Social media monitoring, data harvesting and racial profiling', look at one of your own social media accounts. What can you learn about yourself by looking at your content and connections? What conclusions might different people come to from the same exercise (e.g. law enforcements, prospective employers, future peers, romantic interests)?

4   In addition to using group accounts on Instagram, how else could people subvert dataveillance and data tracking on social media?

5   Julie Cohen is one of the many scholars arguing that privacy is an important condition for human flourishing. Discuss and evaluate.

Further Reading

Cohen, J. E. 2017. Surveillance vs. privacy: effects and implications, in David Gray and Stephen E. Henderson (Eds.), *Cambridge Handbook of Surveillance Law*. New York. https://ssrn.com/abstract=3212900

Dencik, L., Hintz, A.; Cable, J. 2016. Towards data justice? The ambiguity of anti-surveillance resistance in political activism, *Big Data & Society*, 3 (2). https://doi.org/10.1177/2053951716679678

Sujon, Z. 2018. The triumph of social privacy: understanding the privacy logics of sharing behaviors across social media, *International Journal of Communication*, 12, pp. 3751–71. https://ijoc.org/index.php/ijoc/article/view/9357/2453

Williams, P.; Kind, E. 2019. Data-driven policing: the hardwiring of discriminatory policing practices across Europe, *European Network Against Racism*. https://www.enar-eu.org/IMG/pdf/data-driven-profiling-web-final.pdf

Zuboff, S. 2015. Big other: surveillance capitalism and the prospects of an information civilization, *Journal of Information Technology*, 30, pp. 75–89. Available online at: https://papers.ssrn.com/sol3/papers.cfm?abstract_id=2594754

SOCIAL SCREENS: FROM YOUTUBE TO TIKTOK

Chapter Overview

Introduction: Social Screens, Social Media Entertainment and YouTube   206
YouTube: Platform, Creation and Affective Labour   207
     Platform origins and features   207
     Content and creators   211
Affective Labour and Social Relations   221
Emerging Trends in Social Video: Rise of Live and TikTok   224
Conclusion   226
Questions and Activities   227
Further Reading   227

Chapter Objectives

- Introduce social video as a broad field at the intersection of screen industries and social media
- Identify unique aspects of YouTube, the industry defining social video platform, in terms of its origins, its content and creators, and its impact on social interactions
- Outline the impact of YouTube, as part of the social media ecosystem, on the rise of 'influence' and affective labour
- Explore emerging trends in social video such as the rise of the live (Periscope, Facebook Live, Twitch) and ultra short-form video app TikTok

Introduction: Social Screens, Social Media Entertainment and YouTube

Streaming, portals, user-generated video content platforms and mobile phone cameras have been hugely disruptive technologies, converging screen and entertainment industries with social media, and reconfiguring viewing habits and creative practices. Streaming and social video are increasingly part of twenty-first-century media landscapes, and have transformed film, television, music, gaming and the cultural industries. While many may attribute the beginning of these changes to YouTube and streaming portals like Netflix, this chapter introduces the role of social media in this ecosystem.

Stuart Cunningham and David Craig, two well-established researchers focusing on the juncture between North California (Silicon Valley) and South California (Hollywood), define this convergence as 'social media entertainment', quite distinct from 'portals' (e.g. Hulu, Netflix, Amazon, etc.). Cunningham and Craig (2019: 5), helpfully, define social media entertainment (SME) as:

> … an emerging proto-industry fueled by professionalizing, previously amateur content creators using new entertainment and communicative formats, including vlogging, gameplay, and do-it-yourself (DIY) … Featuring online video players with social networking affordances including YouTube, Facebook, Instagram, Twitter, Snapchat, and Vimeo … And their counterparts in China, YouKu and Weibo.

Amanda Lotz, a professor who specializes in internet distributed television, what she calls 'portals', argues that instead of killing legacy television, internet TV is evolving the industry and audio-visual practices:

> Media cannot be killed. The written word, sound, still pictures or moving images and the complex of industrial formations, audience practices, and textual attributes that come to define them as particular media persist. *The distribution systems used to circulate media, however, evolve with considerable regularity.* (2017, emphasis added)

Streaming services are more important than ever, and they are not merely distribution services either. Netflix, Hulu, Amazon, Vimeo, Tudou and others are developing original content. The market is thriving, and social media platforms are trying to secure their share of this market. Facebook has launched Facebook Watch and Facebook Live as well as Facebook camera. Instagram has IGTV, and Twitter, once proud owner of the now defunct Vine, has Periscope. In gaming there is Twitch, and music streaming services are also abundant – Soundcloud, Spotify, GooglePlay, iTunes and many other podcasting apps. New short-form video apps like TikTok and Byte are also captivating users' attention, and introducing new ways of making, creating and engaging content. All of these point not only to the disruption of film, television and entertainment industries, but also to the development of new and often cross-platform industries.

In addition, there is also 'social TV', i.e. the use of social media channels to enhance or promote television or even multi-platform presences. For example, reality television cast members and sports figures use television as a platform to launch sophisticated transmedia careers, anchored through social media where they can secure paid partnerships, flog merchandise and accrue followers. More and more 'television' content, especially for big dramas and sporting events, increasingly includes hashtags and social media handles, so that programme makers can track viewing metrics, device use, user engagement and measure 'success' through social media analytics (Kosterich and Napoli 2016). This has given rise to the second and third screen phenomenon, what broadcasters are calling the 'media mesh' as audiences turn to social media on their phones and tablets, while watching video content (Blake 2017; Holt and Sanson 2014; Sørensen 2016: 382). In addition, audio-visual content can be repurposed, mixed, edited and reshared, through screenshots, memes, gifs and embedded video.

According to national research conducted by Ofcom in 2018, 'subscription services now account for 18 minutes of our daily viewing, YouTube 29 minutes, and all non-TV viewing a total of 89 minutes of our time every day' (2018: 4). Indeed, UK TV broadcasting revenue has decreased year on year, for an almost 4% decline in annual revenue in 2017 and 2018, marked further by TV's declining advertising revenues and the rise of streaming content (Ofcom 2018, 2019). Following the COVID-19 lockdown in the UK, Ofcom (2020) found that people spent 40% of their day 'watching TV and online video'. These services are more important than ever. Having established the breadth of this area, this chapter focuses on YouTube, where it came from, what we can learn from its content and creators, including those malevolent influencers, and what these mean for changing social relations. From here, we consider emerging trends and how these fit into the social screen ecosystem.

YouTube: Platform, Creation and Affective Labour

Platform origins and features

Before it was launched in 2005, YouTube began as a video dating site with the slogan 'Tune in, Hook Up' which, despite its founders offering $20 to girls and women to post video profiles on the site, failed to attract any daters (Dredge 2016; Koebler 2015). As a result, the three co-founders, all PayPal employees at the time, Steve Chen, Chad Hurley and Karim Jawal, had to rethink the purpose of the site, reimagining it as a video sharing platform for ordinary people. The emphasis was on *social* connection and an easy-to-use site for uploading video content, browsing and commenting on material, kind of like the video equivalent to Flickr (Burgess and Green 2018: 3–4).

Certainly, YouTube was not the first of its kind, and was launched in an already crowded online video market. The 2000s saw the launch of many video players, such as QuickTime and Real Media, followed by Divx in 2001, and Vimeo, Grouper and Flickr in 2004 – to name but a few (Roettgers 2010; Stokel-Walker 2019). Even Google entered the market with *Google Video*, also a video hosting service that allowed users to upload and embed on websites very similar to YouTube, in early 2005 (Burgess and Green 2018; Stokel-Walker 2019: 27). Thus, when YouTube was created in February 2005, it featured the brand caption 'your digital video repository', as shown in Figure 9.1 (a WayBackMachine screen shot from July 2005). Following a number of changes, the founders settled on the brand caption 'Broadcast Yourself. Watch and share videos worldwide' in December 2005. This variation around the core brand message shows that it took time for the site to decide on its purpose and focus which were shrouded in a 'fog of uncertainty and contradiction' (Burgess and Green 2009: 3).

Figure 9.1 YouTube front page, featuring the motto 'YouTube: Your Digital Video Repository'

Source: as captured by WayBackMachine, June 18, 2005 (https://web.archive.org/web/20050618025635/http://www.youtube.com:80/)

Despite the number of other video sharing sites in the market in the early 2000s, YouTube offered a number of things other video sharing sites did not. The easy usability meant anyone, even those with few technical skills or no experience, could use YouTube. It also offered a number of user functions, such as sharing, commenting, number of public views, the option to embed videos on other sites, tagging and a 'recommendation' system in some form (e.g. features, most popular, recently viewed). These were important features, and quickly became popular with users, supporting a community orientation with users who felt compromised by YouTube's escalating commercialism.

In addition to its easy user interface and useful functionality, YouTube's founders were also closely connected to the tech community with links to established media, which helped boost their visibility and reputation. As former PayPal employees, YouTube's three founders were well connected, and YouTube was featured in influential tech news sites like *TechCrunch* and *SlashDot* (Burgess and Green 2009). Its visibility in popular culture was amplified when it was used to share established media content like the hit late-night comedy video 'Lazy Sunday' from *Saturday Night Live* in 2005, as well as the Nike ad featuring Ronaldinho Gaúcho, the famous Brazilian footballer, in 2006. YouTube's convenient usability features and its buzzy visibility in and through media helped magnify its impact. These connections between legacy media continue to be important for YouTube. Indeed, it is well known for circulating highly professional content alongside amateur content, as discussed further a bit later on.

By mid-2006, YouTube was getting almost half of all the online video traffic (46%), compared to MySpace at 23% and Google Video with only 10% (Sorkin and Peters 2006). In October 2006, 18 months after it had been created, and after a battle with other media companies like Yahoo!, Microsoft, Viacom and News Corporation, Google bought YouTube for USD $1.65 billion (Burgess and Green 2018: 4; Sorkin and Peters 2006).

While this provides a brief introduction to the technical background and context of YouTube and online video, Henry Jenkins offers a cultural context for YouTube's origins, which also provides another explanation for its triumph over other online video sites – its capacity to draw a new generation of creators. Burgess and Green (2018) suggest that YouTube fosters a 'vernacular creativity', an everyday language for being creative. Henry Jenkins (2009b) situates this particular creative affinity as coming from the active communities of 'vidders', sci-fi fans dedicated to film-making, Youth Internet Radio Network (YIRN), and the DIY ethos of zine culture, 'garage cinema' and multi-media casting. Jenkins, struck by the diversity of voices on the platform, argued that:

> … YouTube has become the home port for lip-syncers, karaoke singers, trainspotters, birdwatchers, skateboarders, hip hoppers, small time wrestling federations, educators, third wave feminists, churches, proud parents, poetry slammers, gamers, fans, Ron Paul supporters, human rights activists, collectors, hobbyists and each of these groups has a longer history of media production. (2009b: 110)

Burgess and Green, leading YouTube researchers, describe YouTube as a 'dynamic cultural system' with 'participatory culture' at the heart of its business model (2018: vii). In order to understand this business model, I turn to two points. The first is YouTube's shift from a meta-business to a profit-generating one based on advertising, significantly bolstered by Google's considerable technological advantage. The second is its 'YouTube Partner Program' allowing creators to monetize their work, while also enrolling them in the platform and its business logics.

In its first five to ten years in business, YouTube was understood as part of the many digital companies shifting the standard media business model based on media production (on *making* video) to media curation (and on *hosting* video). Based on this shift, Burgess and Green refer to YouTube as a 'meta-business', which is a business that actually produces none of its own products or content (Burgess and Green 2008: 8). This model drives the gig or sharing economy. For example, Uber, 'the world's largest taxi company owns no vehicles… and AirBnB, the largest accommodation provider, owns no property' (Goodwin 2015, cited in Srnicek 2016: 76). Yetas the company has matured, YouTube has rolled out many different ways of making money, such as the subscription service YouTube Red and YouTube Originals, based on partnerships with relationships with legacy and established media. However, its most successful partnerships are with its creators (discussed below).

In addition, once purchased by Google, YouTube was able to benefit from Google's resources, advanced search, massive database of personalized user data for targeted advertising and recommender algorithms – all of which helped cement YouTube's position as a major player in the digital space. As James Williams, former Googler turned technology critic, argues:

> … one of the first projects that Google's DeepMind division put their 'AlphaGo' system to work on was enhancing YouTube's video recommendation algorithm. In other words, it now seems the same intelligence behind the system that defeated the human world champion at the game Go is sitting on the other side of your screen and showing you videos that it thinks will keep you using YouTube for as long as possible. (Williams 2018: 90–91)

As such, YouTube may have started out with some usability and functionality advantages, but once purchased by Google the site was able to maximize these advantages with virtually unlimited resources and tech power.

The second major aspect of YouTube's business model is its partner programme (YPP). YouTube launched advertising in 2007, shortly followed by the YPP, which 'gives creators greater access to YouTube resources and features' and allows them to monetize their content through a percentage of ad revenues (YouTube Help 2020a; see also Burgess and Green 2018: 55). For an overview of the minimum requirements creators need to meet to join YPP, see Box 9.1, YouTube's Partner Programme minimum entry requirements. Notably, these requirements are subject to change and are different from the 2017 entry requirements of 10,000 'lifetime views', reported by researchers (Burgess and Green 2018: 55).

Box 9.1 YouTube's Partner Programme (YPP), minimum entry requirements

Minimum eligibility requirements to join:

- Follow all the YouTube monetisation policies.
- The YouTube monetisation policies are a collection of policies that allow you to monetise on YouTube. If you're a YouTube partner, your agreement including the YouTube partner programme policies require compliance with these monetisation policies in order to potentially earn money on YouTube.
- Live in a country or region where the YouTube Partner Programme is available.
- Have more than 4,000 valid public watch hours in the last 12 months.
- Have more than 1,000 subscribers.
- Have a linked AdSense account. (YouTube Help 2020a)

The introduction of targeted advertising from 2007 meant that YouTube could monetize its website traffic, and also provided creators with a legitimate source of income (Cunningham and Craig 2019: 42). Popular YouTubers had a chance to make a living from their video creation work, a possibility inspiring many creators, despite the hard labour and high burn-out rates involved in this kind of creative work (Kyncl, with Peyvan 2017; Stokel-Walker 2019). YouTube content is discussed further in the next section, but it is worth noting that although there has been debate around whether YouTube does generate any profits for Google, it seems that from 2015 it shifted from a loss leader to lucrative Google product (Cunningham and Craig 2019: 42–43). Google's net digital ad revenues made up 32% of the worldwide market in 2019 (Clement 2019a), closely followed by Facebook and Amazon (Sterling 2019). Between 2017 and 2019, YouTube generated USD $5.1 billion dollars of the global advertising market share showing strong progress (Clement 2019a, 2020c). Based on this level of profitability, many have referred to Google (and Facebook) as *advertising* platforms (Srnicek 2016; Zuboff 2015, 2019) rather than as tech or social platforms, because this is where they make their money.

Despite YouTube's dominance in advertising, it is also a site where people can go to create, consume or share content that relates to their identities and lives. In this sense, YouTube has a long history of providing a space for people to develop or participate in shared communities, and the next section addresses this by looking more closely at its content and creators.

Content and creators

YouTube videos range from the wild and wonderful to the most banal and horrifying. Spanning every possible genre and look, from a slick and professional aesthetic to an amateur style characteristic of home video, YouTube videos have something for everyone. As a platform, it also made a significant impact on how people create and consume music, entertainment, politics, information and gaming – as well as how professional gate-keepers in each of these genres are able to manage, promote and capitalize on talent. In this section, I introduce some of YouTube's key trends, followed by select examples of its content creators in order to gain a broad sense of the platform.

These examples include an introduction to some of the top content and trends, as well as a number of more detailed examples of the rise-to-celebrity-from-humble-YouTube-beginnings. Justin Bieber may be one of the best-known celebrities, but the same story is told about others who began their creative careers on YouTube, like mega-YouTubers Smosh, the Fine Brothers, Rooster Teeth, Lily Singh, to name but a few. Discussed further below, we look more closely at Issa Rae who began her career with the web series *Awkward Black Girl,* and YouTube game vlogging giant PewDiePie.

However, some YouTube creators work towards promoting white supremacy via the 'alternative influencer network' (Lewis 2018) as experienced by Caleb Cain, reformed Alt-Right racist who is now taking on what he refers to as the 'decentralized cult' of white extremists (Cain 2019; Lewis 2018). In addition, child exploitation and paedophile networks are active on YouTube, and these creators are also amplified through its recommendation algorithm. All of these examples highlight very different aspects of YouTube, and in the case of extremism and abuse, demonstrate its prioritization of targeted advertising revenue over the public good.

Top trends and YouTubers

According to Google, the top trend from 2007 to 2020, culminating in over 4 billion views, is a genre of videos that they label 'with me'. These are videos that invite viewers to do a range of different things with the video maker, such as 'get ready with me', 'clean with me', 'plan with me', 'drive with me' and even 'YouTube with me' (YouTube 2020d). One example of this is London-based beauty vlogger Lucy Moon's 'cgrwm' videos, an acronym for 'chat and get ready with me' (Moon 2020). For *YouTube Culture and Trends*, this is a longstanding trend covering a huge range of activities while also highlighting a trend towards viewers' 'solitary interaction' with YouTube. This trend is distinct from the many tutorials and DIY content on YouTube, one that seems to be highly gendered in terms of its creators and viewers. Related to this, there are many more girls and women, like Zoella or Michelle Phan, making beauty tutorials, and many more boys and men making gaming tutorials supporting traditional gendered content norms (Bishop 2019). However, there are also trans or non-binary beauty vloggers like Gigi Gorgeous or Jeffree Star, who tend to bend and break both genre and gender conventions.

New trends and genres are also constantly evolving, some of which are dangerous or offensive. For example, the 'prank wars' genre can include harmless tricks, or they can show disturbing videos of harmful pranks gone too far. According to YouTube journalist and researcher Chris Stokel-Walker, this particular genre clearly shows an escalating logic where both aspiring and established YouTubers broadcast more and more extreme behaviour in the hopes of getting more views (2019: 164–69). One example of this genre is *DaddyOFive*, a YouTube channel owned by two parents who were dedicated to playing cruel tricks on their children to get more views and monetize their content. Following complaints of child abuse, the parents lost custody of their youngest children and were court ordered to remove their YouTube channels and videos (Hale 2019; Leaver and Abidin 2017).

To begin exploring YouTube content, it's useful to look at recent trends on YouTube, including its most viewed channels, videos with most global views and top earners (see Table 9.1).

Table 9.1 Comparing YouTube's 'most viewed channels worldwide' with the 'most viewed videos globally' and the 'top earners' in 2019

Most viewed YouTube channels as of January 2020	Billions of views per month	Videos with most global views as of December 2019	Billions of views over time	YouTube's Top Earners	2018/ 2019 USD in millions
T-Series	3.23	Luis Fonsi - Despacito ft. Daddy Yankee	6.55	Ryan Kaji	26
Cocomelon - Nursery Rhymes	2.36	Ed Sheeran - Shape of You	4.51	Dude Perfect	20
Like Nastya Vlog	2.01	Waz Khalifa - See You Again ft. Charlie Puth	4.31	Anastasia Radzinskaya (Like Nastya Vlog)	18
Kids Diana Show	1.73	Masha and the Bear - Recipe for Disaster	4.18	Rhett and Link	17.5
SET India	1.57	Pinkfong Kids' Songs and Stories - Baby Shark Dance	4.06	Jeffree Star	17
cocoz toon	1.54	Mark Ronson ft. Bruno Mars - Uptown Funk	3.73	Preston	14
Zee TV	1.48	PSY - Gangnam Style	3.47	PewDiePie	13
Chiko TV	1.13	Justin Bieber - Sorry	3.22	Markiplier	13
Familia Vogel - Speil mit mir Kinderspielzeug	1.08	Marron S - Sugar	3.08	DanTDM	12
SAB TV	1.08	Katy Perry - Roar	2.97	VanossGaming	11.5

Sources: Clement 2019b, 2020a; Armstrong 2020

Note: Light grey cells indicate children's content. Dark grey cells indicate gaming YouTubers.

As Statista researcher J. Clement (2020a) argues, looking at the most viewed YouTube channels, most viewed videos and highest paid YouTubers reveals an interesting snapshot of the most popular content, clearly 'dominated by music and children's content'. All the cells highlighted in light grey show content produced for children, making up six of the most viewed YouTube channels, two of the most viewed videos and two of the top earners. Cocomelon, a channel featuring nursery rhymes and original animated content for kids, has 74 million subscribers and 52 billion views. Like Nastya Vlog is a 6-year-old making videos about their life, has 2 billion views per month, and Ryan Kaji, also a child vlogger, is the top YouTube earner for 2019. Both of these young children are famous for unboxing and play videos among other content. Child-oriented YouTube videos and channels represent 26% of the most viewed and most paid sections on YouTube, as shown in Table 9.1. In the most viewed channel category, the remaining four channels feature Indian content, made in India, and all of which are 'multi-channel networks' (MCNs), which Ramon Lobato defines as:

> … intermediary firms that operate in and around YouTube's advertising infrastructure. A common business model is for MCNs to sign up a large number of popular channels to their network, then, using YouTube's content management system, to sell advertising and cross-promote their affiliated channels across this network, while also working with popular YouTube celebrities to develop them into fully fledged video brands, (Lobato 2016: 349)

This is important, as MCNs are influential structures shaping video content, as well as media structures. Notably, the four 'most viewed YouTube channels' are not native to YouTube. T-Series, SET India, Zee TV and SAB TV all use YouTube to build on their already well-established media networks and audience reach, and illustrate YouTube's partnerships with legacy media.

There are a few other content creators worth discussing further. The first is Dude Perfect, a channel featuring 'five best buds just kickin it' with headers featuring overly excited white men interested in comedy and sports. This channel represents one of the biggest genres on YouTube. Sophie Bishop, a critical YouTube researcher, notes that 'content is highly gendered on YouTube', explaining that 43 of the 50 most subscribed to 'vloggers are male, producing content across diverse themes including gaming, football, technology, pranks, comedy, politics, news and sketch humour' (Bishop 2018: 70). In line with this, five of the highest YouTube earners are also gamers or at least began their YouTube careers as gamers, including Preston, PewDiePie, Markiplier, DanTDM and VanossGaming.

Yet, almost directly in contrast to this, Jeffree Star is the fifth highest YouTube earner for 2018–2019, and as a male beauty vlogger breaks these gendered conventions. With a full face of make-up, Star is not your typical male YouTuber, and has launched his own cosmetic line which he promotes on and off of YouTube. Thus, Star breaks the apparent cis-gendered and heterosexual normativity of top YouTubers, and provides a peek into YouTube's rich and diverse cultural life, albeit amidst some controversy and accusations of racism (e.g. Lawson 2020).

These tensions between convention and disruption are fairly typical of YouTube, as it is as a site marked by a long history of hosting both commercial, for-profit content and grassroots, non-profit content which reflects users' genuinely diverse stories. As Jane Arthurs and colleagues argue:

> YouTube is now characterized as a paradigmatic example of a hybrid commercial environment where user-generated content production is efficiently tied to forms of monetization. Lobato (2016) has pointed out that the evolution of YouTube through the introduction of paid advertising is shifting ... [from] participatory culture towards an analysis of a 'hybrid cultural–commercial space'. (Lobato, 2016: 357, cited in Arthurs et al. 2018: 7)

There are also tensions between the commercialized and community orientation of YouTube, repeatedly identified as a central feature of YouTube (Burgess and Green 2009, 2018). While this tension may not be apparent while looking at the top and highest earning YouTubers, the diversity of content from Indian drama, music, kids' content, gamers and a gay beauty vlogger is much more diverse than traditional network television and the screen industries more broadly (even though much more work on diversity still needs to be done). One particularly interesting example is Issa Rae's rise from *Awkward Black Girl* web series star and director, to the star and writer of HBO's hit dramedy *Insecure*. In contrast, Felix Kjellberg, known as PewDiePie, represents the cis-gendered norms particularly popular in YouTube's gaming and vlogging genres. (See Box 9.2 for a brief introduction to Issa Rae's remarkable screen achievements and journey from YouTuber to internet celebrity, as well as a brief comparison with PewDiePie's pathway to celebrity, as one of YouTube's homegrown talents.)

Box 9.2   Issa Rae and PewDiePie

Issa Rae is an actor, writer, film-maker and co-founder of *Color Creative*, a content start-up for women and people of colour meant to support its artists and amplify 'diverse, emerging writers and exceptional storytelling for Film TV and Digital' (https://colorcreative.tv/). Self-described as a 'social media addict' whose life wouldn't be what it was without the internet, Rae has long relied on YouTube as a creative outlet for her creative ideas (IMDB 2020). Rae began to take drama and acting seriously in secondary school, but it wasn't until she was in university that she began making her own YouTube content (Wortham 2015). Beginning with 'raunchy music videos' and parodies, Rae also developed a 'mockumentary series she wrote about student life at Stanford called "Dorm Diaries"' (Wortham 2015). Modelled after reality television, the series gained traction at her university, and Rae 'learned that she had a knack for portraying everyday Black life' (Wortham 2015).

Yet it was with her 2011 YouTube web series *The Misadventures of an Awkward Black Girl* that she really began to draw attention (Nwandu 2018). She wanted to depict 'a three-dimensional woman of color' living an ordinary life (cited in Iqbal 2018). The web-series went viral, gaining millions of views and winning a Shorty Award for best web show. Building on this interest and attention, Rae went on to write, direct and star in an HBO

(Continued)

series, *Insecure*, which draws on similar themes, and in the process representing more ordinary depictions of everyday Black life. *Insecure* has been well received, inspiring rave reviews, and was nominated for a Golden Globe award. In addition to these accomplishments, Issa Rae has used her growing recognition to boost minority voices in media and the world of content creation. Her current YouTube channel, *Issa Rae Presents*, has 488K subscribers and over 54 million views (August 2020).

Although Rae began her content creation career on YouTube, she has extended her reach and impact beyond YouTube to become an 'internet celebrity', working across platforms in social and traditional media (Abidin 2018: 16). There are many other celebrities who began explosive music, acting or entertainment careers on YouTube, such as Justin Beiber, Grace Helbig, Ed Sheeran, Shawn Mendes and many more (see Cunningham and Craig 2019; Kyncl 2017; Stokel-Walker 2019).

Felix Kjellberg, known as PewDiePie, is one of the most famous and well-paid homegrown YouTube stars. While PewDiePie's YouTube career is well documented, it is worth noting that he began his channel with game play videos, which then evolved into a vlog with cultural commentary, general opinion, animated shorts and gaming. PewDiePie was on the top of the YouTube charts for many years, and was only recently overtaken in views and subscribers by T-Series, a multichannel network featuring 'India's largest music label and movie studio' (https://www.youtube.com/user/tseries/about). Like many other YouTubers, PewDiePie has launched his own merchandise line and has an intense relationship with his enormous audience, whom he affectionately calls his 'bro army' (Cunningham and Craig 2019: 162). PewDiePie has been at the centre of many public controversies, including public accusations of anti-semitism, which he countered with accusations of a media conspiracy working to limit his reach and power (Abidin 2018: 64–67). As a result of these accusations, PewDiePie lost a lucrative contract with Disney (MCN Maker Studios) but did not lose too many followers, illustrating his influential position with audiences, which seems to increasingly be the case with 'technologically adept and savvy' YouTubers (Deller and Murphy 2019: 127).

It is worth noting that while trends and celebrities tell us a great deal about YouTube there are two other points worth raising. The first of these is that YouTube offers a rich *cultural system,* as Burgess and Green suggest. Part of this rich cultural system is made up of the ordinary people who use YouTube to connect with others, as well as to make their own content even when that content does not go viral or reach wider audiences. There are many communities and people making content and connecting over YouTube, not always in pursuit of fame and influence. Bearing this in mind, there are new kinds of celebrity and whole ranges of influencers (e.g. Abidin 2018), yet only a small percentage of creators are able to achieve celebrity status. Brooke Erin Duffy, a researcher examining aspirational labour, finds that only 8–17% of social media bloggers are able to support themselves through their content, while 81% have not made anything (2017: 16). Duffy refers to this group of aspirational labourers as 'the new precariat', one that spans many platforms, genres and sectors (cited in Stokel-Walker 2019: 86).

Second, despite how easy it looks and in addition to the incredibly challenging odds, being a successful YouTuber is incredibly hard work. Most celebrities and influencers are exceptionally talented at hiding the time and effort involved in making regular videos. Yet, when you dig down into how YouTubers (and other influencers and celebrities) achieve their success, it usually only follows determination and consistency. For example, even Justin Bieber, before he found his big break via YouTube, had been playing music as much as he could, wherever he could. Once he was 'discovered' by Scooter Braun, both of them worked relentlessly to develop a YouTube catalogue which helped soon-to-be-fans get to know Bieber's music and literally *grow* his audience (Kynckl 2017: 214). Although this is often not part of the story YouTubers tell until they reach their breaking point, it is one that is very real. Stokel-Walker observes this, dedicating a whole chapter to 'burnout: the slaves of the algorithm'. In this chapter, Stokel-Walker recounts Michael Buckley's story, from *What The Buck's* legendary YouTube channel, that after a few years of success, he began to feel as if he were 'making a living out of [his] soul… [as well as feeling] constrained and exhausted by the high workload' (Stokel-Walker 2017: 189). There are many stories like Buckley's, and this is an important part of influencer and celebrity culture on YouTube and other social media (see Chapter 7).

While this section has focused on some of the recent trends linked to YouTube, such as the '_____ with me' videos, the top earners and most viewed videos, there are many other aspects to YouTube. As many have argued, it cultivates a hybrid cultural and commercial space, and a continual tension between community and commodity (Arthurs et al. 2018; Burgess and Green 2009, 2018; Lobato 2016). So far, I have introduced the content and creators who have been able to take advantage of the more commercial aspects of YouTube. It seems that its creators, especially those that gain public recognition, also reflect social concerns and moral anxieties (see moral panics, discussed in Chapter 7). Despite volatile controversies, mega YouTubers and social video creators are gaining clout and economic power in the world. The next section takes a different perspective, focusing on YouTube's relation to radicalization and extremism, child sexual abuse and the platform's lukewarm response to these troubling social issues.

Malevolent influencers and users

Bearing in mind the role of moral panics in shaping cultural views of new technologies and youth cultures, it is important to note that community is not always positive and not always about building a better world, but instead can also include building communities who value hate, who promote white supremacy and anti-feminist ideologies. Many people have reported on YouTube's 'rabbit hole', the algorithmic loop-hole that recommends increasingly radical, abusive or disturbing content, also confirmed by researchers (Lewis 2018; Rieder et al. 2018; Tufecki 2018). These kinds of 'sticky' videos are more likely to keep viewers on YouTube for longer periods of time, and as a result generate more advertising based profits. Thus extreme content can be much more profitable for YouTube, as it is across social media platforms (see also Chapter 3).

Social media are often blamed for the rise of fake news and misinformation, but also for spreading right-wing propaganda used to radicalize viewers. This section looks at two cases, red-pilling and child sexual exploitation. The first case is that of reformed racist and avid YouTube user Caleb Cain, and his experience of 'red-pilling', a metaphor referring to *The Matrix* film, where the lead character takes a red pill exposing the illusion of reality as just that: a carefully crafted illusion set by feminists, liberals and people of colour (Cain 2019). The second case involves the use of YouTube's comments section by child sex predators to mark and share abusive content. Both of these cases end up being profitable for YouTube by increasing social video views, audience engagement, advertising revenues and time spent on the platform.

While these cases raise serious issues, these are not unique to YouTube as harm, abuse, bullying, harassment and trolling are endemic across social platforms. Yet the participatory nature of YouTube means people can upload videos featuring abuse, extremism, bullying, violence and dangerous material as easily as they can create tutorials or life vlogs. In some cases, videos show blatant profiteering at the expense of others (e.g. *DaddyOFive* discussed above, and the prank war genre more broadly), or extreme violence, as seen in videos showing Islamic State beheadings (Andre 2012; Koch 2018).

Red-pilling: Extremism and radicalization

Caleb Cain, a fairly unassuming and self-proclaimed liberal young man, posted a 38-minute YouTube video titled 'My descent into the Alt-Right pipeline' in March 2019. The video detailed Cain's increasing alienation and what he describes as a slow descent into a:

> … 'decentralized cult' of far-right YouTube personalities, who convinced him that Western civilization was under threat from Muslim immigrants and cultural Marxists, that innate I.Q. differences explained racial disparities, and that feminism was a dangerous ideology. (Cited in Roose 2019)

With honest reflection and candour, Cain (2019) describes his experience of 'buying into' dangerous and scientifically discredited ideologies like 'race realism' and exposure to anti-Semitic Jewish conspiracy. He reflects on how this 'terrifying' world 'preyed upon his biases' while also providing him with 'a sense of belonging' he could not find anywhere else (Roose 2019). However, following the Christchurch mosque shooting where a white supremacist murdered 50 people, Cain said he saw these views reflected in the killer's manifesto and weaponized memes.[1] For him, this was a horrible revelation. All of a sudden, the Alt-Right

---

1 Following advice to avoid amplifying hate by not naming mass murderers and to remember victims from Jacinda Arden, New Zealand prime minister, and reinforced by Whitney Phillips, expert on internet hate, I am not naming the shooter in this chapter. Instead, here is a list of the victims who were murdered on March 15 in the Christchurch mosque shootings: Mucaad Ibrahim, Haji-Daoud Nabi, Husna Ahmed, Lilik Abdul Hamid, Sayyad Milne, Atta Elayyan, Amjad Hamid, Ansi Alibava, Ali Elmadani, Naeem Rashid, Talha Naeem, Khaled Mustafa, Hamza Mustafa, Linda Armstrong, Farhaj Ahsan, Syed Jahandad Ali, Hafiz Musa Patel, Tariq Omar, Junaid Ismail, Hussein Moustafa, Zeeshan

was not just a set of ideas, but also a destructive ideology fuelling real hatred used to justify murder and violence. Kevin Roose (2019), a journalist reporting on Cain's story, claims that this is only one of many similar stories told by young people, especially young men, as they get sucked into a deeply prejudiced and closed world view.

Becca Lewis, a Data & Society researcher, looked into far-right networks on YouTube, confirming many of Cain's experiences. Lewis examined the YouTube networks of 65 'political influencers' and 80 of their YouTube channels, finding dense clusters of interaction. Lewis refers to these as 'Alternative Influence Networks' (AINs), which make up 'an alternative media system that adopts the techniques of brand influencers to build audiences and "sell" them political ideology' (2018: n.p.). She also notes that in addition to hate, AINs are also good at cultivating a sense of 'belonging', especially for those, like Cain, who feel alienated and alone. According to Lewis, this sense of belonging is important, and AINs:

> ... provide a metaphorical 'family' [along with a] sense of identity, place, and belonging; emotional, social, and cultural support and security; and gives rise to political and social affiliations and beliefs. (Lewis 2018: 20)

Key people in these networks, like Carl Benjamin, Richard Spencer or Dave Rubin, combine celebrity 'with the intimacy of influencer culture', YouTubing nationalism and bigotry, along with tips for self-care and white belonging, in an 'aspirational' tone (Lewis 2018: 28; cf. Duffy 2017).

Lewis's work maps links with Milo Yiannopoulos, infamous far-right political commentator and troll hero, along with right-wing and self-professed culture warrior Jordan Peterson. As Lewis carefully documents, these far-right influencers are working together to make up 'an intellectual dark web' to make 'polished ... captivating videos that are easily available on the pages of the internet's most popular video platform' (Lewis 2018: 5, 11).

Lewis finds that YouTube's algorithm consistently returns AIN influencers and extremist content related to 'gamergate' and 'refugees', all of which points to an algorithmic recommendation system directly users toward an ideological 'rabbit hole' which has the potential to radicalize viewers *and* increase YouTube's advertising revenue (2018: 30, 36; see also Rieder et al. 2018; Tufecki 2018). However, and this is important, Lewis also argues that AINs are not technical problems. Fixing YouTube's algorithm may provide a quick fix, but in reality, these are deeply social issues and far-right political influencers are maximizing YouTube's promotional culture for their own ideological ends.

Raza, Ghulam Hussain, Karam Bibi, Hussein Al-Umari, Kamel Darwish, Suhail Shahid, Abdelfattah Qasem, Arifbhai Vora, Ramiz Vora, Haroon Mahmood, Syed Areeb Ahmed, Mohsin Al-Harbi, Ahmed Gamal Eldin Mohamed Abdel Ghany, Abdukadir Elmi, Osama Adnan Yousef Abukwaik, Muse Nur Awale, Mounir Guirgis Soliman, Muhammad Abdus Samad, Ashraf Ali, Matiullah Safi, Ashraf El-Moursy Ragheb, Mohamad Moosid Mohamedhosen, Dr Mojammel Hoq, Ozair Kadir and Muhammad Haziq Mohd-Tarmizi (*Guardian* n.d.; Phillips 2018: 14 ff.).

Comments and recommendations: Child sexual exploitation and abuse

Despite the fact that so much of YouTube's top content involves kids as viewers or creators (see Table 9.1), YouTube maintains that its services should not be used by those under 13 years old. This claim is made even more problematic when its algorithms have been found to recommend violent and disturbing content to children (Bridle 2017; Lomas 2017). More recently, YouTube enabled sexual predators to use 'the site's comments section to leave predatory messages on videos containing and uploaded by children, and to share links to child sexual abuse material' (Martineau 2019; Orpahnides 2019; Winder and Farid 2019). Disturbingly, its algorithm recommends these videos to other sexual predators, revealing networks of abuse partially connected via this platform.

Researchers from Harvard University's prestigious Berkman Klein Centre found YouTube's 'recommendation algorithm drives engagement with content that enables child sexual exploitation' (Kaiser and Córdova 2019). Jonas Kaiser, one of these researchers, notes that ordinary YouTube content featuring children in family-style videos are often embedded within a relatively ordinary family-video-for-family-members context. What helped Kaiser and his colleague Cordova flag the recommendation algorithm was that some of these videos, particularly those that feature children 'swimming or doing the splits', will have hundreds of thousands of views (as cited in Field 2019). Jonas's very measured explanation for this astonishing discrepancy in views is this:

> The way YouTube's recommendations usually work is that it optimizes for people staying on the site, getting recommended content that is more likely to keep them watching. In this context it seems to be, but obviously we don't know, that YouTube's algorithm or machine learning algorithm optimizes basically on paedophile behavior … but if YouTube takes this video and connects it with videos of other small children, that's a totally different story. (Field 2019)

In addition to enabling recommendations for sexual predators, there are longer-standing issues around violent and disturbing content made for children. James Bridle (2017), writer and author of *The New Dark Age*, argues that 'someone or something or some combination of people and things is using YouTube to systematically frighten, traumatise, and abuse children, automatically and at scale'. In a viral post on Medium, he documents a seriously disturbing and extensive trend in both human and algorithmically generated videos for kids. Table 9.1 shows how important children's channels and content are for YouTube. Yet some of these channels feature knock-offs of popular characters like Peppa Pig or Spider-man, for example, to maximize views and subscribers. These videos 'capitalize on violence and dark humour', showing things like 'Peppa eating her father or drinking bleach' as well as unsettling things like having 'the wrong heads' on characters. In addition, some of these videos show bizarre ads of old men in diapers or t-shirts with 'keep calm and rape a lot' slogans on the front (Bridle 2017). Bridle clearly makes the point that there is a world of disturbing if not dangerous content hiding within children's YouTube. While this in itself is disturbing, Bridle's key point is that these videos are being monetized, and algorithmically recommended to children, showing that YouTube favours profits over the public good, and that YouTube 'is complicit in the abuse' (Bridle 2017).

Affective Labour and Social Relations

So far, in this chapter, I have introduced the broader context of social television and online video, focusing on YouTube as a major platform in this landscape. I've discussed key themes related to its content and creators. YouTube creators experience the best and the worst of labour relations, and this is closely related to changing social relations and the rise of affective labour. This 'intimate work of connection' is not unique to YouTube but is perhaps most visible here and through influencer work (Baym 2018; Duffy 2017). YouTube's partner programme enrols its creators and users into a particular kind of promotional logic, which requires platform specific visual and advertising literacies. Like the increased demand for relational labour, these visual and promotional literacies are apparent in YouTubers' accounts of their work and experience on the platform. Finally, although hotly debated, the last of these themes concerns the debate on its role in contributing to more or less diversity and inclusion.

In terms of affective and relational labour, creative work increasingly requires producing a feeling of connection between creators and audiences. While this is not an entirely new phenomenon, it has become an accepted strategy for growing and engaging audiences. For example, writing in 1956, two social scientists were fascinated with the illusion of the 'face-to-face' closeness of 'the new mass media – radio, television, and the movies', so they proposed that this closeness was actually a 'parasocial relationship' (Horton and Wohl 1956: 215). Parasocial relations, a theory used to explain feelings of intimacy and closeness with celebrities and public figures, helps explain the asymmetric and often one-directional relationships between audiences and those in the media. Often cited examples of a parasocial relationship include the mass outpouring of grief when a celebrity or public figure dies, like Kobe Bryant who was killed in a tragic accident early in 2020 (see also Amy Winehouse, David Bowie and the often cited Princess Diana). Parasocial relations also help explain the intense perception of intimacy many people feel for their favourite celebrities and public figures, especially those who appear in visual media (Turner 2013).

Crystal Abidin (2015), a senior research fellow and important voice on internet celebrity, updates this theory for the social media age, arguing that we have moved from parasocial relations to 'perceived interconnectedness'. She argues that there is a shift from 'fans', a word which alludes to a relatively one-sided relationship marked by big asymmetries in admiration and respect, to followers, readers, viewers, friends or other slightly more egalitarian descriptions. For Abidin (2015), 'perceived interconnectedness' is about actively building more 'reciprocal and disclosive intimacies', marking a shift from a one-directional flow of communication to one that is much more multi-directional. (See Table 9.2 for an overview of the primary elements of both Horton and Wohl's parasocial relations and Abidin's 'perceived interconnectedness'.)

Table 9.2 From parasocial relations to perceived interconnectedness

Element	Parasocial Relations	Perceived Interconnectedness
Medium	TV/radio technology	Social media platforms
Primary strategy	Theatrics	Intimacies
Origin of strategy	Constructed by producer	Co-constructed by producer and audience
Organization of actors	Hierarchical	Flat
Authority of dissemination	Broadcast	Interactive
Flow of dialogue	Unidirectional	Bi-directional
Conversational structure	One-to-many	One-to-many, One-to-one

Source: adapted from Abidin (2015)

This shift toward the *work* of intimacy as identified in Abidin's 'perceived interconnected-ness' is widespread. For example, in her analysis of musicians and audiences, Nancy Baym argues that musicians no longer play the role of the distant idol. Instead, they are deeply engaged in relational work, where audiences expect musicians to be 'constantly accessible, especially on social media, offering unique and intimate moments to their fans' (2018: 1). Baym proposes the term 'affective labour' or 'relational labour' to describe this work, and it clearly applies to influencers and creators who constantly engage their audiences on social media in many ways. While both Abidin and Baym are writing about multiple platforms, this is important for YouTube.

Abidin observes that creating a sense of intimacy with audiences is a key strategy for internet celebrities as this is the way performers, YouTubers, musicians, influencers and social media's new entrepreneurs, or whatever you call them, are able to monetize talent, material and social media labour. As such, relational labour is a key characteristic of interaction on social media (cf. Berryman and Kavka 2018; Raun 2018; Woodcock and Johnson 2019). As we can see with the case of malevolent influencers, this also applies to extremists, predators, trolls, abusers and other harmful content makers.

Issa Rae, PewDiePie, Justin Bieber, and even Jordan Petersen and other Alt-Right influenc-ers are able to capitalize on the kind of intimacy work and relational labour needed to develop a following and grow audiences. Each of these celebrities, some of whom primarily used YouTube as a launch pad for a multi-platform career, and those who are primarily just YouTubers, have all successfully been able to be relatable, use humour, demonstrate grati-tude, successfully promote themselves and make the shift from non-professional to professional content creation. Although this is only a brief introduction to the complexities of relational labour, it is apparent that it is an important part of the digital skill sets required for visibility and connection in a social media age. YouTube may only be a part of the broader social video landscape, but it has set the milestones for others in the industry, as well as reflecting broad cultural shifts in labour and connection.

Building on this, the third theme emerging from this chapter is about those required skill sets. YouTube and social video foster and demand new literacies and skill sets, not only for those making visual content, but also for those viewing it (see also Lange 2014). For Baym and Abidin, 'relational labour' is not just about the technical or social skills required to grow and maintain audiences, but also about navigating platforms, offline audiences, negotiating the terms of monetization and succeeding as an entrepreneur (Abidin 2015; Baym 2018). Tobias Raun, based on research with transgender vloggers, notes that intimacy and authenticity work are prerequisites for success in monetizing content, visibility and even for 'advocacy work' (2018: 99). Sophie Bishop, YouTube researcher and lecturer in digital marketing, argues that visibility labour:

> ... necessitates in-depth and timely comprehension of YouTube's algorithmic changes, likely obtained through regularly reading trade journals and annual attendance at industry conventions, mostly held in media centres in the Global North such as Los Angeles, London and New York (Duffy, 2015). For entrepreneurial vloggers, algorithmic understanding will shape their practice, a process I term algorithmic 'selfoptimization'. (Bishop 2018: 73)

Thus, whether it is called 'self-optimization', 'relational labour' or the 'work of intimacy', it is clear that this kind of work demands a wide range of skills and literacies. Patricia Lange, anthropologist of visual culture, argues that some of these literacies are unique to YouTube, because it enables 'personally expressive media' which do not have to adhere to the promotional logics of monetization, but do involve a vast set of skills involving 'construction, maintaining, and negotiating a technologized identity' (2014: 11). Lange's point, based on an extensive ethnography of kids on YouTube, is that YouTubing demands the development of technical, visual and performative literacies. This is also an important point. YouTube may set the aesthetic standards for social video, but each visual platform has its own affordances, cultural norms and standards – all of which involve specific literacies which must bridge technical, algorithmic, metric, aesthetic, identity and visual communication skills.

Finally, one of the key debates around YouTube and streaming on demand services is whether or not content reflects more diversity or more hegemony. There are radically alternating views on this issue. Neil Landau, speaking about the new streaming services displacing network giants, points out that there are more shows with a wider range of characters, including more trans and LGBTQI characters (e.g. Amazon's *Transparent*), more shows featuring female leads from wider age ranges and with differing body types (e.g. Netflix's *Orange is the New Black*, *Jessica Jones* and *Grace and Frankie*) and more shows starring racially diverse casts (e.g. *Seven Seconds*, *AJ and the Queen* and *Dear White People*, all on Netflix). Yet, looking at the most viewed videos and channels on YouTube, as well as the top earners, presents a different and less diverse story. Based on her YouTube research, Bishop argues that there is a heavily gendered divide between beauty and gaming on YouTube, and that:

> YouTubers who do not fit within an existing genre will be punished. This excludes channels outside of popular genres in playlists and actively demotes channels if users end a viewing session with a given video. (Bishop 2018: 80)

For Bishop, these gendered distinctions, are reinforced by tagging and algorithmic visibility which 'actively promotes hegemonic, feminized cultural outputs .... [that] privileges and rewards feminized content deeply entwined with' typical feminized categories and YouTube tags around beauty, fashion and friendships (2018: 69). Her point here reflects old-fashioned and highly gendered assumptions shaping children's toy marketing, and the persistence of such assumptions for the social video ecosystem (see Chapter 4).

In contrast to Bishop's work on YouTube's strictly gendered genres, Maloney et al. argue that YouTube promotes radical change around gender. Based on YouTube gaming play, a genre which is often understood as hypermasculine and traditionally gendered, Maloney et al. find nuance and considerable openness. For them, the social video and gaming videos from PewDiePie, VanossGaming and Sky Does Minecraft show an:

> ... ironic heterosexual recuperation and changing gay discourse, affectionate homosociality and the satirical rejection of hypermasculinity [and as a result], we lean towards an understanding that culturally exalted masculinities are in transition, becoming more inclusive. (Maloney et al. 2018: 1710)

Certainly, when compared to the last bastions of network and even cable television and film, YouTube's new generations of creators come across as much more diverse, and with a wider array of talents. This progress, shaped by the seemingly infinite opportunities for anyone to represent themselves on YouTube, has little to do with YouTube success. Based on the top earners, most viewed videos and channels (see Table 9.1), traditional hegemonies are overlaid and interwoven with changing social relations, affective labour and new literacies – all of which are integrated with visibility and the politics of identity. The next section examines emerging trends not just for YouTube, but also in social video more broadly.

Emerging Trends in Social Video: Rise of Live and TikTok

Social video is a complicated area with lots of convergence between television, streaming, apps and social media. As YouTube and Facebook are dominant platforms in this field, this chapter has focused on YouTube, even though many more sites and apps are relevant to this discussion. In addition, the pandemic of 2020 involved global lockdowns, heightening the importance of social media, streaming and live video chat providers like Zoom, Microsoft Teams, Jitsi, Google Meet and many more. Given this context, there are three emerging trends worth considering beyond YouTube, including the rise of live video, the impact of new players like TikTok and the extension of densely networked platform media.

The rise of live is one of the emerging trends, informing a range of social media platforms (e.g. Facebook, Periscope, Snapchat, Meerkat, YouTube, Twitch), as well as established screen industries like film and television (Rein and Venturini 2018; van Es 2017: 1245). For example, for the BBC live streaming provides a foothold in the crowded streaming and video-on-demand (COF) market. Inge Sørensen argues that the:

> … BBC regards live TV as core to its multi-platform strategy. Today, the BBC uses two of television's traditional traits – liveness and reach – to crowd out and gain a competitive edge on streamed content and VOD providers like YouTube, Netflix and Amazon Prime. (2016: 381)

Thus it is not just social media that are concerned with live content. Indeed, Rein and Venturini argue that 'live-streaming may well be the current next big thing' (2018: 3374), but it is so only because it is driven by big players like Facebook. Based on research with Twitch users, Wulf et al. (2018) find that live streaming is enjoyable for users and contributes to a real-time sharing of experience. In this sense, live content on social or broadcast media holds the potential to drive new directions in social video.

TikTok, the new short-form social media app launched in 2016 but making 2020 headlines, is the number one most downloaded app on the App Store and Google Play, reaching '1.5 billion downloads worldwide' (Davis 2019: 60; Williams 2020). TikTok clips are much shorter than YouTube's, averaging 15 seconds, and meaning users can see many more videos than other social video sites and apps. In addition, TikTok offers a 'Go Live' feature, where users can live stream content to their followers, and this puts them in direct competition with Facebook, Instagram, Twitter and other social media. Like YouTube, TikTok offers a simple interface, easy to use editing and content creation tools, personalized and algorithmic content filtering, as well as easily *shareable* content across the web and other social platforms (Glatt, as cited in Stokel-Walker 2020). All of these features have been a hit with younger users.

TikTok 'uses AI technologies to assess users' preferences through their interactions with the content and provide a personalized content feed to each user', so users do not have to manually input any of their interests or preferences (Li 2019: 334). TikTok will do this for them, based on their in-app behaviour. Therefore, despite TikTok's 'new' features, it also conforms to the data-gathering norms set by other social media platforms and the social quantification sector (see Chapter 8). Perhaps because TikTok is Chinese, or perhaps because it is owned by 'artificial intelligence firm ByteDance', many users are concerned about its data-collection practices (Davis 2019: 60). Indeed, TikTok is being sued by a 'class action lawsuit filed in California' for collecting personally identifiable data about its users and including spyware in the app (2019: 60). Yet as we know from Chapter 8, these data-extraction practices are commonplace.

Finally, it is clear that platforms and users are part of a densely networked platform ecosystem. Whether we are looking at YouTube, TikTok, the BBC, Netflix or other social video apps or platforms, users are embedding content across sites, using Twitter or Instagram to interact with users, while filming YouTube videos. Social video, perhaps like other social media, are most successful when they can be used across the web and social media. As Sørensen points out, '57% of 16- to 24-year-olds, habitually *"media mesh"* on two or more screens simultaneously', a phenomenon reproduced by creators as they navigate complex social ecosystems marked by intense creative and affective labour (2015: 382, emphasis added). Looking at two live-streaming apps, Meerkat and Periscope, Rein and Venturini argue that these apps did well 'because they were constructed to integrate smoothly with Twitter', making it much easier for users to connect with their followers across platforms (2018: 3363). As such, integrating into the 'media mesh' is important for publishers when deciding what platforms to use, as was demonstrated by The Verge when they 'adopted YouTube's live feature' (see also Mashable and Twitter, Rein and Venturini 2018: 3368). In closing, while new players like TikTok may seem to take the world by storm, it is often because of the meshing with existing platforms and legacy media.

Conclusion

Screen industries have shifted from well-defined divisions between film and television, now including a greater degree of conversion across sectors and integration with social media, as seen with the emergence of the proto-industry 'social media entertainment' (Cunningham and Craig 2019). In terms of 'social screens', many social media platforms are not only developing or working with their own social video, but are also working a wide range of players in this field. Thus, this chapter has laid out the broader context for understanding not only social video, but also the increasingly social nature of the screens in our lives.

As one of the earliest and most dominant social video platforms, this chapter has focused on YouTube, from its origins in 2005, its key platform features, and a look at key content and creators. YouTube, like every other long or short-form social video app, enables a creative vernacular where video makers can express their identities, their perspectives, their creations and the everyday language of their lives in many different ways (Burgess and Green 2018). Yet, as in the cases of malevolent influencers and users, the story of social video enables reactionary and anti-social ideologies, as much as it does capitalist and community oriented perspectives.

The lack of regulation, particularly when compared to TV and film ratings systems and content restrictions, means that YouTube is responsible for protecting children and vulnerable people. This responsibility is in direct opposition to how it makes it profits, and may explain the lack of action on this matter. Unlike twentieth-century screen culture, twenty-first-century screens position users as data points, embedding them into a set of data relations (see Chapters 3, 7 and 8). YouTube, along with other social video and streaming sites, chose to track, monetize and profile users' behaviours, generating massive amounts of data.

Based on this exploration of YouTube, I introduced some of the ways YouTube and social video are impacting on human interactions and social relations, notably through the rise of affective and relational labour (e.g. Baym 2018), as well Abidin's (2018) reworking of parasocial relations as 'perceived interconnectedness'. Both of these frameworks provide valuable insights not only on social video, but also on changing norms and lived practices experienced through social video and platforms more broadly. Of course, in line with the broader field of social video, this chapter ends by looking at some of the key trends and emerging practices. These include the rise of live – as seen in social video apps, as well as in driving new multi-platform strategies for established broadcasters. New players like TikTok may change the stakes of the game, but also reiterate many of the things apparent in other social video platforms, such as data collection and the extension of data relations. It certainly has become clear that for creators and for platforms, social video is about connecting to and integrating in what Sørensen refers to as the 'media mesh' – the densely interconnected mix of apps, platforms and networks demanding easy use and navigation.

Questions and Activities

1   In small groups, make your own short YouTube video answering the questions: What is YouTube and why does it matter? The video should be 1–2 minutes long. Script your answers, pay attention to lighting and sound, and take advantage of YouTube's editing tools. Report back what you learned from the experience.
2   How is YouTube (or another digital video platform) changing the screen industries?
3   Using an example, evaluate the role of influencers on YouTube. What do you think is happening in these examples, and what impact does that have on society?
4   Using one of the examples from this chapter or an example based on your own experience with social video, evaluate relational labour. What kind of 'intimate work of connection' do you see?
5   What are the key visual literacy skills required for your generation? What is the same or different for the skills needed by younger generations?

Further Reading

Abidin, C. 2018. *Internet Celebrity: Understanding Fame Online*. Emerald Publishing.
Bishop, S. 2018. Anxiety, panic and self-optimization: inequalities and the YouTube algorithm, *Convergence*, 24 (1), pp. 69–84. https://doi.org/10.1177/1354856517736978
Burgess, J. Green, J. 2018. *YouTube: Online Video and Participatory Culture*, 2nd edn. Polity.
Cunningham, S.; Craig, D. 2019. *Social Media Entertainment: The New Intersection of Hollywood and Silicon Valley*. New York University Press.
Lewis, B. 2018. Alternative influence: broadcasting the reactionary right on YouTube, *Data & Society*, September 18. https://datasociety.net/library/alternative-influence/
Phillips, W. 2018. The oxygen of amplification: better practices for reporting on extremists, antagonists, and manipulators, *Data & Society*, May 22. https://datasociety.net/library/oxygen-of-amplification/

10

LOVE, INTIMACY AND PERSONAL CONNECTIONS

Chapter Overview

Introduction	230
Personal Connections: Interpersonal Relations Across Social Media	230
Love and Intimacy	231
Dating industries: From sites to apps	234
Tinder	238
Gamification and swipe logic	240
Abuse and harassment	242
Personal Disconnections: Breaking Up and Defriending on Social Media	244
Conclusion: Shifting Intimacies	246
Questions and Activities	247
Further Reading	247

┤Chapter Objectives├

- Introduce personal connections and theories of love
- Examine the dating industry from sites to apps, and the role of social media in this industry
- Explore Tinder as an app and its unique affordances
- Introduce disconnection on social media (e.g. breaking up and defriending)
- Evaluate the changing nature of personal connection and disconnection in relation to social media

Introduction

Many have argued that screens, apps and social media technologies are contributing to a decline in social cohesion, resulting in a loss of communicative capacities and meaningful connections with others. Social dating apps, like Tinder, have made it easier to make quick connections across a wider geographic area and social groups. As a result, dating apps have also often been attributed with the rise of 'hook-up culture', ghosting, and the increased casualization and disposability of relationships. At the other end of the scale, online abuse, harassment, trolling and mass public shaming are also on the rise. All of these phenomena point to the ways social and digital media play an increasingly affective role in our lives, impacting on human intimacy and personal connections. This chapter examines theories of love, recent research on Tinder and dating apps, as well as the impact of disconnections, such as breaking up and defriending, on mediated personal connections.

Personal Connections: Interpersonal Relations Across Social Media

When it comes to thinking about personal connections, many people tend to prioritize face-to-face communication as the most genuine and personal. Digital and social media have exponentially increased the number of available sites and channels that can be used to communicate with others, and this can make it more difficult to make sense of interpersonal relations. Nancy Baym, a leading internet researcher specializing in personal connection, argues that every new medium rewrites the boundaries around what we understand as 'real' and what we understand as mediated. For example, the advent of the telephone prompted concerns about the dissolution of 'real relationships' because there would no longer be a need to see people face to face (Marvin 1988). Similarly, when it was new, some argued that television was a key driver for 'dumbing down' the population and to a loss of literacy (Postman 1985). These fears were also expressed about reading, writing and photography, and indicate anxiety over the changing personal boundaries related to new communication technologies (Baym 2015a: 1). Indeed, for Baym, every new medium calls into question how we understand ourselves, others and our relationships with them (2015a: 1–3). She suggests that people tend to respond to new communication innovations in one of two ways: to focus on the decline of quality and meaning; or to focus on the promise of more connections, made faster and over a greater geographic area (2015a: 1). Both of these positions reflect longstanding cultural concerns on the nature of personal connections in relation to technological change, and succinctly sum up a huge range of scholarship, media commentary and personal responses.

In terms of our current era of social media, we find ourselves in a state of 'perpetual contact' marked by the blurring of mass and interpersonal media (Baym 2015a: 2–3). Thus, while YouTube videos or Instagram selfies, for example, can be intended only for a small audience, they also have the potential to quite quickly reach mass audiences – making communication simultaneously interpersonal and public. Baym argues that these dynamics raise questions around the 'true self', and what is understood by presence and absence. These are important points. If, for example, we are speaking on the phone in the presence of other people, where are we? Are we with the people in the room, or are we with the people we are speaking to? When we use social media, are our profiles and pages genuine or do they reflect idealized reflections of our selves? In terms of how we connect with others, are we more or less 'real' on social media than we are in person? Baym states that every new medium raises these kinds of profound questions, raising moral panics and deep anxieties.

Baym argues that to understand 'how we use media and with what consequences', we need to bear in mind historical continuities as well as innovations (2015a: 19). In principle, this is quite straightforward, but in actuality it is a difficult task, particularly given the degree to which social media are deeply embedded within personal communications and connections to others. To do this, this chapter begins with theories of love and intimacy, providing a framework for making sense of what is new, what is historically continuous, and what is unique to social media and mediated personal connections. Next, it introduces the dating industry, providing an overview of how this has changed from the twentieth to the twenty-first centuries, highlighting the rising importance of apps in this crowded space. Focusing on Tinder as an important social dating app, we look at some of the key trends in dating, such as gamification, swipe logic and the rise in online abuse – all of which are part of both the app's unique affordances and the broader social context of social media. Yet understanding personal connection also means understanding disconnection, so the last section looks at why this is important, as well as specific practices such as breaking up and defriending. Finally, the conclusion links these sections, offering an analysis of social media and personal connections.

Love and Intimacy

but my tongue breaks down, and then all at once a

subtle fire races inside my skin, my

eyes can't see a thing and a whirring whistle

thrums at my hearing,

cold sweat covers me and a trembling takes

ahold of me all over: I'm greener than the

grass is and appear to myself to be little

short of dying (Sappho, excerpt from 'Like the Gods', 6th century BCE)

There are an almost infinite number of stories, poems and songs dedicated to love. The above poem fragment by ancient Greek poet Sappho is only one of these, and may resonate with some people's idea or experience of love. While often the subject of poetry, love is less frequently the subject of social or economic theory. However, there are those that have looked at love in terms of *social* rather than individual relations. For example, Mihai Rusu (2017) provides a useful overview of sociological approaches to love, ranging from classical sociologists like Max Weber and Emile Durkheim to contemporary theorists like Zygmunt Bauman's widely cited work *Liquid Love* (2003) and Eva Illouz's body of work on love (1997, 2013, 2019). Rusu gives a clear overview of the development of a 'sociology of love', often grounded in the study of other social structures and relationships, such as kinship and the family, ethics and morality, and social cohesion more often seen in the work of classic sociologists (Rusu 2018: 5–6). In recent years, social theorists like Anthony Giddens (1992), and Ulrich Beck and Elisabeth Beck-Gernshein (1995) have contributed to this in their collective works on the transformation of love and intimacy. All of this work grounds love as much more than a set of powerful *individual* emotions, and instead as an interior and interiorizing experience at the meeting points between social norms, conventions and the political organization of the social world.

Take, for example, Sappho, who became known as a lesbian poet, one of the first to be publicly lauded. However, as evidenced by the civil rights struggles around the cultural and legal recognition of lesbian, gay, bisexual, transexual, queer and intersex (LGBTQI) rights, who one is able to love is not just an individual choice. Instead, heterosexual and cis-gendered relationships have been legally and socially sanctioned at the expense of those who don't identify as heterosexual. Indeed, there is a much broader spectrum of gendered identities and sexual orientations. In the UK the first same-sex marriage bill became law in 2013, resulting in the first legal same-sex marriage in 2014 (Gov.uk 2013). In 2015, the US legalized same-sex marriage (Masci et al. 2019). While these changes mark huge gains in securing human rights for LGBTQI communities, these same rights are far from global. This is only one example of the ways in which love and relationships are bound up in political and social structures.

While this example focuses on romantic or passionate love, there are many different kinds of love, including love for family, for friendships and for humanity. These different kinds of love have different names, of which there are four worth mentioning: *eros, storge, philia* and *agape*. *Eros* refers to erotic love, *storge* to affection, *philia* to friendship and *agape* to a spiritual form of love, which could also be understood as a love for the greater good (Lewis 1960; Rusu 2018). All of these kinds of love are individually experienced within the social institutions of marriage, family, community, affinity and society.

Focusing on *eros* and romantic love, Eva Illouz, who has dedicated her career to the study of love and relationships, argues this link is important. For Illouz, love and relationships 'intersect with the culture, the economy, and the social organization of advanced capitalism' (1997: 1, 2013, 2019). She offers a critical account not only of love in the contemporary moment, what she calls 'hyperconnective modernity', but also of its historical development (2019). Drawing from the work of historian Theodor Zeldin, Illouz defines marriage as primarily serving an economic function, binding the estates and wealth of families together up until the early twentieth century (1997: 9). She argues that in this context, romantic love threatened to challenge the established social order, which was built upon humans' subjugation to God and the redistribution of wealth along class lines – all maintained by traditional marital arrangements. As such, romantic love facilitated the 'formation of emotional individualism' and of an interiority free from traditional constraints (2019: 6). In the early twentieth century, romantic love was radical and liberating.

At the same time, many feminist thinkers challenge the transcendental narrative of romantic love as the pathway to happiness and self-fulfilment, arguing that love is instead:

> … one of the main causes of the divide between men and women, as well as one of the cultural practices through which women are made to accept (and 'love') their submission to men. For, when in love, men and women continue to perform the deep divisions that characterize their respective identities: in Simone de Beauvoir's famous words, even in love men retain their sovereignty, while women aim to abandon themselves. (Illouz 2013: 4–5)

In this way, romantic love also conforms to and instantiates class, gender and power structures (Illouz 2019: 6). Given this tension between freedom and submission, the idea and practice of romantic love is far more than just an individual and intense experience of feeling 'greener than grass' as Sappho describes above. Instead, love is hugely complex and mediates between the interior self, social experience and social structures.

Based on this development and nature of love, Illouz argues that there is something 'qualitatively new in the modern experience' of love, to the 'romantic imagination' and indeed to the suffering so frequently attached to desire and connection (2013: 16–17).

Zygmunt Bauman, a famous social philosopher, takes a different position, claiming this qualitative new kind of romantic love is one part of 'a liquid modern life setting' where romance is now 'hoped to come and go with ever greater speed' (2003: xii). Bauman's argument that we are in an age of 'liquid love' means that relationships that are no longer primarily bound by the traditional obligations of courtship or relational commitments, and are instead marked by momentary networked connections rather than primarily through fixed dyads, characteristic of marriage. Bauman's notion of liquid love fits with Illouz's vision of hyperconnective modernity, although Illouz characterizes hyperconnective love as marked by 'negative bonds', such as:

> ... the one-night stand, the zipless fuck, the hook-up, the fling, the fuck-buddy, the friends with benefits, casual sex, casual dating, cybersex, [which] are only some of the names of relationships defined as short-lived, with little or no involvement of the self, [and are] often devoid of emotions. (2019: 21)

Although some may disagree with Illouz's characterization of 'short-lived' relationships as 'often devoid of emotion', her point, along with Bauman's, is that *eros* and dating rituals are shifting towards a new era of amplified connection through a series of networked interactions, as much experienced through easy disconnection as it is through successive relationships.

While Illouz notes the role networked media, dating apps and sites, social platforms and other digital media play in 'hyperconnectivity', Zizi Papacharissi, professor of communication and editor of *The Networked Self and Love*, takes a different stance. Papacharissi claims that love has little to do with technology because 'technology cannot predict love, algorithms cannot render it out of databased profiles, and platforms cannot fix love that is broken' (2018: 4). Neither Illouz or Bauman attribute these broader social changes entirely to networked and connective technologies, but they do position these technologies as impacting on personal relationships within the context of advanced capitalism. Love and intimacy are informed by the armies of counsellors, psychoanalysts, psychologists, advice columns, and dating apps, sites and services – all contributing to the 'qualitatively new' romantic industries available to those seeking momentary or permanent matches.

Despite Papacharissi's rational reminder that technology does not create, predict or fix love, whole industries have dedicated themselves to making a profit from those who think they can use it to find love and intimate connection. The next section introduces dating industries from their somewhat stigmatized beginnings as newspaper ads in the 1700s to their current role as a standard entry point into the dating world.

Dating industries: From sites to apps

Since the early 1700s, personal ads in newspapers have been one of many approaches to meeting new romantic interests and early courtship (Reimann 2016). For a long time personal and dating ads were stigmatized, carrying with them the presumption that anyone who needed to resort to such extreme measures must be both desperate and incapable of finding a love interest in the more 'normal' ways. Fast forward to centuries later when Grindr, Tinder, Bumble, Lumen, Bristlr and many other dating apps are commonplace. In the US, three in ten adults have used dating sites or apps, a figure that increases to almost one in two for young and LGBTQI people (Anderson et al. 2020). In the UK, 31% of adult females and 42% of adult males claim that they are currently using or had used dating sites or apps in the past (Kunst 2019).

Indeed, the online dating space is a fiercely competitive marketplace dominated by large global players, marked by the rapid growth of niche services for highly personalized tastes. The largest global player is InterActiveCorp (IAC), which owns the Match Group and controls 25% of the online dating and dating app market share (Lin 2019). IAC owns the following influential dating brands (among others):

- Match.com
- Meetic
- OkCupid
- PlentfyOfFish
- Tinder
- OurTime
- Hinge (https://www.iac.com/brands)

The second largest competitor is eHarmony, with just under 12% of the market, and which is both a dating site and app (Lin 2019). Taken together, online dating and dating apps generate a worldwide revenue of US $6.1 billion, with a year-on-year growth of 8% (Statista 2020).

In terms of niche markets, in addition to an impressive range of highly differentiated apps and services, there is significant growth in apps for those in the 50+ age range (e.g. Lumen or Stitch), and a rise in 'real time' dating apps using location to connect people as they cross paths or share neighbourhoods (e.g. Happn, Spark or TubeCrush; see Thomas 2014). There is also a rise in those sites or apps catering to specific lifestyles based on religious beliefs (e.g. JDate, Minder or Christian Mingle), diet choice (e.g. Veggie Romance, or Veggly for vegetarians and vegans), musical taste (e.g. Tastebuds or CLiKD), and many more. Bumble, founded by a former Tinder co-founder, lets female users make the first move, effectively aiming to empower and protect women in a dating context which can sometimes feel risky and hostile (Anderson et al. 2020). In addition, there are several elite dating apps, such as The Inner Circle or The League, as well as numerous LGBTQI sites and apps, such as Grindr, Her and Transdr. One of these niche apps, Bristlr, allows people to sign up based on whether they have or are interested in those with beards, rather than on their gender or sexual orientation. All of these illustrate the breadth and size of the dating industry and its growing market. Jumping on the dating bandwagon in September 2018, Facebook launched 'Facebook dating' first in Columbia and then in the US. This Tinder-style app-within-an-app was intended to extend Facebook's social real estate and monetize those users seeking love connections directly through Facebook. (See Table 10.1 for an overview of the top ten dating apps on the App Store and Google Play Store in 2020.)

Table 10.1 Top ten dating apps on the App Store and Google Play Store

	App Store	Google Play Store	Overall worldwide
1	Tinder	Tinder	Tinder
2	Bumble	Badoo	Badoo
3	Tantan	Hily	Hily
4	Hingo	Happn	Bumble
5	Badoo	Dating app: Chat	Azar
6	Azar	Azar	Happn
7	Plenty of Fish	OkCupid	Dating app: Chat
8	Happn	Free Dating App	Hinge
9	Hily	Bumble	OkCupid
10	Grindr	Lovoo	Tantan

Source: adapted from data compiled by Mobile Action in January 2020

Sam Yagan, co-founder of OkCupid and Vice-Chair of Match, argues that there are three eras in online and app-based dating (as reported by Bercovici 2014). The first of these is the search approach in the 1980s–1990s, where filtering for age, sex and location was not only the peak functionality of the time, but was also limited to only those with computing skills and who Yagan terms the 'geeks and freaks'. For Yagan, this was an important era that provided the basis for the second 'algorithmic' age (2000s–2010s), when both eHarmony and OkCupid were launched and which matched daters using many criteria (e.g. demographics, personality tests, wide-ranging interests) using proprietary software. The third 'IRL' (in real life) era saw the rise of apps such as location-based dating like Tinder and Grindr for real-world meet-ups, accelerated by instant communication made possible by the stratospheric take-off of smart phones (as reported by Bercovici 2014).

While these three eras correspond well with the rise of dating apps in the western world, the story looks quite different in the east and what researchers Ramina Sotoudeh, Roger Friedland and Janet Afary (2017) refer to as 'socially conservative countries'. (See Box 10.1 for an overview of online dating in five Muslim countries. Following this, the next section takes a closer look at Tinder, the game-changing and most downloaded dating app.

Box 10.1 Dating in socially conservative countries

Using Facebook banner ads to reach respondents, Ramina Sotoudeh, Roger Friedland and Janet Afary (2017) examined attitudes towards love and dating by surveying 20,000 people from five Muslim countries: Algeria, Pakistan, Palestine, Tunisia and Turkey. Sotoudeh et al. found that as in the west the internet provides an important part of the dating experience, although unlike in the west Facebook plays a much more central role, often making up 'the internet' for young people as well as providing an alternative space for hanging out with and meeting peers.

The authors define 'socially conservative' as a belief that the hijab is obligatory for women, and is a 'marker of piety and Muslim identity' (Sotoudeh et al. 2017: 432). In accordance with the socially conservative values of these countries, the results of the survey were also highly gendered, with men being much more active both online and offline. Although online spaces, like Facebook, provide spaces that are less observable to parents and authority figures, and as such are also considered safer dating spaces than real life alternatives, this is much more the case for men who are more active in making contact and arranging dates (2017: 432).

As such, Sotoudeh et al. note a 'gendered double standard' where women living in their home countries were much more likely to face serious consequences for 'immodest behaviour' and were less likely to access dating sites or arrange dates (2017: 437). This was different for Muslim women based in the west, who were more likely to use the internet to meet potential love interests. (See Table 10.2 for an overview of 'intimate internet use in the Muslim world', which summarizes these gendered differences.)

Table 10.2 Intimate internet use in the Muslim world

	Pakistan	Palestine	Algeria	Turkey	Tunisia
Access to online dating sites					
Female	3%	21%	24%	29%	29%
	(10)	(55)	(326)	(182)	(226)
Male	8%	37%	38%	11%	40%
	(41)	(167)	(407)	(33)	(136)
Arranging dates Female					
Female	2%	12%	6%	30%	10%
	(6)	(31)	(84)	(191)	(83)
Male	5%	25%	15%	7%	20%
	(41)	(167)	(407)	(33)	(136)
Total female	301	261	1381	629	791
Total male	862	662	2768	483	697

Source: Sotoudeh et al. (2017: 431)

Needless to say, Sotoudeh et al. argue that Muslims turned to the internet to seek out love despite the 'gender restrictiveness' of their offline worlds, and Facebook, in particular, broadened users' dating pools and matchmaking activities (2017: 437). Since this research was conducted, there has also been an explosion of Muslim dating apps, such as Minder, MuzMatch, Crescent and Salaam Swipe. Dating site giants Match and eHarmony are also popular for those seeking Muslim matches (see http://www.muslimdating-sites.org/muslim-dating-apps.html for an overview of the top Muslim dating apps).

Tinder

Often referred to as a 'hook-up' app for those looking for a quick no-commitment connection, Tinder feels like the 'defining app of the online dating era' (Iqbal 2019). It is the first swiping app, and since it was launched in 2012, it has been downloaded more than 340 million times on both Android and iOS (Dating Site Review 2020). In 2019, Tinder was processing 1.6 billion swipes on a daily basis, and its users were collectively going on a million dates a week (Iqbal 2019). Tinder is available in 190 countries and in over 40 languages, all of which illustrate its huge popularity with prospective daters. In addition, it has been popular in the app scene as well, inspiring the look and feel of many other dating apps (e.g. fh6, Skout, POF, Lovoo, Woo). For all intents and purposes, Tinder was a game changer for dating, for algorithms and for social technologies. It used a location-based algorithm to match users with nearby users and was smart phone based, and in these ways introduced the app-driven social experience to the dating sector. (See Box 10.2 for some key information on Tinder.)

Box 10.2 Tinder: Key info

Founded: 2012

Founders: Sean Rad, Justin Mateen, Joe Munoz, Dinesh Moorjani and Whitney Wolfe

Owner: Match Group Inc. (which is owned by InterActiveCorp (IAC))

CEO: Elie Seidman from 2017, formerly Sean Rad (2012–2016)

Cost: Free to use, premium subscription service Tinder Plus launched in 2014, followed by Tinder Gold in 2017

Headquarters:

- Tinder: Los Angeles, California United States
- Match Group: Dallas, Texas, United States

Number of Employees: 320

Unique features:

1. Location-based algorithm: Tinder uses location in part to match members
2. Swipe interface: This interface allows users to use the 'swipe' to like or dislike other profiles on Tinder. Swiping right indicates 'liking' someone, whereas swiping left is a 'nope' or dislike of someone's profile. It is also possible to 'super like' another user by swiping up. If two users both 'like' or 'super like' each other, they can begin sending messages to each other, a feature that is only activated when a 'like' is mutual.

3. Two-factor and/or social authentication: Tinder was one of the first dating apps to use two-factor authentication. At first, it required users to sign in using their Facebook account, verifying their name, contacts, likes, interests and photos. As it has evolved, it is possible to create an account with just a phone number, rather than an additional account. Once this has been done, users are able to link their Instagram, Facebook and/or Spotify accounts, sharing a vast amount of information which can be used to identify common friends and interests with other Tinder users.

4. Continual development: For example, there is: double opt-in Tinder VR ('real' VR); 'boosts' (paid bumps to a user's profile so it will be more widely circulated to other Tinder users); super likes; premium services (e.g. Tinder Plus and Tinder Gold).

Overall value: US $10 billion

(*Sources*: Iqbal 2019; Dating Site Review 2020; Tinder LinkedIn page (March 2020))

Certainly, Tinder captured the 2012 ethos of mobile communication for dating, concretizing a shift away from computers that were often fixed in the bedroom or office. According to Andrew Schrock, a digital scholar, mobile media enable four key affordances: 'portability, availability, locatability, and multimediality' (2015, cited in Ranzini and Lutz 2017: 82). Giulia Ranzini and Chritoph Lutz find that 'Tinder relies on all four of these communicative affordances', allowing users to move around and engage Tinder at their convenience, unlike landline phones or desktop computers (2017: 82). These affordances came together in its easy convenience, sparking a lot of media attention and many claims that it was responsible for the rise of 'hook-up culture', as well as increasing risk to female users. (See Figure 10.1 for just a few headlines which represent widely circulated concerns about the impact of Tinder and other dating apps.)

Figure 10.1 Selection of headlines identifying Tinder and other dating apps as cause for a decline in the quality of dating relationships

Of the growing body of research on Tinder and dating apps, there are two areas worth a further look: gamification and swipe logic; and the increase of abuse and harassment experienced by mostly female users. Each of these is addressed in turn below, followed by an exploration of what disconnection, breaking up and defriending mean for personal connections.

Gamification and swipe logic

Tinder's primarily visual interface invites users to engage in a playful mode of interaction based on quick visual judgements and a simple, tactile navigational path through the app (swiping right means 'like' and left means 'nope'). Once a user makes their choice, they are notified of their choice in big letters. If they have swiped right on a user's profile who also happened to like them, they are greeted with the congratulatory message, 'It's a MATCH!' Users are then able to 'say something nice' or to 'KEEP SWIPING'. The seemingly endless stream of profiles and simple tactility invite the user to keep going and to keep choosing their way through Tinder and their dating experience. These characteristics gamify the Tinder experience, enticing users with bold messages and easy tactile decision making. Sean Rad, Tinder co-founder and former CEO, confirms this when he describes the Tinder experience as:

> … a casting session and you're in the director's chair … At the end of the day, it's just one big party, and you're just sitting there saying, "Yes, no, yes, no" … The irony of Tinder is that in some ways the lack of information, or text, is actually less superficial than having the information. (Sean Rad, Tinder's co-founder and former CEO, cited in David and Cambre 2016: 5)

According to Rad, the easy and playful interface helps people connect based on instinct rather than over-thinking or analysing too much information. Garda and Karhulahti, two game researchers, argue that Tinder is full of 'gameplay' features that are both personally expressive, and position romantic interaction 'as play' (2019: 1). For these researchers, people are motivated to use Tinder to play, just as much if not more than they are motivated by finding a match. Indeed, the repetitive swiping is reminiscent of a slot machine, leading to 'uninterrupted engagement' which is 'is strongly related to the contingency factor of providing the individual with an endless chain of semi-random stimuli: a new profile image or hand of cards' that demands little in exchange for a reward (2019: 5). In this sense, whether Tinder feels like a slot machine or card play, the heightened uncertainty around finding a match is similar to gambling, comforting users through repetitive movements and exhilarating them through the excitement of a possible match.

Related to Tinder, many people describe it as 'more like a game', even placing the app in gaming folders on their phones so it is easy to reach when users want entertainment (e.g. 'Elmer', cited in Garda and Karhulahti 2019: 8). On Tinder, the ultimate prize game players might win is 'the promise of happiness' and of meaningful connection with a desirable partner, whether that partner is for the long or short term (2019: 10). It is this promise, along with the tactile swiping similar to gambling, that keeps many users coming back. In this sense, Tinder is not about personal connection but about playing with others, and exploring the dynamics and limits of connection made possible through networked media. This kind of play resonates with what Illouz refers to as 'hyperconnective modernity', in that it is not about finding lasting or even fulfilling bonds, but more about the pursuit of connection.

Although briefly touched upon above, Tinder was one of the first to introduce 'swiping' as a key element of its user interface. In terms of the binary yes or no, it built upon the 'hot or not' precedents set by the pre-Facebook site Facemash circa 2003 and Grindr, also a location-based and real time app for gay men (launched in 2009; see David and Cambre 2016: 3). Based on a six-month ethnography of 'mobile image-sharing practice' and eight interviews with Tinder users, digital researchers Gaby David and Carolina Cambre found the swiping interface led to a 'swipe logic' – which they describe as a particular set of behavioural relations driven by the app's affordances and limitations, such as the interface's pace, quantity, stream and visuality. In other words, the swipe interface compresses a series of actions – what they call a 'figuration of intimacy' – into a binary set of decisions (yes or no) (2016: 9). According to David and Cambre, Tinder curates platform specific 'social dynamics' by algorithmically circulating some profiles and limiting others (2016: 9).

Swipe logic incorporates some elements of gamification as mentioned above, but it also engages familiar and memorable gestures, like 'turning magazine pages' while browsing profile after profile, 'reducing an individual to the status of "one wave lost in a multitude of waves"' (Featherstone 2003: 441, cited in David and Cambre 2016: 6). In addition, many find this motion delightful and compulsive, in part because of its familiarity and in part because of its association with matching. By amplifying this familiar gesture, Tinder also incorporates speed into the interface design, encouraging immediacy and fast swiping through other users' profiles. Here the pace is related to the consumption of a greater number of profiles, and deeper engagement with Tinder's stream of profiles. All of these things contribute to its 'feel' and 'swipe logic'.

In addition to setting up a particular social dynamic between users, David and Cambre argue that Tinder is based on 'excessive visuality', where profile images are symbolically linked to a fixed set of choices that at one point were binary ('like' or 'nope') in 2016, and in early 2020, included 'super like', 'like' or 'nope'. For David and Cambre, this configuration of visuality and fixed set of gestural choices may broaden one's potential matches, but it also abstracts and depersonalizes other users. According to David and Cambre, Tinder's swipe logic disrupts traditional ideas of intimacy and facilitates a 'screened intimacy', which they describe as:

> ... the mediatization and depersonalization that is encouraged as a result of the speed of profile-viewing enabled by the swipe logic and thus as a top-down discursive hindrance to intimacy. At the same time ... [it can include] meaningful connections. (David and Cambre 2016: 2)

Thus, screened intimacies capture both the gestural motions of swipe logic, along with the social affordances entwined with Tinder's particular interface and technical features. Despite these apparent limitations on meaningful connections, dating apps and sites are increasingly important spaces for starting romantic partnerships. Research finds that 39% of Americans who use dating apps or sites claim they have married or been in a committed relationship with 'someone they met on a dating site or app' (Anderson et al. 2020). As Tinder is one of the most popular of these services, its role, particularly in heterosexual relationships, is important. Despite this, and perhaps because of the depersonalization David and Cambre note as part of 'screened intimacies', Tinder is also a site of sexual harassment and online abuse, particularly for female users.

Abuse and harassment

Another significant area of research in relation to Tinder is the extensive abuse and harassment experienced by its many female users. Two noteworthy Instagram sites, *Bye Felipe* and *Tinder Nightmares*, have grown significant followings by posting crowdsourced screenshots of male responses to women who ignore or reject their advances on Tinder. Both sites recognize that these responses reveal a social misogyny, as well as widespread male sexual entitlement to women's attention.

Many researchers have examined discourses on *Tinder Nightmares*, finding frequent illustrations of 'toxic masculinity' and highly 'patriarchal logics' (Hess and Flores 2018: 1085; Thompson 2018: 69). Started in 2014 by Elan Gale, the executive producer of serial reality shows *The Bachelor* and *The Bachelorette*, *Tinder Nightmares* has become a popular site with 2 million followers on Instagram (as of August 2020), and is part of the 'unspirational family'. In his book, titled after the site, Gale describes the page as '... all those shitty, misshaped, little puzzle pieces along the way [in the search for 'the happily after'] ... They're gross and hilarious and weird and they make you wonder what the fuck is even going on' (2015: n.p.). Others describe the site as 'a discursive space that challenges particular masculinist performances', particularly those that 'encourage men to be sexually aggressive, to value dominance and control, and to position women as inferior, especially in digital spaces' (Banet-Weiser and Miltner 2016 as referenced in Hess and Flores 2018: 1087).

A quick browse of *Tinder Nightmares* reveals screenshot after screenshot of aggressive sexual come-ons and excessive unwarranted hostility, so the observations about toxic masculinity are not made lightly. Based on an analysis of the subreddit forum '/r/Tinder', Jin Lee argues that people talk about their success on Tinder in terms of 'coolness' – a highly 'gendered code of conduct' which justifies the kind of sexist hostility observed on *Tinder Nightmares* (2019: 2). Lee analyses the 'cool girl figure' as a frequently occurring script which articulates gendered ideas of coolness in /r/Tinder talk. For Lee, this figure features a postfeminist ideal of a sexually liberated female whose 'freedom and pleasure are celebrated' as long as they are laid back enough to 'accommodate male culture ... (e.g. laughing at men's dirty jokes, joining hookups)' (2019: 3). As such, Lee argues that talk on /r/Tinder reveals a double standard around sexual behaviours and hook-up culture, one where girls and women going off the 'cool girl' script risk being attacked for their transgression, often in the form of name calling along the lines of sexual permissiveness (e.g. 'slut' or 'whore') or based on appearance (e.g. 'ugly' or 'bitch') (2019: 3–4).

Tinder Nightmares is only one of many sites documenting abusive online behaviour towards women. Frances Shaw, an interdisciplinary digital media researcher, adds *Bye Felipe* to a long list of sites like *Tinder Nightmares*, such as *Feminist Tinder, Fedoras of OKCupid* and *Trans Men on Grindr*, all of which 'draw attention to the sexual politics of online dating in similar ways' (2016: 5). Alexandra Tweten, founder and author of *Bye Felipe*, describes the site as a place 'to call out men who turn hostile when they're rejected or ignored' (2018: 2). As Shaw argues, sites like these are not only repositories for documenting abuse, but also function as spaces for consciousness raising and for drawing attention to the very real threats women face online, as well as to the broader social problems of sexism and misogyny (2016: 8).

On this note, online misogyny is a serious problem, one that can include extreme harassment and violence. For example, Gamergate, the massive and coordinated harassment campaign targeting female video-game makers and feminist commentators, involved death and rape threats as well as doxxing, publishing people's real addresses and contact details on sites like 8Chan and 4Chan (Dewey 2014; Gillespie 2018a; Quinn 2017; Wu et al. 2019). Amnesty International's (2018) work on 'Toxic Twitter' documents the serious sexist and racist abuse endured on Twitter by female public figures like UK Labour MP Diane Abbott and activists like Laura Bates, the founder and author of *Everyday Sexism*. In the UK, following her marriage to Prince Harry, Meghan Markle was subjected to racist mainstream media attacks as well as on social media (Foster, with Megan 2019; Hounsell 2019; Rodriguez 2019). All of these examples point to *Tinder Nightmares* as a microcosm of a larger internet culture, replete with the same social issues, hierarchies and inequalities.

Yet *Tinder Nightmares, Bye Felipe* and other similar sites do facilitate an active collective and feminist response to what would normally be privately experienced. While not a solution or quick fix to the broader problem of misogyny, these sites do help name and identify abuse and related experiences as *social* rather than as individual. Indeed, social media have also opened up spaces to reveal the scope of these social problems, and collectively mobilize against them as seen in #MeToo, #GirlsLikeUs and #SayHerName. As Sarah Jackson et al. argue, these sites, like hashtags, can 'center the politics of counterpublics, develop repertoires of political contention, and attract allies' (see Jackson et al. 2020: 185). In this way, such sites offer a space for identifying and reflecting on shared experiences, as well as activating a collective awareness about the many links between gender and social structures (cf. Illouz 1997, 2013, 2019).

In the next section, we look beyond Tinder and at practices of disconnecting and breaking up on dating apps, sites and social media.

Personal Disconnections: Breaking Up and Defriending on Social Media

Just as social media and dating apps have been used to connect romantically, and are part of a changing dating sector increasingly reliant on algorithms, data collection and mobile apps to reach clients and users, people also use social media and dating apps to *disconnect* from others. There is much less scholarship on this aspect of Tinder, dating sites and social media, although it is a fascinating and important topic – one that highlights the broader social context of 'connection' alongside the individual experiences of disconnection.

Bernie Hogan, Oxford Internet Institute research fellow, argues that break-ups require de-linking users within social networks, and that this breaks the logic of connectivity 'that powers much of network society' (2018: 113). Tero Karppi, a new media scholar, takes this research further, stating that connection is 'the cultural logic' of social media, and while defriending, detoxing, breaking up, unfollowing and logging out are not the only kinds of disconnections, they also work in opposition to this logic (2018: 2). For Karppi, disconnections 'are tools to think about the outside; they destroy the all too perfect and totalizing images of the world connected' (2018: 24). Any disconnective activity requires intentional labour to remove or change the links making up people's relational status. Ben Light, professor of digital society, places these kinds of activities as part of a broader genre of disconnective practices, that should also include disconnecting from platforms themselves. These practices provide important opportunities for making visible social media's dominant ideology of connection and their affordances. For Light, 'connection cannot exist without disconnection', and as such, is a crucial part of social media and networked experience (2014: 159; cf. Quinn and Papacharissi 2017).

Focusing on individual users rather than the cultural logics of disconnection, Ilana Gershon, an anthropology professor, published a book called *The Breakup 2.0: Disconnecting over New Media* (2010; see also Gershon 2020). She found that people had particular expectations for mediated communications, and were pretty much uniformly horrified by 'bad breakups' taking place over text or on Facebook (2010: 2–3). Her key argument is that break-ups revealed particular affiliations and expectations about what, how and when to communicate via different platforms – a set of beliefs that she calls 'media ideologies' (2010: 6). For example, email was viewed as a formal kind of communication, one that was not appropriate for personal talk between friends. Similarly, text and instant messenger were highly informal, and although they were appropriate for casual interactions, were much less so for 'breaking up' communications. While face to face was considered the ideal way to break up with someone, text or instant messenger could be used to start more serious talk about relationships (Gershon 2010). Gershon argues that connective and disconnective work is complex, on or off of social media. Her key point is that the medium matters, and looking at how people break up on media reveals unwritten rules and expectations about media and about how to use them to communicate (2010: 15).

For example, in Gershon's research one respondent, Leslie, found out she was breaking up with her partner when he changed his relationship status on Facebook to 'single', simultaneously notifying shared friends (2010: 37). This experience raised many questions about how Leslie should navigate the personal nature of this public communication, while also working out how to interpret and react to her now ex. Other respondents, like Keith, complained about the ambiguity of 'it's complicated' as a relationship status, arguing that this marks a lack of basic 'social skills' (as cited in Gershon 2010: 47). Gershon also documents unfriending practices, noting that some of her respondents actively culled people from their friends lists without ever providing an explanation, although some others viewed defriending as 'an excessive act of hostility', not worth the effort of delinking their connections in the network (2010: 42). Yet 'ghosting', i.e. disappearing from a relationship with no communication, is also an increasingly popular way to end a relationship, whether that is through defriending, unfollowing, blocking, breaking up or just ceasing to communicate (e.g. LeFebvre et al. 2019). These early silent defriending behaviours seem to be an early precursor of 'ghosting', illustrating just some of the complexities around disconnecting and breaking up.

Following up her 2010 research with *The Break-up 2.1* (2020), Gershon notes that although US undergraduates may have broadened the range of media used for interpersonal communications, now including 'Snapchat, Twitter, Instagram, Tinder (and so on)', they still navigate breakups in similar ways. She finds that people still invest a lot of time deciphering communication, including its medium of delivery, and also on managing and/or disconnecting shared photos, friendships, groups and messages, sometimes deciding to unfriend, block or unfollow (2020: 2–3). As in 2010, people also monitored their ex's social media accounts and other 'digital traces', sometimes through their friends' accounts if they had lost access by unfriending or blocking (2020: 3). Gershon found that people used different social media for different stages in their relationships. For example, using Tinder or Bumble for initial contact, moving to Snapchat or Instagram for the 'getting to know you' chat, before exchanging phone numbers and switching to texting for longer-term communication (2020: 20). She refers to this as 'media-switching', observing that moving the communicative medium could be as much a part of breaking up as it could be about solidifying a relationship (2020: 5).

In her 2010 work, Gershon found that many young people used Facebook to legitimize their relationships with romantic partners, and Facebook's relationship status feature was used to announce when people were 'in a relationship', thereby making it 'Facebook official' (2010: 37, 65; see also Robards and Lincoln 2016). In 2018, Gershon finds that Facebook relationship statuses are still used to legitimize well-established relationships *with family* rather than friend networks, marking a shift in platform audience (2020: 4). Snapchat streaks, i.e. the number of consecutive days users send daily messages to each other, were also spoken about as cementing both relationships and friendships (2020: 5). Once streaks were broken or were shared with others outside of the relationship, the relationship could become visible, illustrating flows of connection on social media. As Gershon explains:

> People do not always automatically stop a streak just because they have broken up, and thus breaking up can now involve various stages of disentangling by media. First, people start to suspect the breakup might be about to happen, because as a couple they are texting more infrequently. Or perhaps, as happened for one interviewee, someone notices that her boyfriend has a Snapchat streak going with another girl. (2020: 5)

Thus, while there is a proliferation of media, Gershon argues that there are continuities across the decade that she's been researching breakups on social media. However, there have been many events revealing social media's systems of dataveillance (see Chapter 8) which may impact the ways people make and refrain from public disclosures. For example, in work on privacy and sharing culture, I have found that users see their relationship status as personal information, which they are less likely to share on publicly visible social media sites (e.g. Sujon 2018).

Conclusion: Shifting Intimacies

In this chapter we have looked at personal connections, and the ways these are mediated through social media, finding that the dating industry has grown in size and scope – transitioning from a set of sites for 'freaks and geeks' to mainstream apps helping people make romantic connections. We have also looked at love, which although experienced as intensely individual is also intensely social. Eva Illouz, introduced at the beginning of this chapter, develops a theory of 'hyperconnective modernity', which argues that 'the increase of social networks, real or virtual' is directly connected to the *unmaking of bonds'* (original emphasis, 2019: 4). Illouz suggests love and intimacy have merged with the 'consumer market', made visible through the dating and therapy industries alongside greater uncertainty in long-term relationships – all of which could be linked to the changing dynamics of dating through Tinder, Bumble, Hinge, Grindr or others apps (2019: 5). Given the historical transformation of love from a marital consolidation of estates and family wealth to an individualistic twenty-first-century experience based on choice, love is 'a powerful agent of social change' (2019: 7), one that reflects, refracts and re-creates power hierarchies and social relations. Zygmunt Bauman, on the other hand, leaves behind Illouz's erosion of bonds, arguing that 'liquid love' fits networked connections rather than the traditional dyads of heterosexual marriage. Both agree that love and connection are not just about individuals.

For Illouz and Bauman, love, intimacy, personal connections and disconnections are also about the social fabric, tying together intimate interactions with the socio-economic conditions of the market. Dating apps have become hugely influential for 'modern courtship and sexual activity', which, according to political media researchers Hobbs et al., show a widened pool of prospective partners, rather than the dissolution of social bonds as envisioned by Illouz (Hobbs et al. 2017: 272). Indeed, Hobbs and his colleagues argue that dating apps illustrate Bauman's concept of liquid love, where 'networked intimacy' allows daters to benefit from an extended pool of prospective partners and increased romantic freedom (2017: 271).

Dating sites and apps have 'displaced the role of traditional "matchmakers", such as family, friends and community leaders', and this points to a shifting pattern around how people make, communicate with, and maintain or break off their intimate connections (2017: 272).

Apps, platforms and websites are not 'neutral conduits'; instead they have 'animating logics' and 'economic imperatives' which leave an imprint 'on the dynamics of sociality and public discourse' (Gillespie 2018a: 14). Many agree with Illouz's link between economics and love, easily apparent in app 'dating culture' and 'market logics' (Lee 2019: 2). As we have learned from Tinder, 'swipe logic' and 'screened intimacies' are pervasive features informing personal connections and dating relationships (David and Cambre 2016). While the research presented in this chapter does not support the link between Tinder, Grindr, Bumble, Her, and the legion of other dating apps and the rise of hook-up culture, each of these offers different 'media ideologies' and affordances (Gershon 2010, 2020). Users do rely on dating apps to make connections, before switching to other mediums which better suit their current relationship stage. There may be many more ways to communicate, but the ways in which relationships start and end on social media must be negotiated, within the bounds set by a pervasive ideology of connection.

Questions and Activities

1. Debate: 'Social media offers the illusion of intimacy rather than genuine connection'. Explain why you agree or disagree.
2. Ilana Gershon argues that we see more continuities in the last decade of dating and breaking-up experiences. Using examples, explain why you agree or disagree.
3. In your view, what is the most significant impact of social media on love relationships?
4. In this chapter, we looked at a number of theoretical concepts, such as Eva Illouz's 'hyperconnective modernity' and Zygmunt Bauman's 'liquid love'. Which of these concepts best explains the way we make and maintain personal connections?

Further Reading

David, G.; Cambre, C. 2016. Screened intimacies: Tinder and the swipe logic, *Social Media + Society*, 2 (2). http://journals.sagepub.com/doi/full/10.1177/2056305116641976

Gershon, I. 2020. The Breakup 2.1: the ten-year update, *The Information Society.* DOI: 10.1080/01972243.2020.1798316

Rusu, M. S. 2018. Theorising love in sociological thought: classical contributions to a sociology of love, *Journal of Classical Sociology,* 18 (1), pp. 3–20. https://doi.org/10.1177/1468795X17700645

REFERENCES

Abbate, Janet. 2017. What and where is the Internet? (Re)defining Internet histories, *Internet Histories: Digital Technology, Culture and Society*, 1 (1–2). www.tandfonline.com/doi/full/10.1080/24701475.2017.1305836

Abbate, Janet. 2000. *Inventing the Internet*. The MIT Press

Abdulla, Rasha; Poell, Thomas; Rieder, Bernhard; Woltering, Robert; Zack, Liesbeth. 2018. Facebook polls as proto-democratic instruments in the Egyptian revolution: the 'We Are All Khaled Said' Facebook page, *Global Media and Communication*, 14 (1), pp. 141–60. https://doi.org/10.1177/1742766518760085

Abidin, Crystal. 2015. Communicative <3 intimacies: influencers and perceived interconnectedness. *Ada: A Journal of Gender, New Media, and Technology*, 8. DOI: 10.7264/N3MW2FFG

Abidin, Crystal. 2016. 'Please subscribe!: influencers, social media, and the commodification of everyday life', Doctor of Philosophy, The University of Western Australia. https://doi.org/10.26182/5ddc899d698cb

Abidin, Crystal. 2017. 'YouTuber influencers vs. legacy media: PewDiePie, weaponized microcelebrity, and cross-media politics', Wishcrys Blog. https://wishcrys.com/2017/02/22/youtuber-influencers-vs-legacy-media-pewdiepie-weaponized-microcelebrity-and-cross-media-politics/

Abidin, Crystal. 2018. *Internet Celebrity: Understanding Fame Online*. Emerald Press.

Abidin, Crystal. 2020. Meme factory cultures and content pivoting in Singapore and Malaysia during COVID-19, *The Harvard Kennedy School Misinformation Review*, 1, July, pp. 1–20. https://misinforeview.hks.harvard.edu/article/meme-factory-cultures-and-content-pivoting-in-singapore-and-malaysia-during-covid-19/

Aday, Sean; Farrell, Henry; Freelon, Deen; Lynch, Marc; Sides, John; Dewar, Michael. 2013. Watching from afar: media consumption patterns around the Arab Spring, *American Behavioral Scientist*, 57 (7), pp. 899–919. https://doi.org/10.1177/0002764213479373

Adorno, Max; Horkheimer, Theodor. 2005 [1944]. The culture industry: enlightenment as mass deception, trans. Andy Blunden, in *Dialectic of Enlightenment*. https://www.marxists.org/reference/archive/adorno/1944/culture-industry.htm

Alaimo, Kara. 2015. How the Facebook Arabic page 'We Are All Khaled Said' helped promote the Egyptian revolution, *Social Media + Society*. https://doi.org/10.1177/2056305115604854

Albarran, Alan B. (Ed.) 2013. *The Social Media Industries*. Routledge.

Albrechtslund, Anders. 2008. Online social networking as participatory surveillance, *First Monday*, 3 (13). https://journals.uic.edu/ojs/index.php/fm/article/view/2142/1949

Alderman, John. 2001. *Sonic Boom: Napster, MP3, and the New Pioneers of Music*. Perseus.

Alexander, Cynthia J.; Pal, Leslie A. 1998. *Digital Democracy: Policy and Politics in the Wired World*. Oxford University Press.

Alhabash, Saleem; Ma, Mengyan. 2017. A tale of four platforms: motivations and uses of Facebook, Twitter, Instagram, and Snapchat among college students?, *Social Media + Society*, 3 (1). http://journals.sagepub.com/doi/full/10.1177/2056305117691544

Amnesty International. 2018. #ToxicTwitter: violence and abuse against women online, Amnesty International. https://docs.house.gov/meetings/IF/IF00/20180905/108642/HHRG-115-IF00-20180905-SD015.pdf

Amnesty International. 2019. China human rights, Amnesty International. https://www.amnestyusa.org/countries/china/

Anderson, Benedict. 2006. *Imagined Communities,* revised edition. Verso.

Anderson, Monica; Toor, Skye; Rainie, Lee; Smith, Aaron. 2018. Activism in the social media age, Pew Research Center. July 11. https://www.pewresearch.org/internet/2018/07/11/an-analysis-of-blacklivesmatter-and-other-twitter-hashtags-related-to-political-or-social-issues/

Anderson, Monica; Vogels, Emily A.; Turner, Erica. 2020. The virtues and downsides of online dating, Pew Internet Research. February 6. https://www.pewresearch.org/internet/2020/02/06/the-virtues-and-downsides-of-online-dating/

Andre, Virginie. 2012. 'Neojihadism' and YouTube: patani militant propaganda dissemination and radicalization, *Asian Security*, 8 (1), pp. 27–53. DOI: 10.1080/14799855.2012.669207

Ang, Ien. 1996. *Desperately Seeking the Audience*. Routledge.

Annenberg Inclusion Initiative. 2019. *Inequality Across 1,200 Popular Films: Examining Gender and Race/Ethnicity of Leads/Co Leads from 2007 to 2018*. USC Annenberg. http://assets.uscannenberg.org/docs/inequality-in-1200-films-research-brief_2019-02-12.pdf

Anon. 2009. The history and evolution of social media, Web Designer Depot. https://www.webdesignerdepot.com/2009/10/the-history-and-evolution-of-social-media/

AP. 2014. Cogent CEO: comcast purposefully slowed down Netflix, *The Mercury News*. May 8. http://www.mercurynews.com/2014/05/08/cogent-ceo-comcast-purposefully-slowed-down-netflix-streaming/

Apperley, Thomas; Moore, Kyle. 2019. Haptic ambience: ambient play, the haptic effect and co-presence in Pokémon GO, *Convergence*, 25 (1), pp. 6–17. https://doi.org/10.1177/1354856518811017

Armstrong, Martin. 2020. YouTube's top-earners 2019, Statista. January 3, https://www.statista.com/chart/12247/youtubes-highest-paid-stars/

Arnstein, Sherry R. 1969. A ladder of citizen participation, *Journal of the American Planning Association*, 35 (4), pp. 216–24. DOI: 10.1080/01944366908977225

Arthur, Charles. 2012. The history of the smartphone, *Guardian*. January 24. https://www.theguardian.com/technology/2012/jan/24/smartphones-timeline

Arthurs, Jane; Drakopoulou, Sophia; Gandini, Alessandro. 2018. Researching YouTube, *Convergence*, 24 (1), pp. 3–15. https://doi.org/10.1177/1354856517737222

Associated Press. 2012. Beyond Facebook: a look at social network history, *The Economic Times*, May 19. https://economictimes.indiatimes.com/slideshows/corporate-industry/beyond-facebook-a-look-at-social-network-history/a-look-at-social-network-history/slideshow/13296931.cms

Auerbach, Karl. 2014. Severe tire damage, the internet's first live band, History of the Internet 1965–1995, July 20. https://history-of-the-internet.org/videos/std/

Ausserhofer, Julian; Maireder, Axel. 2013. National politics on Twitter, *Information, Communication & Society*, 16 (3), pp. 291–314. DOI: 10.1080/1369118X.2012.756050

Aytes, Ayhan. 2013. Return of the crowds: mechanical Turk and neoliberal states of exception', in Trebor Scholz (Ed.), *Digital Labor: The Internet as Playground and Factory*. Routledge.

Baer, Dave. 2015. Emoticons have basically saved human communication, *Business Insider*, September 24. https://www.businessinsider.com/emoji-were-invented-33-years-ago-heres-why-theyre-so-crucial-today-2015-9

Bainbridge, Jason. 2014. 'It is a Pokémon world': the Pokémon franchise and the environment, *International Journal of Cultural Studies*, 17 (4), pp. 399–414. https://doi.org/10.1177/1367877913501240

Baker, Stephanie A.; Walsh, Michael J. 2018. 'Good morning fitfam': top posts, hashtags and gender display on Instagram, *New Media & Society*, 20 (12), pp. 4553–70. https://doi.org/10.1177/1461444818777514

Banet-Weiser, Sarah; Baym, Nancy; Coppa, Francesca; Gauntlett, David; Gray, Jonathan; Jenkins, Henry; Shaw, Adrienne. 2014. Participations: dialogues on the participatory promise of contemporary culture and politics, PART I: CREATIVITY, *International Journal of Communication*, 8, pp. 1069–88. https://ijoc.org/index.php/ijoc/article/view/2721/1117

Baran, Paul. 1964. On distributed communications: 1. introduction to distributed communication networks. Memorandum, Rand Corporation. https://www.rand.org/content/dam/rand/pubs/research_memoranda/2006/RM3420.pdf

Barassi, Veronica. 2019. Datafied citizens in the age of coerced digital participation, *Sociological Research Online*. DOI: 10.1177/1360780419857734

Barker, Alex. 2020. Digital ad market set to eclipse traditional media for first time, *Financial Times*, June 23. https://www.ft.com/content/d8aaf886-d1f0-40fb-abff-2945629b68c0

Barker, Meg-John; Gill, Rosaline; Harvey, Laura. 2018. Mediated intimacy: sex advice in media culture, *Sexualities*, 21 (8), pp. 1337–45. https://doi.org/10.1177/1363460718781342

Barney, Darin; Coleman, Gabriella; Ross, Christine; Sterne, Jonathan; Tembeck, Tamar (Eds.) 2016. *The Participatory Condition in the Digital Age*. University of Minnesota Press.

Barwise, Patrick. 2018. The evolution of digital dominance: how and why we got to GAFA, martin moore and damian tambini (Eds.), *Digital Dominance: The Power of Google, Amazon, Facebook, and Apple*. Oxford University Press.

Bastow, Clem. 2016. From Pokéstops to Pikachu: everything you need to know about Pokémon GO, *Guardian*, July 11. https://www.theguardian.com/technology/2016/jul/11/from-pokestops-to-pikachu-everything-you-need-to-know-about-pokemon-go

Bauman, Zygmunt. 2000. *Liquid Modernity*. Polity.

Bauman, Zygmunt. 2003. *Liquid Love: On the Frailty of Human Bonds*. Polity.

Bauman, Zygmunt. 2005. *Liquid Life*. Polity.

Baym, Nancy. 2006. Interpersonal life online, in Leah Lievrouw and Sonia Livingstone (Eds.), *The Handbook of New Media*, updated student edn. Sage.

Baym, Nancy. 2015a. *Personal Connections in the Digital Age*, 2nd edn. Polity.

Baym, Nancy. 2015b. Social media and the struggle for society, *Social Media + Society*, 1 (1). http://journals.sagepub.com/doi/full/10.1177/2056305115580477

Baym, Nancy. 2018. *Playing to the Crowd: Musicians, Audiences, and the Intimate Work of Connection*. New York University Press.

BBC. 2018. Vero: The 'new Instagram' everyone's talking about, *BBC News*, February 27. https://www.bbc.com/news/newsbeat-43208162

Beck, Ulrich; Beck-Gernsheim, Elisabeth. 1995. *The Normal Chaos of Love*. Polity.

Beer, David. 2008. Social network(ing) sites ... revisiting the story so far: a response to danah boyd and nicole ellison, *Journal of Computer Mediated Communication*, 13 (2), pp. 516–29. http://onlinelibrary.wiley.com/doi/10.1111/j.1083-6101.2008.00408.x/full

Bene, Marton. 2017. Influenced by peers: Facebook as an information source for young people, *Social Media + Society*, 3 (2). DOI: 10.1177/2056305117716273

Benjamin, Ruha (Ed.) 2019a. *Captivating Technology*. Duke University Press.

Benjamin, Ruha. 2019b. *Racer After Technology*. Polity.

Benjamin, Walter. 1999 [1972] *The Arcades Project*. Harvard University Press. https://monoskop.org/images/e/e4/Benjamin_Walter_The_Arcades_Project.pdf

Benkler, Yochai. 2006. *The Wealth of Networks: How Social Production Transforms Markets and Freedoms*. Yale University Press.

Benkler, Yochai. 2012. Sharing nicely: on shareable goods and the emergence of sharing as a modality of economic production, in Michael Mandiberg (Ed.), *The Social Media Reader*. New York University Press.

Benkler, Yochai. 2013. Wikileaks and the networked Fourth Estate, in Benedetta Brevini, Anne Hintz and Patrick McCurdy (Eds.), *Beyond Wikileaks*. Palgrave Macmillan.

Bennett, Jessica. 2014. With some selfies, the uglier the better, *The New York Times*. February 21. https://www.nytimes.com/2014/02/23/fashion/selfies-the-uglier-the-better-technology.html

Bennett, Lance W.; Segerberg, Alexandra. 2012. The logic of connective action, *Information, Communication & Society*, 15 (5), pp. 739–68. DOI: 10.1080/1369118X.2012.670661

Bennett, Lance W.; Segerberg, Alexandra. 2013. *The Logic of Connective Action: Digital Media and the Personalization of Contentious Politics*. Cambridge University Press

Bercovici, Jeff. 2014. Love on the run: the next revolution in online dating, *Forbes*, February 14. http://www.forbes.com/sites/jeffbercovici/2014/02/14/love-on-the-run-the-next-revolution-in-online-dating/

Bergvall-Kåreborn, Birgitta; Howcroft, Debra. 2013. 'The future's bright, the future's mobile': a study of Apple and Google mobile application developers, *Work, Employment and Society*, 27 (6), pp. 964–81. https://doi.org/10.1177/0950017012474709

Bernstein, Jay M. 1991. Introduction, in *Theodor W. Adorno: The Culture Industry*. Routledge.

Berryman, Rachel; Kavka, Misha. 2018. Crying on YouTube: vlogs, self-exposure and the productivity of negative affect, *Convergence*, 24 (1), pp. 85–98. https://doi.org/10.1177/1354856517736981

Bidgoli, Hossein. 2006. *Handbook of Information Security*, Volume 1. Wiley.

Bijker, Wiebe E.; Hughes, Thomas Parke; Pinch, Trevor J. 1989. *The Social Construction of Technological Systems: New Directions in the Sociology and History of Technology*. The MIT Press.

Biolcati, Roberta; Passini, Stefano. 2018. Narcissism and self-esteem: different motivations for selfie posting behaviors, *Cogent Psychology*, 5 (1). DOI: 10.1080/23311908.2018.1437012

Birkinshaw, Julian; Sheehan; Tony. 2002. Managing the knowledge life cycle, *MIT Sloan Management Review*. https://sloanreview.mit.edu/article/managing-the-knowledge-life-cycle/

Bishop, Sophie. 2018. Anxiety, panic and self-optimization: inequalities and the YouTube algorithm. *Convergence*, 24 (1): pp. 69–84. https://doi.org/10.1177/1354856517736978

Bishop, Sophie. 2019. Managing visibility on YouTube through algorithmic gossip, *New Media & Society*, 21 (11–12), pp. 2589–2606. DOI: 10.1177/1461444819854731

Blank, Grant; Bolsover, Gillian; Dubois, Elizabeth. 2014. A new privacy paradox: young people and privacy on social network sites, *Annual Meeting of the American Sociological Association*, August 17, San Francisco, CA. http://dx.doi.org/10.2139/ssrn.2479938

Blake, James. 2017. *Television and the Second Screen: Interactive TV in the Age of Social Participation*. Routledge.

Blood, Rebecca. 2000. Weblogs: a history and perspective, Rebecca's Pocket, September 7. http://www.rebeccablood.net/essays/weblog_history.html

Blumenthal, Eli. 2019. Apple names best apps and games of 2019, *CNET*, December 2, https://www.cnet.com/news/apple-announces-its-best-apps-and-games-as-2019-winds-down/

Blumer, Herbert. 1969. *Symbolic Interactionism: Perspective and Method*. University of California Press.

Bogle, Ariel (2016) How the gurus behind Google Earth created 'Pokémon GO', Mashable. July 11. https://mashable.com/2016/07/10/john-hanke-pokemon-go/

Boing Boing. 2017. An hour with Ev Williams: founder of Medium, Twitter, and Blogger, Boing Boing, June 11. https://boingboing.net/2017/11/06/an-hour-ish-with-ev-williams.html

Bond, Shannon. 2017. Google and Facebook build digital ad duopoly, *Financial Times*. March 14. https://www.ft.com/content/30c81d12-08c8-11e7-97d1-5e720a26771b

Bosch, Tanja Estella; Admire, Mare; Ncube, Meli. 2020. Facebook and politics in Africa: Zimbabwe and Kenya, *Media, Culture & Society*, 42 (3), pp. 349–64. https://doi.org/10.1177/0163443719895194

Bourdieu, Pierre. 1986. The forms of capital, in John Richardson (Ed.), *Handbook of Theory and Research for the Sociology of Education*. Greenwood. https://www.marxists.org/reference/subject/philosophy/works/fr/bourdieu-forms-capital.htm

boyd, danah. 2006a. Friends, friendsters, and top 8: writing community into being on social network sites, *First Monday*, 11, 12, December 4. https://firstmonday.org/ojs/index.php/fm/article/download/1418/1336

boyd, danah. 2006b. The significance of social software, BlogTalk Reloaded, October 2. https://www.danah.org/papers/BlogTalkReloaded.html

boyd, danah. 2012. Networked privacy, *Surveillance and Society*, 10 (3–4), pp. 348–50. http://ojs.library.queensu.ca/index.php/surveillance-and-society/article/view/networked/networked

boyd, danah. 2014. *It's Complicated: The Social Lives of Networked Teens*. Yale University Press.

boyd, danah; Ellison, Nicole. 2007. Social network sites: definition, history, and scholarship, *Journal of Computer Mediated Communication*, 13 (1), pp. 210–30. http://onlinelibrary.wiley.com/doi/10.1111/j.1083-6101.2007.00393.x/full

Brake, David. 2014. *Sharing Our Lives Online: Risk and Exposure in Social Media*. Palgrave Macmillan.

Bratton, Benjamin H. 2015. *The Stack: On Software and Sovereignty*. The MIT Press.

Bresnahan, Krystal M. 2016. From portraits to selfies: family photo-making rituals, ProQuest Dissertations Publishing. University of South Florida. 10243540

Briant, Emma. 2018. As Cambridge Analytica and SCL elections shut down, SCL Group's defence work needs real scrutiny, Open Democracy. May 4. https://www.opendemocracy.net/en/opendemocracyuk/as-cambridge-analytica-and-scl-elections-shut-down-scl-groups-defence-work-needs-re/

Bridle, James. 2017. Something is wrong on the internet, Medium, November 6. https://medium.com/@jamesbridle/something-is-wrong-on-the-internet-c39c471271d2

Brock, André. 2020. *Distributed Blackness: African American Cybercultures*. New York University Press.

Brown, Barry. 2000. The artful use of groupware: an ethnographic study of how Lotus Notes is used in practice, *Behaviour & Information Technology*, 19 (4), pp. 263–273. DOI: 10.1080/01449290050086372

Bruns, Axel. 2008. FCJ-066 The future is user-led: the path towards widespread produsage, *The FibreCulture Journal*, 11. http://eleven.fibreculturejournal.org/fcj-066-the-future-is-user-led-the-path-towards-widespread-produsage/

Brügger, Niels. 2015. A brief history of Facebook as a media text, *First Monday*, 20 (5). http://firstmonday.org/ojs/index.php/fm/article/view/5423/4466

Bruns, Axel. 2015. Making sense of society through social media, *Social Media + Society*, 1 (1). http://journals.sagepub.com/doi/abs/10.1177/2056305115578679

Brunsdon, Charlotte; Morley, David. 1978. *Everyday Television: Nationwide*. British Film Institute.

Bryant, Peter. 2014. If a tree falls in the forest: the role of community formation and the power of the individual in zine making participation, *Online Journal of Communication and Media Technologies*, 4 (3). ISSN 1986–3497.

Bucher, Taina. 2015. Networking, or what the social means in social media, *Social Media + Society*, May 11. https://doi.org/10.1177/2056305115578138

Bucher, Taina. 2018a. *If…Then: Algorithmic Power and Politics*. Oxford University Press.

Bucher, Taina; Helmond, Anne. 2018b. The affordances of social media platforms, in Jean Burgess, Thomas Poell and Alice Marwick (Eds.), *The SAGE Handbook of Social Media*. Sage.

Buckingham, David (Ed.). 2008. *Youth, Identity, and Digital Media*. The John D. and Catherine T. MacArthur Foundation Series on Digital Media and Learning. The MIT Press. DOI: 10.1162/dmal.9780262524834.001

Bucy, Eric P.; Gregson, Kimberly S. 2001. Media participation: a legitimizing mechanism of mass democracy, *New Media & Society*, 3 (3), pp. 357–80. https://doi.org/10.1177/1461444801003003006

Buoalamwini, Joy; Gebru, Timnit. 2018. Gender shades: intersectional accuracy disparities in commercial gender classification, *Proceedings of Machine Learning Research*, 81, pp. 1–15. http://proceedings.mlr.press/v81/buolamwini18a/buolamwini18a.pdf

Burgess, Jean. 2015. From 'broadcast yourself' to 'follow your interests': making over social media, *International Journal of Cultural Studies*, 18 (3): pp. 281–85. https://doi.org/10.1177/1367877913513684

Burgess, Jean; Green, Joshua. 2009. *YouTube: Online Video and Participatory Culture*. Polity.

Burgess, Jean; Green, Joshua. 2018. *YouTube: Online Video and Participatory Culture*, 2nd edn. Polity.

Burgess, Jean; Marwick, Alice; Poell, Thomas. 2018. Editors' introduction, *The SAGE Handbook of Social Media*. Sage.

Cadwalladr, Carole. 2018. 'I made Steve Bannon's psychological warfare tool': meet the data war whistleblower, *Guardian*. March 18. https://www.theguardian.com/news/2018/mar/17/data-war-whistleblower-christopher-wylie-faceook-nix-bannon-trump

Cadwalladr, Carole. 2019. Facebook's role in Brexit — and the threat to democracy, TED 2019, April. https://www.ted.com/talks/carole_cadwalladr_facebook_s_role_in_brexit_and_the_threat_to_democracy/transcript?language=en

Cain, Caleb. 2019. My descent into the alt-right pipeline, YouTube, March 22. https://youtube.com/watch?v=sfLa64_zLrU&t=2030s

Calhoun, Craig (Ed.). 1992. *Habermas and the Public Sphere*. The MIT Press.

Callinicos, Alex. 2004. *Making History: Agency, Structure, and Change in Social Theory*, 2nd edn. Koninklijke Brill NV.

Callon, Michel. 1986. Some elements of a sociology of translation: domestication of the scallops and the fishermen of St Brieuc Bay, in John Law (Ed.), *Power, Action and Belief: a New Sociology of Knowledge?* Routledge.

Caoduro, E. 2014. Photo filter apps: understanding analogue nostalgia in the new media ecology, *Networking Knowledge: Journal of the MeCCSA Postgraduate Network*, 7 (2). https://doi.org/10.31165/nk.2014.72.338

Caralucci, Tony. 2014. Ello, the social network alternative to Facebook, *Global Research*, September 27. https://www.globalresearch.ca/ello-the-social-network-alternative-to-facebook/5404499

Carpentier, Nico. 2004. Coping with the agoraphobic media professional: a typology of journalistic practices reinforcing democracy and participation, *CeMeSo Working Paper*, 2 (34). http://nicocarpentier.net/workpap/cemeso-02-agoraphobic.pdf

Carpentier, Nico. 2007. Participation and media, in B. Cammaerts and N. Carpentier (Eds.), *Reclaiming the Media: Communication Rights and Democratic Media Roles*. Intellect.

Carpentier, Nico. 2011. *Media and Participation: A Site of Ideological-Democratic Struggle*. Intellect.

Carpentier, Nico. 2016. Beyond the ladder of participation: an analytical toolkit for the critical analysis of participatory media processes, *Javnost – The Public*, 23 (1), pp. 70–88. 10.1080/13183222.2016.1149760

Carr, Caleb T.; Hayes, Rebecca A. 2015. Social media: defining, developing, and divining, *Atlantic Journal of Communication*, 23 (1), pp. 46–65.

Cassiano, Marcella Siqueira. 2019. China's Hukou platform: windows into the family, *Surveillance and Society*, 17 (1/2). DOI: https://doi.org/10.24908/ss.v17i1/2.13125

Castells, Manuel. 1996. *Rise of the Network Society Volume 1: Economy, Society and Culture*. Blackwell.

Cath, Corinne; Ten Oever, Niels; O'Maley, Daniel. 2017. Media development in the digital age, Center for International Media Assistance (CIMA), March. http://www.cima.ned.org/wp-content/uploads/2017/03/CIMA-Internet-Governance_150ppi-for-web_REV.pdf

CBS News. 2014. Then and now: a history of social networking sites, CBS News, February 4. https://www.cbsnews.com/pictures/then-and-now-a-history-of-social-networking-sites/12/

CCCS. 1982. *Empire Strikes Back: Race and Racism in 70s Britain*. Hutchinson and Co.

CERN. No date. The Birth of the Web, CERN: Accelerating Science. https://home.cern/topics/birth-web

Cha, Jiyoung. 2016. Television use in the 21st century: an exploration of television and social television use in a multiplatform environment, *First Monday*, 21 (2). http://firstmonday.org/ojs/index.php/fm/article/view/6112

Chacon, Benjamin. 2017. Everything you need to know about Instagram's new paid partnership feature, Later.com, October 15. https://later.com/blog/paid-partnership-feature/

Chamary, J. V. 2018. Why 'Pokémon GO' is the world's most important game, *Forbes*, February 10. https://www.forbes.com/sites/jvchamary/2018/02/10/pokemon-go-science-health-benefits/#34f91b7c3ab0

Chan, Lik Sam. 2018. Ambivalence in networked intimacy: observations from gay men using mobile dating apps, *New Media & Society*, 20 (7), pp. 2566–81. https://doi.org/10.1177/1461444817727156

Chang, Alvin. 2018. The Facebook and Cambridge Analytica scandal, explained with a simple diagram, Vox, May 2. https://www.vox.com/policy-and-politics/2018/3/23/17151916/facebook-cambridge-analytica-trump-diagram

Chase, Garrett. 2018. The early history of the Black Lives Matter movement, and the implications thereof, *Nevada Law Journal*, 18 (3), pp. 1091–1112. https://scholars.law.unlv.edu/nlj/vol18/iss3/11

Chavez, Ivana. 2019. We're Not Really Strangers x Bumble: HOLR chats with Koreen Odiney, *HOLR Magazine*, November 5. https://www.holrmagazine.com/were-not-really-strangers-wnrs-collab-bumble/

Chen, Jenn. 2020. Social media demographics to inform your brand's strategy in 2020, Sprout Social, January 15. https://sproutsocial.com/insights/new-social-media-demographics/#IG-demos

China Labour Watch. 2018. Amazon profits from secretly oppressing its supplier's workers: an investigative report on Hengyang Foxconn, June 10. http://www.chinalaborwatch.org/report/132

Cho, Junghoo; Tomkins, Andrew. 2007. Guest editor's introduction: social media and search, *IEEE Internet Computing*, 11 (6), pp. 13–15.

Cho, Sumi; Crenshaw, Kimberlé; McCall, Leslie. 2013. Toward a field of intersectionality studies: theory, application, praxis, *Signs: Journal of Women in Culture and Society*, 38 (4), pp. 785–819.

Chong, Gladys Pak Lee. 2019. Cashless China: securitization of everyday life through Alipay's social credit system—Sesame Credit, *Chinese Journal of Communication*. DOI: 10.1080/17544750.2019.1583261

Chouliaraki, Lillie. 2006. *The Spectatorship of Suffering*. Sage.

Chouliaraki, Lilie. 2013. *The Ironic Spectator: Solidarity in the Age of Post-Humanitarianism*. Polity.

Claements, M. 2013. From Star Trek to Fifty Shades: how fanfiction went mainstream, *Guardian*, August 8. https://www.theguardian.com/books/2018/aug/08/fanfiction-fifty-shades-star-trek-harry-potter

Clark, Jessica; Couldry, Nick; De Kosnik, Abigail; Gillespie, Tarleton; Jenkins, Henry; Kelty, Christopher; Papacharissi, Zizi; Powell, Alison; van Dijck, Jose. 2014. Participations: dialogues on the participatory promise of contemporary culture and politics PART 5: PLATFORMS, *International Journal of Communication*, 8, pp. 1446–73. https://ijoc.org/index.php/ijoc/article/view/2905/1143

Clarke, Laurie. 2019. How Yahoo's prudish policies pushed Tumblr into obscurity, *Wired*, August 14. https://www.wired.co.uk/article/tumblr-sold-to-wordpress?utm_content=buffer081fa&utm_medium=social&utm_source=twitter.com&utm_campaign=buffer

Clement, J. 2019a. Net digital ad revenues of Google as percentage of total digital advertising revenues worldwide from 2016 to 2019, Statista, July 23. https://www.statista.com/statistics/193530/market-share-of-net-us-online-ad-revenues-of-google-since-2009/

Clement, J. 2019b. Most viewed YouTube videos of all time 2019, Statista, December 3. https://www.statista.com/statistics/249396/top-youtube-videos-views/

Clement, J. 2020a. Most popular social networks worldwide as of October 2019, Ranked by Number of Active Users, Statista, October. https://www.statista.com/statistics/272014/global-social-networks-ranked-by-number-of-users/

Clement, J. 2020b. Most viewed YouTube channels worldwide as of January 2020, by monthly views, Statista, January 6. https://www.statista.com/statistics/373729/most-viewed-youtube-channels/

Clement, J. 2020c. Global YouTube advertising revenues 2017–2019, Statista, February 4. https://www.statista.com/statistics/289658/youtube-global-net-advertising–revenues/

Clement, J. 2020d. Number of apps available in leading app stores as of 1st quarter 2020, Statista. August 11, https://www.statista.com/statistics/276623/number-of-apps-available-in-leading-app-stores/

Cockburn, Cynthia. 1997. Domestic technology: Cinderella and the engineers, *Women's Studies International Forum*, 20 (3), pp. 361–71. ftp://ftp.ige.unicamp.br/pub/CT001%20SocCiencia/25%20de%20Outubro/Cockburn%20domestic%20technology.pdf

Cohen, Ira. 2006a. Agency and structure, in Bryan S. Turner (Ed.), *The Cambridge Dictionary of Sociology*. Cambridge University Press.

Cohen, Ira. 2006b. Structuration, in Bryan S. Turner (Ed.), *The Cambridge Dictionary of Sociology*. Cambridge University Press.

Cohen, Julie E. 2012. Configuring the networked citizen, in Austin Sarat, Lawrence Douglas and Martha Merrill Umphrey (Eds.), *Imagining New Legalities: Privacy and Its Possibilities in the 21st Century*. Stanford University Press.

Cohen, Julie E. 2015. The networked self in the modulated society, in Wouter de Been and Mireille Hildebrandt (Eds.), *Crossroads in New Media, Identity and Law: The Shape of Diversity to Come*. Palgrave, pp. 67–79

Cohen, Julie E. 2017. Surveillance vs. privacy: effects and implications, in David Gray and Stephen E. Henderson (Eds.), *The Cambridge Handbook of Surveillance Law*. Cambridge University Press. https://ssrn.com/abstract=3212900

Cohen, Julie E. 2019. The emergent limbic media system, in Mireille Hildebrandt and Kieron O'Hara (Eds.), *Life and the Law in the Era of Data-Driven Agency*. http://dx.doi.org/10.2139/ssrn.3351918.

Confessore, Nicholas. 2018. Cambridge Analytica and Facebook: the scandal and the fallout so far, *The New York Times*, April 4. https://www.nytimes.com/2018/04/04/us/politics/cambridge-analytica-scandal-fallout.html

Connolly, Amanda. 2016. Happy birthday, Twitter: 10 years of famous first tweets, The Next Web, March 21. https://thenextweb.com/twitter/2016/03/21/happy-birthday-twitter/

Constine, Josh. 2017. AOL Messenger shutting down after 20 years, *TechCrunch*, October 6. https://techcrunch.com/2017/10/06/aol-instant-messenger-shut-down/

Cook, James. 2016. Cheezburger used to run a viral publishing empire–now it's been sold to an Israeli media company, *Business Insider*, April 21. https://www.businessinsider.com/cheezburger-used-to-run-a-viral-publishing-empire-now-its-been-sold-2016-4

Couldry, Nick. 2000. *The Place of Media Power: Pilgrims and Witnesses of the Media Age*. Routledge.

Couldry, Nick. 2012. *Media, Society, World: Social Theory and Digital Practice*. Polity.

Couldry, Nick; Jenkins, Henry. 2014. Participations: dialogues on the participatory promise of contemporary culture and politics. *International Journal of Communication*. 8 Forum, pp. 1107–1112. https://ijoc.org/index.php/ijoc/article/view/2748/1119

Couldry, Nick. 2017. Deep mediatization: social order in the age of datafication, Berkman Klein Center, Harvard University, October 8. https://cyber.harvard.edu/events/2017/10/CouldryHepp

Couldry, Nick; Curran, James (Eds.) 2003. *Contesting Media Power: Alternative Media in a Networked World*. Rowman & Littlefield.

Couldry, Nick; Hepp, Andreas. 2017. *The Mediated Construction of Reality*. Polity.

Couldry, Nick; Livingstone, Sonia; Markham, Tim. 2018. The public connection project ten years on, in M.A. Guerrero and A. Arriagada (Eds.), *Conexión Pública: prácticas cívicas y uso de medios en cinco países*. Universidad Ibero Americana. [Accepted version: http://eprints.lse.ac.uk/88284/1/Livingstone_Public%20Connection%20Project_Accepted.pdf]

Couldry, Nick; Mejias, Ulises Ali. 2019a. *The Costs of Connection: How Data is Colonizing Human Life and Appropriating if for Capitalism*. Stanford University Press.

Couldry, Nick; Mejias, Ulises Ali. 2019b. Data colonialism: rethinking big data's relation to the contemporary subject, *Television & New Media*, 20 (4), pp. 336–49. DOI: 10.1177/1527476418796632

Couldry, Nick; Van Dijck, José. 2015. Researching social media as if the social mattered, *Social Media + Society*, September 30. https://doi.org/10.1177/2056305115604174

Creemers, Rogier. 2018. China's social credit system: an evolving practice of control, SSRN. http://dx.doi.org/10.2139/ssrn.3175792

Crenshaw, Kimberlé. 1989. Demarginalizing the intersection of race and sex: a Black feminist critique of antidiscrimination doctrine, feminist theory and antiracist politics, *University of Chicago Legal Forum*, 1 (8). http://chicagounbound.uchicago.edu/uclf/vol1989/iss1/8

Crenshaw, Kimberlé. 1991. Mapping the margins: intersectionality, identity politics, and violence against women of color, *Stanford Law Review*, 43 (6), pp. 1241–99. http://ec.msvu.ca:8080/xmlui/bitstream/handle/10587/942/Crenshaw_article.pdf?sequence=1

Cunningham, Stuart; Craig, David. 2019. *Social Media Entertainment: The New Intersection of Hollywood and Silicon Valley*. New York University Press.

Curran, James. 1991. Rethinking the media as a public sphere, in Peter Dahlgren and Colin Sparks (Eds.), *Communication and Citizenship: Journalism and the Public Sphere in the New Media Age*. Routledge.

Curran, James. 2006. *Media and Power*. Routledge.

Das, Ranjana. 2017. Audiences: a decade of transformations – reflections from the CEDAR network on emerging directions in audience analysis, *Media, Culture & Society*, 39 (8), pp. 1257–67. https://doi.org/10.1177/0163443717717632

Das, Ranjana. 2019. A field in flux: the intriguing past and the promising future of audience analysis, *Television & New Media*, 20 (2), pp. 123–29. https://doi.org/10.1177/1527476418814592

Das, Ranjana; Ytre-Arne, Brita. 2016. After the excitement: an introduction to the work of CEDAR, *Participations*, 13 (1), pp. 280–88.

Danet, Brenda. 1995. Playful expressivity and artfulness in computer-mediated communication, *Journal of Computer-Mediated Communication*, 1 (2). http://onlinelibrary.wiley.com/doi/10.1111/j.1083-6101.1995.tb00323.x/full. DOI: 10.1111/j.1083-6101.1995.tb00323.x

Daubs, Michael S.; Manzerolle, Vincent R. 2016. App-centric mobile media and commoditization: implications for the future of the open web, *Mobile Media and Communications*, 4 (1), pp. 52–68.

Davenport, Thomas; Patil, Dhanurjay. 2012. Data scientist: the sexiest job of the 21st century, *Harvard Business Review*, October. https://hbr.org/2012/10/data-scientist-the-sexiest-job-of-the-21st-century

David, Gaby; Cambre, Carolina. 2016. Screened intimacies: Tinder and the swipe logic, *Social Media + Society*, 2 (2). http://journals.sagepub.com/doi/full/10.1177/2056305116641976

Davies, William. 2003. *You Don't Know Me, But… Social Capital and Social Software*. The Work Foundation.

Davis, Rebecca. 2019. TikTok goes viral, *Variety*, 346 (12), pp. 59–61.

Dawkins, Richard. 1976. *The Selfish Gene*. Oxford University Press.

De Beauvoir, Simone. 2010 [1949]. *The Second Sex*. Trans. Constance Borde and Sheila Malovany-Chevalier. Vintage.

De Certeau, Michel. 2011 [1984]. *The Practice of Everyday Life*. University of California Press.

De Kosnik, Abigail. 2013. Fandom as free labour, in Trebor Scholz (Ed.), *Digital Labor: The Internet as Playground and Factory*. Routledge.

De Seta, Gabriele. 2015. Postdigital Wangluo: the internet in Chinese everyday life, *Anthropology Now*, 7 (3), pp. 106–117. DOI: 10.1080/19428200.2015.1103621

Deahl, Dani. 2017. Snapchat's newest feature is also its biggest privacy threat, *The Verge*, June 23. https://www.theverge.com/2017/6/23/15864552/snapchat-snap-map-privacy-threat

Deffree, Suzanne. 2018. Emoticons debut at Carnegie Mellon, September 19, 1982, EDN Network, September 19. https://www.edn.com/electronics-blogs/edn-moments/4396667/Emoticons-debut-at-Carnegie-Mellon--September-19--1982

Deller, Ruth A.; Murphy, Kathryn. 2020. 'Zoella hasn't really written a book, she's written a cheque': mainstream media representations of YouTube celebrities, *European Journal of Cultural Studies*, 23 (1), pp. 112–32. https://doi.org/10.1177/1367549419861638

Delwiche, Aaron. 2018. Early social computing: the rise and fall of the BBS scene, in Jean Burgess, Alice Marwick and Thomas Poell (Eds.), *The Social Media Handbook*. Sage.

DeNardis, Laura. 2010. The emerging field of internet governance, Yale Information Society Project Working Paper Series, September 17. https://papers.ssrn.com/sol3/papers.cfm?abstract_id=1678343

DeNardis, Laura. 2012. Hidden levers of internet control: an infrastructure-based theory of internet governance, *Information, Communication and Society*, 15 (5), pp. 720–38.

Dencik, L., Hintz, A.; Cable, J. 2016. Towards data justice? The ambiguity of anti surveillance resistance in political activism, *Big Data & Society*, 3 (2). https://doi.org/10.1177/2053951716679678

Dencik, Lina. 2018. Surveillance realism and the politics of imagination: is there no alternative?, *Krisis: Journal for Contemporary Philosophy*, 1. https://krisis.eu/surveillance-realism-and-the-politics-of-imagination-is-there-no-alternative/

DeShong, Travis. 2020. A wave of super earnest card games want you to bare your soul on game night, *The Washington Post*, January 8. https://www.washingtonpost.com/lifestyle/style/a-wave-of-super-earnest-card-games-want-you-to-bare-your-soul-on-game-night/2020/01/08/4a908c50-1614-11ea-9110-3b34ce1d92b1_story.html?arc404=true

Dewey, C. 2014. The only guide to gamergate you will ever need to read, *Washington Post*, October 14. https://www.washingtonpost.com/news/the-intersect/wp/2014/10/14/the-only-guide-to-gamergate-you-will-ever-need-to-read/

Dhalla, Nariman K., Yuspeh, Sonia. 1976. Forget the product life cycle concept!, *Harvard Business Review*, January 1. https://hbr.org/1976/01/forget-the-product-life-cycle-concept

Ditchfield, Hannah. 2019. Behind the screen of Facebook: identity construction in the rehearsal stage of online interaction, *New Media & Society*. https://doi.org/10.1177/1461444819873644

Donovan, Joan; Wardle, Claire. 2020. Misinformation is everybody's problem now, *Social Science Research Council*. August. https://items.ssrc.org/covid-19-and-the-social-sciences/mediated-crisis/misinformation-is-everybodys-problem-now/

Donovan, Laura. 2016. Pokémon Go is having an effect on players' mental health, ATTN, July 8. https://archive.attn.com/stories/9779/pokemon-go-affecting-players-mental-health

Dredge, Stuart. 2016. YouTube was meant to be a video-dating website, *Guardian*, March 16. https://www.theguardian.com/technology/2016/mar/16/youtube-past-video-dating-website

Drotner, Kristen. 1999. Dangerous media? Panic discourses and dilemmas of modernity, *Paedagogica Historica*, 35 (3), pp. 593–619. DOI: 10.1080/0030923990350303

Duffy, Brooke Erin. 2017. *(Not) Getting Paid to Do What You Love: Gender, Social Media, and Aspirational Work*. Yale University Press.

Duffy, Brooke Erin; Poell, Thomas; Nieborg, David B. 2019. Platform practices in the cultural industries: creativity, labor, and citizenship, *Social Media + Society*. https://doi.org/10.1177/2056305119879672

Duffy, Ronan. 2017. Humans of New York has launched its own series that streams for free on Facebook, *The Journal.ie*, September 3. https://www.thejournal.ie/humans-of-new-york-the-series-3576802-Sep2017/

du Gay, Paul (Ed). 1997. *Production of culture/Cultures of production*. Sage.

Duguay, Stefanie; Burgess, Jean; Suzor, Nicholas. 2018. Queer women's experiences of patchwork platform governance on Tinder, Instagram, and Vine, *Convergence*. https://doi.org/10.1177/1354856518781530

Dunham, Ian. 2016. Fight for the future and net neutrality: a case study in the origins, evolution, and activities of a digital-age media advocacy organization, *International Journal of Communication*, 10 (5), pp. 5826–38. http://ijoc.org/index.php/ijoc/article/view/4636/1863

Durkheim, Émile. 1982 [1917]. The rules of sociological method, in Steven Lukes (Ed.), W.D. Halls (Trans.), *Bulletin de la Sociéte française de philosophie*, 15, p. 57.

Dwilson, Stephanie Dube. 2019. Cambridge Analytica's SCL Group & Emerdata: who are they?, Heavy, July 29. https://heavy.com/entertainment/2019/07/cambridge-analytica-scl-emerdata/

Editorial. 1992. *Computer Supported Cooperative Work* (CSCW), 1, pp. 1–5. https://link.springer.com/article/10.1007/BF00752448

Editors of Encyclopaedia Britannica. 2019a. Arab spring, *Encyclopædia Britannica*, August 23. https://www.britannica.com/event/Arab-Spring

Editors of Encyclopaedia Britannica. 2019b. Egypt uprising of 2011, *Encyclopædia Britannica*, January 18. https://www.britannica.com/event/Egypt-Uprising-of-2011

Ehrlich, Brenna. 2013. I can haz $$$: cheezburger network scores $30 million in funding, Mashable, January 18. https://mashable.com/2011/01/17/cheezburger-funding/

Eikren, Emill; Ingram-Waters, Mary. 2016. Dismantling 'you get what you deserve': towards a feminist sociology of revenge porn, *Ada: A Journal of Gender, New Media, and Technology*, 10. DOI:10.7264/N3JW8C5Q, URL: http://adanewmedia.org/2016/10/issue10-eikren-ingramwaters/

Eisenstein, Elizabeth L. 1980. *The Printing Press as an Agent of Change*. Cambridge University Press. DOI: 10.1017/CBO9781107049963

Ellis, Clarence A.; Gibbs, Simon; Rein. Gail. 1991. Groupware: some issues and experiences, *Communications of the ACM*, January, 38 ff. Accessed via Business Insights: Global. Web. November 25, 2017.

Ellison, Nicole B.; boyd, danah. 2013. Sociality through social network sites, in William Dutton (Ed.), *The Oxford Handbook of Internet Studies*. Oxford University Press. http://www.danah.org/papers/2013/SocialityThruSNS-preprint.pdf

Emejulu, Akwugo. 2020. George Floyd: why the sight of these brave, exhausted protesters gives me hope, *The Conversation*, June 2. https://theconversation.com/george-floyd-why-the-sight-of-these-brave-exhausted-protesters-gives-me-hope-139804

Esguerra, Richard. 2009. Google CEO Eric Schmidt dismisses the importance of privacy, Electronic Frontier Foundation, December 10. https://www.eff.org/deeplinks/2009/12/google-ceo-eric-schmidt-dismisses-privacy

Eubanks, Virginia. 2018. *Automating Inequality: How High-Tech Tools Profile, Police and Punish the Poor*. St. Martin's Press

Evans, Sandra K.; Pearce, Katy E.; Vitak, Jessica; Treem, Jeffrey W. 2016. Explicating affordances: a conceptual framework for understanding affordances in communication research, *Journal of Computer-Mediated Communication*, 22 (1), pp. 35–52. https://doi.org/10.1111/jcc4.12180

REFERENCES

Facebook. 2007a. Facebook unveils platform for developers of social applications, Facebook Newsroom, May 24. https://newsroom.fb.com/news/2007/05/facebook-unveils-platform-for-developers-of-social-applications/

Facebook. 2007b. Facebook platform for mobile, Facebook Newsroom, October 24. https://newsroom.fb.com/?s=facebook+platform&post_type=any

Facebook. 2008a. Facebook expands its social platform across the web through general availability of Facebook Connect, Facebook Newsroom, December 4. https://newsroom.fb.com/news/2008/12/facebook-expands-its-social-platform-across-the-web-through-general-availability-of-facebook-connect/

Facebook. 2008b. People You May Know, May 2. https://www.facebook.com/notes/facebook/people-you-may-know15610312130/

Facebook. 2013a. Updates to Facebook login, Facebook Newsroom, August 22. https://newsroom.fb.com/news/2013/08/updates-to-facebook-login/

Facebook. 2013b. Important message from Facebook's White Hat program, June 21. https://www.facebook.com/notes/facebook-security/important-message-from-facebooks-white-hat-program/10151437074840766

Facebook. 2016. Reactions now globally available, Facebook Newsroom, February 24. https://newsroom.fb.com/news/2016/02/reactions-now-available-globally/

Facebook. 2017. 58 million people are active on Facebook, December 1, 2007, Facebook Newsroom, February 15. https://newsroom.fb.com/company-info/

Facebook. 2020a. Data policy, February 2. https://www.facebook.com/privacy/explanation

Facebook. 2020b. People You May Know, Help Centre, February 15. https://www.facebook.com/help/163810437015615?helpref=uf_permalink

Facebook. 2020c. Privacy basics, February 15. https://www.facebook.com/about/basics

Facebook 2020d. Your privacy, February 2. https://www.facebook.com/help/238318146535333?helpref=hc_global_nav

Fahlman, Scott E. 1982. Smiley lore. http://www.cs.cmu.edu/~sef/sefSmiley.htm

Fang, Liu. 2018. Feature: delving deep into manuscripts of Marx and Engels, *China – Europe*, February 24. http://www.xinhuanet.com/english/2018-02/24/c_136995124.htm

Farley, Amy. 2020. Meet the computer scientist and activist who got big tech to stand down, *Fast Company*. August 4. https://www.fastcompany.com/90525023/most-creative-people-2020-joy-buolamwini

Farman, Jason. 2015. The materiality of locative media: on the invisible infrastructure of mobile networks, in Andrew Herman (Ed.), *Theories of the Mobile Internet: Materialities and Imaginaries*. Routledge.

Ferris, Lindsay; Duguay, Stefanie. 2020. Tinder's lesbian digital imaginary: investigating (im)permeable boundaries of sexual identity on a popular dating app, *New Media & Society*, 22 (3), pp. 489–506. https://doi.org/10.1177/1461444819864903

Ferwerda, B.; Schedl, M.; Tkalcic, M. 2016. Using Instagram picture features to predict users' personality, in Q. Tian, N. Sebe, G.J. Qi, B. Huet, R. Hong, X. Liu (Eds.), *MultiMedia Modeling. MMM 2016, Lecture Notes in Computer Science*, 9516. Springer.

Field, Matt. 2019. How YouTube was recommending kids' videos to pedophiles, *Bulletin of the Atomic Scientists*, June 13. https://thebulletin.org/2019/06/how-youtube-was-recommending-kids-videos-to-pedophiles/

Fischer, Claude S. 1992. *America Calling: A Social History of the Telephone to 1940*. University of California Press.

Fisher, Mark. 2009. *Capitalist Realism: Is There No Alternative?* Zero Books.

Foote, Jeremy; Shaw, Aaron; Mako Hill, Benjamin. 2018. A computational analysis of social media scholarship, in Jean Burgess, Thomas Poell, and Alice Marwick (Eds.), *The SAGE Handbook of Social Media*. Sage.

Fornaciari, Federica. 2014. Pricey privacy: framing the economy of information in the digital age, *First Monday*, 19 (12). https://doi.org/10.5210/fm.v19i12.5008

Foster, Max; with McGann, Hilary. 2019. The racist online abuse of Meghan has put royal staff on high alert, CNN News. https://www.cnn.com/2019/03/07/uk/meghan-kate-social-media-gbr-intl/index.html

Foucault, Michel. 1972. *The Archaeology of Knowledge*, Allan Sheridan (trans.), Harper & Row.

Foucault, Michel. 1975. *Discipline and Punish*. Alan Sheridan (trans.), Pantheon Books.

Foucault, Michel. 1976, *History of Sexuality*. Robert Hurley (trans.), Pantheon Books.

Foucault, Michel. 1984 *The Uses of Pleasure*. Robert Hurley (trans.), Pantheon Books.

Foucault, Michel. 1986. *Care of the Self*. Robert Hurley (trans.), Pantheon Books.

Franklin, M.J. 2018. 'People You May Know' is the perfect demonstration of everything that's wrong with Facebook, Mashable, May 15. https://mashable.com/2018/05/15/people-you-may-know-facebook-creepy/?europe=true

Fraser, Nancy. 1990. Rethinking the public sphere: a contribution to the critique of actually existing democracy, *Social Text*, 25/26, pp. 56–80. DOI:10.2307/466240

Freedman, Des. 2014. *The Contradictions of Media Power*. Bloomsbury.

Freelon, Dean; McIlwain, Charlton D.; Clark, Meredith. 2016. Beyond the hashtags: #Ferguson, #Blacklivesmatter, and the online struggle for offline justice, Center for Media & Social Impact, American University. https://papers.ssrn.com/sol3/papers.cfm?abstract_id=2747066

Frieling, Rudolf; Grays, Boris. 2008. *The Art of Participation: 1950 to Now*. Thames & Hudson.

FTC. 2019. FTC's $5 billion Facebook settlement: record-breaking and history-making, Federal Trade Commission, July 24. https://www.ftc.gov/news-events/blogs/business-blog/2019/07/ftcs-5-billion-facebook-settlement-record-breaking-history

Fuchs, Christian. 2012. Dallas Smythe today – the audience commodity, the digital labour debate, Marxist political economy and critical theory. Prolegomena to a digital labour theory of value, *tripleC*. 10 (2), pp. 692–740.

Fuchs, Christian. 2014. *Social Media: A Critical Introduction*. Sage.

Fuchs, Christian. 2015a. *Culture and Economy in the Age of Social Media*. Routledge.

Fuchs, Christian. 2015b. *Reading Marx in the Information Age: A Media and Communication Studies Perspective on Capital*, Volume 1. Routledge.

Fuchs, Christian. 2017. *Social Media: A Critical Introduction*, 2nd edn. Sage.

Furlong-Mitchell, Hayley. 2019. 10 questions with Koreen Odiney, The Nue Co. April 10. https://www.thenueco.com/blogs/journal/10-questions-with-koreen-odiney

Gale, Elan. 2015. *Tinder Nightmares*. Abrams.

Galič, Maša; Timan, Tjerk; Koops, Bert-Japp. 2017. Bentham, Deleuze and beyond: an overview of surveillance theories from the panopticon to participation, *Philosophy and Technology*, 30, pp. 9–37. https://doi.org/10.1007/s13347-016-0219-1

Gallagher, Billy. 2018. How Reggie Brown invented Snapchat, *TechCrunch*, February 10. https://techcrunch.com/2018/02/10/the-birth-of-snapchat/

Gandini, Alessandro. 2016. *The Reputation Economy: Understanding Knowledge Work in Digital Society*. Palgrave Macmillan.

Garda, Maria B.; Karhulahti, Veli-Matti. 2019. Let's play Tinder! Aesthetics of a dating app, *Games and Culture*, pp. 1–14. https://journals.sagepub.com/doi/pdf/10.1177/155541 2019891328

Garza, Alicia. 2015. A love note to our folks, Alicia Garza on the organizing of #BlackLivesMatter, *N + 1 Magazine*, January 20. https://nplusonemag.com/online-only/online-only/a-love-note-to-our-folks/

Gauntlett, David. 2010. Making is connecting: everyday creativity, social capital and digital media, MeCCSA Annual Conference, London School of Economics, January. https://www.youtube.com/watch?v=nF4OBfVQmCI&feature=channel_page

Gauntlett, David. 2011. *Making is Connecting: The Social Meaning of Creativity, from DIY and Knitting to YouTube and Web 2.0*. Polity.

Gehl, Robert W. 2015. The case for alternative social media, *Social Media + Society*. https://doi.org/10.1177/2056305115604338

Gehl, Robert W. 2018. *Weaving the Dark Web: Legitimacy on Freenet, Tor and I2P*. The MIT Press.

Gerbaudo, Paolo. 2017. *The Mask and the Flag: Populism, Citizenism and Global Protest*. Oxford University Press.

Gerlitz, Caroline; Helmond, Anne. 2013. The like economy: social buttons and the data intensive web, *New Media and Society*, 15 (8), pp. 1348–65. DOI: https://doi.org/10.1177/1461444812472322

Gershon, Ilana. 2010. *Break-up 2.0: Disconnecting Over New Media*. Cornell University Press.

Gershon, Ilana. 2020. The breakup 2.1: the ten-year update, *The Information Society*. DOI: 10.1080/01972243.2020.1798316

Giddens, Anthony. 1984. *The Constitution of Society: Towards a Theory of Structuration*. Polity.

Giddens, Anthony. 1986. *The Constitution of Society: Outline of a Theory of Structuration*. University of California Press.

Giddens, Anthony. 1991. *The Consequences of Modernity*. Polity.

Giddens, Anthony. 1992. *The Transformation of Intimacy: Sexuality, Love and Eroticism in Modern Societies*. Stanford University Press.

Giddings, Seth. 2017. Pokémon GO as distributed imagination. *Mobile Media & Communication*, 5 (1), pp. 59–62. https://doi.org/10.1177/2050157916677866

Gillespie, Tarleton. 2010. The politics of platforms, *New Media and Society*, 12 (3), pp. 347–64.

Gillespie, Tarleton. 2018a. *Custodians of the Internet: Platforms, Content Moderation, and the Hidden Decisions that Shape Social Media*. Yale University Press.

Gillespie, Tarleton. 2018b. Regulation of and by platforms, in Jean Burgess, Alice Marwick and Thomas Poell (Eds.), *The SAGE Handbook of Social Media*. Sage.

Gilroy, Paul. 1987. *There Ain't No Black in the Union Jack: The Cultural Politics of Race and Nation*. Hutchinson.

Glasser, Theodore L. (Ed.) 1999. *The Idea of Public Journalism*. Guilford Press.

Goffman, Erving. 1959. *The Presentation of Self in Everyday Life*. Doubleday Anchor Books.

Goffman, Erving. 1990 [1959]. *The Presentation of Self in Everyday Life*, new edn. Penguin.

Goggin, Gerard. 2011. *Global Mobile Media*. Routledge.

Goggin, Gerard. 2014. Facebook's mobile career, *New Media and Society*, 16 (7), pp. 1068–86. https://doi.org/10.1177/1461444814543996.

Golbeck, Jennifer. 2013. Your social media 'likes' expose more than you think, TEDx Mid-Atlantic, October. https://www.ted.com/talks/jennifer_golbeck_your_social_media_likes_expose_more_than_you_think

Golbeck, Jennifer. 2014. The internet, suicide, & how sites like PostSecret can help, *Psychology Today*, October 14. https://www.psychologytoday.com/us/blog/your-online-secrets/201410/the-internet-suicide-how-sites-postsecret-can-help

Google. 2020. Privacy policy, February 12. https://policies.google.com/privacy?hl=en-GB&gl=uk

Gorman, Alyx. 2019. From sponsors to socialism: the return of Instagram star Essena O'Neill, *Guardian*, November 19. https://www.theguardian.com/lifeandstyle/2019/nov/19/sponsors-socialism-return-instagram-star-essena-oneill

Gov.UK. 2013. Same sex marriage becomes law, Gov.UK, July 17. https://www.gov.uk/government/news/same-sex-marriage-becomes-law

Gramsci, Antonio. 2005. *The Prison Notebooks*. Lawrence & Wishart.

Granovetter, Mark. 1973. The strength of weak ties, *American Journal of Sociology*, 78 (6), pp. 1360–80. URL: https://sociology.stanford.edu/sites/default/files/publications/the_strength_of_weak_ties_and_exch_w-gans.pdf

Green, Hank. 2014. Pre-history of online video, YouTube, June 20. https://www.youtube.com/watch?v=Qfooiifd2v0

Greenberg, Saul. 1991. Computer supported cooperative work and groupware: an introduction to the special edition, *International Journal of Man Machine Studies*, 34 (2), pp. 133–43.

Greenwald, Glenn. 2014. *No Place to Hide: Edward Snowden, the NSA and the U.S. Surveillance State*. Macmillan US.

Greenwald, Glenn; MacAskill, Ewen. 2013. NSA Prism program taps in to user data of Apple, Google and others, *Guardian*. June 7, https://www.theguardian.com/world/2013/jun/06/us-tech-giants-nsa-data

Gruzd, Anatoily; Mai, Philip. 2020. Going viral: how a single tweet spawned a COVID-19 conspiracy theory on Twitter, *Big Data & Society*, July. https://doi.org/10.1177/2053951720938405

Grzanka, Patrick R. 2014. Power/knowledge/position, in Patrick R. Grzanka (Ed.), *Intersectionality: A Foundations and Frontiers Reader*. Westview.

Guardian. n.d. We shall speak their names. https://www.theguardian.com/world/ng-interactive/2019/mar/21/christchurch-shooting-remembering-the-victims

Gunter, Barrie. 2013. The study of online relationships and dating, in William H. Dutton (Ed.), *Oxford Handbook of Internet Studies*. Oxford University Press.

Habermas, Jürgen; Lennox, Sara; Lennox, Frank. 1974 [1964]. The public sphere: an encyclopedia article, *New German Critique*, 3, pp. 49–55. DOI:10.2307/487737

Haddad, Charles; Hill, Jennifer. 1997. Several members of our personal technology staff tell us about their favorite web sites, *The Atlanta Journal and Constitution*, Sunday, December 28.

Hafner, Katie. 1997. The epic saga of the well, *Wired*, November 5. https://www.wired.com/1997/05/ff-well/

Hale, Johnny. 2019. DaddyOFive' parents' sentences reduced despite allegations they broke court order, continued to vlog children, *TubeFilter*, January 9. https://www.tubefilter.com/2019/01/11/daddyofive-youtube-sentence-reduced/

Hall, Stuart. 1980. Cultural studies: two paradigms, *Media, Culture & Society*, 2, pp. 57–72.

Hall, Stuart. 1999. Encoding/decoding, in Simon During (Ed.), *The Cultural Studies Reader*, 2nd edn. Routledge.

Hall, Stuart (Ed.). 2012. *Representation: Cultural Representations and Signifying Practices*. Sage.

Halpern, Daniel; Valenzuela, Sebastián; Katz, James E. 2016. 'Selfie-ists' or 'Narci-selfiers'?: a cross-lagged panel analysis of selfie taking and narcissism, *Personality and Individual Differences*, 97, pp. 98–101. https://doi.org/10.1016/j.paid.2016.03.019

Hammerman, Robin; Russell, Andrew L. 2016. *Ada's Legacy: Cultures of Computing from the Victorian to the Digital Age*. Association for Computing Machinery.

Han, Rongbin. 2018. *Contesting Cyberspace in China: Online Expression and Authoritarian Resilience*. Columbia University Press.

Haraway, Donna. 1988. Situated knowledges: the science question in feminism and the privilege of partial perspective. *Feminst Studies*, 14 (3), pp. 575–99.

Harbison, Niall. 2010. 2010: the year of epic photo sharing apps, The Next Web, December 28. https://thenextweb.com/socialmedia/2010/12/28/2010-the-year-of-epic-photo-sharing-apps/

Hartley, John. 2018. Pushing back: social media as an evolutionary phenomenon, in Jean Burgess, Thomas Poell and Alice Marwick (Eds.), *The SAGE Handbook of Social Media*. Sage.

Hauben, Michael; Hauben, Ronda. 1998. On the early days of Usenet: the roots of cooperative online culture, *First Monday*, 3 (8). http://firstmonday.org/ojs/index.php/fm/article/view/613/534

Haugaard, Mark (Ed.). 2002. *Power: A Reader*. Manchester University Press.

Heaney, Katie; Misener, Jessica. 2013. The 7 types of crying selfies you've probably seen on Facebook, *Buzzfeed News*. April 23, https://www.buzzfeednews.com/article/katieheaney/the-7-types-of-crying-selfies-youve-probably-seen-on-faceboo

Hearn, Alison. 2010. Structuring feeling: web 2.0, online ranking and rating, and the digital 'reputation' economy, *Ephemera: Theory & Politics in Organization*, 10 (3/4), pp. 421–38.

Helmond, Anne. 2015. The platformization of the web: making web data platform ready, *Social Media + Society*, September 1–11. DOI: 10.1177/2056305115603080

Henthorn, Jamie; Kulak, Andrew; Purzycki, Kristopher; Vie, Stephanie (Eds.) 2019. *The Pokémon GO Phenomenon: Essays on Public Play in Contested Spaces*. McFarland.

Hern, Alex. 2016. Pokémon GO becomes global craze as game overtakes Twitter for US users, *Guardian*, July 12. https://www.theguardian.com/technology/2016/jul/12/pokemon-go-becomes-global-phenomenon-as-number-of-us-users-overtakes-twitter

Hess, Aaron; Flores, Carlos. 2018. Simply more than swiping left: a critical analysis of toxic masculine performances on Tinder nightmares, *New Media & Society*, 20 (3), pp. 1085–1102. https://doi.org/10.1177/1461444816681540

Highfield, Tim. 2016. *Social Media and Everyday Politics*. Polity.

Hill, Annette. 2004. *Reality TV Audiences and Popular Factual Television*. Routledge.

Hill, Kashmir. 2016. Facebook recommended that this psychiatrist's patients friend each other, *Splinter News*, August 29. https://splinternews.com/facebook-recommended-that-this-psychiatrists-patients-f-1793861472

Hill, Kashmir. 2017. How Facebook figures out everyone you've ever met, Gizmodo, July 11. https://gizmodo.com/how-facebook-figures-out-everyone-youve-ever-met-1819822691

Hill, Kashmir. 2018. 'People You May Know': a controversial Facebook feature's 10-year history, Gizmodo, August 18. https://gizmodo.com/people-you-may-know-a-controversial-facebook-features-1827981959

Hills, Matt. 2002. *Fan Cultures*. Routledge.

Hindman, Mark Jr.; Bukowitz, Alison E.; Reed, Brent N.; Mattingly, Joseph. 2017. No filter: a characterization of #pharmacist posts on Instagram, *Journal of the American Pharmacists Association*, 57 (3), pp. 318–25. https://doi.org/10.1016/j.japh.2017.01.009

Hinton, Sam; Hjorth, Larissa. 2013. *Understanding Social Media*. Sage.

Hjorth, Larissa; Burgess, Jean; Richardson, Ingrid (Eds.) 2012. *Studying Mobile Media: Cultural Technologies, Mobile Communication and the iPhone*. Routledge.

Hjorth, Larissa; Hendry, Natalie. 2015. A snapshot of social media: camera phone practices, *Social Media + Society*, 1 (1). https://doi.org/10.1177/2056305115580478

Hjorth, Larissa; Hinton, Sam. 2019. *Understanding Social Media*, 2nd edn. Sage.

Hjorth, Larissa; Jiminez, Jordi Piera. 2019. Meet Sofia: A 67-year-old widow who uses Pokémon GO to reconnect with her city, *The Conversation*, July 1. https://theconversation.com/meet-sofia-a-67-year-old-widow-who-uses-pokemon-go-to-reconnect-with-her-city-119389

Hjorth, Larissa; Richardson, Ingrid. 2017. Pokémon GO: mobile media play, place-making, and the digital wayfarer, *Mobile Media & Communication*, 5 (1), pp. 3–14. DOI: 10.1177/2050157916680015

Hobbs, Mitchell; Owen, Stepehn; Gerber, Livia. 2017. Liquid love? Dating apps, sex, relationships and the digital transformation of intimacy, *Journal of Sociology*, 53 (2), pp. 271–84. https://doi.org/10.1177/1440783316662718

Hochman, Nadav. 2014. The social media image, *Big Data & Society*. https://doi.org/10.1177/2053951714546645

Hogan, Bernie. 2018. Break-ups and the limits of encoding love, in Zizi Papacharissi (Ed.), *A Networked Self and Love*. Routledge.

Holt, Jennifer; Sanson, Kevin. (Eds.) 2014. *Connected Viewing: Selling, Streaming and Sharing Media in a Digital Age*. Routledge.

Honor. 2019. HONOR 9X research reveals europeans now post a staggering 597 photos of themselves every year, *Honor*. https://www.hihonor.com/global/news/honor-9x-research-reveals-europeans-now-post-a-staggering-597-photos-of-themselves-every-year/

Horkheimer, Max; Adorno, Theodor W. 2002 [1948]. *Dialectic of Enlightenment: Philosophical Fragments*. Gunzelin Schmid Noerr (Ed.) and Edmund Jephcott (Trans.). Stanford University Press.

Horton, Donald; Wohl, Richard R. 1956. Mass communication and para-social interaction, *Psychiatry*, 19 (3), pp. 215–29. DOI: 10.1080/00332747.1956.11023049

Hounsell, Kayla. 2019. 'There's no shortage of negative things': pregnant Meghan faces online bullying, CBC News, March 1. https://www.cbc.ca/news/world/meghan-markle-duchess-of-sussex-faces-online-bullying-1.5037143

Hu, Tung-Hui. 2015. *A Prehistory of the Cloud*. The MIT Press.

Hughes, John; Randall, Dave; Shapiro, Dan. 1991. CSCW: discipline or paradigm? A sociological perspective, in Liam Bannon, Mike Robinson and K. Schmidt (Eds.), *ECSCW'91, Proceedings of the Second European Conference on Computer-Supported Cooperative Work*, Amsterdam. https://pdfs.semanticscholar.org/f550/5301ff7f7795adcb823d184144597230f40e.pdf

Human Rights Watch. 2019. China: events of 2018, *World Report 2019*. https://www.hrw.org/world-report/2019/country-chapters/china-and-tibet

Humphreys, Ashlee. 2016. *Social Media: Enduring Principles*. Oxford University Press.

Humphreys, Lee. 2013. Mobile social media: future challenges and opportunities, *Mobile Media and Communication*, 1 (1), pp. 20–25. http://journals.sagepub.com/doi/full/10.1177/2050157912459499

Humphreys, Lee. 2018. *The Qualified Self: Social Media and the Accounting of Everyday Life*. The MIT Press.

Hunsinger, Jeremy. 2014. Interface and infrastructure in social media, in Jeremy Hunsinger and Theresa Senft (Eds.), *The Social Media Handbook*. Routledge.

Hunsinger, Jeremy; Senft, Theresa (Eds.) 2014. *The Social Media Handbook*. Routledge.

Hunt, Elle. 2015. Essena O'Neill quits instagram claiming social media 'is not real life', *Guardian*, November 3. https://www.theguardian.com/media/2015/nov/03/instagram-star-essena-oneill-quits-2d-life-to-reveal-true-story-behind-images

ICO. 2018. ICO issues maximum £500,000 fine to Facebook for failing to protect users' personal information, Information Commissioner's Office, October 25. https://ico.org.uk/facebook-fine-20181025

Illouz, Eva. 1997. *Consuming the Romantic Utopia: Love and the Cultural Contradictions of Capitalism*. University of California Press.

Illouz, Eva. 2013. *Why Love Hurts: A Sociological Explanation*. Polity.

Illouz, Eve. 2019. *The End of Love: A Sociology of Negative Relations*. Oxford University Press.

Instagram. 2020. About us. https://about.instagram.com/about-us

Instagram Business Team. 2019. Helping creators turn their passion into a living, Get The Latest From Instagram, December 18. https://business.instagram.com/blog/helping-creators-turn-their-passion-into-a-living/#

IPSOS MORI. 2017. Mobile payment usage in China, Ipsos Game Changers, August 17. https://www.ipsos.com/en/mobile-payment-usage-china

Iqani, Mehita; Schroeder, Jonathan E. 2016. #selfie: digital self-portraits as commodity form and consumption practice, *Consumption Markets & Culture*. 19:5, pp. 405–415, DOI: 10.1080/10253866.2015.1116784

Iqbal, Monsoor. 2019. Tinder revenue and usage statistics (2018), Business of Apps, February 22. https://www.businessofapps.com/data/tinder-statistics/

Iqbal, Nosheen. 2018. How Insecure made TV gold with 'a show about regular Black people being basic', *Guardian*, August 12. https://www.theguardian.com/tv-and-radio/2018/aug/12/issa-rae-television-show-insecure-black-people

Isbister, Katherine (2016) Why Pokemon GO became an instant phenomenon, *The Conversation*, July 15. https://theconversation.com/why-pokemon-go-became-an-instant-phenomenon-62412

Jackson, Sarah; Bailey, Moya; Foucault Welles, Brooke. 2020. *#Hashtag Activism: Networks of Race and Gender Justice*. The MIT Press.

Jarrett, Kylie. 2016. *Feminism, Labour and Digital Media: The Digital Housewife*. Routledge.

Jemielniak, Dariusz. 2014. *Common Knowledge? An Ethnography of Wikipedia*. Stanford University Press.

Jenkins, Henry. 1992. *Textual Poachers: Television Fans and Participatory Culture*. Routledge.

Jenkins, Henry. 2006. *Convergence Culture: Where and Old Media Collide*. New York University Press.

Jenkins, Henry. 2007. 'Vernacular creativity': an interview with Jean Burgess (part one), Confessions of an Aca-Fan, October 7. http://henryjenkins.org/blog/2007/10/vernacular_creativity_an_inter.html

Jenkins, Henry. 2009a. *Confronting the Challenges of Participatory Culture: Media Education for the 21st Century*. MacArthur Foundation.

Jenkins, Henry. 2009b. What happened before YouTube?, in Jean Burgess and Joshua Green (Eds.), *YouTube: Online Video and Participatory Culture*. Polity.

Jenkins, Henry; Carpentier, Nico. 2013. Theorizing participatory intensities: a conversation about participation and politics, *Convergence*, 19 (3), pp. 265–86. https://doi.org/10.1177/1354856513482090

Jenkins, Henry; Ito, Mizuko; boyd, danay. 2015. *Participatory Culture in a Networked Era: A Conversation on Youth, Learning, Commerce, and Politics*. Polity.

Jenkins, Henry; with Ravi Purushotma, Margaret Weigel, Katie Clinton, Alice J. Robison. 2009. *Confronting the Challenges of Participatory Culture: Media Education for the 21st Century*. The MIT Press.

Jennings, Rebecca. 2019. Facetune and the internet's endless pursuit of physical perfection, Vox.com. July 25, https://www.vox.com/the-highlight/2019/7/16/20689832/instagram-photo-editing-app-facetune

Jeong, Sarah. 2015. Hunter Moore revenge porn victim got a whopping $145.70 in restitution, *Vice*, December 3. https://www.vice.com/en_us/article/xygzz7/hunter-moore-revenge-porn-victim-got-a-whopping-14570-in-restitution

Jin, Dal Yong 2017. Evolution of Korea's mobile technologies: a historical approach, *Mobile Media & Communication*, September 25. DOI: 2050157917727319, https://doi.org/10.1177/2050157917727319

Jin, Dal Yong 2017. Critical interpretation of the Pokémon GO phenomenon: the intensification of new capitalism and free labor, *Mobile Media & Communication*, 5 (1), pp. 55–58. https://doi.org/10.1177/2050157916677306

Jin, Huimin. 2011. British cultural studies, active audiences and the status of cultural theory: an interview with david morley, *Theory, Culture & Society*, 28 (4), pp. 124–44. DOI: 10.1177/0263276411398268

John, Nicholas A. 2012. Sharing and Web 2.0: the emergence of a keyword, *New Media and Society*, 15 (2), pp. 167–82. https://doi.org/10.1177/1461444812450684

John, Nicholas A. 2016. *The Age of Sharing*. Wiley.

Johnson, Bobbie. 2010. Privacy no longer a social norm, says Facebook founder, *Guardian*, January 11. https://www.theguardian.com/technology/2010/jan/11/facebook-privacy

Jones, Steve. 2006. *Antonio Gramsci*. Routledge.

Jones, Steve; Latzko-Toth, Guillaume. 2017. Out from the PLATO cave: uncovering the pre-Internet history of social computing, *Internet Histories*, 1 (1–2), pp. 60–69. DOI: 10.1080/24701475.2017.1307544, http://www.tandfonline.com/doi/full/10.1080/24701475.2017.1307544,

Jordan, Scott. 2007. A layered network approach to net neutrality, *International Journal of Communication*, 1 (1), pp. 427–60. http://ijoc.org/index.php/ijoc/article/view/168/88

Kaiser, Jonas; Córdova, Yasodara. 2019. On YouTube's digital playground: YouTube's recommendation algorithm is under scrutiny for surfacing harmful content, Berkman Klein Centre, June 3. https://cyber.harvard.edu/story/2019-06/youtubes-digital-playground

Kantor, Kevin. 2015. People you may know, YouTube, April 6. https://www.youtube.com/watch?v=LoyfunmYIpU

Karppi, Tero. 2018. *Disconnect: Facebook's Affective Bonds*. University of Minnesota Press.

Katz, James E.; Schroeder, Elizabeth Thomas. 2015. Selfies and photo messaging as visual conversation: reports from the United States, United Kingdom and China, *International Journal of Communication*, 9, pp. 1861–72. https://ijoc.org/index.php/ijoc/article/view/3180/1405

Keating, Laruen. 2017. Facebook users shared 300 billion reactions in one year, *Tech Times*, February 24. https://www.techtimes.com/articles/199136/20170224/facebook-users-shared-300-billion-reactions-one-year.htm

Keller, Evelyn Fox. 1983. *A Feeling for the Organism*. Henry Hold.

Kelly, Séamus; Jones, Matthew. 2001. Groupware and the social infrastructure of communication, *Communications of the ACM*, 44 (12), pp. 77–79.

Kemp, Simon. 2019. Digital 2019: global internet use accelerates, *We Are Social*, January 30. https://wearesocial.com/blog/2019/01/digital-2019-global-internet-use-accelerates

Kent, Mike; Ellis, Katie; Xu, Jian (Eds.) 2017. *Chinese Social Media: Social, Cultural and Political Implications*. Routledge.

Keogh, Brendan. 2017. Pokémon GO, the novelty of nostalgia, and the ubiquity of the smartphone, *Mobile Media & Communication*, 5 (1), pp. 38–41. https://doi.org/10.1177/2050157916678025

Kim, Ji Won. 2018. Rumor has it: the effects of virality metrics on rumor believability and transmission on Twitter. *New Media & Society*, 20 (12), pp. 4807–25. https://doi.org/10.1177/1461444818784945

Kim, Larry. 2014. Is Ello the new Facebook killer or a 15 minute fame flame?, *Search Engine Journal*, October 29. https://www.searchenginejournal.com/ello-new-facebook-killer-15-minute-fame-flame/118002/#close

Kimball, Diana. 2012. Case study: Cards Against Humanity, The Kickstarter Blog, July 26. https://www.kickstarter.com/blog/case-study-cards-against-humanity

Kloet, Jeroen de; Poell, Thomas; Guohua, Zeng; Fai, Chow Yiu. 2019. The platformization of Chinese Society: infrastructure, governance, and practice, *Chinese Journal of Communication*. DOI: 10.1080/17544750.2019.1644008

Kobie, Nicole. 2016. Linked to bullying and even murder, can anonymous apps like Kik ever be safe?, *Guardian*, March 7. https://www.theguardian.com/sustainable-business/2016/mar/07/anonymous-apps-cyber-bullying-security-safety-kik-yik-yak-secret

Kobie, Nicole. 2019. The complicated truth about China's social credit system, *Wired*, June 7. https://www.wired.co.uk/article/china-social-credit-system-explained

Koch, Ariel. 2018. Jihadi beheading videos and their non-Jihadi echoes, *Perspectives on Terrorism*, 12 (3), pp. 24–34. www.jstor.org/stable/26453133

Koebler, Jason. 2015. 10 years ago today, YouTube launched as a dating website, Motherboard Vice, April 23. https://www.vice.com/en_us/article/78xqjx/10-years-ago-today-youtube-launched-as-a-dating-website

Koetse, Manya. 2018. Insights into Sesame Credit, What's on Weibo, November 7. https://www.whatsonweibo.com/insights-into-sesame-credit-top-5-ways-to-use-a-high-sesame-score/

Kogan, Aleksandr. 2018. Written evidence submitted by Aleksandr Kogan, text submitted to the The Digital, Culture, Media and Sport Committee of the UK Parliament. https://www.parliament.uk/globalassets/documents/commons-committees/culture-media-and-sport/Written-evidence-Aleksandr-Kogan.pdf

Kolko, Beth; Nakamura, Lisa; Rodman, Gilbert (Eds.) 2000. *Race in Cyberspace*. Routledge.

Kollowee, Julia. 2017. Google and Facebook bring in one fifth of global ad revenue, *Guardian*, May 2. https://www.theguardian.com/media/2017/may/02/google-and-facebook-bring-in-one-fifth-of-global-ad-revenue

Korn, Jeny Ungbha. 2016. 'Genderless' online discourse in the 1970s: muted group theory in early social computing, in Robin Hammerman and Andrew L. Russell (Eds.), *Ada's Legacy: Cultures of Computing from the Victorian to the Digital Age*. Association for Computing Machinery.

Kosterich, Allie; Napoli, Phillip M. 2016. Reconfiguring the audience commodity: the institutionalization of social TV analytics as market information regime, *Television & New Media*, 17 (3), pp. 254–71. https://doi.org/10.1177/1527476415597480

Kotliar, Dan M. 2020. The return of the social: algorithmic identity in an age of symbolic demise, *New Media & Society*, 22 (7), pp. 1152–67. https://doi.org/10.1177/146144 4820912535

Kramer, Adam D.I.; Guillory, Jamie E.; Hancock, Jeffrey T. 2014. Experimental evidence of massive-scale emotional contagion through social networks, *Proceedings of the National Academy of Sciences of the United States of America (PNAS)*, 111 (24), pp. 8788–90. DOI: 10.1073/pnas.1320040111

Kumparak, G. 2019. Instagram will now hide likes in 6 more countries, *TechCrunch*, July 14. https://techcrunch.com/2019/07/17/instagram-will-now-hide-likes-in-6-more-countries/

Kunst, Alexander. 2019. Share of individuals who used online dating sites and apps in the United Kingdom (UK) in June 2017, by gender, Statista, December 20. https://www.statista.com/statistics/713874/online-dating-site-and-app-usage-in-the-united-kingdom-by-gender/

Kurose, James F.; Ross, Keith W. 2013. *Computer Networking*, 6th edn. Pearson.

Kurzweil, Ray. 1992. The future of libraries part 1: the technology of the book, *Library Journal*, 117 (1) 1: 80.

Kyncl, Robert; with Peyvan, Maany. 2017. *Streampunks: YouTube and the Rebels Remaking Media*. Virgin Books.

Lambert, Alexander. 2013. *Intimacy and Friendship on Facebook*. Palgrave Macmillan.

Landau, Neil. 2016. *TV Outside the Box: Trailblazing in the Digital Revolution*. Focal Press.

Lange, Patricia G. 2014. *Kids on YouTube: Technical Identities and Digital Literacies*. Left Coast Press.

Lapowsky, Issie; Thompson, Nicholas. 2019. Facebook's pivot to privacy is missing something crucial, *Wired*, March 6. https://www.wired.com/story/facebook-zuckerberg-privacy-pivot/?verso=true

Latour, Bruno [Johnson, Jim]. 1988. Mixing humans and nonhumans together: the sociology of a door-closer, *Social Problems*, 35 (3), pp. 298–310. DOI: 10.2307/800624

Law, John (Ed.). 1986. *Power, Action and Belief: A New Sociology of Knowledge?* Routledge.

Law, John. 2004. *After Method: Mess in Social Science Research*. Routledge.

Lawson, Caitlin E. 2020. Skin deep: callout strategies, influencers, and racism in the online beauty community, *New Media & Society*. https://doi.org/10.1177/1461444820904697

Leaver, Tama; Abidin, Crystal. 2017. When exploiting kids for cash goes wrong on YouTube: the lessons of DaddyOFive, *The Conversation*, May 2. https://theconversation.com/when-exploiting-kids-for-cash-goes-wrong-on-youtube-the-lessons-of-daddyofive-76932

Leaver, Tama; Highfield, Tim; Abidin, Crystal. 2020. *Instagram: Visual Social Media Cultures*. Polity.

LeCun, Yann; Pesenti, Jerome; Schroepfer, Mike. 2018. FAIR turns five: what we've accomplished and where we're headed, Facebook Engineering, December 5. https://engineering.fb.com/ai-research/fair-fifth-anniversary/

Lee, Jin. 2019. Mediated superficiality and misogyny through cool on Tinder, *Social Media + Society*. https://doi.org/10.1177/2056305119872949

LeFebvre, Leah E. 2018. Swiping me off my feet: explicating relationship initiation on Tinder, *Journal of Social and Personal Relationships*, 35 (9), pp. 1205–29. https://doi.org/10.1177/0265407517706419

LeFebvre, Leah E.; Allen, Mike; Rasner, Ryan D.; Garstad, Shelby; Wilms, Aleksander; Parrish, Callie. 2019. Ghosting in emerging adults' romantic relationships: the digital dissolution disappearance strategy, *Imagination, Cognition and Personality*, 39 (2), pp. 125–50. DOI:10.1177/0276236618820519

Lehman-Wilzig, Sam; Nava Cohen-Avigdor. 2004. The natural life cycle of new media evolution: inter-media struggle for survival in the internet age, *New Media & Society*, 6 (6): 707–30. https://doi.org/10.1177/146144804042524

Lenhart, Amanda; Madden, Mary. 2007. Social networking websites and teens, Pew Internet Research, January 7. http://www.pewinternet.org/2007/01/07/social-networking-websites-and-teens/

Lenhart, Amanda; Ybarra, Michele; Price-Feeney, Myeshia. 2016. Nonconsensual image sharing, *Data & Society*. https://datasociety.net/pubs/oh/Nonconsensual_Image_Sharing_2016.pdf

Lessig, Lawrence. 2001. *The Future of Ideas: The Fate of the Commons in a Connected World*. Random House. http://www.the-future-of-ideas.com/download/lessig_FOI.pdf

Lessig, Lawrence. 2005. *Free Culture: How Big Media Uses Technology and the Law to Lock Down Culture*. Penguin. http://www.free-culture.cc/freecontent/

Lessig, Lawrence. 2008. *Remix: Making Art and Commerce Thrive in the Hybrid Economy*. Bloomsbury Academic. https://textbookequity.org/Textbooks/Remix.pdf

Levitt, Theodore. 1969. Putting the product life cycle to work, *Management Review*, 55 (1), p. 19.

Lewis, Becca. 2018. Alternative influence: broadcasting the reactionary right on YouTube, *Data & Society*, September 18. https://datasociety.net/library/alternative-influence/

Lewis, Clive Staples. 1960. *The Four Loves*. Harcourt.

Li, Hairong. 2019. Special section introduction: artificial intelligence and advertising, *Journal of Advertising*, 48, pp. 333–37. DOI: 10.1080/00913367.2019.1654947

Liang, Fan; Das, Vishnupriya; Kostyuk, Nadiya; Hussain, Muzammil M. 2018. Constructing a data-driven society: China's social credit system as a state surveillance infrastructure, *Policy & Internet*, 10: 415–53. DOI: https://doi.org/10.1002/poi3.183

Lievrouw, Leah; Livingstone, Sonia (Eds.) 2006. *The Handbook of New Media*, updated student edn. Sage.

Light, Ben. 2014. *Disconnecting with Social Networking Sites*. Palgrave Macmillan.

Light, Jennifer S. 1999. When computers were women, *Technology and Culture*, 40 (3), pp. 455–83. http://beforebefore.net/scima200/media/light.pdf

Lih, Andrew. 2009. *The Wikipedia Revolution: How a Bunch of Nobodies Created the World's Greatest Encyclopedia*. Hyperion.

Lin, Melissa. 2019. Online dating industry: the business of love, Finance. https://www.toptal.com/finance/business-model-consultants/online-dating-industry

Lin, Serena C.; Coleman, Miles C. 2019. (Selfie)ishness: using the I-It/I-Thou distinction to parse an ethics of self-portraiture, *Consumption Markets & Culture*. DOI: 10.1080/10253866.2019.1586679

Lingel, Jessa. 2017. *Digital Countercultures and the Struggle for Community*. The MIT Press.

LinkedIn. 2012. People you may know, LinkedIn, September 24, as captured by the WayBackMachine. https://web.archive.org/web/20120924040616/http://data.linkedin.com/projects/pymk

Livingstone, Sonia. (Ed.). 2005. *Audiences and Publics: When Cultural Engagement Matters for the Public Sphere*. Intellect Press.

Livingstone, Sonia. 1994. The rise and fall of audience research: an old story with a new ending, in Mark R. Levy and Michael Gurevitch (Eds.), *Defining Media Studies: Reflections on the Future of the Field*. Oxford University Press.

Livingstone, Sonia. 1998. Relationships between media and audiences: prospects for future audience reception studies, in Tamar Liebes and James Curran (Eds.), *Media, Ritual and Identity: Essays in Honor of Elihu Katz*. Routledge. https://core.ac.uk/download/pdf/92945.pdf

Livingstone, Sonia. 2007. Do the media harm children?, *Journal of Children and Media*, 1 (1), pp. 5–14. DOI: 10.1080/17482790601005009

Livingstone, Sonia. 2015. From mass to social media? Advancing accounts of social change, *Social Media + Society*, April–June, pp. 1–3. http://sms.sagepub.com/content/1/1/2056305115578875.full.pdf

Livingstone, Sonia. 2019. Audiences in an age of datafication: critical questions for media research, *Television & New Media*, 20 (2), pp. 170–83. DOI: 10.1177/1527476418811118

Livingstone, Sonia; Lunt, Peter. 2014. Mediatization: an emerging paradigm for media and communication studies, in K. Lundby (Ed.), *Mediatization of Communication: Handbook of Communication Science* (21). De Gruyter Mouton. http://eprints.lse.ac.uk/62122/1/Mediatization_in%20lundby.pdf

Livingstone, Sonia; Witschge, Tamara; Das, Ranjana; Hill, Annette; Kavada, Anastasia; Hallett, Lawrie; Starkey, Guy; Lunt, Peter. 2009. *Existing and emerging audience research in the UK: a review for the Transforming Audiences, Transforming Societies COST Action, August*

2010. COST (European Cooperation in Science and Technology). http://eprints.lse. ac.uk/41863/

Lobato, Roman. 2016. The cultural logic of digital intermediaries: YouTube multichannel networks, *Convergence*, 22 (4), pp. 348–60. https://doi.org/10.1177/1354856516641628

Lomas, Natasha. 2017. I watched 1,000 hours of YouTube kids' content and this is what happened… *TechCrunch*, November 12. https://techcrunch.com/2017/11/12/i-watched-1000-hours-of-youtube-kids-content-and-this-is-what-happened/

Longo, John. 2020. With fikfoks, aka 'fake tiktoks,' influencers expand their empire, *Mel Magazine*, February 12. https://melmagazine.com/en-us/story/fikfok-fake-tiktok-influencers/amp?__twitter_impression=true

Losh, Elizabeth. 2015. Feminism reads big data: "social physics," atomism, and *Selfiecity, International Journal of Communication*. 9, pp. 1647–1659. https://ijoc.org/index.php/ijoc/article/view/3152/1390

Lotz, Amanda. 2017. *Portals: A Treatise on Internet-Distributed Television*. Michigan Publishing.

Lovink, Geert. 2011. *Networks Without a Cause*. Polity.

Lovink, Geert; Rasch Miriam (Eds.) 2013. *Unlike Us: Social Media Monopolies and Their Alternatives*. Institute of Network Cultures. https://monoskop.org/images/7/7b/Lovink_Geert_Rasch_Miriam_eds_Unlike_Us_Reader_Social_Media_Monopolies_and_Their_Alternatives.pdf

Lukes, Steven. 2005 [1974]. *Power: A Radical View*. Macmillan.

Lukosch, Stephen; Sümmer, Till. 2006. Groupware development support with technology patterns, *International Journal of Human–Computer Studies*, 64 (7), pp. 599–610.

Lunt, Peter; Livingstone, Sonia. 1994. *Talk on Television: Audience Participation and Public Debate*. Routledge.

Lunt, Peter; Livingstone, Sonia. 2013. Media studies' fascination with the concept of the public sphere: critical reflections and emerging debates, *Media, Culture and Society*, 35 (1), pp. 87–96. ISSN 0163-4437

Lupton, Deborah. 2016. *The Quantified Self*. Polity.

Lupton, Deborah. 2020. *Data Selves*. Polity.

Mac, Ryan; Warzel, Charlie; Kantrowitz, Alex. 2018. Growth at any cost: top Facebook executive defended data collection in 2016 memo — and warned that Facebook Could get people killed, *Buzzfeed News*, March 29. https://www.buzzfeednews.com/article/ryanmac/growth-at-any-cost-top-facebook-executive-defended-data#.op7KL6Zno

MacAskill, E; Dance, G. 2013. NSA files: decoded, *Guardian*. November 1, https://www.theguardian.com/world/interactive/2013/nov/01/snowden-nsa-files-surveillance-revelations-decoded

Mackenzie, Donald; Wajcman, Judy. 1999 [1985]. *The Social Shaping of Technology*, 2nd edn. Open University Press.

Madden, Mary. June 2009. The state of music online: ten years after Napster, Pew Internet Report. http://www.pewinternet.org/2009/06/15/the-state-of-music-online-ten-years-after-napster/

Madianou, Mirca. 2015. Polymedia and ethnography: understanding the social in social media, *Social Media + Society*, 1 (1). http://journals.sagepub.com/doi/full/10.1177/2056 305115578675

Madianou, Mirca; Miller, Daniel. 2012. Polymedia: towards a new theory of digital media in interpersonal communication, *International Journal of Cultural Studies*, 16 (2), pp. 169–87. DOI: https://doi.org/10.1177/1367877912452486

Makuch, Ben; Pearson, Jordan. 2019. Minds, the 'anti-Facebook,' has no idea what to do about all the neo-Nazis, *Vice*, May 28. https://www.vice.com/en_ca/article/wjvp8y/minds-the-anti-facebook-has-no-idea-what-to-do-about-all-the-neo-nazis

Maloney, Marcus; Roberts, Steve; Caruso, Alexandra. 2018. 'Mmm … I love it, bro!': performances of masculinity in YouTube gaming, *New Media & Society*, 20 (5), pp. 1697–1714. https://doi.org/10.1177/1461444817703368

Mandiberg, Michael (Ed.) 2012. *The Social Media Reader*. New York University Press.

Martin, Michèle. 1991. *'Hello Central?': Gender, Technology and Culture in the Formation of the Telephone System*. McGill-Queen's University Press.

Martineau, Paris. 2019. YouTube has kid troubles because kids are a core audience, *Wired*, June 6. https://www.wired.com/story/youtube-kid-troubles-kids-core-audience/

Marvin, Carolyn. 1988. *When Old Technologies Were New: Thinking About Electric Communication in the Late Nineteenth Century*. Oxford University Press.

Marwick, Alice. 2013. *Status Update: Celebrity, Publicity, and Branding in the Social Media Age*. Yale University Press.

Marx, Karl; Engels, Friedrich. 1998 [1888]. *The Communist Manifesto*. Trans. Samuel Moore. Oxford World's Classics.

Masci, David; Brown, Anna; Kiley, Jocelyn. 2019. 5 facts about same-sex marriage, Pew Research Centre, June 24. https://www.pewresearch.org/fact-tank/2019/06/24/same-sex-marriage/

Massanari, Adrienne L. 2015. *Participatory Culture, Community and Play: Learning from Reddit*. Peter Lang.

Mathiesen, Thomas. 1997. The viewer society: Michel Foucault's 'Panopticon' revisited, *Theoretical Criminology*, 1 (2), pp. 215–34. DOI: 10.1177/1362480697001002003

Matsakis, Louise. 2018. Minds is the anti-Facebook that pays you for your time, *Wired*, April 19. https://www.wired.com/story/minds-anti-facebook/?verso=true

McCay-Peet, Lori; Quan-Haase, Anabel. 2017. What is social media and what questions can social media research help us answer?, Luke Sloan and Anabel Quan-Haase (Eds.), *The SAGE Handbook of Social Media Research Methods*. Sage.

McGlynn, Clare; Rackley, Erika; Houghton, Ruth. 2017. Beyond 'revenge porn': the continuum of image-based sexual abuse, *Feminist Legal Studies*, 25, pp. 25–46. https://doi.org/10.1007/s10691-017-9343-2

McHugh, Molly. 2017. There are no new social networks, The Ringer, April 14. https://www.theringer.com/2017/4/14/16038242/social-media-invention-facebook-twitter-snapchat-tech-e40178df183

McLellan, David. 1998. Introduction, Karl Marx and Friedrich Engels, *The Communist Manifesto*. Oxford World's Classics.

McLelland, Mark; Yu, Haiqing; Goggin, Gerald. 2018. Alternative histories of social media in Japan and China, in Luke Sloan and Anabel Quan-Haase (Eds.), *The SAGE Handbook of Social Media Research Methods*. Sage.

McLuhan, Marshall. 1964. *Understanding Media: The Extensions of Man*. Signet.

McLuhan, Marshall. 2001. *Understanding Media: The Extensions of Man*. Routledge.

McMillan, Robert. 2013. The Friendster autopsy: how a social network dies, *Wired*, February 27. https://www.wired.com/2013/02/friendster-autopsy/

McMullan, John. 2017. A new understanding of 'New Media': online platforms as digital mediums, *Convergence: The International Journal of Research into Media Technologies*, November 5. DOI: https://doi.org/10.1177/1354856517738159

Memmott, Mark. 2011. Little Egyptian girl named Facebook to honor site's role in revolution, NPR, January 22. https://www.npr.org/sections/thetwo-way/2011/02/22/133959319/little-egyptian-girl-named-facebook-to-honor-sites-role-in-revolution?t=1578778039729

Metz, Cade. 2009. Google chief: only miscreants worry about net privacy, The Register, December 7. https://www.theregister.co.uk/2009/12/07/schmidt_on_privacy/

Meyer, Robinson. 2016. The Forrest Gump of the internet, *The Atlantic*, June 6. https://www.theatlantic.com/technology/archive/2016/06/ev-williams-is-the-forrest-gump-of-the-internet/486899/

Mihailidis, Paul. 2014. A tethered generation: exploring the role of mobile phones in the daily life of young people, *Mobile Media and Communication*, 2 (1), pp. 58–72. https://doi.org/10.1177/2050157913505558

Miller, Daniel. 2011. *Tales from Facebook*. Polity.

Miller, Jason. 2014. The fourth screen: mediatization and the smart phone, *Mobile Media and Communication*, 2 (2), pp. 209–26. https://doi.org/10.1177/2050157914521412

Miller, Toby. 2007. *Cultural Citizenship: Cosmopolitanism, Consumerism, and Television in a Neoliberal Age*. Temple University Press.

Milligan, Ian. 2018. Welcome to the web: the online community of GeoCities during the early years of the World Wide Web, in Niels Brügger and Ralph Schroeder (Eds.), *The Web as History*. UCL Press. http://discovery.ucl.ac.uk/1542998/1/The-Web-as-History.pdf

Milner, Ryan M. 2016. *The World Made Meme: Public Conversations and Participatory Media*. The MIT Press.

Miltner, Kate M. 2014. There's no place for lulz on LOLCats: the role of genre, gender and group identity in the interpretation and enjoyment of an internet meme, *First Monday*, 19 (8), August 4. http://firstmonday.org/ojs/index.php/fm/article/view/5391/4103

Miltner, Kate M.; Baym, Nancy. 2015. The selfie of the year of the selfie: reflections on a media scandal, *International Journal of Communication*, 9, pp. 1701–15. https://ijoc.org/index.php/ijoc/article/view/3244/1394

Mobile Action. 2020. Top 10 dating apps worldwide for January 2020, February 11. https://www.mobileaction.co/blog/app-marketing/top-dating-apps-january-2020/

Molloy, Mark. 2017. Who owns Snapchat and when was it created?, *The Telegraph*, July 25. https://www.telegraph.co.uk/technology/0/owns-snapchat-created/

Molteni, Megan; Rogers, Adam. 2017. The actual science of James Damore's Google memo, *Wired*, August 15. https://www.wired.com/story/the-pernicious-science-of-james-damores-google-memo/

Moon, Lucy. 2020. Chatty GRWM | Megxit, Tiktok, Is skiing just for rich people? YouTube, January 16. https://www.youtube.com/watch?v=RRSnuUFDEWw

Moore, Martin; Tambini, Damian (Eds.) 2018. *Digital Dominance: The Power of Google, Amazon, Facebook and Apple*. Oxford University Press.

Moran, Padraig. 2019. How China's 'social credit' system blocked millions of people from travelling, CBC The Current, March 7. https://www.cbc.ca/radio/thecurrent/the-current-for-march-7-2019-1.5046443/how-china-s-social-credit-system-blocked-millions-of-people-from-travelling-1.5046445

Morley, David. 2001. Belongings: place, space and identity in a mediated world, *European Journal of Cultural Studies*, 4 (4), 425–48. https://doi.org/10.1177/1367549 40100400404

Morozov, Evgeny. 2012. *The Net Delusion: How Not to Liberate the World*. Penguin.

Morris, Sue. 2003. WADs, Bots and Mods: multiplayer FPS games as co-creative media, DiGRA Conference. http://www.digra.org/wp-content/uploads/digital-library/05150.21522.pdf

Murphy, Margi. 2017. Net neutrality: what the US overhaul of internet laws will mean for the web, *The Telegraph*, December 15. http://www.telegraph.co.uk/technology/2017/12/14/net-neutrality-will-us-overhaul-internet-laws-affect-web/

Murray, Rhea. 2015. Instagram star quits social media, reveals her 'dream life' was all a sham, *Today*, November 3. https://www.today.com/news/instagram-star-quits-social-media-reveals-her-dream-life-was-t53721

Murthy, Dhiraj. 2013. *Twitter: Social Communication in the Twitter Age*. Polity.

Nagle, Angela. 2017. *Kill All Normies: Online Culture Wars from 4Chan and Tumblr to Trump and the Alt-Right*. Zero Books.

Nakamura, Lisa; Kolko, Beth; Rodman, Gil (Eds.) 2000. *Race in Cyberspace*. Routledge

Nakamura, Lisa; Chow-White, Peter. 2011. *Race After the Internet*. Routledge.

Neff, Gina. 2012. *Venture Labor: Work and the Burden of Risk in Innovative Industries*. The MIT Press.

Newman, Jared. 2018. Google admits to potential Google+ data leak after getting caught, The Fast Company, August 10. https://www.fastcompany.com/90248177/google-admits-to-potential-google-data-leak-after-getting-caught

Newton, Casey. 2018. As controversy swirls, social network Vero is closing in on 3 million users, *The Verge*, March 2. https://www.theverge.com/2018/3/2/17067610/vero-social-media-ayman-hariri-downloads

Ng, Alfred. 2020. Teens have figured out how to mess with Instagram's tracking algorithm, *CNet*, February 4. https://www.cnet.com/news/teens-have-figured-out-how-to-mess-with-instagrams-tracking-algorithm/

Niea, Kho Suet; Keea, Chang Peng; Ahmada, Abdul Latiff. 2014. Mediatization: a grand concept or contemporary approach. *Procedia: Social and Behavioural Sciences*, the International Conference on Communication and Media, i-COME' 14, 18–20 October, Langkawi, Malaysia, pp. 362–67.

Nissenbaum, Helen. 2010. *Privacy in Context: Technology, Policy, and the Integrity of Social Life*. Stanford University Press.

Noble, Safiyah Ugoma. 2018. *Algorithms of Oppression: How Search Engines Reinforce Racism*. New York University Press.

Norman, Don A. 2013 [1988]. *The Design of Everyday Things*, revised and expanded edn. Basic Books.

Nothias, Toussaint. 2020. Access granted: Facebook's free basics in Africa, *Media, Culture & Society*, 42 (3), pp. 329–48. https://doi.org/10.1177/0163443719890530

Nwandu, Angelica. 2018. Issa Rae: 'there was no blueprint for my career', *Glamour*, September 4. https://www.glamour.com/story/issa-rae-october-2018-cover-story

O'Brien, Dennis. 1996. Six degrees of Bacon, *The Daily Telegraph (Sydney Australia)*, July 20, Features, p. 103.

O'Neill, Lauren. 2016. The Pokemon GO phenomenon, explained by a millennial, CBC News, July 11. https://www.cbc.ca/news/trending/pokemon-go-obsession-explained-who-what-why-how-1.3673279

O'Reilly, Tim. 2005. What is Web 2.0: design patterns and business models for the next generation of software, O'Reilly. http://www.oreilly.com/pub/a/web2/archive/what-is-web-20.html

O'Reilly, Tim; Battelle, John. 2009. Web squared: Web 2.0 five years on, *O'Reilly Media*. http://www.web2summit.com/web2009/public/schedule/detail/10194

Ofcom. 2008. Social networking: a quantitative and qualitative research report into attitudes, behaviours and use. Ofcom, Office of Communications. https://www.ofcom.org.uk/__data/assets/pdf_file/0015/24063/report1.pdf

Ofcom. 2018. *The Communications Market 2018*, August 2. https://www.ofcom.org.uk/__data/assets/pdf_file/0022/117256/CMR-2018-narrative-report.pdf

Ofcom. 2019. *The Communications Market 2019*, July 4. https://www.ofcom.org.uk/__data/assets/pdf_file/0028/155278/communications-market-report-2019.pdf

Ofcom. 2020. Lockdown leads to surge in TV screen time and streaming, August 5. https://www.ofcom.org.uk/about-ofcom/latest/features-and-news/lockdown-leads-to-surge-in-tv-screen-time-and-streaming

Ohlberg, Marieke. 2019. China's social credit system: what you should know and how you can prepare, American Chamber Shanghai – *Insight Magazine*, January/February, pp. 23–25. https://www.amcham-shanghai.org/sites/default/files/2019-01/AmCham_InsightMagazine_JanFeb_2019.pdf#page=23

Olsson, Tobias (Ed.) 2013. *Producing the Internet: Critical Perspectives of Social Media*. Nordicom.

Ong, Jonathan Corpus. 2015. *The Poverty of Television: The Mediation of Suffering in Class-divided Philippines*. Anthem Press.

Orgad, Shani. 2012. *Media Representation and the Global Imagination.* Cambridge University Press.

Orphanides, K. G. 2019. On YouTube, a network of paedophiles is hiding in plain sight, *Wired,* February 20. https://www.wired.co.uk/article/youtube-pedophile-videos-advertising

Osborne, Hilary. 2018. What is Cambridge Analytica? The firm at the centre of Facebook's data breach, *Guardian,* March 18. https://www.theguardian.com/news/2018/mar/18/what-is-cambridge-analytica-firm-at-centre-of-facebook-data-breach

Oxford Dictionary of Sociology, 2018. Oxford University Press.

Paasonen, Susanna; Jarrett; Kylie; Light, Ben. 2019. *#NSFW: Sex, Humor, and Risk in Social Media.* The MIT Press.

Padilla, M. 2019. Instagram is hiding likes: will that reduce anxiety?, *The New York Times,* July 18. https://www.nytimes.com/2019/07/18/world/instagram-hidden-likes.html

Page, Sarah. 2020. The racism faced by teenagers in the UK: new research, *The Conversation,* July 23. https://theconversation.com/the-racism-faced-by-teenagers-in-the-uk-new-research-142596

Pal, Leslie Alexander; Alexander, Cynthia Jacqueline (Eds.). 1998. *Digital Democracy: Policy and Politics in the Wired World.* Oxford University Press.

Papacharissi, Zizi. (Ed.) 2011. *A Networked Self: Identity, Community and Culture on Social Network Sites.* Routledge.

Papacharissi, Zizi. 2011. Conclusion: a networked self, in Zizi Papcharissi (Ed.), *A Networked Self: Identity, Community, and Culture on Social Network Sites.* Routledge.

Papacharissi, Zizi. 2015. 'We have always been social', *Social Media + Society,* 1 (1). DOI: https://doi.org/10.1177/2056305115581185, http://journals.sagepub.com/doi/full/10.1177/2056305115581185#articleCitationDownloadContainer

Papacharissi, Zizi. 2018. Introduction, in Zizi Papacharissi (Ed.), *A Networked Self, and Platforms, Stories, Connections.* Routledge.

Parkinson, Hannah Jane. 2015. Tinder Nightmares founder: 'I hate dating so much', *Guardian,* December 7. https://www.theguardian.com/technology/2015/dec/07/elan-gale-tinder-nightmares-interview

Paßmann, Johannes; Schubert, Cornelius. 2020. Liking as taste making: social media practices as generators of aesthetic valuation and distinction, *New Media & Society.* https://doi.org/10.1177/1461444820939458

Patella-Rey, P. J. 2018. Beyond privacy: bodily integrity as an alternative framework for understanding non-consensual pornography, *Information, Communication & Society,* 21 (5), pp. 786–91. DOI: 10.1080/1369118X.2018.1428653

Peterson, Soren Mørk. 2008. Loser-generated content: from participation to exploitation, *First Monday,* 13 (3). http://www.firstmonday.dk/ojs/index.php/fm/article/view/2141/1948

Phillips, Whitney. 2013. *This is Why We Can't Have Nice Things: Mapping the Relationship Between Online Trolling and Mainstream Culture.* The MIT Press.

Phillips, Whitney. 2018. The oxygen of amplification: better practices for reporting on extremists, antagonists, and manipulators, *Data & Society*, May 22. https://datasociety. net/library/oxygen-of-amplification/

Phillips, Whitney; Milner, Ryan. 2017. *The Ambivalent Internet: Mischief, Oddity, and Antagonism Online*. Polity.

Phillips, Whitney; Milner, Ryan. 2021. *You Are Here: A Field Guide for Navigating Polarized Speech, Conspiracy Theories, and Our Polluted Media Landscape*. The MIT Press.

Picone, Ike; Kleut, Jelena; Pavlíčková, Tereza; Romic, Bojana; Hartley, Jannie Møller; De Ridder, Sander. 2019. Small acts of engagement: reconnecting productive audience practices with everyday agency, *New Media & Society*. DOI: 10.1177/1461444819837569

Pinch, Trevor J.; Bijker, Wiebe E. 1984. The social construction of facts and artefacts: or how the sociology of science and the sociology of technology might benefit each other, *Social Studies of Science*,14 (3), pp. 399–441. DOI: https://doi. org/10.1177/030631284014003004

Plantin, Jean-Christophe; de Seta, Gabriele. 2019. WeChat as infrastructure: the techno-nationalist shaping of Chinese digital platforms, *Chinese Journal of Communication*, 12 (3), pp. 257–73. DOI: 10.1080/17544750.2019.1572633

Plantin, Jean-Christophe; Lagoze, Carl; Edwards, Paul N.; Sandvig, Christian. 2016. Infrastructure studies meet platform studies in the age of Google and Facebook, *New Media and Society*, August 4. DOI: https://doi.org/10.1177/1461444816661553

Portnoy, Erica; Gillula, Jeremy. 2017. EFF – explanation of mobile services, Electronic Frontier Foundation, December 6. https://www.eff.org/document/explanation-mobile-services

Postill, John; Pink, Sarah. 2012. Social media ethnography: the digital researcher in a messy web, *Media International Australia*, 145, pp. 123–34.

Postman, Neil. 1985. *Amusing Ourselves to Death: Public Discourse in the Age of Show Business*. Penguin.

Powell, Anastasia; Henry, Nicola; Flynn, Asher. 2018. Image based sexual abuse, in Walter S. DeKeseredy and Molly Dragiewicz (Eds.), *Routledge Handbook of Critical Criminology*, 2nd edn. Routledge.

Proulx, Mike; Shepatin, Stacey. 2012. *Social TV: How Marketers Can Reach and Engage Audiences by Connecting Television to the Web, Social Media, and Mobile*. Wiley.

Puglise, Nicole. 2016. Cards Against Humanity raises $100,000 to dig 'tremendous hole', *Guardian*, November 28. https://www.theguardian.com/technology/2016/nov/28/cards-against-humanity-hole

Qui, Jack Linchuan. 2017. *Goodbye iSlave: A Manifesto for Digital Abolition*. University of Illinois Press.

Qui, Jack Linchuan. 2018. Labor and social media: the exploitation and emancipation of (almost) everything, in Jean Burgess, Alice Marwick and Thomas Poell (Eds.), *The SAGE Handbook of Social Media*. Sage.

Quinn, Kelly; Papacharissi, Zizi. 2017. Our networked selves: personal connection and relational maintenance in social media use, in Jean Burgess, Alice Marwick and Thomas Poell (Eds.), *The SAGE Handbook of Social Media*. Sage.

Quinn, Zoe. 2017. *Crash Override: How Gamergate (Nearly) Destroyed My Life, and How We Can Win the Fight Against Online Hate*. Public Affairs.

Quodling, Andrew. 2018. Shadow profiles – Facebook knows about you even if you're not on Facebook, *The Conversation*, April 13. http://theconversation.com/shadow-profiles-facebook-knows-about-you-even-if-youre-not-on-facebook-94804

Rainie, Lee; Wellman, Barry. 2012. *Networked: The New Social Operating System*. The MIT Press.

Ranzini, Giulia; Lutz, Christoph. 2017. Love at first swipe? Explaining Tinder self-presentation and motives, *Mobile Media & Communication*, 5 (1), pp. 80–101. https://doi.org/10.1177/2050157916664559

Raun, Tobias. 2018. Capitalizing intimacy: new subcultural forms of micro-celebrity strategies and affective labour on YouTube, *Convergence*, 24 (1), pp. 99–113. https://doi.org/10.1177/1354856517736983

Raynes-Goldie, Kate. 2010. Aliases, creeping, and wall cleaning: understanding privacy in the age of Facebook, *First Monday*, 15. http://firstmonday.org/ojs/index.php/fm/article/view/2775/2432

Raynes-Goldie, Kate. 2012. Privacy in the age of Facebook: discourse, architecture, consequences. PhD. Perth, Australia: Curtin University. http://www.k4t3.org/facebookphd/

Reagle, Joseph M. Jr. 2010. *Good Faith Collaboration: The Culture of Wikipedia*. The MIT Press. https://reagle.org/joseph/2010/gfc/

Reiff, Nathan. 2019. Top companies owned by Facebook, Investopedia, June 25. https://www.investopedia.com/articles/personal-finance/051815/top-11-companies-owned-facebook.asp

Reimann, Matt. 2016. The chatty, charming history of personal ads, Medium, Timeline, September 22. https://timeline.com/tinder-personal-ads-history-4c34c7d6dbcb

Rein, Kathatrina; Venturini, Tomasso. 2018. Ploughing digital landscapes: how Facebook influences the evolution of live video streaming, *New Media & Society*, 20 (9), pp. 3359–80. https://doi.org/10.1177/1461444817748954

Rettberg, Jill Walker. 2014. *Seeing Ourselves Through Technology: How We Use Selfies, Blogs and Wearable Devices to See Ourselves*. Palgrave Macmillan. https://link.springer.com/book/10.1057%2F9781137476661

Rettberg, Jill Walker. 2017. Biometric citizens: adapting our selfies to machine vision, in Adi Knutsman (Ed.), *Selfie Citizenship*. Palgrave Macmillan.

Rheingold, Howard. 1993. *Virtual Community: Homesteading on the Electronic Frontier*. Addison-Wesley.

Rieder, Bernhard; Matamoros-Fernández, Ariadna; Coromina, Òscar. 2018. From ranking algorithms to 'ranking cultures': investigating the modulation of visibility in YouTube search results, *Convergence*, 24 (1), pp. 50–68. https://doi.org/10.1177/1354856517736982

Rink, David R.; Swan, John E. 1979. Product life cycle research: a literature review, *Journal of Business Research*, 7 (3): 219–42. https://doi.org/10.1016/0148-2963(79)90030-4

Rios, Juan Sebastian; Ketterer, Daniel John; Wohn, Donghee Yvette. 2018. How users choose a face lens on Snapchat, in *Companion of the 2018 ACM Conference on Computer Supported Cooperative Work and Social Computing (CSCW '18)*, Association for Computing Machinery, New York, pp. 321–24. DOI: https://doi.org/10.1145/3272973.3274087

Robards, Brady; Lincoln, Siân. 2016. Making it 'Facebook Official': reflecting on romantic relationships through sustained Facebook use, *Social Media + Society*, 2 (4). http://journals.sagepub.com/doi/full/10.1177/2056305116672890

Rodriguez, Cecilia. 2019. Meghan Markle, Kate Middleton and the trolls that abuse them, *Forbes*, February 3. https://www.forbes.com/sites/ceciliarodriguez/2019/02/03/meghan-markle-kate-middleton-and-the-trolls-that-abuse-them/#1c570c817845

Roettgers, Janko. 2010. The decade in online video, part 1: the early years, GigaOm, January 1. https://gigaom.com/2010/01/01/the-decade-in-online-video-part-1-the-early-years/

Rogers, Richard. 2014. Foreword: debanalising Twitter: the transformation of an object of study, in Katrin Weller, Axel Bruns, Jean Burgess, Merja Mahrt and Cornlius Puschmann (Eds.), *Twitter and Society*. Peter Lang.

Rogers, Richard. 2018a. Digital methods for cross-platform analysis, in Jean Burgess, Thomas Poell and Alice Marwick (Eds.), *The SAGE Handbook of Social Media*. Sage.

Rogers, Richard. 2018b. Otherwise engaged: social media from vanity metrics to critical analytics, *International Journal of Communication*, 12, pp. 450–72. https://ijoc.org/index.php/ijoc/article/view/6407/2248

Roose, Kevin. 2019. The making of a YouTube radical, *The New York Times*, June 8. https://www.nytimes.com/interactive/2019/06/08/technology/youtube-radical.html

Russell, Jylian. 2017. Facebook reactions: what they are and how they impact the feed, Hootsuite, May 15. https://blog.hootsuite.com/how-facebook-reactions-impact-the-feed/

Rusu, Mihai Stelian. 2018. Theorising love in sociological thought: classical contributions to a sociology of love, *Journal of Classical Sociology*, 18 (1), pp. 3–20. https://doi.org/10.1177/1468795X17700645

Safranova, Valeriya. 2015. On fake Instagram, a chance to be real. *The New York Times*. November 18, https://www.nytimes.com/2015/11/19/fashion/instagram-finstagram-fake-account.html

Safranova, Valeriya. 2017. The rise and fall of Yik Yak, the anonymous messaging app, *The New York Times*, May 27. https://www.nytimes.com/2017/05/27/style/yik-yak-bullying-mary-washington.html?

Saker, Michael;Evans, Leighton. 2018. Pokémon GO is not dead, it has 5m loyal players and it's changing people's lives, *The Conversation*, October 22. https://theconversation.com/pokemon-go-is-not-dead-it-has-5m-loyal-players-and-its-changing-peoples-lives-104095

Sandoval, Marisol. 2014. *From Corporate to Social Media: Critical Perspectives on Corporate Social Responsibility in Media and Communication Industries*. Routledge.

Sandvig, Christian. 2013. The Internet as infrastructure, in William H. Dutton (Ed.), *The Oxford Handbook of Internet Studies*. Oxford University Press.

Sandvig, Christian. 2015. The social industry, *Social Media + Society*. DOI: 10.1177/2056305 115582047.

Sandvoss, Cornell. 2005. *Fans: The Mirror of Consumption*. Polity.

Schaffer, Jennifer. 2014. What we talk about when we talk about PostSecret, *Buzzfeed*, December. https://www.buzzfeed.com/jenniferschaffer/what-we-talk-about-when-we-talk-about-postsecret

Schilt, K. 2003. 'I'll resist with every inch and every breath': girls and zine making as a form of resistance, *Youth & Society*, 35 (1), pp. 71–97. https://doi.org/10.1177/0044118X0 3254566

Schmidt, Kjeld; Bannon, Liam. 1992. Taking CSCW seriously: supporting articulation work, *Computer Supported Cooperative Work (CSCW)*, 1: 7–40. https://link.springer.com/article/10.1007/BF00752449

Scholz, Trebor. 2008. Market ideology and the myths of Web 2.0, *First Monday*, 13 (3). http://firstmonday.org/ojs/index.php/fm/article/view/2138

Scholz, Trebor (Ed.). 2013. *Digital Labor: The Internet as Playground and Factory*. Routledge.

Schonig, J. 2020. 'Liking' as creating: on aesthetic category memes, *New Media & Society*, 22 (1), pp. 26–48. https://doi.org/10.1177/1461444819855727

Sedghi, Amy. 2014. Facebook: 10 years of social networking in numbers, *Guardian*, February 4. https://www.theguardian.com/news/datablog/2014/feb/04/facebook-in-numbers-statistics

Selwyn, Neil; Pangrazio, Lucy. 2018. Doing data differently? developing personal data tactics and strategies amongst young mobile media users, *Big Data & Society*. https://doi.org/10.1177/2053951718765021

Sen, Amartya. 1999. *Development as Freedom*. Oxford University Press.

Senft, Theresa; Baym, Nancy. 2015. What does the selfie say? Investigating a global phenomenon, *International Journal of Communication*, 9, pp. 1588–1606. https://ijoc.org/index.php/ijoc/article/viewFile/4067/1387

Shamsian, Jacob. 2016. The story of Pokemon GO's creation explains the oddest thing about the game, *Insider*, July 10. https://www.insider.com/why-are-pokemon-go-locations-random-2016-7

Sharon, T. and Zandbergen, D. (2016) From data fetishism to quantifying selves: self-tracking practices and the other values of data, *New Media & Society*, 19 (11), pp. 1695–1709. https://doi.org/10.1177/1461444816636090

Shaw, France. 2016. 'Bitch I Said Hi': the Bye Felipe campaign and discursive activism in mobile dating apps, *Social Media + Society*, pp. 1–11. https://doi.org/10.1177/20563 05116672889

Shi-Kupfer, Kristin; Ohlberg, Mareike. 2019. China's digital rise: challenges for Europe, *Mercator Institute for China Studies*, April 4. https://www.merics.org/en/papers-on-china/chinas-digital-rise

Shifman, Limor. 2013. Memes in a digital world: reconciling with a conceptual troublemaker, *Journal of Computer Mediated Communication*, 18 (3), pp. 362–77. http://onlinelibrary.wiley.com/doi/10.1111/jcc4.12013/full

Shifman, Limor. 2014. *Memes in Digital Culture*. Wiley.

Shirky, Clay. 2003. Social software and the politics of groups, Clay Shirky's Writings About the Internet, March 9. http://shirky.com/writings/group_politics.html

Shirky, Clay. 2008. *Here Comes Everybody: The Power of Organizing Without Organizations*. Allen Lane.

Shirky, Clay. 2009. *Here Comes Everybody: The Power of Organizing Without Organizations*, reprint edn. Penguin.

Shu, Catherine. 2014. Watch John Oliver's brilliant concise primer on net neutrality, *TechCrunch*, June 3. https://techcrunch.com/2014/06/03/watch-john-olivers-brilliant-concise-primer-on-net-neutrality/

Siapera, Eugenia. 2012. *Understanding New Media*. Sage.

Siegelman, Wendy. 2018. Cambridge Analytica is dead – but its obscure network is alive and well, *Guardian*, May 5. https://www.theguardian.com/uk-news/2018/may/05/cambridge-analytica-scl-group-new-companies-names

Silverstone, Roger. 1994. *Television and Everyday Life*. Routledge.

Silverstone, Roger. 1999. *Why Study the Media?* Sage.

Silverstone, Roger; Hirsch, Eric (Eds.). 1993. *Consuming Technologies: Media and Information in Domestic Spaces*. Routledge.

Simmel, Georg. 1987 [1949/1950]. The sociology of sociability, *American Journal of Sociology*, reprinted in David Frisby and Mike Featherstone (Eds.), *Simmel on Culture: Selected Writings*. Sage.

Singer, Natasha. 2017. How google took over the classroom, *The New York Times*, May 13. https://www.nytimes.com/2017/05/13/technology/google-education-chromebooks-schools.html

Sloan, Luke; Quan-Haase, Anabel (Eds.) 2017. *The SAGE Handbook of Social Media Research Methods*. Sage.

Smahel, David; Machackova, Hanna; Mascheroni, Giovanna; Dedkova, Lenka; Staksrud, Elisabeth;Ólafsson, Kjarta; Livingstone, Sonia; Hasebrink, Uwe. 2020. EU Kids online 2020: survey results from 19 countries, EU Kids Online. DOI: 10.21953/lse.47fdeqj01ofo

Smith, Crystal. 2011. *The Achilles Effect: What Pop Culture is Teaching Young Boys About Masculinity*. Iuniverse Inc.

Smith, Crystal. 2017. Word cloud: how toy ad vocabulary reinforces gender stereotypes, Crystal Smith, September 20. http://crystalsmith.ca/word-cloud-toy-ad-vocabulary-reinforces-gender-stereotypes/

Smith, Richard. 2013. So what? Why study mobile media and communication?, *Mobile Media and Communication*, 1 (1), pp. 38–41.

Smith, Stacy; Choueiti, Marc; Pieper, Katherine; Case, Ariana; Choi, Angel. 2018. *Inequality in 1,100 Popular Films: Examining Portrayals of Gender, Race/Ethnicity, LGBT & Disability from 2007 to 2017*. Annenberg Foundation & USC Annenberg Inclusion Initiative. http://assets.uscannenberg.org/docs/inequality-in-1100-popular-films.pdf

Smythe, Dallas W. 1981. On the audience commodity and its work, in *Dependency Road: Communications, Capitalism, Consciousness, and Canada*. Ablex.

Snapchat. 2020. Our privacy principles, February 12. https://www.snap.com/en-GB/privacy/privacy-center/

Snider, Mike. 1997. Easing new users onto the internet, *USA Today*, Life section, March 6.

Soffer, Oren. 2016. The oral paradigm and Snapchat, *Social Media + Society*. https://doi.org/10.1177/2056305116666306

Solon, Olivia. 2017a. 'It's digital colonialism': how Facebook's free internet service has failed its users, *Guardian*, July 27. https://www.theguardian.com/technology/2017/jul/27/facebook-free-basics-developing-markets

Solon, Olivia. 2017b. Snapchat's new map feature raises fears of stalking and bullying, *Guardian*, June 23. https://www.theguardian.com/technology/2017/jun/23/snapchat-maps-privacy-safety-concerns

Solon, Olivia. 2018. FaceTune is conquering Instagram – but does it take airbrushing too far?, *Guardian*, March 9. https://www.theguardian.com/media/2018/mar/09/facetune-photoshopping-app-instagram-body-image-debate

Solove, Daniel J. 2007. 'I've got nothing to hide', and other misunderstandings of privacy, *San Diego Law Review*, GWU Law School Public Law Research Paper No. 289, 44, p. 745. https://ssrn.com/abstract=998565

Sørensen, Inge Ejbye. 2016. The revival of live TV: liveness in a multiplatform context, *Media, Culture & Society*, 38 (3), pp. 381–99. https://doi.org/10.1177/0163443715608260

Sorkin, Andrew Ross; Peters, Jeremy W. 2006. Google to Acquire YouTube for $1.65 Billion, *The New York Times*, October 9. https://www.nytimes.com/2006/10/09/business/09cnd-deal.html

Sotoudeh, Ramina; Friedland, Roger; Afary, Janet. 2017. Digital romance: the sources of online love in the Muslim world, *Media, Culture and Society*, 39 (3), pp. 429–39. https://doi.org/10.1177/0163443717691226

Sovacool, Benjamin K.; Hess, David J. 2017. Ordering theories: typologies and conceptual frameworks for sociotechnical change, *Social Studies of Science*, 47 (5), pp. 703–50. DOI: https://doi.org/10.1177/0306312717709363

Sproull, Lee; Kiesler, Sara. 1991. *Connections: New Ways of Working in the Networked Organization*. The MIT Press

Srnicek, Nick. 2017. *Platform Capitalism*. Polity.

Star, Susan Leigh. 1990. Power, technology and the phenomenology of conventions: on being allergic to onions, *The Sociological Review*, 38 (1), pp. 26–56. DOI: https://doi.org/10.1111/j.1467-954X.1990.tb03347.x

Stark, Luke. 2019. Facial recognition is the plutonium of AI, *XRDS: Crossroads, The ACM Magazine for Students*, 25 (3), pp. 50–55. DOI: 10.1145/3313129

Starosielski, Nicole. 2015a. *The Undersea Network*. Duke University Press.

Starosielski, Nicole. 2015b. Fixed flow: undersea cables as media infrastructures, in Lisa Parks and Nicole Starosielski (Eds.), *Signal Traffic: Critical Studies of Media Infrastructures*. University of Illinois Press.

Statista. 2017a. Number of apps available in leading app stores as of March 2017, Statista: The Statistics Portal. https://www.statista.com/statistics/276623/number-of-apps-available-in-leading-app-stores/

Statista. 2017b. 'Number of mobile phone users worldwide from 2013 to 2019 (in billions)', Statista: The Statistics Portal. https://www.statista.com/statistics/274774/forecast-of-mobile-phone-users-worldwide/

Statista.2017c. Market share held by the leading social networks in the United Kingdom (UK) as of July 2017. https://www.statista.com/statistics/280295/market-share-held-by-the-leading-social-networks-in-the-united-kingdom-uk/

Statista. 2020. Online dating worldwide, *Statista*. https://www.statista.com/outlook/372/100/online-dating/worldwide

Statt, Nick. 2014. Google's April Fools' prank puts Pokemon in the real world, *CNET*, March 31. https://www.cnet.com/news/googles-april-fools-prank-puts-pokemon-in-the-real-world/

Sterling, Greg. 2019. Almost 70% of digital ad spending going to Google, Facebook, Amazon, Says Analyst Firm, *Marketing Land*, June 17. https://marketingland.com/almost-70-of-digital-ad-spending-going-to-google-facebook-amazon-says-analyst-firm-262565

Stevenson, Michael. 2018. From hypertext to hype and back again: exploring the roots of social media in early web culture, in Jean Burgess, Alice Marwick and Thomas Poell (Eds.), *The SAGE Handbook of Social Media*. Sage.

Stevenson, Nick. 2003a. *Cultural Citizenship: Cosmopolitan Questions*. Open University Press.

Stevenson, Nick. 2003b. Cultural citizenship in the 'cultural' society: a cosmopolitan approach, *Citizenship Studies*, 7 (3), pp. 331–48. DOI: 10.1080/1362102032000098904

Stoilova, Mariya, Livingstone, Sonia; Nandagiri, Rishita. 2019a. Children's data and privacy online: growing up in a digital age: research findings, London School of Economics and Political Science. http://eprints.lse.ac.uk/101282/1/Livingstone_childrens_data_and_privacy_online_research_findings_published.pdf

Stoilova, Mariya; Nandagiri, Rishita; Livingstone, Sonia. 2019b. Children's understanding of personal data and privacy online – a systematic evidence mapping, *Information, Communication & Society*. DOI: 10.1080/1369118X.2019.1657164

Stokel-Walker, Chris. 2018. Why YouTubers are feeling the burn, *Guardian*, August 12. https://www.theguardian.com/technology/2018/aug/12/youtubers-feeling-burn-video-stars-crumbling-under-pressure-of-producing-new-content

Stokel-Walker, Chris. 2019. *YouTubers: How YouTube Shook Up TV and Created a New Generation of Stars*. Canbury Press

Stokel-Walker, Chris. 2020. The bloodiest battle in the shortform video app war will be fought through off-platform embeds, FFWD, Medium, January 27. https://ffwd.medium.com/the-bloodiest-battle-in-the-shortform-video-app-war-will-be-fought-through-off-platform-embeds-704091445594

Stoycheff, E. (2016) Under surveillance: examining Facebook's spiral of silence effects in the wake of NSA internet monitoring, *Journalism & Mass Communication Quarterly*, 93 (2), pp. 296–311. https://doi.org/10.1177/1077699016630255

Streeter, Thomas. 2017. The internet as a structure of feeling, *Internet Histories: Digital Technology, Culture and Society*, 1 (1–2). http://www.tandfonline.com/doi/full/10.1080/24 701475.2017.1306963

Sujon, Zoetanya. 2018. The triumph of social privacy: understanding the privacy logics of sharing behaviors across social media, *International Journal of* Communication, 12, pp. 3751–71. https://ijoc.org/index.php/ijoc/article/view/9357/2453

Sujon, Zoetanya. 2019a. Disruptive play or platform colonialism?: the contradictory dynamics of Google expeditions and educational virtual reality, *Digital Culture & Education*, 11 (1), pp. 1–22. https://static1.squarespace.com/static/5cf15af7a259990001706378/t/5d2 4c64e71bd370001520db8/1562691157533/Final+Sujon.pdf

Sujon, Zoetanya. 2019b. Facebook's privacy turn: new protections or new markets? *Notes from a Digital Explorer*, June 7. https://sujonz.wordpress.com/2019/06/07/facebooks-privacy-turn-new-protections-or-new-markets/

Sujon, Zoetanya. 2019c. The rise of platform empires: sociality as mass deception, *Living in an Age of Surveillance Capitalism*, University of Glasgow. http://ualresearchonline.arts.ac.uk/14480/

Sujon, Zoetanya; Viney, Leslie; Toker-Turnalar, Elif. 2018. Domesticating Facebook: the shift from compulsive connection to personal service platform, *Social Media + Society*. https://doi.org/10.1177/2056305118803895

Sulleyman, Aatif. 2017. Net neutrality repeal: what is it and why will it make the internet much worse?, *Independent*, December 15. http://www.independent.co.uk/life-style/gadgets-and-tech/net-neutrality-what-is-it-repeal-latest-meaning-define-trump-internet-rules-why-explained-a8111066.html

Sundararajan, Arun. 2016. *The Sharing Economy: The End of Employment and the Rise of Crowd-Based Capitalism*. The MIT Press.

Taylor, Astra. 2014. *The People's Platform: Taking Back Power and Culture in the Digital Age*. Picador.

Taylor, Astra; Gessen, Keith. 2011. *Occupy: Scenes from Occupied America*. Verso.

Taylor, David G. 2020. Putting the 'self' in selfies: how narcissism, envy and self-promotion motivate sharing of travel photos through social media, *Journal of Travel & Tourism Marketing*, 37 (1), pp. 64–77. DOI: 10.1080/10548408.2020.1711847

Taylor, Margaret; Taylor, Andrew. 2012. The technology life cycle: conceptualization and managerial implications, *International Journal of Production Economics*, 140 (1): 541–53.

Taylor, T. L. 2018. *Watch Me Play: Twitch and the Rise of Game Live Streaming*. Princeton University Press.

TeleGeography. 2017. Submarine cable frequently asked questions, *TeleGeography*. https://www2.telegeography.com/submarine-cable-faqs-frequently-asked-questions

Tencent QQ. 2017. Social networks, Tencent. https://www.tencent.com/en-us/system. html

Terranova, Tiziana. 2000. Free labor: producing culture for the digital economy, *Social Text*, 63, 18 (2), pp. 33–58. http://web.mit.edu/schock/www/docs/18.2terranova.pdf

Terranova, Tiziana. 2004. *Network Culture: Politics for the Information Age*. Pluto Press.

Terranova, Tiziana. 2013. Free labour, in Trebor Scholz (Ed.), *Digital Labor: The Internet as Playground and Factory*. Routledge.

Thatcher, Mandy. 2007. Delegates gather for social media forum in London, *Strategic Communication Management*, 11 (3), p. 2.

Thomas, Charlie. 2014. The £2bn relationship – the business of online dating, *The Huffington Post*, October 26. http://www.huffingtonpost.co.uk/2012/10/26/the-2bn-relationship-the-business-of-online-dating_n_2024458.html

Thomas, Sara E. 2018. 'What should I do?': young women's reported dilemmas with nude photographs, *Sexuality Research and Social Policy*, 15, pp. 92–207. https://doi.org/10.1007/s13178-017-0310-0

Thompson, John B. 1995. *The Media and Modernity: A Social Theory of the Media*. Polity.

Thompson, Laura. 2018. 'I can be your Tinder nightmare': harassment and misogyny in the online sexual marketplace, *Feminism & Psychology*, 28 (1), pp. 69–89. https://doi.org/10.1177/0959353517720226

Thumim, Nancy. 2012. *Self Representation and Digital Culture*. Palgrave Macmillan.

Thumim, Nancy. 2017. Self-(re)presentation now, *Popular Communication*, 15 (2), pp. 55–61. DOI: 10.1080/15405702.2017.1307020

Tiefentale Alise; Manovich Lev. 2015. Selfiecity: exploring photography and self-fashioning in social media, in D.M. Berry and M. Dieter (Eds.), *Postdigital Aesthetics*. Palgrave Macmillan, London

Tiefentale, Alise; Manovich, Lev. 2018. Competitive photography and the presentation of the self, in Julia Eckel, Jens Ruchatz and Sabine Wirth (Eds.), *Exploring the Selfie: Historical, Theoretical, and Analytical Approaches to Digital Self-Photography*. Palgrave Macmillan.

Tiidenberg, Katrin. 2018. *Selfies: Why We Love (and Hate) Them*. Emerald Publishing.

Tilic, Gorkem. 2017. Snapchat as an advertising platform, *New Trends and Issues Proceedings on Humanities and Social Sciences*, 4 (11), pp. 122–29. https://un-pub.eu/ojs/index.php/pntsbs/article/view/2866

Tinder. 2020. Tinder information, statistics, facts and history, Dating Sites Reviews. https://www.datingsitesreviews.com/staticpages/index.php?page=Tinder-Statistics-Facts-History

Tippet, K. 2016. Jimmy Wales: the sum of all human knowledge, On Being. September 8, https://onbeing.org/programs/jimmy-wales-the-sum-of-all-human-knowledge-2/

Titcomb, James. 2017. How the world reacted to the first iPhone 10 years ago, *The Telegraph*, Technology, September 12. http://www.telegraph.co.uk/technology/2017/01/09/world-reacted-first-iphone-10-years-ago/

Tkacz, Nathaniel. 2015. *Wikipedia and the Politics of Openness*. University of Chicago Press.

Tönnies, Ferdinand. 2002 [1887]. *Community and Society: Gemeinschaft und Gesellschaft*. Charles P. Loomis (Trans. and Ed.). Dover Publications.

Trivundža, Ilija T.; Nieminen, Hannu; Carpentier, Nico; Trappel, Josef. 2017. *Critical Perspectives on Media, Power and Change*. Taylor & Francis.

Tufecki, Zeynep. 2017a. Facebook's ad scandal isn't a 'fail,' it's a feature, *The New York Times*, September 23. https://www.nytimes.com/2017/09/23/opinion/sunday/facebook-ad-scandal.html

Tufecki, Zeynep. 2017b. *Twitter and Tear Gas: The Power and Fragility of Networked Protest*. Yale University Press. https://www.twitterandteargas.org/downloads/twitter-and-tear-gas-by-zeynep-tufekci.pdf

Tufecki, Zeynep. 2018. YouTube, the great radicalizer, *The New York Times*, March 10. https://www.nytimes.com/2018/03/10/opinion/sunday/youtube-politics-radical.html

Tumblr. 2018. Hey Tumblr, Tumblr Staff Blog, December 17. https://staff.tumblr.com/post/181199101690/hey-tumblr-a-couple-of-weeks-ago-we-announced-an

Turkle, Sherry. 2011. *Alone Together: Why We Expect More From Technology and Less From Each Other*. Basic Books.

Turner, Graeme. 2013. *Understanding Celebrity*, 2nd edn. Sage.

Tweten, Alexandra. 2018. *Bye Felipe: Disses, Dick Pics, and Other Delights of Modern Dating*. Hachette Books.

Twitter. 2020. Content on the services, Terms and Conditions, February 12. https://twitter.com/en/tos

Udell, John. 1999. *Practical Internet Groupware*. O'Reilly Media.

UK Parliament. 2019. *Disinformation and 'fake news': Final Report*. (Feb), https://publications.parliament.uk/pa/cm201719/cmselect/cmcumeds/1791/179102.htm

Universal Declaration of Human Rights. 1948. https://www.un.org/en/universal-declaration-human-rights/

Urry, John. 1998. The concept of society and the future of sociology, *Dansk Sociologie*, special issue, pp. 29–41. htps://rauli.cbs.dk/index.php/dansksociologi/article/view/746/777

Urry, John. 2005. Beyond the science of society, *Sociological Research Online*, 10 (2). www.socresonline.org.uk/10/2urry.html

Uusitalo, Olavi. 2014. Technological change: dominant design approach, in *Float Glass Innovation in the Flat Glass Industry*, Springer Link, pp. 15–24.

Vaidhyanathan, Siva. 2011. *The Googlization of Everything*. University of California Press.

Vaidhhyanathan, Siva. 2018. *Antisocial Media: How Facebook Disconnects Us and Undermines Democracy*. Oxford University Press.

Vanderklippe, Nathan. 2018. Chinese blacklist an early glimpse of sweeping new social-credit control, *The Globe and Mail*, January 13. https://www.theglobeandmail.com/news/world/chinese-blacklist-an-early-glimpse-of-sweeping-new-social-credit-control/article37493300/

VanderMay, Anne. 2014. PostSecret founder has a few things to say about new anonymous apps, *Fortune*, August 9. https://fortune.com/2014/08/09/postsecret-founder-has-a-few-things-to-say-about-new-anonymous-apps/

Van, Dijck, José. 2013. *The Culture of Connectivity: A Critical History of Social Media*. Oxford University Press.

Van Dijck, José. 2015. After connectivity: the era of connectication, *Social Media + Society*, May. https://doi.org/10.1177/2056305115578873

Van Dijck, José; Poell, Thomas; De Waal, Martin. 2018. *The Platform Society: Public Values in a Connective World*. Oxford University Press.

van Es, Karin. 2017. Liveness redux: on media and their claim to be live, *Media, Culture & Society*, 39(8), pp. 1245–56. https://doi.org/10.1177/0163443717717633

Van Schewick, Barbara. 2010. *Internet Architecture and Innovation*. The MIT Press.

Venturini, Tomasso; Rogers, Roger. 2019. 'API-based research' or how can digital sociology and journalism studies learn from the Facebook and Cambridge Analytica data breach, *Digital Journalism*, 7 (4), pp. 532–40. DOI: 10.1080/21670811.2019.1591927

Voakes, Paul S. 2004. A brief history of public journalism, *National Civic Review*, 93 (3), pp. 25–35. https://doi.org/10.1002/ncr.58

Wang, Yuhua; Minzner, Carl. 2015. The rise of the Chinese security state, *The China Quarterly*, 222 (June), pp. 339–59. DOI: https://doi.org/10.1017/S0305741015000430

Wardle, Claire. 2017. Fake news. It's complicated, *First Draft News*, February 16. https://medium.com/1st-draft/fake-news-its-complicated-d0f773766c79

Warfield, Katie; Cambre, Crystal; Abidin, Carolina 2016. Introduction to the Social Media + Society special issue on selfies: me-diated inter-faces, *Social Media + Society*, pp. 1–5. https://doi.org/10.1177/2056305116641344

Warren, Frank. 2012. Half a million secrets, TED, February. https://www.ted.com/talks/frank_warren_half_a_million_secrets/transcript

Warren, Frank. 2014. *The World of PostSecret*. William Morrow.

Warren, Samuel D.; Brandeis, Louis D. 1890. The right to privacy, *Harvard Law Review*, 4 (5), pp. 193–220. http://www.cs.cornell.edu/~shmat/courses/cs5436/warren-brandeis.pdf

Wasserman, Todd. 2012. Facebook outs suspected bigamist leading double life, Mashable, March 12. https://mashable.com/2012/03/12/facebook-outs-suspected-bigamist/?europe=true

Wasserman, Todd. 2015. The revolution wasn't televised: the early days of YouTube, Mashable, February 14. https://mashable.com/2015/02/14/youtube-history/?europe=true#5mMBLe2hhsqX

Watts, Duncan. 2004. *Six Degrees: The Science of a Connected Age*. Vintage.

Weber, Max. 1995 [1922]. Basic categories of social organization, in W. G. Runciman (Ed.), E. Matthews (Trans.), *Weber: Selections in Translation*. Cambridge University Press.

Webster, Andrew. 2017. Pokémon GO's wild first year: a timeline, *The Verge*, July 6. https://www.theverge.com/2017/7/6/15888210/pokemon-go-one-year-anniversary-timeline

Webster, Andrew. 2019. Pokémon GO spurred an amazing era that continues with Sword and Shield, *The Verge*, February 28. https://www.theverge.com/2019/2/28/18243332/pokemon-go-sword-shield-franchise-history-niantic-nintendo-switch

Wei, Ran. 2013. Mobile media: coming of age with a big splash, *Mobile Media and Communication*, 1 (1), pp. 50–56. https://doi.org/10.1177/2050157912459494.

Weller, Katrin; Bruns, Axel; Burgess, Jean; Mahrt, Merja; Puschman, Cornelius (Eds.). 2014. *Twitter and Society*. Peter Lang.

Wellman, Barry. 1997. An electronic group is virtually a social network, in Sara Kiesler (Ed.), *Culture of the Internet*. Lawrence Erlbaum. http://citeseerx.ist.psu.edu/viewdoc/download?doi=10.1.1.28.4128&rep=rep1&type=pdf

Wellman, Barry. 2004. The three ages of internet studies: ten, five and zero years ago, *New Media and Society*, 6 (1), pp. 123–29.

WhatsApp. 2020. WhatsApp privacy, February 12. https://www.whatsapp.com/privacy

Willems, Wendy. 2016. Beyond free basics: Facebook, data bundles and Zambia's social media internet. Africa at LSE, September 1. http://eprints.lse.ac.uk/76384/

Williams, James. 2018. *Stand Out of Our Light: Freedom and Resistance in the Attention Economy*. Cambridge University Press.

Williams, Katie. 2020. Top social media apps worldwide for January 2020 by downloads, Sensor Tower Blog, February 21. https://sensortower.com/blog/top-social-media-apps-worldwide-january-2020

Williams, Patrick; Kind, Eric. 2019. Data-driven policing: the hardwiring of discriminatory policing practices across Europe, *European Network Against Racism*. https://www.enar-eu.org/IMG/pdf/data-driven-profiling-web-final.pdf

Williams, Raymond. 2005 [1980]. *Culture and Materialism*. Verso Books.

Williams, Raymond. 2015 [1976]. *Keywords: A Vocabulary of Culture and Society*, new edn. Oxford University Press.

Winder, Belinda; Farid, Hany. 2019. YouTube's paedophile problem is only a small part of the internet's issue with child sexual abuse, *The Conversation*, March 5. https://theconversation.com/youtubes-paedophile-problem-is-only-a-small-part-of-the-internets-issue-with-child-sexual-abuse-94126

Winseck, Dwayne; Pike, Robert M. 2007. *Communication and Empire: Media, Markets, and Globalization, 1860–1930*. Duke University Press.

Witte, Ray. 2018. 'We're Not Really Strangers' Koreen Odiney – interview, *ILY Mag*. https://ilymag.com/2019/11/07/were-not-really-strangers-koreen-odiney-interview/

Wolf, Christine T. 2016. DIY videos on YouTube: identity and possibility in the age of algorithms, *First Monday*, 21 (6). http://firstmonday.org/ojs/index.php/fm/article/view/6787

Wolin, Richard. 2019. Max Horkheimer, *Encyclopaedia Brittanica*. https://www.britannica.com/biography/Max-Horkheimer

Wong, Julia Carrie. 2019a. Zuckerberg says Facebook is pivoting to privacy after year of controversies, *Wired*, March 6. https://www.theguardian.com/technology/2019/mar/06/mark-zuckerberg-facebook-privacy-vision

Wong, Julia Carrie. 2019b. The Cambridge Analytica scandal changed the world – but it didn't change Facebook, *Guardian*, March 18. https://www.theguardian.com/technology/2019/mar/17/the-cambridge-analytica-scandal-changed-the-world-but-it-didnt-change-facebook

Wong, K. L. X. and Dobson, A. S. 2019. We're just data: exploring China's social credit system in relation to digital platform ratings cultures in Westernised democracies, *Global Media and China*, 4 (2), pp. 220–232. DOI: 10.1177/2059436419856090.

Woodcock, Jamie; Johnson, Mark R. 2019. The affective labor and performance of live streaming on Twitch.tv, *Television & New Media*, 20 (8), pp. 813–23. https://doi.org/10.1177/1527476419851077

Woolf, Nicky. 2015. 'Revenge porn king' Hunter Moore pleads guilty to hacking charges, *Guardian*. February 19, https://www.theguardian.com/technology/2015/feb/19/revenge-porn-hunter-moore-pleads-guilty-hacking-identify

Wortham, Jenna. 2010. Once just a site with funny cat pictures, and now a web empire, *The New York Times*, June 13. https://www.nytimes.com/2010/06/14/technology/internet/14burger.html

Wortham, Jenna. 2015. The misadventures of Issa Rae, *The New York Times*, August 4. https://www.nytimes.com/2015/08/09/magazine/the-misadventures-of-issa-rae.html

Wu, Brianna; Warzel, Charlie; Donovan, Joan; Jeong, Sarah. 2019. How an online mob created a playbook for a culture war, *The New York Times*, August 15. https://www.nytimes.com/interactive/2019/08/15/opinion/what-is-gamergate.html

Wu, Yan; Wall, Matthew. 2019. The ties that bind: how the dominance of WeChat combines with guanxi to inhibit and constrain China's contentious politics, *New Media & Society*, 21(8), 1714–33. https://doi.org/10.1177/1461444819830072

Wulf, Tim; Schneider, Frank M.; Beckert, Stefan. 2018. Watching players: an exploration of media enjoyment on Twitch, *Games and Culture*. DOI:10.1177/1555412018788161

Wynne, Sharon Kennedy. 1995. Six degrees of Kevin Bacon, *St Petersburg Times* (Florida), December 4, City Edition.

Yeo, Tien Ee Dominic; Fung, Tsz Hin. 2018. 'Mr Right Now': temporality of relationship formation on gay mobile dating apps, *Mobile Media & Communication*, 6 (1), pp. 3–18. https://doi.org/10.1177/2050157917718601

YouTube Creator Blog. 2019. More updates on our actions related to the safety of minors on YouTube, YouTube Creator Blog, February 28. https://youtube-creators.googleblog.com/2019/02/more-updates-on-our-actions-related-to.html

YouTube Help. 2020a. YouTube Partner Programme overview and eligibility, Help Centre. https://support.google.com/youtube/answer/72851?hl=en-GB

YouTube Help. 2020b. Set your channel or video's audience, Help Centre. https://support.google.com/youtube/answer/9527654

YouTube Help. 2020c. Determining whether your content is made for kids, Help Centre. https://support.google.com/youtube/answer/9528076

YouTube Culture and Trends. 2020d. 'With me': how sole activities brought ... YouTube Culture and Trends. https://www.youtube.com/trends/articles/with-me-interactive/

Zeller, Samuel. 2018. Goodbye Instagram, hello Ello, Medium, January 12. https://medium.com/swlh/goodbye-instagram-hello-ello-45df3d8754ec

Zimmer, Michael. 2008. Preface: critical perspectives on Web 2.0, *First Monday*, 13 (3). http://firstmonday.org/ojs/index.php/fm/article/view/2137

Zittrain, Jonathan. 2018. Mark Zuckerberg can fix this mess, *The New York Times*, April 7. https://www.nytimes.com/2018/04/07/opinion/sunday/zuckerberg-facebook-privacy-congress.html?smid=tw-nytopinion&smtyp=cur

Zuboff, Shoshana. 2015. Big other: surveillance capitalism and the prospects of an information civilization, *Journal of Information Technology*, 30 (1), pp. 75–89.

Zuboff, Shoshana. 2019. *The Age of Surveillance Capitalism: The Fight for the Future at the New Frontier of Power*. Profile Books.

Zuckerberg, Mark. 2017. Facebook community now officially 2 billion people, Facebook, June 27. https://www.facebook.com/zuck/posts/10103831654565331?pnref=story

Zuckerberg, Mark. 2019. A privacy-focused vision for social networking, Facebook, March 6. https://www.facebook.com/notes/mark-zuckerberg/a-privacy-focused-vision-for-social-networking/10156700570096634/

Zuckerman, Ethan. 2015. Cute cats to the rescue? Participatory media and political expression, in Danielle Allen and Jennifer Light (Eds.), *From Voice to Influence: Understanding Citizenship in a Digital Age*. University of Chicago Press. https://dspace.mit.edu/bitstream/handle/1721.1/78899/cutecats2013.pdf?sequence=1&isAllowed=y

Zulli, Diana; Liu, Miao; Gehl, Robert. 2020. Rethinking the 'social' in 'social media': insights into topology, abstraction, and scale on the mastodon social network, *New Media & Society*. July. https://journals.sagepub.com/doi/full/10.1177/1461444820912533

INDEX

Page numbers in *italics* refer to figures and tables

Abbate, Janet 33
Abdulla, Rasha et al. 145–6
Abidin, Crystal 133, 164, 216, 221–2, 223, 226–7
'about us'/mission statements 73, *90*, *91*, 164, 166, 173
active audience tradition 76–9, 134
Adorno, Max and Horkheimer, Theodor 70–2, 79
advertising revenues 50, 211
affective labour and social relations 221–4, 226–7
affordances 47
  and tactics of belonging 98–103
  Tinder 239, 241–2
Alaimo, Kara 145
algorithmic power 66–7
algorithmic sociality 92
algorithms 4, 11, 26, 41, 54, 66–8, 77, 89, 97, 100–1, 170, 180, 210, 212, 223–5, 234, 236, 238, 241
  facial recognition biases 174–5
  recommendation 210, 219, 220–1
  sexism and racism of 89, 174–5
  surveillance 198
  YouTube 217–19, 220–1
Alibaba 50
Alt-Right extremism and radicalization 218–19, 222
'Alternative Influence Networks'(AINs) 219
alternative social media 12, 123–4
ambivalent cultures 79–80
Anderson, Benedict 89
anonymous apps 139–40
antitrust law 55–6
App Store 172, 225, *236*
application layer of internet 114
Application Processing Interfaces (API) 120, 121
apps
  filters and lenses (selfies) 170–2, 173
  mobile networks and 47, 49, 119, 120–1
Arab Spring and Egyptian Revolution (2011) 142–7, 151
ARPANET 111, 113, 117
Arthurs, Jane et al. 214–15

artificial intelligence (AI)
  and facial recognition 173–5, 176
  TikTok 225
aspirational labourers 216
audience, active 76–9, 134
audience commodity 71–2
authenticity
  Instagram 165–6
  personal connections and technologies 230–1

Bannon, Steve 7
Baran, Paul 111–13, 119, 120
Bastow, Clem 15
BATX platforms, China 9, 10, 19, 51, 54, 123
Bauman, Zygmunt 233–4, 246
Baym, Nancy 27, 100, 117, 133, 222, 223, 231
BBC live streaming 225
Beer, David 45, 46
belonging, tactics of 98–103
Benjamin, Ruha 31, 54, 89, 174
Bentham, Jeremy 194, *195*
Berner-Lee, Tim 33, 117
Bieber, Justin 217, 222
biometric grid and facial recognition 170
Bishop, Sophie 223–4
#BlackLivesMatter 147–9, 151
Black software 32–3, 54
'Black Twitter' 135
Black/women of color 54, 61–2, 68, 215–16
blogging 36, 99
Bosworth, Andrew 201
boyd, danah 38, 185
  and Ellison, Nicole 45–6, 48, 49, 52
Brock, André 31, 54, 135
Bryant, Emma 6–7
Bucher, Taina 66–7, 88
  and Helmond, Anne 100
Bumble 141, 234–6, 245–7
Buolamwini, Joy and Gebru, Timnit 174–5
Burgess, Jean 101–2
  et al. 26, 31, 45, 52, 56
  and Green, Joshua 208, 209–10, 215, 216
Bye Felipe 242, 243

Cadwalladr, Carole 6–7
Cain, Caleb 218–19
Cambridge Analytica (CA) 6–8, 19,
    181, 193
capitalism
    and ideology 60–2, 70–1, 72, 79
    platform empires as new stage of 73–5
Cards Against Humanity (CAH) 142n
Carpentier, Nico 130, 134, 150
Cath, Corrine et al. 114
celebrities
    affective labour and social relations 221–3
    and influencers 216–17
censorship/blackouts 9, 137, 147
Cheezburger Network 17–18
Chen, Steve 208
children
    sexual exploitation and abuse of 220–1
    YouTube content 213–14
China
    BATX platforms 9, 10, 19, 51, 54, 123
    censorship 9, 137
    social credit systems (SCS) 8–11, 19
Chong, Gladys 8, 10–11
Cockburn, Cynthia 96, 97
coercive power 63
Cohen, Ira 95
Cohen, Julie E. 185, 202, 203
community and connection 11–12
    memes 16–19, 102–3, 133–4
    Pokémon Go 12–16, 19, 133–4
computer mediated communication (CMC) 29,
    33–4, 38, 45–6
computer-supported cooperative work (CSCW)
    29, 33–4, 35, 38
connective media 52–3
connectivity/connection see community and
    connection; ideology of connection; 'social'
    in social media
content creators see user generated content
    (UGC); specific platforms
content layer of internet 114
Couldry, Nick 59, 67–8, 98
    and Hepp, Andreas 88, 98
    and Mejias, Ulises Ali 73, 74–5, 91, 103,
        123, 169
    and Van Dijck, José 88, 98
COVID-19 pandemic 86, 207
creative agency vs free labour 131–2
Crenshaw, Kimberlé 61–2
critical race studies 54
Cullors, Patrisse 148
cultural power see symbolic power

culture industries 70–1
Cunningham, Stuart and Craig, David
    206, 211, 226
cute cat theory of political activism 137, 147

data aggregation 192–3
data categorization 188–92
data colonialism 53–4, 73, 74–5, 91
data selfies 169–75
dataveillance/surveillance 5, 194–201
    China's social credit systems (SCS) 8–11, 19
    Facebook 100–1, 121–2
        and Cambridge Analytica (CA) 6–8, 19,
            181, 193
    geo-location 15–16
    TikTok 225
    see also privacy
dating industries
    sites to apps 234–7, 246–7
    Tinder 238–43, 247
Daubs, Michael S. and Manzerolle, Vincent R. 119
David, Gabi and Cambre, Carolina 240, 241–2, 247
Dawkins, Richard 16
'deep mediatization' 98
defriending and breaking up 244–6
DeNardis, Laura 108–9
Dencik, Lina 197–8, 203
Dorsey, Jack 142
'dramaturgical approach' (front/back stage
    presentation) 162, 176
Drotner, Kristen 161, 163
Duffy, Brooke Erin 216

early internet history and infrastructures 110–13
    'stack' and global megastructures 113–18, 124–5
    telephony and mobile social media 118–20
early internet/virtual communities 32–3
economic power 63
ego based networks 38–9
Egyptian Revolution (2011) 142–7, 151
Eisenstein, Elizabeth L. 128
Ellison, Nicole and boyd, danah 52, 56
embedded technologies and overlapping
    networks 109–22
emoticons/emojis 17, 100
End User Licence Agreements (EULAs) 90–1
European Network Against Racism 196–7
exploitative connectivity 91, 92

Facebook
    'about us'/mission statement 73, 90, 91, 173
    Arab Spring and Egyptian Revolution
        145–6, 147

#BlackLivesMatter 148
and Cambridge Analytica (CA) 6–8, 19,
    181, 193
and Cornell University 'mood manipulation'
    study 181
dating app 235
development 44, 47, 49–50, 51
facial recognition and AI 173
free internet 122
ideology of connection 76, 94
and Instagram 164, 173, 187, *190–1*
like buttons 100–1, 121
mobile strategy 120
privacy and data policies 187, 189,
    190–1, 192
'relational and productive' algorithmic
    power 66–7
shadow profiles and PYMK feature 199–201
socially conservative countries and online
    dating 236–7
and WhatsApp 187, 189, 192
Facebook Connect (now called Facebook Login)
    47–8, 121–2
Facetune 171–2
facial recognition
    lenses and filters 170–2, 173
    tagging and artificial intelligence 173–5, 176
Fahlman, Scott E. 17
fan culture 135, 136
Federal Communications Commission, US
    116–17
feminist perspective 61–2, 233
    see also entries beginning gendered
Field, Matt 220
filters 170–2, 173
flame wars 17
Floyd, George 148
Foucault, Michel 64–6, 79, 194–6
four stage model of social media 28–9, *30–1*,
    55–6
    1. pre-history and ferment (1980s–90s) 29–34
    2. early development (19902–2006) 34–43
    3. consolidation and growth (2007–12) 44–9
    4. maturation (2013–present) 49–54
free labour vs creative agency 131–2
Freelon, Dean et al. 95, 148–9
Fuchs, Christian 9, 12, 76, 88, 95, 100, 135

Gab 143
GAFA platforms 9, 19, 51, 54–5, 123
Gamergate 243
games/gaming 12–16, 19, 38–9, 133–4
    gender issues 224, 243

gamification and swipe logic of dating apps 240–2
Garza, Alicia 147–8
Gehl, Robert 12
gendered content: YouTube 212, 214, 223–4
gendered double standard: dating sites and apps
    237, 242–3
gendered technologies: social vs individual 96–7
General Data Protection Regulation (GDPR),
    EU 193
geo-location 15–16
Gerbaudo, Paolo 144, 145, 151
Gershon, Ilana 244–6, 247
gesellschaft and *gemeinschaft* 88
Giddens, Anthony 94–5, 130, 232
Gilmore, Myron 128
global megastructures 113–18, 124–5
Goffman, Erving 162, 176
Goggin, Gerard 119, 120
Google
    advertising revenue 50
    and Pokémon Go 13, 15, 19
    privacy and data policies 187, 189
    and YouTube 210, 211
Google+ 181
Google Cardboard 136
Google for Education 122
Google Play Store 225, *236*
Google Search 68
governments
    censorship/blackouts 9, 137, 147
    and power of social media platforms 193
Grindr 137, 234–6, 241, 243, 246
groupware 35–6

Habermas, Jürgen 89
Hall, Stuart 77
Hauben, Ronda and Hauben, Michael 32
Helmond, Anne 120, 121
    Bucher, Taina and 100
Henthorn, Jamie et al. 14
historical perspective 24–6
    life cycles of technology, knowledge, and
        products 27–8
    participation 128–9
    privacy 181–2
    see also early internet history and infrastructures;
        four stage model of social media
Hjorth, Larissa 15
Horton, Donald 221
Human Computer Interaction (HCI) 29,
    33–4, 99
Humphreys, Lee 118
'hyperconnective modernity' 233, 234

ideology of connection 69–70, 75–6
  ambivalent cultures and 79–80
  audience commodity 71–2
  culture industries 70–1
  platform empires 73–5
  see also power; 'social' in social media
Illouz, Eva 233, 234, 246, 247
influencers
  and celebrities 216–17
  malevolent users and 217–21
Information Commissioner's Office (ICO),
    UK 7, 8
infrastructures of everyday life 94–8
infrastructures and platformatization 108–9,
    124–5
  embedded technologies and overlapping
      networks 109–22
  platform empires 122–4
  see also early internet history and
      infrastructures
Instagram 99, 101
  'about us'/mission statement 90, 91, 164
  Bye Felipe 242–3
  Finstas 198–9
  selfies 163–6, 169, 170, 173, 176
  subverting dataveillance (Finstas) 198–9
  Tinder Nightmares 242–3
  We're Not Really Strangers (WNRS) 140–1, 142
institutional privacy 185–6
internet censorship/blackouts 9, 137, 147
internet communication network structure
    (Baran model) 111–13, 119, 120
Internet Protocol (IP) 111, 113, 114, 118
Internet Service Providers (ISPs) 111, 116–17
interoperability 113
intersectionality 61–2
intimacy
  affective labour and social relations
      221–2, 223
  'screened intimacy' 241–2
  see also love and intimacy
iPhone
  global impact of mobile phones 118–20
  PostSecrets app 140
  release of 44, 47, 48, 118
Iqani, Mehita and Schroeder, Jonathan E.
    159, 161

Jackson, Sarah et al. 138, 143
Jarrett, Kylie 97, 132
Jenkins, Henry 43, 101, 129, 134, 135, 136, 138,
    150, 209
Jiminez, Jordi Piera 15

Katz, James E. and Schroeder, Elizabeth Thomas
    168–9
Kjellberg, Felix (PewDiePie) 215, 216, 222
knowledge
  life cycles of technology, products and 27–8
  and power 64–7
Kogan, Aleksandr 6, 7
Kotliar, Dan M. 67
Kramer, Adam D.I. et al. 181
Krieger, Mike 163

language: new vernaculars and literacies 101–3
Leaver, Tama et al. 164
lenses 170–2, 173
Lessig, Lawrence 37, 114, 134–5
Lewis, Becca 219
LGBTQI communities 223, 232, 235
life cycles of technology, knowledge, and
    products 27–8
'like' buttons/metrics 100–1, 121–2, 166
Linked-In 200
'liquid love' 233–4
live streaming/streaming services 207, 223,
    224–5
Livingstone, Sonia 77–8, 98
  and Lunt, Peter 97–8
Lobato, Roman 214
logical layer of internet 114
LOLcats 17–19
Lotus Notes 35, 36
Lotz, Amanda 206
love and intimacy 230, 231–4
  breaking up 244–6
  dating industries
    sites to apps 234–7, 246–7
    Tinder 238–43, 247
  defriending 244–6
  personal connections and technologies 230–1
  personal disconnections 244–6

machine vision 173–4, 176
Madden, Mary 37
Madianou, Mirca and Miller, Daniel 48, 52
malevolent influencers and users 217–21
Maloney, Marcus et al. 224
Martin, Trayvon 147–8
Marwick, Alice 53
Marx, Karl, and Marxism 60–1, 79
Marx, Karl and Engels, Friedrich 60
massification 49–51
  of creative agency 135
Mastodon 12, 50, 123, 138, 143
McGlynn, Clare et al. 183

McIlwain, Charlton 31, 33, 54
McLuhan, Marshall 110
'media mesh' 207, 226, 227
mediatization 97–8
memes 16–19, 102–3, 133–4
mental health 140–2
metrics: 'like' buttons 100–1, 121–2, 166
Milner, Ryan M. 19, 103
  Phillips, Whitney and 78–9, 103, 136
Miltner, Kate M. 17, 18–19, 103
  and Baym, Nancy 158
mission/'about us' statements 73, *90*, *91*, 164, 166, 173
mobile networks and apps 47, 49, 119, 120–1
mobile/smart phones
  global impact of 118–20
  see also iPhone
monopsonies 123–4
'mood manipulation' study 181
Moore, Hunter 182–3
Moore, Martin and Tambini, Damian 75, 120, 123
moral panics 161, 163
'multi-channel networks' (MCNs) 214
Murthy, Dhiraj 128–9, 146, 147
music 36–8, 70
musicians 222
Muslim countries: online dating 236–7
Muslims: Christchurch mosque shooting 218–19
MySpace 38

Napster 36–8, *40*
net neutrality principle 116–17
new vernaculars and literacies 101–3
Niantic 13, 15–16
Niea, Kho Suet et al. 97
Nintendo 13, 14
Nissenbaum, Helen 184–5
Noble, Safiyah 68, 89
non-consensual image sharing 182–3
Norman, Don 99
NSFNET (National Science Foundation) 111, 113

Odiney, Koreen 140, 141, 142
Ofcom 44–5, 47, 207
O'Neill, Essena 165–6
Open Systems Innovation (OSI) model 113, *114*, 115, 118
O'Reilly, Tim 43, 47, 110
overlapping networks and embedded technologies 109–22
ownership 55
Oxford English Dictionary (OED) word of the year (2013) 156

packet switching 111, 113
panopticon 194–6
Papacharissi, Zizi 11, 48–9, 234
parasocial relations and perceived interconnectedness 221–2
participation
  history of 128–9
  meaning of 130–6
  and play 135–6
participatory culture 129
  and creative agency 133–5
  making sense of 150–1
participatory turn in culture and politics 136–49
  Egyptian Revolution (2011) 142–7
  PostSecrets 139–40, 151
  We're Not Really Strangers (WNRS) 140–2, 151
peer-to-peer file sharing 36–8
'People You May Know' (PYMK) 199–201
perceived interconnectedness 221–2
personal connections/disconnections *see under* love and intimacy
PewDiePie 215, 216, 222
Phillips, Whitney 218–9
  and Milner, Ryan 78–9, 103, 136
photo-editing selfies 171–2
photographic technologies 181–2
physical layer of internet 114
Picone, Ike et al. 78
Plantin, Jean-Christophe 121
  and de Seta, Gabriele 9
  et al. 110, 120, 124
platform empires 73–5, 122–4
platformatization 120–2
'platformed sociality' 52–3
play and participation 135–6
Pokémon Go 12–16, 19, 133–4
police dataveillance 196–7
political issues *see* dataveillance/surveillance; governments; social movements
political power 63
polymedia 48, 52
  single sites to 48–9
PostSecret 139–40, 151
power 59
  capitalism and ideology 60–2, 70–1, 72
  critiques 76–9
  forms of 62–4
  governments and social media platforms 193
  of infrastructures and technologies 108–9, 111–13
  intersectionality 61–2
  and knowledge 64–7
  media and symbolic 67–9

programmed sociality 66–7
of tech companies 50–1
'prank wars' 212–13
presentation of self in everyday life (front/
    back stage) 162, 176
printing technologies
    and photography 181–2
    and 'small media' 128–9
privacy 180
    defining 184–6
    'future is private' claim 202–3
    history of 181–3
    rights and 'nothing to hide' argument 192–4
    and social media platforms 186–92
    see also dataveillance/surveillance
programmed sociality 66–7
public good 103–4

Qui, Jack Linchuan 5, 132

racial profiling 196–7
racism 54, 218–19
    and sexism 68, 89, 174–5, 243
Rad, Sean 240
Rae, Issa 215–16, 222
Raynes-Goldie, Kate 185–6
recommendation algorithms 210, 219, 220–1
red-pilling 218–19
relational labour see affective labour and social
    relations
Rettberg, Jill Walker 36, 102, 170–1, 172,
    173, 176
revenge porn to non-consensual image
    sharing 182–3
Rheingold, Howard 30–2
Rogers, Richard 45, 51, 100, 166
romantic love 233
Roose, Kevin 218, 219

Sandvig, Christian 124
Sappho 231–2
Scholz. Trebor 28, 48, 131–2, 135
selfies 102
    data 169–75
    definitions
        and rise of 156–8
        scholarly 158–63
    platforms 163–9
    sub-types 156
    visual logics of selfie culture 175–6
Senft, Theresa and Baym, Nancy 158, 159,
    160–1
Sesame Credit, China 10–11

sexism and racism 68, 89, 174–5, 243
sexual abuse
    and exploitation of children 220–1
    and harassment 242–3
shadow profiles 199–201
Shifman, Limor 16–7
Shirky, Clay 46–7, 76–7
Silverstone, Roger 94, 136
Simmel, Georg 88
single sites to polymedia platforms 48–9
SixDegrees 25, 42, 51, 54
'small acts of engagement' (SAOE) 76–9, 80,
    133–4, 138
'small media' 128–9
Smythe, Dallas 71–2, 79
Snapchat 55
    'about us'/mission statement 90, 91, 166
    privacy and data policies 189, 190–1
    selfies 166–9, 170, 176
    Snap Map 181
Snowden, Edward 5, 180, 181
social credit systems (SCS), China 8–11, 19
'social entrepreneurship' 53
social and institutional privacy 185–6
social media, definition and features of 26
social media entertainment 206, 226
social media scholarship
    birth of field and dedicated 51–2
    critical turn 52–4
    peer reviewed publications 44–5
social movements 77, 138
    #BlackLivesMatter 147–9, 151
    Egyptian Revolution (2011) 142–7, 151
social network sites (SNSs) 44, 45–6, 48–9, 52
    social software and 38–42
social networks
    rise of 44–6
    to social media 46–8
social plug-ins 121–2
social screens 206–7
    affective labour and social relations 221–4,
        226–7
    emerging trends 224–6
    TikTok 225, 226, 227
    YouTube 207–21
'social' in social media 86–7
    affordances 98–103
    defining 87–9
    infrastructure of everyday life 94–8
    and social media platforms 90–2
    social solidarities and public good 103–4
    structure and agency 92–5
    tactics of belonging 98–103

social software and social network sites (SNSs) 38–42
social solidarities and public good 103–4
'social TV' 207
socially conservative countries: online dating 236–7
socio-technical systems 33–4, 109–10
Solove, Daniel J. 184–5, 192–3, 196
Sørensen, Inge 225, 226, 227
Sotoudeh, Ramina et al. 236–7
Spiegel, Evan 166, 167
Srnicek, Nick 69, 73, 74, 210, 211
'stack' and global megastructures 113–18, 124–5
Stark, Luke 174, 176
Starosielski, Nicole 115, 117, 120
   Parks, Lisa and 109–11, 120
Stoilova, Mariya et al. 188–9
Stokel-Walker, Chris 97, 208, 211–2, 216–7, 225
Strategic Communications Laboratory (SCL Group) 6–7, 8
streaming services/live streaming 207, 223, 224–5
structuration to deep mediatization 94–8
structure and agency 92–5
Sujon, Zoetanya 167, 168, 185
   et al. 94, 136
'submarine cables' 109, 115–6
surveillance capitalism 53–4, 73, 75, 92
surveillance and data see dataveillance/ surveillance
surveillance realism 198
swipe logic of dating apps 240–2
symbolic power 63–4
   and media 67–9
Systrom, Kevin 163

tactics of belonging 98–103
television/TV 206
   'multi-channel networks' (MCNs) 214
   streaming services/live streaming 207, 223, 224–5
Tencent 9–10, 40–41, 51, 54, 123
Terranova, Tiziana 35, 132
Thompson, John B. 62–4, 67, 79, 88–9
Tiefentale, Alise and Manovich, Lev 161–2
Tiidenberg, Katrin 159, 175
TikTok 225, 226, 227
Tinder 238–43, 247
Tinder Nightmares 242–3
Tonnies, Ferdinand 88
Transmission Control Protocol/Internet Protocol (TCP/IP) 111, 113, 114, 118
Tufecki, Zeynep 12, 52, 77, 181, 217, 219

Tumblr 140, 143, 168
Tunisia 137
Twitter 99, 101, 142–3
   'about us'/mission statement 90, 91
   Arab Spring and Egyptian Revolution 145, 146, 147
   #BlackLivesMatter 148–9
   privacy and data policies 187–8, 189–92

UK Brexit 181
   and EU General Data Protection Regulation (GDPR) 193
UK Parliament 6, 8
Universal Declaration of Human Rights (UDHR) 180
UNIX 32
Urban Dictionary 157
Usenet 32–3
user generated content (UGC) 123–4
   diversity issues 135
   free labour vs creative agency 131–2
   PostSecrets 139–40
   see also specific platforms

Vaidhyanathan, Siva 103, 164, 196
Van Dijck, José 52–3, 75, 91, 92, 100–1, 103
   Couldry, Nick and 88, 98
   et al. 123
'vanity metrics' 100, 166
vernaculars and literacies, new 101–3
video see social screens
vloggers 212, 214, 215–16, 223

Wales, Jimmy 11–12
Warfield, Katie et al. 160–1
Warren, Frank 139, 140
Web 2.0 42–3, 46, 47, 48, 51, 110
web-browsers 33, 34
   and networks 34–5
WeChat 9–10, 20, 49, 50–51
   WeChatPay 9, 10
Well (Whole Earth 'Lectronic Link) 32–3
Wellman, Barry 110, 118
We're Not Really Strangers (WNRS) 140–2, 151
WhatsApp 30, 49–50, 56, 117, 122, 187, 189, 190–1, 192, 201
Whisper 140
Wikipedia 11–12
Williams, Evan 142, 143
Williams, James 210
Williams, Patrick and Kind, Eric 196–7
Wohl, Richard R. 221

women
    of color *see* Black/women of color
    feminist perspective 61–2, 233
    sexism and racism 68, 89, 174–5, 243
    see also entries beginning gendered
World Wide Web (WWW) 33, 34–5, 117, 118, 119
Wylie, Christopher 7

Yagan, Sam 236
YikYak 140
#Yolocaust and 'selfiegate' 157–8
YouTube 101, 207–21
    'about us'/mission statement *90, 91*
    affective labour and social relations 221–4

content, creators and trends 211–17
and emerging trends in social video
        224–6
malevolent influencers and users 217–21
origins and features 207–11
privacy and data policies 187, 189,
        190–1
YouTube Partner Programme (YPP) 210–11

Zuboff, Shoshanna 15–16, 53–4, 73, 74, 91, 92,
    186, 197
Zuckerberg, Mark 47, 92, 192, 200, 202–3
Zuckerman, Ethan 137, 147
Zulli, Diana et al. 12, 123–4, 138, 143